World View: War Between China And Japan

Why America Must Be Prepared

John J. Xenakis

Xenakis Publishing — Generational Theory Book Series

Paperback ISBN: 978-1-7327386-3-8

Edition 1

Table of Contents

[Updated: Thursday, June 06, 2019, 15:16:11 190606 3L6xl ET, 120570 words]

Map of East Asia conflict area

Part I. Introduction

Chapter 1. China today

China is like a beautiful child, a helpless child, and you yearn to reach out to help her, so that she can become an equally beautiful adult. But every time you reach out to help her, you get your hand scratched and your face bloodied, and she ends up as helpless as ever.

The history of China is monumental and fascinating, going back at least three millennia. To the modern audience, the most important part of China's history is the part since the Opium Wars of the 1840s, as it moved through stages from dynasty rule, to a republic, to a nationalist dictatorship, and finally to a Communist dictatorship.

Today that beautiful child has grown up. But she hasn't grown up to be a beautiful, well-adjusted woman. Instead, she's grown to be a paranoid schizophrenic monster, just as lost and helpless as she was as a child, but without the charm. She's driven by a vitriolic hatred of Japan; she suffers from the cognitive dissonance of believing that all other people are inferior barbarians, but in the real world being repeatedly beaten economically and diplomatically by Japan, Taiwan, and South Korea; she fears a mass rebellion by her own people that overthrows the government; and she has no clue how to govern herself except by preparing to launch a world war.

China's history is monumental, and I've tried to reflect that monumental history in this book. But let's face it, my main objective has been to deal with the paranoid monster that China has become. I hope that readers will learn from both of these views.

1.1. China since World War II

It is a conclusion of this book that China's policy since the end of World War II has been nothing but disastrous. While China's government has starved and oppressed its own people, the people in Japan, Taiwan, colonial Hong Kong and South Korea have experienced one "economic miracle" after another, and the people in those countries are happier and wealthier than the citizens of China.

China blames the starvation, poverty and oppression of its people on "unfair treaties" imposed by the West. We'll describe the history of these unfair treaties in great detail later in this book, but we'll also show that the starvation, poverty and oppression of China's citizens are entirely the fault of the Chinese Communist Party (CCP).

For now, we'll summarize some of China's policies since the end of World War II. We'll describe these in detail in later chapters.

One of the most barbaric and disastrous government policies of any government in world history was Mao Zedong's Great Leap Forward in 1958-59. The Chinese people were exhausted from China's civil war, and Mao confiscated all farmland, forced hundreds of thousands of Chinese into "battalions," with men, women and children all living apart and allowed them to see each other only once per month. Everyone was responsible for working every waking hour to produce food on the farm. This was supposed to prove that communism was better than capitalism, but it was a complete disaster, with tens of millions of Chinese dying of starvation. It proved in fact that communism itself was a disaster, far worse than capitalism.

Mao was thoroughly humiliated by the Great Leap Forward disaster, and anti-Mao sentiment began to grow. In response, Mao launched the Great Cultural Revolution 1966. He shut down the nation's schools, and called for a massive youth mobilization to form paramilitary groups called the Red Guards to attack any citizens, especially older citizens, who might oppose Mao's policies. Mao used violence to form a personality cult to protect his own power, and attack anyone who didn't fall in line. Mao brought the country to chaos, with industrial production for 1968 dropping 12 percent below that of 1966.

So Mao's Great Leap Forward (1958-59) destroyed China's agricultural production, while Mao's Great Cultural Revolution (1966-76) destroyed China's industrial production. So the destruction of China's economy was not caused by "unequal treaties," but by the barbaric policies of Mao Zedong.

When Mao finally died in 1976, the country was finally rid of its worst monster, and a new leader, Deng Xiaoping in 1978 was able to institute an "Opening up and reform" policy that completely reversed Socialism and opened up China to free markets and capitalism. However, it was still a CCP dictatorship, and the phrase "Socialism with Chinese characteristics" came into use, even though it was no longer socialism, but was the same as Hitler's National Socialism.

The next major turning point in China's society was the 1989 Tiananmen Square massacre of thousands of young students who were holding peaceful pro-democracy demonstrations. This was followed in 1991 by the collapse of China's mentor, the Soviet Union.

This turned the CCP insanity into full-fledged paranoia, as they adopted policies of violent suppression of anything that could be interpreted as "pro-democracy," including the violent suppression of religions.

At the same time, the CCP adopted a vitriolic anti-Japan hate campaign, in order to stoke nationalism instead of pro-democracy feelings.

These violent policies have grown only worse since then, especially since Xi Jinping came to power in 2013. Here's a summary of the policies that the CCP has adopted since then:

- Document Number 9 (2013): A nationwide education program clamping down on Western ideas — democracy, "universal values," "neo-liberalism," free press, criticism of the CCP's violent crackdown on Christianity, Buddhism and Islam. In particular, there was a major crackdown on the press in Hong Kong.
- At a September 25, 2015, press conference on the White House lawn, Xi Jinping blatantly lied to Barack Obama, saying that China had no intention to militarize the South China Sea, at a time when China was moving rapidly to militarize the South China Sea. This was a significant lie about a major military matter.
- In July 2016, the United Nations Permanent Court of Arbitration in The Hague issued a ruling that all China's activities were illegal. This decision infuriated the CCP, and they began openly turning the South China Sea into a major militarized region. The CCP had changed from subterfuge to open contempt for the West and for international law.
- In June 2017, China passed into law the National Intelligence Law, which requires any Chinese citizen or business to cooperate with the military in stealing intelligence information from another country, even when doing so is illegal. The law also promises that China's military will protect anyone who does this. I've described this law as a real "f--k you" to the West, because of the contempt it shows for the rest of the world.
- In 2017, China became far more active in building concentration camps and crematoria in East Turkistan (Xinjiang Province), and began the process of genocide and ethnic cleansing of Muslim Uighurs and Kazakhs.
- On March 20, 2018, Xi Jinping became "dictator for life," attempting to adopt the same kind of cult status that Mao Zedong had.
- In June 2018, China passed a "Sinicization" law that required all religious practices to conform strictly to harsh CCP regulations, including forbidding worship of "outsiders," such as Jesus Christ. This was accompanied by violent crackdowns on Christians, Buddhists and Muslims.
- In May 2019, after months of US-China trade negotiations, China reneged on all the written agreements it had made. This is a typical pattern for China, where it makes commitments and then ignores them, while expressing outrage when other countries don't meet their commitments. This is similar to the practice of ignoring international law, while demanding that all other countries obey international law.

In recent years, particularly since the 2016 Hague Tribunal ruling that all of China's South China Sea activities were illegal in international law, China has become increasingly belligerent and, in my opinion, increasingly preparing to launch a war.

1.2. Chinese people vs China's government

The following table appears later in this book, but I'm repeating it here to make an important point. The table shows the average IQ (intelligence) and income for several countries, ranked by IQ, based on 9 international studies conducted between 1990-2010: [170]

Rank	Country	IQ	Income per cap
1	Singapore	108	$25,407
2	Hong Kong	108	$25,419
3	Taiwan	106	$25,000
4	South Korea	106	$13,710
5	Japan	105	$36,785
6	China	104	$ 1,375
27	United States	98	$36,609 [170]

You can see from this table that the Chinese people are extremely intelligent, but that the income of the Chinese people in Taiwan and Hong Kong is ten times as great as that of the Chinese people in China, and the quality of life is much better. The same is true of Hong Kong, which was a British colony until 1997.

Since 2010, all of these countries have higher per capita incomes, according to the CIA World Factbook: China $16,700, Taiwan $50,500, Hong Kong $61,500, Japan $42,900 and South Korea $39,500. China is the sick man of Asia, with incomes a small fraction of those of other Asian countries.

This is an important point. Some people who reviewed early versions of this book criticized it because it seemed to be racist to say that the Chinese people were totally incompetent. But this is not about race. The Chinese are great people, and very intelligent. The really stupid people in China are those in the CCP, who only care about keeping their power and their money and their mistresses, and don't care about the devastation they're causing to the great Chinese people.

Every year, the Chinese people in Taiwan (and Hong Kong) are substantially more successful than the Chinese people in China. This is a major embarrassment and humiliation to the CCP. No wonder the CCP would like to destroy Taiwan's government, so that the Chinese people in Taiwan will be as poor and miserable as the Chinese people in China.

Chapter 2. Evolution of this book

2.1. Three objectives

Originally this was to be a book about China's claims to the South China Sea. I was going to find out who was right, and who was spinning fake news.

So I researched all of China's history going back thousands of years and multiple dynasties, as well as the histories of China's religions — Confucianism, Daoism, Buddhism, Catholicism, Islam, Protestantism, and Falun Gong.

I discovered that China had no claim at all to the South China Sea. I mean, it isn't even arguable. China's claim to Taiwan, whether valid or not, is at least arguable. But the claim to the South China Sea isn't even arguable. It is completely nonexistent. It is a complete hoax.

This means that China's activities in the South China Sea are criminal, as the Chinese themselves realize. The Chinese know this. That's why China's president Xi Jinping on September 25, 2015, blatantly lied to the face of Barack Obama during a joint press conference on the White House lawn about China's intentions, just as Adolf Hitler lied to Neville Chamberlain in 1938 about "Peace in our time." Xi said that there were no plans to militarize the South China Sea, even though they were actively militarizing it. In July 2016, the United Nations Permanent Court of Arbitration in The Hague issued a ruling that all China's activities were illegal, reaffirming their criminal nature.

China blames this and other criminal activities on its "Unequal Treaties" and its "Century of Humiliation." All of that research from the first objective is included in this book.

So that evolved to become the second objective of this book. I wanted to focus on China's history since the Opium Wars in order to determine exactly how the unequal treaties occurred, how China was humiliated over the period of a century, and by whom, and how that led to China's behavior today.

So I discovered that there were indeed "unequal treaties," especially the 1860 Treaty of Tianjin and the 1915 Twenty-One Demands that gave concessions to foreign powers in a way that was humiliating to China. I followed this history through the late 1800s to the Republican Revolution of 1911, through World War I and the Versailles betrayal, into the rise of communism, and then the brutal Sino-Japanese war (1937-45), in which the Japanese committed brutal atrocities, and in which the United States saved China from a humiliating defeat.

I also followed China's history after WW II — the Great Leap Forward and the Cultural Revolution that killed tens of millions of Chinese through government-forced starvation, executions, and rioting. Then there was the bloody Tiananmen Square massacre in 1989, where thousands of peacefully protesting college students were mercilessly slaughtered by China's military.

So the second objective of the book was achieved, and I had researched the causes of China's claims to Unequal Treaties and a Century of Humiliation. All of that research from the second objective is also included in this book.

However, I began to see the results of the second objective of the book — that most of the humiliation was caused by China's own faults.

And that led me to an important and obvious question that I've never seen discussed anywhere. The West tried to impose the same Unequal Treaties on Japan as on China. Why didn't Japan also suffer a "Century of Humiliation"?

That led to the third objective of this book — to compare Japan and China. The research from that objective is also included in this book.

What I discovered is that Japan has repeatedly and consistently bested China in all areas — economically, diplomatically, militarily, and in governance. The bottom line appears to be the fact that the reason that China suffered a "Century of Humiliation" is because they were inferior to Japan, time after time.

This is not because the Chinese people are inferior. In fact, the same Chinese people in Taiwan and colonial Hong Kong have also beaten the Chinese people in China, by a factor of ten. It's the Chinese government that's inferior to the governments of Japan, Taiwan and South Korea. The great and brilliant Chinese people are being led by corrupt idiots in the CCP.

In fact, it's been a lot worse than that for China. Since World War II ended, Japan, South Korea, Taiwan and Hong Kong all had "economic miracles," while China's economy languished for decades. Mao's Great Leap Forward was supposed to prove that Marxism, Communism and Socialism are better than anything else, but instead it was a total disaster, causing the deaths of tens of millions through starvation and execution.

After Mao's disaster totally discredited Marxism, Socialism and Communism, once Mao died in 1976, Deng Xiaoping was able to institute an "Opening up and reform" policy that completely reversed Socialism and opened up China to free markets and capitalism. They started using the phrase "Socialism with Chinese Characteristics," which is laughable because it means "Socialism that's really capitalism, but we don't want to call it that." However, China retained its governmental dictatorship, and "Socialism with Chinese Characteristics" is really the same as Adolf Hitler's "National Socialism."

2.2. Historical imperative of world wars

There are a lot of people today who feel at least a level of queasiness and perhaps more over the concern that we're headed for a war with China - a world war. So it's not completely far-fetched to have a book that discusses that possibility.

Unfortunately, history tells us that something like that has to happen. There were two world wars in the last century, as well as numerous other massive related wars (Russian civil war, Spanish civil war, Cambodian civil war, Rwandan genocide, etc.) on every continent, and in every region.

The 20th century was not unique. In every century for millennia, there have been massive wars on every continent in every region, such as China's Taiping rebellion, Africa's Mfecane, India's sepoy rebellion, the 30 years war, the 100 years war, the Punic wars in ancient Rome, and so forth.

It's 100% certain that there will be massive wars, including one or two world wars in this century. So the world war with China that this book is about is actually quite likely. The only thing that can't be predicted is the exact timing or the precise scenario. But there will be a world war pitting America and China against each other.

However, my research also reveals that the Chinese have no desire for war against America. For the most part, the Chinese actually like Americans — as well they should — and have no desire for war.

But my research has also revealed that the Chinese have a vitriolic hatred for the Japanese, and are thirsting for a war in revenge for the atrocities committed by the Japanese during World War II.

The Chinese government — though not the Chinese people as far as I can tell — is also thirsting for a war to invade Taiwan and annex it by force to China.

But China's government are well aware that a war with Japan and Taiwan will mean war with America, since America will defend Japan and Taiwan. That's where the world is headed.

It's a cruel irony of the current situation that American and Chinese people greatly like other, but are going to war anyway because China's incompetent government is destined to go to war with Japan and Taiwan.

This book uses the tools of generational theory to analyze the history of China and Japan. The web site GenerationalDynamics.com contains 6,000 articles written since 2003, containing thousands of analyses and forecasts of hundreds of countries at many points in history. Those analyses and forecasts have all come true or are trending true — none has been proven wrong. The same tools will be used to analyze the history of China, and why we're headed for war.

2.3. China's preparations for war

Based on my research, I've concluded that China does not really want war with America, though I've said so in the past. Also, I've concluded that China is not trying to gain hegemony over the entire world, though I've said so in the past.

What the Chinese do have is a vitriolic hatred for the Japanese, and what they want is a war of revenge, even though they realize that will mean a war with America as well. They also want a war with Taiwan, in order to annex it to China, and that also means war with America.

The Japanese committed numerous grotesque atrocities against the Chinese in WW II, and every major action taken by China since then, starting with the Great Leap Forward, was taken with a desire for revenge against the Japanese.

The 1989 Tiananmen Square massacre was a turning point for China, because they were pro-democracy protests. The Chinese Communist Party (CCP) leaders realized that young people were becoming contemptuous of communist ideology, and they made a decision to replace it with highly nationalistic anti-Japanese hate ideology. Since then, they've conducted a vitriolic anti-Japanese hate campaign which has been successful in the sense that most Chinese hate the Japanese.

China has been preparing for war for decades. But things appear to have taken a turn for the worse in July 2016, when the United Nations Permanent Court of Arbitration in The Hague issued a ruling that completely eviscerated China's claims to the South China Sea. The decision infuriated the Chinese, even more so because the court case had been brought and won by the hated Philippines barbarians. Almost every Chinese claim to the South China Sea was declared invalid, unfounded and illegal.

This appears to have been a turning point for the Chinese. Suddenly, they seemed to double down on their preparations for war. China's president Xi Jinping in 2015 had promised US president Barack Obama that the artificial islands that China was building would be for tourists. This was a lie, but at least China was maintaining a public fiction.

But after the Hague Tribunal ruling, China went all out on preparations for war without any pretense. They've rapidly built up military bases in the South China Sea, they've issued a violent "Sinicization" policy for all religions, essentially to the effect that Xi Jinping is higher than God, and they built huge concentration camps and crematoria in East Turkistan (Xinjiang province) to conduct genocide and ethnic cleansing of Uighurs, a Turkic minority with historic enmity to the Chinese. One apparent purpose of the ethnic cleansing policy is to open the route through Pakistan to Gwadar and Karachi seaports, for access to the Pacific Ocean.

The following are some of the activities that China is taking to actively prepare for war:

- by building illegal military bases in the South China Sea, to prevent the US from defending Taiwan and Japan from Chinese attack. [194]
- by building and deploying numerous powerful nuclear missile systems with no purpose other than to attack and destroy American cities, bases, and aircraft carriers [195] [196]
- by using hundreds of thousands of Chinese students and workers, which they call "magic weapons," to infiltrate colleges and businesses in numerous countries, under the control of the military-controlled United Front Work Department (UFWD) [197] [198]
- by actively hacking computer databases in thousands of western businesses and government agencies [199]
- by building computer databases containing detailed personal information on tens of millions of Westerners, including Americans [199]
- by using Huawei chips and phones and routers to install "backdoors" in order to spy on and control significant portions of the internet [200]
- by passing the National Intelligence Law, which demands that all organizations, including Huawei, "support, cooperate with, and collaborate with" China's military in collecting intelligence, even when doing so is illegal. [160] "
- by using "debt trap diplomacy" to gain control of infrastructure projects and install large communities of Chinese families in dozens of countries through the Belt and Road Initiative (BRI) [201]
- by conducting genocide and ethnic cleansing of Uighurs and Kazakhs in East Turkistan to gain access to mining and energy projects in Central Asia and to have a clear path to Gwadar port in Pakistan [202] [203] [204]

These subjects will be discussed in detail in later chapters. I could easily lengthen this "rap sheet" by a dozen more criminal activities. What is abundantly clear is that the Chinese Communist Party (CCP) has become an international criminal organization, who doesn't care who knows.

2.4. China's historic incompetence compared to Japan

As I wrote earlier, my objectives in writing this book have evolved, and the third objective came after the startling realization that China's desire for revenge for its "Century of Humiliation" comes from the fact that China has consistently and repeatedly been bested by Japan since 1870. And this is not because of the lack of brilliant Chinese people, but because of the stupid and corrupt Chinese government.

Prior to World War II, the last time that Japan lost a major war in Asia was the Imjin Wars with Korea that climaxed on October 26, 1597, with the Battle of Myongnyang (Myeongnyang), possibly the most significant battle in Asia during the entire millennium (until WW II). At that time, Korea was in a tributary relationship with China, meaning that Korea paid China a great deal of money, and in return, China agreed not to invade Korea and also agreed to defend Korea from foreign enemies. The Koreans, supported by the Chinese, won a brilliant naval victory in 1597 against the Japanese, using technologically advanced "turtle ships," believed to be the world's first ironclad warship. [85]

Since that time, China has been consistently bested by Japan over and over, militarily, economically, diplomatically, and in governance.

- Although both China and Japan were weakened by the Imjin Wars, Japan moved into the Tokugawa Era, governed by a Japanese clan, until the Meiji Restoration in 1868, while China allowed itself to be colonized for three centuries by a small army of Manchus (the Qing Dynasty), which it could easily have overthrown, even after the Taiping Rebellion (1850-64), until 1911.
- The political and economic development of Japan stood in stark contrast to that of China. The Meiji Restoration of 1868 had propelled Japan into the modern world. The Japanese had tapped into Western knowledge to develop an industrialized economy. Japan's military, once a barefoot army of samurai, were now a well trained Westernized armed force, equipped with modern weapons. [130]
- After 1870, Japan adopted a constitution while China chose to remain a colony of the Manchus
- Japan navigated international law while China expressed contempt for international law
- Around 1900, China declared war on the West (Boxer rebellion) while Japan embraced the West (Anglo-Japanese Alliance)
- Japan aggressively built its economy while China remained a feudal economy
- Japan modernized its military while China retained ancient military technology and an aging navy
- Japan humiliated and defeated China in the First Sino-Japanese war (1894-95)
- Japan forced China to accept the "21 Demands" (1915)
- Japan outmaneuvered China at the Versailles peace treaty conference and had to be saved by Woodrow Wilson
- Japan invaded and captured Manchuria from China (1931)
- Japan invaded and defeated China with the Second Sino-Japanese War (1937-45), including the "Rape of Nanking," and had to be saved from defeat by the United States.

- Since WW II, Japan has become a respected member of the international community, while China has done one stupid and self-destructive thing after another, including the Great Leap Forward, the Cultural Revolution, and the Tiananmen Square massacre, resulting in the deaths of tens of millions of Chinese from man-made famine, starvation, execution, and rioting.
- Japan has been a "developed" country for over a century, while China is still an "undeveloped" country today.

This last point is worth emphasizing. China says it wants to be "respected," but who can respect a country that BRAGS about being undeveloped, so that it can take advantage of the perks. Japan, of course, is proud to be a developed country.

China should be grateful to the United States, and should be thanking the United States for saving China several times, especially in WW II, but instead, they're developing nuclear missile systems to achieve the "China Dream" of destroying the United States — and themselves in the process.

Even worse, China is turning into the same kind of barbaric monster, with the same kinds of horrific atrocities, as Japan in the 1930s. It's truly sickening to watch. That's why I've concluded that China's demand for revenge against Japan is the crucible of the coming war in Asia.

Ironically, Taiwan has also bested China repeatedly since the end of World War II. Taiwan of course is populated by the same Chinese people as China. This proves that it's China's government, not the Chinese people, that is completely incompetent.

It's really depressing that China is letting itself go down the drain and will drag all the rest of us down with them. At the same time, it's worth pointing out that China will have its hands full fighting Taiwan, Japan, Philippines, Vietnam, India, and Russia. Furthermore, China has no experience fighting an external war, and is currently wasting vast resources building a navy that might be useful in their fantasy scenario of peacetime global force projection, but will not be effective in fight China's neighbors on land.

2.5. China's contempt for international law

We've focused on China's thirst for revenge against Japan for the barbaric things that Japan in World War II, and how China is pursuing the same barbaric policies today against Uighurs, Buddists and Christians.

We'll now look at China's thirst for revenge against the West for "Unequal Treaties" and a "Century of Humiliation."

My research on my book has been to determine from China's history how this happened. I've found so far that almost every CCP policy is connected in some way to the "century of humiliation," and particularly to events surrounding the 1860 Treaty of Tianjin and Japan's "21 Demands" in 1915, almost like a serial killer's actions are linked to some traumatic childhood event. We'll discuss the details of these "Unequal Treaties" later in this book, but here we want to focus how China's thirst for revenge has turned into utter contempt for international law.

In past decades, especially since "Nixon went to China" in 1972 and met Mao Zedong, almost everyone in the world was excited about China and wanted China to succeed in becoming an economic powerhouse and a responsible member of the international community. For this reason, numerous concessions were granted to China and billions of dollars were invested in China to make this happen. This including honoring China's request to take Taiwan's United Nations membership away, and give it to China.

But instead of becoming a responsible member of the international community, the Chinese Communist Party (CCP) have become international outlaws, contemptuous of international law. China's Foreign Ministry is laughably frequently accusing other countries of violating international law, when they violate international law all the time, and think that they are superior to it. It's like a women's rights activist who beats and rapes his own wife because he thinks that those laws don't apply to him.

China's contempt for international law has been exposed in many ways:

- The most obvious way is in the annexation and militarization of the South China Sea. The Chinese Communist Party was deeply humiliated and infuriated in July 2016 when the United Nations Permanent Court of Arbitration in The Hague ruled against China's claims to the South China Sea. And it was not just a partial loss or a vague loss. It was a complete repudiation of all of China's actions and claims, under the United Nations Convention on the Law of the Sea 1982 (UNCLOS). In researching this issue, as I'll describe later in this book, is that China's "historic" claims to the South China Sea are a complete hoax, without even a shred of validity. China's response has been that international law does not apply to it.

- The court also ruled that China's militarization of the South China Sea, by building artificial islands and installing military bases, is also completely a violation of international law. In 2015, China's president Xi Jinping promised US president Barack Obama that there would be no militarization of the South China Sea, and that the artificial islands would be for tourists. This was a lie. The Hague ruling evidently caused China to speed up its militarization of the South China Sea. The artificial islands have been turned into immense military bases, bristling with radar domes, shelters for missiles, warplane runways, and other heavy military equipment. No tourists are welcome. Xi Jinping claims that international law doesn't apply to China, but then lied about violating international law.

- The United States, Australia, Japan, and other countries have been conducting "Freedom of Navigation Operations" (FONOPS) by sending warships through the South China Sea, which the Hague tribunal ruled are international waters. China's Foreign Ministry shows contempt for international law by ignoring the court ruling and threatening military reprisal if the FONOPS continue. Some $5 trillion in trade passes through the South China Sea on ships each year, including $1.2 trillion of US trade, and trillions of Japanese trade. Once hostilities between China and Japan begin, China will use military force to prevent even commercial traffic from passing through.

- China has joined with Russia to cripple the United Nations Security Council. In 2010, Russia and China adopted a policy of using the UNSC to control US, EU and NATO policy, by vetoing resolutions for peacekeeping, but doing whatever they want without even asking the UNSC.

- When the US helped China join the World Trade Organization (WTO) in 2000, it was with the expectation that China would become a full and honest member of the international trading community. But China treated the WTO with the same contempt that it treats everyone and everything else. It has demanded that WTO rules apply to everyone else, but not to them. China repeatedly cheats and lies, and when the WTO rules against China, China just ignores the ruling (as it has ignored the Hague Tribunal ruling that China's activities in the South China Sea are illegal), and continues to lie and cheat.

- A related matter is that China has been stealing intellectual property from the United States and other nations, apparently because the Chinese people are unable to develop their own technology. All of China's neighbors — Japan, Korea, India, Russia, Taiwan, colonial Hong Kong — some of which are populated by the same Chinese people, have been able to develop their own technologies within the bounds of international law, but China seems unable to develop technology without stealing other countries' technologies or breaking international law in other ways.

- China isn't only getting revenge on Western nations. In using "debt trap diplomacy" in its contracts with dozens of countries to build infrastructure for the Belt and Road Initiative (BRI), China uses bribes and corruption to impose contractual debts that can't be repaid. In the case of Kenya, China's contracts stipulate that in case of default, China can take possession of any of Kenya's assets, within the country or abroad. [190]

- Also, the same BRI contracts impose the restriction that all disputes will be settled by courts in China, which means that the results will be completely biased in China's favor. [190]

The period 1840-1870 was a chaotic, traumatizing time for both China and Japan. In both cases, the West used military force to open their markets (through Britain's Opium Wars for China, and Commodore Matthew Perry's "visits" to Japan, respectively). Furthermore, both countries went through bloody generational crisis civil wars (the Taiping Rebellion and the Meiji Restoration, respectively).

After 1870, the two countries diverged. Japan enthusiastically entered the international community, and became a "developed nation" within a few decades (as it unfortunately also turned to militarism). But China is still an "undeveloped nation" today. They brag about it. They claim that they have to be given special concessions in trade negotiations, climate change treaties, and so forth, because they're an "undeveloped nation." The Japanese aren't making a similar claim. Why are the Chinese so far behind Japan after 150 years? What's wrong with the Chinese?

There's no doubt that Western nations took advantage of China's naïveté and credulity in imposing unfair treaties. But it kept happening over and over again, and the Chinese never seemed to learn. By contrast, the Japanese learned how to deal with international law very quickly. Why were the Japanese so much smarter than the Chinese?

Even today, the Chinese are doing one stupid, criminal thing after another — stealing intellectual property, illegally militarizing the South China Sea, violently suppressing Christians, Buddhists and Muslims. These are really stupid acts by a really stupid CCP. Japan isn't doing things like that. Why are the Chinese?

In my opinion, the most important battle in East Asian history for the past millennium was the Battle of Myongnyang (Myeongnyang) on October 26, 1597, the climactic battle of the Imjin Wars. Using superior naval technology and cunning, the Korean navy, with Chinese support, won a historic battle, using an array of 13 warships to destroy Japan's entire navy of 100-300 ships, completely humiliating Japan. It seems likely that by 1870, this battle motivated Japan to become militarily superior, and made China overconfident.

Here's something I'll say several times in this book: Friedrich Nietzsche said, "Insanity in individuals is something rare - but in groups, parties, nations and epochs, it is the rule."

Today, the CCP is deep into full scale insanity. They're planning to pursue the "China dream" — to get revenge by launching a full-scale war on Japan and the West. They think that they're going to win that war. There is no chance at all. They will lose, but not before bringing catastrophe and disaster on themselves and the world.

2.6. Does China deserve sympathy?

There are people who say that my criticisms of the Chinese Communist Party (CCP) are too harsh, and that they deserve our sympathy because of geography, or whatever. But it's very hard to feel sympathy for the CCP when these people repeatedly take actions as barbarians and monsters. They're building huge concentration camps and crematoria in East Turkistan (Xinjiang) and locking up millions of Uighurs and Kazakhs. Their activities in the South China Sea are totally criminal. They violently beat, torture and jail Buddhists and Christians, and destroy temples and churches. And if you're a member of the Falun Gong, then you can be thrown into a pit and have your fingernails removed with a pair of pliers. (Only a slight exaggeration.)

Can you imagine if the United States started building concentration camps and crematoria, and locked up all the Mexican immigrants? Or how about if in Britain, the English started putting Scots into concentration camps? That's what Xi Jinping is doing to Uighurs. These people in the CCP are barbarians and monsters, and deserve no sympathy.

And let's go back to the Great Leap Forward that Mao Zedong implemented in the late 1950s. I have a detailed description of that later in this book. This is not the policy of a civilized nation. It resulted in the death of tens of millions of innocent Chinese through starvation, execution, and murder by the army, because of utter stupidity of Mao Zedong. It's one of the stupidest and most destructive policies in history — though not as stupid as sending millions of Uighurs to concentration camps.

The research in this book shows that Japan has bested China in economy, government, diplomacy, and war. The CCP whine about not being respected, but how can anyone respect someone who brags about being "undeveloped" to get the perks?

These are not racist conclusions, for the reasons that I've stated repeatedly. It's not the Chinese people who are stupid. The same Chinese people live in Taiwan and Hong Kong, and both Taiwan and colonial Hong Kong have been vibrant economic superpowers, where the Chinese people experienced freedom of speech, and political freedom that the people of China can only dream of. It's not the Chinese people who are barbarians and monsters, but the barbarians and monsters in the CCP who are doing this.

In the West it's not politically correct to mention race, but race is everything. In the case of China and Japan, both countries are imbued with and drenched in racism. This book describes the anti-Japan hate campaign that the CCP launched in 1989 after the pro-democracy demonstrations and the Tiananmen Square massacre. This is all about race.

Everyone (including the Chinese) refers to China as the "Middle Kingdom." Most people don't realize that this is a highly racist term, dating back millennia.

The Chinese view the universe in three layers. The highest layer is the Kingdom of Heaven. The second layer is China, the Middle Kingdom — yellow race, black hair, brown eyes, yellow skin. And the bottom layer is you and me — the barbarians. This is ironic because the real barbarians are Xi Jinping and the CCP.

Readers of this book should realize that the Chinese people are being victimized by the barbarians and monsters in the CCP as much as anybody else is, and the CCP deserves no sympathy at all. And it's not the Chinese people but the CCP who are bringing catastrophe to China and to the entire world.

Chapter 3. Brief summary of generational eras

For most of the world, World War II was a generational crisis war. Crisis wars are the worst existential wars, where genocide, rape, mass slaughter and other atrocities become common, and the value of an individual human life goes to zero, and the only thing that matters is the survival of the society or nation and its way of life. A crisis war always ends in what I call an "explosive climax," a genocidal act so great that both the victors and the vanquished are shocked by it. In World War II, these climactic acts included the storming of Normandy beach, the firebombing of Dresden, and the nuking of Japanese cities.

China's history is filled with hundreds of crisis wars in the form of massive internal rebellions (civil wars). The most recent were the White Lotus Rebellion (1796-1805), the Taiping Rebellion (1850-64) and Mao's Communist Revolution (1934-49). China is overdue for a new massive civil war, and any sort of economic setback could be the trigger.

Once a crisis war ends, every nation at every time in history goes through the same series of generational eras:

- **Recovery Era (about 18 years).** Typically, a country is devastated and flat on its back after a crisis war. The traumatized survivors of the war (both winners and losers) institute harsh rules and create institutions to make sure that nothing so horrible ever happens again.
- **Awakening Era (about 20 years).** A new generation of kids make their voices heard, typically in the form of demonstrations and riots by college-age students. These kids have no personal memory of the atrocities of the war, and they're opposing the harsh rules imposed by the survivors. This results in a "generation gap" between the war survivors and their children.
- **Unraveling Era (about 20 years).** As younger generations gain power, the harsh rules imposed by the war survivors unravel. Things like discrimination, ethnic attacks, and fiscal irresponsibility become more common. Older generations begin to feel that a new war is coming. The nation is still being run by war survivors who are capable of negotiating and compromising.
- **Crisis Era.** As the survivors of the previous crisis war all disappear (retire and die), younger generations take power, and they are almost complete unable to negotiate and compromise. A small disagreement between two adversaries can lead to tit-for-tat escalations. At some point, there's a particularly shocking event (known as a "regeneracy event," because it regenerates civic unity for the first time since the end

of the previous crisis war) that signals the beginning of a new generational crisis war.

Understanding these generational eras is the key to understanding the behavior of both China and Japan in the last 150 years.

At the end of this book, there's a chapter describing the theoretical underpinnings of generational theory.

Part II. China and Japan since the end of World War II

Chapter 4. China and Japan during and after World War II

World War II started in 1937 with the Marco Polo Bridge Incident, which triggered the Sino-Japanese war. Japan committed many atrocities during that war — including comfort women, the Nanking massacre, chemical and biological warfare (Unit 731), and the Bataan Death March. In the end, it was America's armed forces that saved China from defeat by the Japanese.

In China, beginning in the 1930s, there was a civil war going on between the Nationalists, led by Chiang Kai-Shek, and the Communists, led by Mao Zedong. Once Japan invaded and the Sino-Japanese, the civil war was paused and a "United Front" was formed in China to fight the Japanese. Actually, the Communists took advantage of the situation by allowing the Nationalists to fight the Japanese alone, so they would be weakened.

Once Japan was defeated in 1945, the civil war resumed and the Communists won. The result was the Communist People's Republic of China, founded on October 1, 1949.

In the following chapters, we're going to describe what happened to China, Japan, Korea, and Hong Kong in the decades following 1945. What we're going to show is that China did made one disastrous, self-destructive mistake after another, with the result that China is still far behind the other nations in terms of the economy, quality of life, and political freedom.

Prior to WW II, Japan already had an advanced industrialized economy, far ahead of China's backward feudal economy. After WW II and the Communist Revolution, Japan continued to advance and the capitalist government became an economic powerhouse, while China's communist government made one stupid, disastrous mistake after another, and remained far behind Japan.

Chapter 5. South Korea's postwar economic miracle

For centuries prior to World War II, Korea was a single, unified country, though acting as a buffer between China and Japan. Japan occupied Korea after the Russo-Japanese war in 1905, and colonized Korea in 1910. Japan was ejected from Korea in 1945, only after losing World War II. [147]

To understand what happened to Korea and why there was a Korean war, you have to understand the anxiety and mood of much of the world after World War II ended. Here's what Hannah Arendt wrote in 1950 in the preface to her book, *The Origins of Totalitarianism*:

"Two world wars in one generation, separated by an uninterrupted chain of local wars and revolutions, followed by no peace treaty for the vanquished and no respite for the victor, have ended in the anticipation of a third World War between the two remaining world powers [America and Soviet Union]. This moment of anticipation is like the calm that settles after all hopes have died. We no longer hope for an eventual restoration of the old world order with all its traditions, or for the reintegration of the masses of five continents who have been thrown into a chaos produced by the violence of wars and revolutions and the growing decay of all that has still been spared. Under the most diverse conditions and disparate circumstances, we watch the development of the same phenomena — homelessness on an unprecedented scale, rootlessness to an unprecedented depth.

Never has our future been more unpredictable, never have we depended so much on political forces that cannot be trusted to follow the rules of common sense and self-interest — forces that look like sheer insanity, if judged by the standards of other centuries. It is as though mankind had divided itself between those who believe in human omnipotence (who think that everything is possible if one knows how to organize masses for it) and those for whom powerlessness has become the major experience of their lives."

This mood is hard to understand today, when the horrors of the war have been all but forgotten except for political clichés, but after years of violence in two world wars, and fear of a new world war versus the communists, the people of the world were all traumatized.

Into this traumatized world guided by "forces that look like sheer insanity," the Soviet Union undertook the goal to spread Communism as much as possible, and the West undertook to stop the spread of Communism, under the assumption that the spread of Communism, like the spread of Nazism and Fascism, could result in a Third World War. In Europe, these powerful emotions led to the Iron Curtain, separating Eastern Europe, under Communist control, from Western Europe.

In Asia, these two opposing forces brought about the partitioning of Korea. If Korea had been left alone, perhaps the Koreans would have formed an economic superpower, just like the Japanese and Taiwanese. But that's not what happened. Over the three years between 1945-48, the Soviet Army and its proxies set up a communist regime in the area north of latitude 38 N, or the 38th parallel. South of that line, a military government was formed, supported directly by the United States. [147]

In 1948, the United States called for a United Nations-sponsored vote for all Koreans to determine the future of the peninsula. After the North refused to participate, the South formed its own government in Seoul, led by the strongly anti-communist Syngman Rhee, and the North responded in kind, installing the former communist guerrilla Kim Il-Sung as the first premier of the Democratic People's Republic of Korea (DPRK) in the capital of Pyongyang. [147]

The Korean War (1950-53), which killed at least 2.5 million people, did little to resolve the question of which regime represented the "true" Korea. It did, however, firmly establish the United States as the permanent protector of South Korea, and China and the Soviets as true protectors of North Korea. Officially, the Korean war never ended, and South Korea, North Korea, China and the United States are still in a state of war. A ceasefire armistice was signed in 1953, and there is a demilitarized zone (DMZ) along the 38th parallel. Anyone who tries to cross the DMZ from either direction will typically be shot dead by the North Korean army. [147]

Since the Korean War, North Korea has been a bloody violent dictatorship in a command economy that ignores consumers and focuses almost exclusively on heavy industry, particularly military hardware, including development of nuclear weapons and intercontinental ballistic missiles. North Korea's people are some of the poorest in the world, even poorer than the people in China.

South Korea was completely different. After the Korean War, the South Korean economy was agriculture-based, and was one of the poorest in the world. South Korea took a different path than China or North Korea, and achieved its own "economic miracle."

South Korea's structural transformation is attributed to policy reforms that opened up the country to foreign investors. Indeed, the export-oriented policies of South Korea are one of the most important factors of its success: South Korea is now one of the top 10 exporters in the world, and its exports as a percentage of GDP increased from 25.9 percent in 1995 to 56.3 percent in 2012.3 [135]

A key to South Korea's success has been a strong business environment that fosters growth in the domestic market and attracts foreign investors. [168]

South Korea is known for its spectacular rise from one of the poorest countries in the world to a developed, high-income country in just a few decades. This economic growth is called by some a miracle, and described as the Miracle on the Han River, which has brought South Korea to the ranks of elite countries in the OECD and the G-20. [168]

Chapter 6. Japan's postwar economic miracle

After Japan surrendered at the end of World War II, US General Douglas MacArthur, the Supreme Commander of Allied Powers, led the occupation of Japan by American forces, and enacted widespread military, political, economic, and social reforms. [133]

As punishment for its war crimes, MacArthur convened war crimes trials in Tokyo in 1945-47. He transformed the economy into a free market capitalist system. He introduced land reform, to reduce the power of rich landowners, many of whom advocated war in the 1930s for their own financial gain. [133]

MacArthur also rewrote Japan's constitution, including Article 9, which prohibits Japan's armed forces s from being involved in military actions except in self-defense:

> "CHAPTER II - RENUNCIATION OF WAR
>
> Article 9. Aspiring sincerely to an international peace based on justice and order, the Japanese people forever renounce war as a sovereign right of the nation and the threat or use of force as means of settling international disputes.
>
> In order to accomplish the aim of the preceding paragraph, land, sea, and air forces, as well as other war potential, will never be maintained. The right of belligerency of the state will not be recognized." http://japan.kantei.go.jp/constitution_and_government_of_japan/const itution_e.html

That clause is still in effect, but in view of today's threat from China, many in Japan wish to revoke that clause, but they are opposed by communists and others sympathetic to China. However, legislation has been passed to re-interpret the self-defense clause to permit "collective self-defense," which would permit Japan to use its armed forces anywhere in the world in support of an ally (usually referring to the United States). [133]

The recovery of Japan's economy from the ashes of WW II has been called an economic miracle. By 1956, real per capita GDP had overtaken the prewar 1940 level, with per capita GDP growth growing at an average 7.1%. [134]

By 1973, Japan's per capita GDP was 95% that of Britain and 69% that of the United States. That was the last year of the so-called rapid-growth era, but the Japanese economy continued to expand at a comparatively brisk rate for almost two more decades. [134]

Japan had a stock market bubble in the 1980s that crashed in 1991. In the bubble economy, Japan's per capita GDP was 120% that of Britain and 85% that of the United States. There was an economic decline after that, but the process of catching up with the West, begun a little more than a century earlier, was basically complete. [134]

Today, there is still some controversy over whether Japan has done enough to atone for its WW II war crimes, but beyond that, Japan has become a respected member of the international community.

Chapter 7. Taiwan's postwar economic miracle

The first Sino-Japanese war occurred in 1894-95, and was a humiliating defeat to China. On April 17, 1895, Japan and China signed the Treaty of Shimonoseki, and gave Japan control of Taiwan. Japan annexed it outright in 1910, and remained in control until 1945.

Ironically, being a colony of Japan between 1895-1945 was economically beneficial to Taiwan. In 1899, for example, the Japanese established a fundamental pillar of the island's economy by creating a central bank called the Bank of Taiwan. By issuing currency, which was first silver-based and then gold-based, the bank established a standard unit of exchange, greatly easing all financial transactions. In the latter years of the Japanese era, fertilizer and textile manufacturing played a prominent role. Living standards improved for most people in Taiwan under Japanese rule, but the average local family remained poor, since a substantial portion of surplus industrial revenue was remitted to Japan. [175]

In 1949, Nationalist leader Chiang Kai-shek fled from China, after being defeated by Mao Zedong's forces in the "Communist Revolution" civil war. Chiang and his army fled to Formosa, which became Taiwan. [178]

Mao's army might have followed them into Formosa and defeated the demoralized and virtually defenseless Chiang Kai-shek-led regime but for an accident of history. America might have been indifferent to Mao's attack on Chiang which, if successful, would have made Taiwan a province of China at that time. But the Korean war, and America's defense of South Korea, followed by a bloody and prolonged military engagement with the new Peoples Republic of China and the People's Liberation Army (PLA) led the Truman administration to order a carrier group in Taiwan Strait and then led the US to become the protector of Chiang's government. [178]

Although Taiwan didn't have a General MacArthur who became the country's dictator, as happened in Japan, Taiwan depended on the United States for foreign aid, and that gave America a great deal of influence in Taiwan's government. [178]

In the 1950s, Taiwan introduced draconian fiscal policies to stabilize the currency. America provided a large military sea and air umbrella to protect Taiwan. [178]

The school system that had begun under the Japanese was expanded and improved upon. Primary schools, middle schools, high schools, colleges and universities were rebuilt and expanded to meet the growing needs of the multi-ethnic population — consisting of Hakka Chinese, Han Chinese and indigenous

Aborigine populations. Modern curriculum—in Mandarin, the common language of the mainlanders and the Minnan and Hakka peoples who had settled the island before 1945, had to be developed. [178]

Thanks to the hostility of the Chinese Communist Party (CCP) on the mainland to religion, Protestant and Catholic missions on the east coast of China were driven from their homes. Taiwan became both refuge for Chinese Christians and the new base for the missionaries. Many of the basic needs of the Taiwan's populace such as education, health care, food, and clothing were provided by members of the Protestant and Catholic missions that moved to the island in the late 1940s and early 1950s and by churches and denominations in the United States that supported this Christian missionary enterprise. [178]

I keep saying that the CCP in Beijing is responsible for one bad policy after another, and this is one more example. Taiwan received a great deal of help, in the form of money and expertise, from the religious groups, but the incompetents in the CCP treated them as enemies. No wonder China remains a backward country.

Prior to WW II, the Japanese colonists controlled Taiwan's economy through direct ownership and indirectly through state-owned businesses. While such control continued after the war under Nationalist rule, by the 1960s the government also started encouraging greater participation by private enterprise and free markets. [175]

Taiwan began manufacturing semiconductors in the 1960s, but did poorly as investors held back since semiconductors typically entail a large capital commitment while offering no guarantee that end products will ever reach stable quality control standards. However, the semiconductor industry took off after 1967, when the American company Philco Corp. initiated the local assembly of integrated circuits (IC). [175]

This opened the floodgates, as other Western companies moved operations into Taiwan to take advantage of lower wages. These companies included Royal Philips Electronics, RCA, TRW Inc., Texas Instruments Inc., and Baso Precision Optics Ltd. Thanks to investments by Philips, Taiwan Semiconductor Manufacturing Co. (TSMC) has grown to become the world's largest dedicated independent semiconductor manufacturer. [176]

Taiwan's Gross National Product recorded an explosive growth of a staggering 360% from 1965-1986. Even more impressive was the country's global industrial production output, which grew by 680% in the 1965-1986 period. [177]

I keep pointing out where the CCP in Beijing is responsible for one disastrous policy after another, and here we see another one. Taiwan has become a manufacturing superpower by inviting investments and licensing agreements from foreign companies, while China steals intellectual property and shows contempt for foreigners, while remaining a mediocre manufacturing nation.

Chapter 8. Colonial Hong Kong's postwar economic miracle

Hong Kong after World War II was fundamentally different from Japan, Taiwan and South Korea because it wasn't an independent entity — it was a colony of Great Britain. But that turned out to be a great opportunity for Hong Kong. After WW II, Britain's government was pursuing all sorts of Socialist and welfare policies at home, but they left Hong Kong alone. As a result, Hong Kong had what was widely believed to be the freest market in the world.

Between 1961 and 2009, Hong Kong's real GDP per capita was multiplied by a factor of nine. Today, its GDP per capita at purchasing power parity is the 13th highest in the world. Hong Kong therefore succeeded, in just a few decades, in transforming its economy into one of the wealthiest in the world, with a much higher standard of living than in mainland China. [136]

China got control of Hong Kong in 1997, with a promise to allow Hong Kong to continue its freedoms. However, the government in Beijing has been increasingly clamping down on political freedom, and has already violated its promise of fair and free elections. Ironically, Hong Kong is still doing well economically, because China has not yet clamped down on Hong Kong economically, as we'll see in the statistics in the next chapter.

Chapter 9. China's postwar economic and governmental disasters

9.1. China's failure at self-government

In my introduction to this book, I described the objectives. At first, it would be a study of China's claims to the South China Sea, until I discovered that it was a total hoax. Then I turned to the question of why China believed that it had been victimized by a "Century of Humiliation" and "Unequal Treaties," and when I researched this, it raised the obvious question of why the same thing didn't happen to the Japanese, since they were subjected to the same kinds of "unequal treaties."

Research into that subject revealed that after 1870, the Japanese continually and repeatedly bested the Chinese in all ways — militarily, diplomatically, economically, and in governance.

But in the last chapter we've seen that since World War II it wasn't just Japan. China was bested not just by Japan, but also by colonial Hong Kong, Taiwan and South Korea — diplomatically, economically and in governance, with military protection provided by the West. So in comparing China with Japan, it's not that Japan is so much better than China, it's that China is so much worse than everyone else.

It's easy enough to attribute China's incompetence to national stupidity, but that doesn't make sense, since the Chinese are known to have a higher IQ than Americans. And yet, the Chinese Communist Party has pursued one unbelievably stupid policy after another. I attribute this to a form of Chinese racism that has crippled the Chinese nation. I'll return to this subject below.

9.2. The Statistics

Let's start with some figures about IQ and income. The following figures are extracted from an analysis of 111 countries, ranking them by IQ, based on 9 international studies conducted between 1990-2010: [170]

Rank	Country	IQ	Income per cap
1	Singapore	108	$25,407
2	Hong Kong	108	$25,419

3	Taiwan	106	$25,000
4	South Korea	106	$13,710
5	Japan	105	$36,785
6	China	104	$ 1,375
27	United States	98	$36,609 [170]

This table shows that the Chinese people aren't stupid — with a national average IQ at 104, which is the sixth largest in the world. So if the Chinese people are so intelligent, then why are they so poor? It's because the Chinese people are smart, but the leaders in the CCP are incredibly corrupt and stupid. One interesting statistic is that the national income in mainland China is only a fraction of that of the people in Hong Kong — who are the same Chinese people, but live in an economically much freer society than the oppressive and corrupt dictatorship of the CCP, because Hong Kong was a British colony until recently.

Since 2010, all of these countries have higher per capita incomes, according to the CIA World Factbook: China $16,700, Taiwan $50,500, Hong Kong $61,500, Japan $42,900 and South Korea $39,500. China is the sick man of Asia, with incomes a small fraction of those of other Asian countries, and a far worse standard of living.

According to the World Bank, South Korea is ranked number 4 in terms of the overall Ease of Doing Business (DB) index in 2018, while the U.S. is ranked No. 6, as seen in the table below. [168]

2018 World Bank Doing Business Rankings

	South Korea	United States	Japan	China
Ease of Doing Business Rank	4	6	34	78
Starting a Business	9	49	106	93
Getting Electricity	2	49	17	98
Getting Credit	55	2	77	68
Trading across Borders	33	36	51	97
Enforcing Contracts	1	16	51	5
Resolving Insolvency	5	3	1	56

SOURCE: World Bank [135]

The same World Bank report finds Hong Kong's Ease of Doing Business Rank at 5, and Taiwan's at 15. [169]

The Human Freedom Index from Fraser Institute evaluates human freedoms in 160 countries, using 79 distinct indicators of personal and economic freedom in the following areas: [171]

- Rule of Law
- Security and Safety

- Movement
- Religion
- Association, Assembly, and Civil Society
- Expression and Information
- Identity and Relationships
- Size of Government
- Legal System and Property Rights
- Access to Sound Money
- Freedom to Trade Internationally
- Regulation of Credit, Labor, and Business [171]

The results are as follows:

```
Country          Human Freedom Index rank
-------------    ------------------------
Hong Kong          3
Taiwan            10
United States     17
Japan             31
South Korea       27
China            135      [171]
```

The web site notes that countries in the top quartile of freedom enjoy a significantly higher average per capita income ($39,249) than those in other quartiles; the average per capita income in the least-free quartile is $12,026. This is one more explanation why Chinese people are so poor, while the people of Hong Kong, Taiwan, Japan and South Korea are much wealthier. [171]

Transparency International draws on 13 surveys and expert assessments to measure public sector corruption in 180 countries and territories, giving each a transparency score of 0 (highly corrupt) to 100 (very clean). Here are the scores for the countries we're interested in: [172]

```
Rank    Country         Transparency Score
----    -------------   ------------------
14      Hong Kong       76
18      Japan           73
22      United States   71
31      Taiwan          63
45      South Korea     57
87      China           39      [172]
```

I've received many messages from Chinese, Taiwanese and South Koreans who state on a personal level what the above statistics describe.

9.3. The Great Leap Forward (1958-60)

Let's now look at some of the disastrous CCP policies since World War II.

Mao Zedong was a very charismatic figure who apparently was able to exert almost total control of the population in the 1950s. However, Mao's time as leader cannot be described as anything short of a total disaster for China and its people. Xi Jinping can whine and moan about unequal treaties, but no unequal treaties did any harm compared to the massive destruction wrought by Mao's policies.

Millions of people died from execution even in the "good times" of Mao's leadership, but no period was worse than the Great Leap Forward, during which some 20 to 30 million people died of starvation and executions in a man-made famine. [34] p. 296

It's really very hard to explain what happened in the Great Leap Forward in any rational way, because the plan was completely insane, as was Mao himself. Mao was crazed with determination to prove that Communism works, and the "Great Leap Forward" was devised to leap China forward ahead of the capitalist countries.

Mao's plan to implement "true" communism in China began in 1958 with the Great Leap Forward. Here's a summary of how the program worked: [35]

- 500,000,000 peasants were taken out of their individual homes and put into communes, creating a massive human work force. The workers were organized along military lines of companies, battalions, and brigades. Each person's activities were rigidly supervised. [35]
- The family unit was dismantled. Communes were completely segregated, with children, wives and husbands all living in separate barracks and working in separate battalions. Communal living was emphasized by eating, sleeping, and working in teams. Husbands and wives were allowed to be alone only at certain times of the month and only for brief periods. (This was also a birth control technique.)
- All workers took part in ideological training sessions, to provide for ideological training of the Chinese masses.

It's completely beyond me how anyone could ever believe that something so insane could ever work, and many people in the West during the 60s and 70s idolized Mao and considered China to be a "people's paradise." It shows how ideology can turn ordinary, educated people into complete idiots. What this experience shows is what a fanatical and desperate maniac Mao was to do something so disastrous.

Mao's stipulated purpose was to mobilize the entire population to transform China into a socialist powerhouse — producing both food and industrial goods — much faster than might otherwise be possible. This would be both a national triumph and an ideological triumph, proving to the world that socialism could triumph over capitalism.

First, Mao dismantled the Central Statistical Bureau, the organization responsible for keeping track of all the economic activity going on in the country. As a result, China's leadership had no real idea whether the Great Leap Forward was meeting its objectives or not. This gives the sense that Mao was playing the part of a desperate gambler who had no idea what he was doing, but closed his eyes and rolled the dice. [34] p. 300

Early in 1959, and again in July 1959, officials in Mao's government had begun to see that the program was failing. Their objections were rewarded with punishment. Mao was determined to follow his ideological course, no matter what else happened. The result was disaster.

The individual peasants and managers were required to report the size of the crop harvests up the line to the central government, but there was no way to guarantee that the reports were accurate.

On the one hand, there was no economic incentive for the farmers and managers to provide accurate reports, since everyone in a socialist society is paid the same ("according to his need").

On the other hand, there was no independent check of the crop harvest estimates. If the population had been much smaller, then the central government might have been able to send out enough bureaucrats to check the reports, or at least do spot checks. But with a billion peasants, no such meaningful checks were possible.

For the farmers and managers themselves, there was plenty of political incentive to overreport the crop harvest results.

As a result, even though actual crop yield in 1959 was a little smaller than it had been in 1958, the crop reports added up to an enormous increase in production, more than a doubling of output. [34] p. 302

By the time that Chairman Mao was finally ready to accept the situation, it was too late. There was too little food to feed everyone, and tens of millions died of starvation.

9.4. Mao's justifications for the Great Leap Forward

Mao pursued the insane Great Leap Forward with the fervor of a religious maniac, even dismantling the Central Statistical Bureau, and then ignoring bad news reports for months (and probably executing anyone who was responsible for the bad news reports).

We don't know Mao's justifications, except for the obvious one to try to prove the superiority of Communism. Here's what Mao wrote in 1939: [137]

"The socialist revolution aims at liberating the productive forces. The change-over from individual to socialist, collective ownership in agriculture and handicrafts and from capitalist to socialist ownership in private industry and commerce is bound to bring about a tremendous liberation of the productive forces. Thus the social conditions are being created for a tremendous expansion of industrial and agricultural production." [137]

This stuff is so completely delusional, so completely out of touch with reality that it's amazing that anyone could believe it, and yet Mao not only believed it but killed tens of millions of Chinese in the pursuit of those beliefs.

On April 15, 1958, Mao wrote "Introducing a Co-operative," saying the following: [137]

Apart from their other characteristics, the outstanding thing about China's 600 million people is that they are "poor and blank". This may seem a bad thing, but in reality it is a good thing. Poverty gives rise to the desire for change, the desire for action and the desire for revolution. On a blank sheet of paper free from any mark, the freshest and most beautiful characters can be written, the freshest and most beautiful pictures can be painted." [137]

This is the cruelest part of Mao's delusion. China's people were flat on their backs from the Sino-Japanese war and the civil war, and they wanted to put their lives back together. Mao took advantage of these poor, credulous people by inflicting on them one of the greatest horrors of any nation in history, an even greater horror than the Holocaust that the Nazis had just inflicted in the previous decade.

As an aside, China's people at this time were in the same generational archetype as America's Silent Generation, the generation that grew up during the Great Depression and World War II. That generation was originally called "Depression Babies," but Time magazine renamed them the Silent Generation in the 1950s because they did their jobs and didn't complain about anything. According to Mao, China's people at the time of the Great Leap Forward were "poor and blank," and a "blank sheet of paper," which is very similar to the description of America's Silent Generation. The generation that grows up during a generational crisis war suffers a kind of generational child abuse, and their trauma affects them for life.

Mao could have tried to prove the superiority of Communism in many other ways, without this insane, disastrous plan.

So even though we can't be sure what justifications Mao gave for his fanaticism, it's worthwhile to speculate on them, because it's pretty clear that Xi Jinping and today's CCP leaders are equally fanatical, and the same justifications are being used today.

Mao certainly would have been aware of the Boxer rebellion 68 years earlier, which failed but had the goal of ejecting foreign traders. Now, in the 1950s, China was still dependent on foreign trade.

Furthermore, China had to be saved by Woodrow Wilson and America after the Versailles betrayal, following World War I.

Then China had to be saved by American-led forces to eject Japanese conquerors in China during World War II.

So China was repeatedly dependent on other nations, especially Western nations, for its own physical and economic survival. This must have infuriated a fanatic like Mao, especially after he had committed mass murder and atrocities during China's civil war, and would not hesitate to do so again.

We can't discuss Mao's motivations without mentioning the racist belief that Chinese were racially superior to any other race on the planet. Mao of course would have been aware of Adolf Hitler's view that German Aryans were the Master Race, and racially superior to any other race on the planet.

But in comparing Hitler's racist views to the racist views of Chinese, we have to mention that Hitler's Master Race views were not very old, and were only part of the German culture for a few years or decades, and so could be forgotten easily after the war. But China's racist views go back three millennia — to the Xia and Zhang dynasties, and to Confucius and to Sun Tzu's Art of War. So Mao and all Chinese were imbued with this Chinese Master Race philosophy, and with all the delusional stuff that goes with it, like the Yellow Emperor and the Mandate from Heaven.

Next, Mao had, of course, fresh memories of the atrocities committed by the Japanese, and undoubtedly was planning China's revenge even at that time.

China had been thoroughly brutalized by Japan, and had lost Taiwan. Mao and the Chinese were full of fury, and were not interested in some theoretical exercise. They did not put everyone on a collective farm as a social experiment. They were bloodthirsty, looking for revenge. Mao was looking for a quick solution to his desire for revenge and launched the Great Leap Forward out of total desperation, and used "Communist theory" as a justification for the media. He may even have believed that he would lose the Mandate from Heaven if he didn't quickly attack the Japanese and get revenge.

And so, putting all this together, Mao's fanaticism in pursuing the Great Leap Forward was a desperate, delusional attempt to instantaneously create a huge economic windfall that he could use to create a military and attack Japan, and get revenge, and thereby keep the Mandate from Heaven.

Suggesting all of Mao's motives may be somewhat speculative, but we do know that all of these motivations are quite real, and remain real today, and we also know that Mao pursued a desperate, disastrous and fanatical policy in the Great Leap Forward, and so it's reasonable to connect the dots between the two.

9.5. Great Cultural Revolution (1966-76)

Mao was thoroughly humiliated by the Great Leap Forward. It showed that Capitalism was vastly superior to Communism. It had proven that the charismatic Mao had no clue what he was doing, and it substantially weakened Mao's political power. Mao decided to try to regain his power after the last disaster by launching an even worse disaster, the Great Cultural Evolution.

Before describing the Great Cultural Revolution, let's put it into a generational context. Mao followed a standard generational pattern that I've written about many times in the context of other leaders during a generational Awakening era when the preceding crisis war was a civil war. The Communist Revolution was just an ordinary civil war, and it followed the ordinary post-civil war pattern. Although both the civil war and its aftermath are "ordinary," they are filled with mass slaughter, rape, torture, and mass executions.

A country and a country's leader behave differently, depending on whether the preceding crisis war was an external war with another country versus an internal crisis civil war between tribes and ethnic groups. In the former case, the two armies each withdraw from the other country, and further contact between the populations is done diplomatically. But in the latter case, the two populations have to live with each other when the war ends — in the same country, the same villages and even on the same streets. This means that the hatred and the desire for revenge continue at a very personal level.

When a crisis civil war ends, the leader of the country, usually from the winning tribe or ethnic group, refuses to give up power, and becomes increasingly violent and authoritarian, using as an excuse that peaceful protests or negative news articles can turn into a new civil war. This excuse provides justification for mass slaughter, rape, torture, mass jailings, mutilations, and so forth. This happens in country after country, differing only in level of violence. Bashar al-Assad in Syria exhibits the most violence, using missiles, barrel bombs, Sarin gas, chlorine gas, and other atrocities on hospitals, marketplaces, schools, and civilian neighborhoods, resulting in genocide and ethnic cleansing of his Sunni Arab political enemies.

In order to illustrate how Mao was nothing more than an ordinary, run of the mill war criminal, let me take as an example Zimbabwe, a small African country that would seem to be as different from China as any country could be, and a leader, Robert Mugabe, who would seem to be as different from Mao Zedong as any leader could be.

The Rhodesia civil war climaxed in 1979, resulting in a new state, Zimbabwe. The victorious leader was Robert Mugabe from the Shona tribe. The Shona and Ndebele tribes had been enemies for centuries, and in order to control the Ndebele tribe, Mugabe ordered "Operation Gukurahundi" (Shona language for "The rain that washes away the chaff (from the last harvest) before the spring rain"). Mugabe's officers had received military training in China in the 1960s, and the new genocide of the Ndebele tribe was accomplished, with tens of thousands from the Ndebele tribe tortured and slaughtered, under orders from Mugabe. Some families were pushed into huts that were set on fire and they either burned to death or were shot dead when they tried to escape.

That wasn't the end of it. Since the 1980s, Mugabe has systematically won every election by marginalizing, jailing and torturing opposition politicians, marginalizing the members of the Ndebele tribe, and rigging elections. This has continued to the present time, until he was forced to step down in 2017.

This is the same pattern that is followed by every country in the decades following a bloody crisis civil war. I've written articles detailing this pattern among in numerous leaders from other countries in modern times, following a civil war, such as Hun Sen in Cambodia, Bashar al-Assad in Syria, Paul Biya in Cameroon, Pierre Nkurunziza in Burundi, Paul Kagame in Rwanda, the military junta in Thailand, Yoweri Museveni in Uganda, Robert Mugabe in Zimbabwe, Salva Kiir in South Sudan, and Joseph Kabila in Democratic Republic of Congo (DRC).

The details may be different, but Mao followed the same pattern. Mao was weakened by the disastrous failure of the Great Leap Forward, and he apparently believed that the leadership in the CCP was becoming too "revisionist," meaning supportive of his enemies, rather than ideological "pure," which means supporting him. In August 1966, Mao gathered a group of supporters to help him attack current party leadership and reassert his authority. [138]

Mao launched the Great Cultural Revolution. He shut down the nation's schools, calling for a massive youth mobilization to take current party leaders to task for their embrace of bourgeois values and lack of revolutionary spirit. In the months that followed, the movement escalated quickly as the students formed paramilitary groups called the Red Guards and attacked and harassed members of China's elderly and intellectual population. A personality cult quickly sprang up around Mao, similar to that which existed for Josef Stalin, with different factions of the movement claiming the true interpretation of Maoist thought. [138]

The Cultural Revolution was particularly harsh on religion. As we've described previously, the CCP cracked down on Chinese Christians in the 1950s, and Taiwan became a refuge for them, and a new base for missionaries. During the Cultural Revolution, any remaining foreign missionaries were imprisoned and tortured. Christian missionaries and charities were an enormous boon to Taiwan's economy, and their expulsion from China was just one more stupid mistake that explains why Taiwan, South Korea and Japan were economically and governmentally superior to China. [178]

The Red Guards, mostly younger students, soon brought the country to the verge of chaos; they fought pitched battles, carried out summary executions, drove thousands to suicide, and forced tens of thousands into labor camps, usually far from home. Intellectuals were sent to the countryside to learn the virtues of peasant life. Countless art and cultural treasures as well as books were destroyed, and universities were shut down. Insulting posters and other personal attacks, often motivated by blind revenge, were mounted against educators, experts in all fields, and other alleged proponents of "old thought" or "old culture," namely, anything pre-Maoist. [36]

With different factions of the Red Guard movement battling for dominance, many Chinese cities reached the brink of anarchy by September 1967, when Mao had Lin send army troops in to restore order. The army soon forced many urban members of the Red Guards into rural areas, where the movement declined. Amid the chaos, the Chinese economy plummeted, with industrial production for 1968 dropping 12 percent below that of 1966. [138]

Mao used the army to resist any attempt to remove him from power, until he died in September 1976, after 1.5 million people had been killed, and millions of others suffered imprisonment, seizure of property, torture or general humiliation in the Cultural Revolution. Deng Xiaoping gained power in 1977, and led the government for the next 20 years. [138]

9.6. Tiananmen Square Incident (April 5, 1976)

The Cultural Revolution brought chaos and destruction to years, leaving China's economy devastated. Prime minister Zhou Enlai was a moderating influence. Working with Deng Xiaoping, the two sought to implement moderate policies, trying to bring the warring political factions together. The result was that Zhou remained relatively popular. [142]

From 1970-76, Mao Zedong was ill, and China was governed by Mao's fourth and current wife, Jiang Qing, along with three men, together known as the "Gang of Four." The Gang of Four opposed the moderate policies of Zhou Enlai. If any more proof is needed that China's government is totally dysfunctional, then this is a perfect example. [140]

Zhou Enlai died on January 8, 1976. Deng Xiaoping gave the eulogy at his funeral.

Jan Wong, a Canadian student at Beijing University, wrote in a book called "Red China Blues": [141]

> "I had never seen such universal grief. It seemed everyone was weeping, men and women, old people and children. Some were almost hysterical.

Bus drivers, street sweepers and shop clerks all went about their chores with swollen red eyes. ...

Of the top Communist leaders, only Zhou had tried to mitigate some of the suffering of the Cultural Revolution, to stem some of the madness and to protect some of his old comrades from Mao's wrath." [141]

Because of his popularity, on the night of April 4, 1976, people laid thousands of wreaths in Tiananmen Square to commemorate Zhou's death. With memories of the May Fourth (1919) Movement still fresh in everyone's mind, the Gang of Four reacted by banning any gatherings in Tiananmen Square, and by removing all the wreaths. This infuriated people, and over 100,000 outraged people returned to Tiananmen Square on April 5. [142]

Although there was relatively little violence, thousands of people were arrested. The Gang of Four blamed Deng Xiaoping for the protests, but the protests exposed how unpopular the Gang of Four were. [141]

The "April 5th Movement" retained an enormous symbolic value, and was a precursor to the Tiananmen Square massacre thirteen years later, on June 4, 1989.

9.7. Tangshan earthquake (July 28, 1976)

After April 5, the chaos in China continued a few weeks later at 3:42 a.m. on July 28, 1976, with a magnitude 7.8 earthquake in the sleeping city of Tangshan, in northeastern China. [143]

Over a million people lay sleeping when the earthquake struck. The earthquake lasted only 14-16 seconds, but in that brief time, the entire city of Tangshan was leveled. A 7.1 magnitude aftershock struck in the afternoon, killing anyone left trapped in the rubble. [143]

9.8. Mao Zedong dies (September 9, 1976)

Once Mao Zedong died on September 9, 1976, the Gang of Four were thrown out of power and jailed by the military. Deng Xiaoping, whom the Gang of Four had blamed for all the chaos ascended to the leadership.

9.9. Deng Xiaoping's 'Reform and Opening Up' of China (1978-1989)

Mao's death in 1976 was a turning point for China. Mao had devastated the country with the Great Leap Forward and the Great Cultural Revolution, and the economy was in shambles. Furthermore, Mao had completely discredited Communism, Socialism and Marxism, because everyone could see that China's capitalist neighbors — Taiwan, colonial Hong Kong, South Korea and Japan — were all surging ahead with economic miracles. By 1978, it was already clear that the "economic miracles" in Japan, South Korea, Hong Kong and Taiwan were taking place, and as those economies grew into economic superpowers, China remained a backwater land of peasants.

The Chinese people believe themselves the superior race, and everyone else being barbarians and vassals. It was completely a violation of Chinese culture to turn to the lessons of other nations, and apply them to themselves. So it must have been an act of total desperation when Deng Xiaoping demanded that China "open up" to other nations, trying to catch up to Japan, which had opened up a century earlier.

Deng Xiaoping embarked China on the road to Economic Reforms and Openness, with new policies that were common in the West but radically new in China: [38]

- The de-collectivization of the countryside, followed with industrial reforms aimed at decentralizing government controls in the industrial sector [38]
- Special Economic Zones, areas where foreign investment would be allowed to pour in without strict government restraint and regulations
- Rapid development of the consumer and export sectors of the economy
- A much wider range of personal rights and freedoms for average Chinese as evidence of the success of the reforms [38]

It's kind of laughable, but this was a complete abandonment and repudiation of Marxism, Socialism and Communism. Recall what Mao wrote in describing Socialism and Communism:

> "The socialist revolution aims at liberating the productive forces. The change-over from individual to socialist, collective ownership in agriculture and handicrafts and from capitalist to socialist ownership in private industry and commerce is bound to bring about a tremendous liberation of the productive forces. Thus the social conditions are being created for a tremendous expansion of industrial and agricultural production." [137]

So Mao's principles were a complete disaster, led to mass starvation and tens of millions of deaths. When Mao finally died in 1976, it was finally possible to abandon Communism, although China continued to call itself a communist country, and the ruling dictatorship continued to call itself the Chinese Communist Party (CCP).

This was when various phrases started being used, like "socialist modernization" and "socialism with Chinese characteristics." What these phrases mean is "Capitalism and free markets and private property, but we're going to call it socialism anyway for public relations purposes."

According to the minutes of the "Third Plenary Session of the 11th Central Committee," meeting from December 18-22, 1978, where the reforms were presented, China must implement "socialist modernization": [139]

> "Socialist modernization requires centralized leadership and strict implementation of various rules and regulations and observance of labor discipline. Bourgeois factionalism and anarchism must be firmly opposed. But the correct concentration of ideas is possible only when there is full democracy. Since for a period in the past democratic centralism was not carried out in the true sense, centralism being divorced from democracy and there being too little democracy, it is necessary to lay particular emphasis on democracy at present, and on the dialectical relationship between democracy and centralism, so as to make the mass line the foundation of the Party's centralized leadership and the effective direction of the organizations of production. In ideological and political life among the ranks of the people, only democracy is permissible and not suppression or persecution. ... The constitutional rights of citizens must be resolutely protected and no one has the right to infringe upon them.

> In order to safeguard people's democracy, it is imperative to strengthen the socialist legal system so that democracy is systematized and written into law in such a way as to ensure the stability, continuity and full authority of this democratic system and these laws; there must be laws for people to follow, these laws must be observed, their enforcement must be strict and law breakers must be dealt with. ... Procuratorial and judicial organizations must maintain their independence as is appropriate; they must faithfully abide by the laws, rules and regulations, serve the people's interests, keep to the facts; guarantee the equality of all people before the people's laws and deny anyone the privilege of being above the law." [139]

There are two important concepts here: "socialist modernization" was necessary to open China to the world, and "democratic centralism" meant that the country was centrally controlled, but democratic in the sense there must be no suppression or persecution. Elsewhere, the same document says: "The Party members' right to make criticisms within the Party concerning the leadership at higher levels, up to Members of the Standing Committee of the Political Bureau of the Central Committee, must be guaranteed and any practice that does not conform to the Party's democratic centralism and the principle of collective leadership should be resolutely corrected."

This is what was meant by Socialism with Chinese Characteristics at the time of Deng Xiaoping in 1978, but none of this is recognizable in today's China, where members of the CCP are clearly above the law, and anyone who criticizes the CCP can be thrown into jail, beaten and tortured.

Furthermore, consider Deng's "24-Character Strategy" (24 Chinese characters):

"Observe calmly; secure our position; cope with affairs calmly; hide our capacities and bide our time; be good at maintaining a low profile; and never claim leadership."

Xi Jinping is certainly not following Deng's advice. China today is belligerent, boastful, and militarily threatening to anyone who does not do as China demands. It's the opposite of Deng's advice.

The fact that Deng's advice has not been followed at all is not surprising, since it contradicts millennia of Chinese culture.

This is a lesson for today as we try to negotiate with China to stop them from cheating at trade or stealing intellectual property. The failure of Deng's "opening up" policy is proof that China is incapable of changing its culture, at least not in a reasonable time frame.

9.10. Socialism with Chinese Characteristics

During the Deng Xiaoping era, the term "Socialism with Chinese Characteristics" entered common usage.

The term is completely double-speak. The defining principle of Marxist Socialism is Marx's Socialist Principle Of Distribution is "From each according to abilities, to each according to needs." In this delusional view, a supposedly benign government assigns work to people according to their abilities, and pays them according to their needs.

Mao Zedong had tried full-scale Communism with the Great Leap Forward, and it was such a total disaster that he totally discredited Communism and Socialism. Then Socialism was further discredited by the Capitalist "economic miracles" in Japan, South Korea, colonial Hong Kong, and Taiwan.

Deng Xiaoping replaced state-owned businesses with open markets, thus throwing out the last vestiges of what can actually be called Communism or Socialism. China was turning from a Communist dictatorship into a Fascist dictatorship. So for Chinese officials to admit that China was no long "Marxist" or "Communist" or "Socialist" would have been a public relations disaster.

So the solution was to say that China was a country following principles of "Socialism with Chinese Characteristics." This meant that China was no longer Socialist at all. Furthermore, the beauty of that phrase is that it can mean anything you want. So if China adopts some socialist policy, then it's a "Socialist" policy. But if China adopts a non-socialist policy, then it's a "Chinese Characteristic" policy. Very convenient.

(As an aside, the government of Cuba in 2011 partially opened up its markets to Capitalism, and specifically rejected any further policies based on Marx's Socialist Principle Of Distribution. However, Cuba still calls itself "Socialist." Maybe they should use the phrase, "Socialist with Cuban Characteristics.")

9.11. One-Child policy

Once Marxism, Socialism and Communism were abandoned in favor of free markets, China began to experience the same kinds of economic growth as its capitalistic neighbors — Japan, South Korea, Taiwan and Hong Kong.

For four decades, China has been attempting to control family planning decisions for individual families through the "one-child policy," announced in 1979, which called for forced abortions, forced sterilizations, and harsh fines to prevent families from having more than one child. It was only revised to a "two-child policy" in March 2016, allowing two children instead of just one. [145]

The two-child policy failed, and in August 2018, China announced in a Weibo social media post on Monday that all family planning matter has been removed from the new draft civil code that is scheduled for enactment in March 2020.

This means that all family planning controls should end. There will be no more one-child policy, no more two-child policy, no more forced abortions, no more forced sterilizations, and no more harsh fines.

According to Zhang Juwei, director of the state-run Chinese Academy of Social Sciences' Institute of Population and Labor Economics, "It has become an irresistible trend to allow people to make their own decisions on fertility, which will be the direction for the adjustment of population policy in the future."

The one-child policy has been a disaster for China's society. Women who had unapproved pregnancies could be violently dragged from their homes and forced to abort and be sterilized. If an unapproved child was born, then the child could not be registered, and essentially did not exist, so could not get schooling or other social benefits.

The negative consequences of the one-child policy were apparent almost as soon as it was adopted in 1979. The policy accelerated the aging of the population, and a decline in the working-age population, which threatened economic growth. Furthermore, with fewer children, fewer elderly people could be cared for by their children.

The one-child policy also had a malevolent effect on the demographics of China's population. The most well-known is that many parents aborted their unborn babies when ultrasounds showed that the babies were girls, because many parents wanted a boy who would take care of his parents when they got old, something that girls rarely did. The sex ratio peaked at 121/100 (121 boys for each 100 girls) in 2005, with recent estimates at 116/100, and as high as 140/100 in parts of rural central China. [146]

We said above that after China abandoned Socialism for open market capitalism, they began to experience the same kind of economic growth as their capitalistic neighbors. Some of this economic growth was accelerated by the one-child policy. Since girls were being aborted or killed, there were more young males, and without the "encumbrance" of girlfriends or wives, these males worked to push the economy forward faster than it might have otherwise. However, those benefits have now evaporated as the young males have gotten older, and there is no similar new generation of young males to take their place.

Aborting girl babies creates a vicious cycle. The number of births in a population grows exponentially based not on the total size of the population, but rather on the number of females in the population. So if there are fewer girls, then there will be fewer females, and fewer births. This vicious cycle is in fact occurring, as statisticians are predicting a sharp fall in China's population in the next decade for exactly this reason.

The two-child policy did little to improve these figures. Many couples chose not to have a second child simply because they don't trust the authorities, and feared reprisals. For those who do have a second child, the birth ratio problem is exacerbated. Those with a daughter, knowing that they could have only one more child, almost universally aborted a female baby.

The population growth rate is below what was promised, and is far from satisfactory. In fact, in some regions the number of births is decreasing. In the first six months of 2018, the number of births in many provinces in mainland China fell by 15-20% from the year before.

It seems that there are a lot of reasons why China's mothers don't want more than one child, according to a web site reader who sent me the following:

"My Chinese wife was an elementary school teacher in Xi'an, China. She says that the biggest reasons why the two-child policy would fail were mostly economic. Consider the following:

(*) Children have to be taken care of when they are born. If the couple does not have relatives nearby when the child is born, then one must leave the workforce. While that is on the face of things the same as in the States, it can be far deeper in China, since the "baby-sitter" is responsible for the academic success or

failure of the children. (My Chinese relatives have both positive and negative examples in their families.)

(*) Contrary to "official belief" by most everybody outside of China, Chinese education is *not* free. (By law, it is *supposed to be free.*) The biggest reasons are that all the schools in a city are ranked in quality. Every parent wants their kids to get into the best quality schools, so as to improve their educational chances later on. It has not been uncommon within Xi'an for parents to pay a bribe to get their kids into a better school in excess of $8,000. That starts first with kindergarten, then for first grade, then again for junior high, and again for senior high.

(*) Many teachers would teach sub-standard classes in the school, and then tell the parents that if they wanted their children to get better chances later on, they would have to attend the teachers' own private lessons after school, which were never free.

(*) Most of the kids in the cities will attend private classes after school in other schools to get an edge over the competition for the limited seats in the best schools.

(*) Students who don't pass the zhongkao don't get into senior high school. They get only one more chance to try the exam a year later if they fail the first time. At this point, schools are very reluctant to allow students into senior high schools through bribes because of Xi's anti-corruption drive.

(*) Then the students have to pass the gaokao or else they don't get into college. More private school expenses. Students may have one or two more chances to pass the gaokao, but most do not; they have been socially placed for life.

(*) Once students graduate from a university, they then have to pass school-specific entrance exams to get into graduate school. And even more bribes and private school expenses.

(*) The parents are responsible for getting their kids their first jobs, based on guanxi. Obtaining that guanxi can be quite expensive and take many years. My wife spent a LOT of time and money to get her son his first job after he graduated from the university with a degree in civil engineering.

(*) Many college-graduate girls will not marry young guys if they don't already have a house and a car. Since both of those are horribly expensive in the city, they have to depend upon their parents to provide the funds and/or credit.

In short, even one child is too expensive for a couple in China.

Then comes the fact that now, a married couple also has to support *two* sets of parents. My wife has four sisters and a brother, so they have no problems taking care of her parents. But her son, and her nieces and nephews, will have to support *two* sets of parents because of the one-child policy in place for their *generation. Add to that the costs of bribing their children through the education system, and you have a completely broken economic system at the family level.*

That is why an increasingly large number of Chinese children are delaying marriage, and often forsaking the entire concept."

Like many CCP policies, the one-child policy was one of the stupidest of any nation in history, and its disastrous consequences are now being felt.

9.12. Tiananmen Square massacre (June 4, 1989)

Deng's reforms came to a halt in 1989, with the Tiananmen Square massacre of thousands of peacefully protesting young college students.

Let's recall the following phrase from Deng Xiaoping's description of "socialist modernization":

"In ideological and political life among the ranks of the people, only democracy is permissible and not suppression or persecution. ... The constitutional rights of citizens must be resolutely protected and no one has the right to infringe upon them."

The last vestiges of democracy were extinguished on June 4, 1989, when China's army slaughtered thousands of peacefully protesting college students making pro-democracy demands.

Students from Beijing's Art College built a gigantic 'Goddess of Democracy' and placed it just opposite the portrait of Mao Zedong on the Gate of Heavenly Peace, infuriating CCP leaders. (RFI/Jan van der Made) [144]

In May 1989, exactly 70 years after the May 4th movement, millions of young Chinese students crowded into Beijing's Tiananmen Square to demand greater democracy and less repression, exactly what Deng Xiaoping had called for. On June 4, Chinese troops and security police stormed through Tiananmen Square, firing indiscriminately into the crowds of protesters. Thousands of students were killed, and tens of thousands were arrested.

Today, it's forbidden in China to talk about the Tiananmen Square massacre, and anyone who does can be punished.

9.13. Collapse of the Soviet Union (December 26, 1991)

That wasn't the only thing that happened around that time. On December 26, 1991, the Soviet Union collapsed, and all the former Soviet republics became independent self-governing nations.

Arguably, the collapse of the Soviet Union was more traumatic to the CCP than even the Tiananmen Square massacre. Suddenly, the leadership of the CCP were staring death in the face, as they considered the fact that something like the Tiananmen Square protests could force the Chinese Communist Party to collapse as well. Ever since the Bolshevik Revolution, Russian communism had always been the role model for Chinese communism. If Russian communism could collapse, then so could Chinese communism.

In the 1990s, Socialism with Chinese Characteristics began to take on a whole new and far darker and more sinister meaning. The CCP leadership became increasingly paranoid, and began seeing ghosts. Centralism was still in play, but democratic centralism was gone. The "right to make criticisms" was gone, and any criticism of the CCP leadership could lead to torture, rape and jailing.

Religious persecution surged, as we described detail in earlier chapters. The Buddhism-based Falun Gong movement was and is particularly targeted, after millions of people became practioners of their form of meditation. The CCP has increasingly cracked down on Christianity and even Daoism, for fear their practice could lead to overthrow of the CCP.

9.14. China's nationalist anti-Japan propaganda (1989-present)

When any country is preparing for war, it's necessary to educate and motivate the public to prepare them for war. If you're going to slaughter, torture and attempt to exterminate the people of another country, you have to convince your own public, including your own army, that those people are worthy of extermination. The tools you would use would be to incite in your own people, nationalism, xenophobia, hatred, and racism toward the people that you want to exterminate.

In the case we're describing, China has been conducting a vitriolic anti-Japan propaganda campaign since 1989, the time of the Tiananmen Square massacre.

The student pro-democracy protests that led to the Tiananmen Square massacre in 1989 frightened CCP officials, who realized that being pro-democracy meant that the young people were becoming increasingly contemptuous of communist ideology. [98]

The CCP decided to replace indoctrination of communist ideology with indoctrination of Chinese nationalism.

The CCP launched the Patriotic Education Campaign, a propaganda campaign designed to restore the legitimacy of the CCP government, according to University of Victoria (Canada) sociology professor Min Zhou: [98]

> "The propaganda has been carried out through both the educational system and the mass media. It is promulgated not only in the form of school curricula (especially officially-sanctioned history textbooks), but also in the form of broadcast media, films, museums and memorials. ...
>
> Although everyone in China can be subject to nationalist propaganda, the Chinese youth have been singled out as the main target group. Accounting for a large part of this nationalist propaganda, patriotic education is incorporated into the entire process of education from "kindergartens all the way through the universities" .... Nationalist propaganda focuses on restoring national pride and eliminating national humiliation. China's official media and its education system propagate nationalism through repeated emphasis on China's humiliation and victimhood caused by foreign powers over the past two centuries.
>
> Within this discourse, a particular emphasis is placed upon China's suffering at the hands of aggressive Japanese imperialists.... Japan figures prominently in China's nationalist propaganda. One essential component of this propaganda is the historical memory of Japan's wartime atrocities and its apparent lack of sincerity in coming to terms with this history." [98]

This anti-Japan propaganda campaign is continuing, and is pursued vigorously today as part of China's preparation for war with Japan.

According to Michael Yon, an American with a Thai family: [96]

> "China is leading a deadly information war. The first target is Japan. The ultimate target is the United States. For more than two years, our research team and I have been warning that a Chinese radicalization program will lead to terrorism against Japanese. These predictions are proving true, so far with minor attacks. In November 2015, a Korean extremist detonated an explosive device inside the grounds of Yasukuni Shrine. He fled to South Korea but was arrested when he returned to Japan the following month." [96]

Yon says that he's personally researched the effectiveness of China's anti-Japan information campaign in eleven countries in the Asia-Pacific region. He says that China's claims about other countries are false: [96]

> "Most countries depicted in propaganda as having anti-Japan grievances are the opposite. For example, Japan fought for Indonesian independence and its soldiers are buried at the Indonesian equivalent of Arlington National Cemetery. A teammate and I saw Japanese buried with honors up front among thousands of Muslim graves.
>
> Thailand is another country believed to harbor animosity. Thais hold no animosity for Japanese. They were allies. Relations are warm at the government level and at the street level. Today, my Thai family (I am American) often vacations in Japan. There is a large memorial in a school for Japanese soldiers in Ban Kat, near my office. Would Thais permit a memorial for 18,000 soldiers in a school if Japanese had ravaged the area? I asked former Thai Prime Minister Abhisit Vejjajiva during a private conversation in Bangkok if Thailand holds any position about Yasukuni Shrine or Comfort Women issues—the answer was no." [96]

Yon's research confirms the statistics in the Pew Global research that appear later in this book. In Indonesia, the percentage of people with a favorable view of Japan is a very high 77%, while for Thailand it's an even higher 81%. [97]

If you look at that table, then there are only two countries listed with an extremely low favorability rating: China at 8%, and South Korea at 22%. That's not surprising, since Japan colonized Korea and invaded China. [97]

Many of Japan's atrocities have been fully and repeatedly verified — the Nanking massacre, Japan's Unit 731, the Bataan Death March. But in one case there is controversy. [184]

China and South Korea have also during the last decades been extremely critical of Japan over the subject of "comfort girls," the accusation that the Japanese abducted Korean and Chinese girls to be used as forced prostitutes. The controversy has to do with the word "abducted," where the word "tricked" might be a better choice, since the girls signed up for the jobs voluntarily, although they the job description was more of a nursemaid, not a prostitute. [95]

In August 1944, the US army interrogated twenty Korean "comfort girls" who had been freed by the Americans from the Japanese in Burma. According to the report: [95]

> "A "comfort girl" is nothing more than a prostitute or "professional camp follower" attached to the Japanese Army for the benefit of the soldiers. The word "comfort girl" is peculiar to the Japanese. ...
>
> Early in May of 1942 Japanese agents arrived in Korea for the purpose of enlisting Korean girls for "comfort service" in newly conquered Japanese territories in Southeast Asia. The nature of this "service" was not specified but it was assumed to be work connected with visiting the wounded in hospitals, rolling bandages, and generally making the soldiers happy. The inducement used by these agents was plenty of money, an opportunity to pay off the family debts, easy work, and the prospect of a new life in a new land, Singapore. On the basis of these false representations many girls enlisted for overseas duty and were rewarded with an advance of a few hundred yen.
>
> The majority of the girls were ignorant and uneducated, although a few had been connected with "oldest profession on earth" before. ...
>
> In Myitkyina the girls were usually quartered in a large two story house (usually a school building) with a separate room for each girl. There each girl lived, slept, and transacted business. In Myitkyina their food was prepared by and purchased from the "house master" as they received no regular ration from the Japanese Army. They lived in near-luxury in Burma in comparison to other places. This was especially true of their second year in Burma. They lived well because their food and material was not heavily rationed and they had plenty of money with which to purchase desired articles. They were able to buy cloth, shoes, cigarettes, and cosmetics to supplement the many gifts given to them by soldiers who had received "comfort bags" from home.
>
> While in Burma they amused themselves by participating in sports events with both officers and men, and attended picnics, entertainments, and social dinners. They had a phonograph and in the towns they were allowed to go shopping. ...
>
> Officers were allowed to come seven nights a week. The girls complained that even with the schedule congestion was so great that they could not care for all guests, thus causing ill feeling among many of the soldiers.

Soldiers would come to the house, pay the price and get tickets of cardboard about two inches square with the prior on the left side and the name of the house on the other side. Each soldier's identity or rank was then established after which he "took his turn in line". The girls were allowed the prerogative of refusing a customer. This was often done if the person were too drunk. ...

The interrogations further show that the health of these girls was good. They were well supplied with all types of contraceptives, and often soldiers would bring their own which had been supplied by the army. They were well trained in looking after both themselves and customers in the matter of hygiene. A regular Japanese Army doctor visited the houses once a week and any girl found diseased was given treatment, secluded, and eventually sent to a hospital. ...

The average Japanese soldier is embarrassed about being seen in a "comfort house" according to one of the girls who said, "when the place is packed he is apt to be ashamed if he has to wait in line for his turn". However there were numerous instances of proposals of marriage and in certain cases marriages actually took place.

All the girls agreed that the worst officers and men who came to see them were those who were drunk and leaving for the front the following day. But all likewise agreed that even though very drunk the Japanese soldier never discussed military matters or secrets with them. Though the girls might start the conversation about some military matter the officer or enlisted man would not talk, but would in fact 'scold us for discussing such un-lady like subjects. Even Col. Maruyama when drunk would never discuss such matters.'" [95]

Returning now to Michael Yon's research on China's anti-Japan propaganda: [96]

"However, propaganda that Japanese kidnapped up to 400,000 sex-slaves for the Comfort Women system is false. There were scattered cases, such as on Java in the Dutch East Indies. I found what appear to be three new cases in Myanmar and I interviewed a 97-year-old survivor. However, they mostly were volunteers. There is evidence that some were tricked, typically by Korean brokers. But the propaganda persists. Just 20 years ago, they were saying 200,000 were kidnapped, and before that 20,000. At this rate of inflation, we will soon reach a million." [96]

We know that the Chinese lie about everything, and so nothing that the Chinese say about comfort women has any credibility at all, and can be completely ignored. It's clear from the US Army report and Michael Yon's research that there were several thousand comfort girls, some had already been prostitutes while others were tricked, and that they were usually treated well by the Japanese soldiers.

The point is that the truth doesn't matter to the Chinese. They are on an anti-Japanese hate propaganda campaign, in preparation for war, and the only thing that matters is what the Chinese people believe, and it's pretty clear that they believe what the CCP tells them to believe.

9.15. Yellow race, black hair, brown eyes, yellow skin

The anti-Japan propaganda hate campaign came several years after a blatantly racist anti-Japan song became popular in China. The concept of "yellow race" and "yellow skin" is a strong part of Chinese chauvinism, with Chinese defined as descendants of the Yellow Emperor, the heirs of a glorious civilization who will recover their preeminence. [2]

This chauvinism was apparent in the lyrics of the popular 1980s song Descendants of the Dragon, "With brown eyes, black hair and yellow skin, we are forever descendants of the dragon":

Heirs of the Dragon

Music and Lyrics by Hou Dejian

In the Far East there is a river,
its name is the Yangtze River
In the Far East there is a river,
its name is the Yellow River

Although I've never seen the beauty of the Yangtze,
in my dreams I miraculously travel the Yangtze's waters
Although I've never heard the strength of the Yellow River,
the rushing and surging waters are in my dreams

In the Ancient East there is a dragon,
her name is China
In the Ancient East there is a people,
they are all the heirs of the dragon

I grew up under the claw of the dragon,
after I grew up I became an heir of the dragon

Black eyes, black hair, yellow skin,
forever and ever an heir of the dragon

One hundred years ago on a tranquil night,
in the deep of the night before enormous changes
Gun and cannon fire destroyed the tranquil night,
surrounded on all sides by the appeasers' swords

How many years have gone by with the gunshots still ringing out,
how many years followed by how many years
Mighty dragon, mighty dragon open your eyes,
forever and ever open your eyes [3]

So after the 1989 pro-democracy demonstrations, this popular song provided the pathway for the CCP's anti-Japan hate propaganda campaign.

This became a popular song in China in the 1980s, almost 100 years after the Sino-Japanese war of 1894-95, in which China was deeply humiliated.

In November, 2017, China's president Xi Jinping explained to Donald Trump, how a "Chinese person" should be defined: a Chinese person, according to Xi, is someone who is a "descendant of the dragon with black hair and yellow skin." [10]

So this attitude explains why the CCP is exterminating the Uighurs in East Turkistan (Xinjiang) and the Tibetans in Tibet. It explains why the CCP has contempt for international law. It explains why the Chinese find it acceptable to steal every country's intellectual property, and why Huawei finds it acceptable to sell subsidized chips and electronic devices that can be controlled remotely by China's military.

Xi Jinping always talks about the "China Dream." This is the dream getting revenge against the Japanese, and, as "Descendants of the Dragon," to gain preeminence of the Chinese people, and set up a tributary systems where leaders of every country in the world pay tribute to Xi Jinping, the new Yellow Emperor of China.

This is probably the closest we're going to get for an explanation of China's delusionally insane behavior. On the one hand, we have the China Dream. On the other hand we have extermination of Uighurs, Tibetans, Buddhists and Christians, relentless contempt for international law, and a monster military buildup in the South China Sea. These two things are connected by a belief in the superiority of the yellow race and an overwhelming desire for revenge for a "century of humiliation," combined with a delusional expectation of "national rejuvenation."

Part II. China and Japan since the end of World War II

I'll repeat what Friedrich Nietzsche said, "Insanity in individuals is something rare - but in groups, parties, nations and epochs, it is the rule."

Chapter 10. Rise of China's dictator Xi Jinping

10.1. Biography of Xi Jinping

Xi Jinping was born on June 15, 1953, the son of Xi Zhongxun, a former comrade of Mao Zedong. However, Xi Zhongxun was purged in 1962, and Xi Jinping was sent to a work camp for seven years during Mao's Great Cultural Revolution. He joined the Communist Party and rose through its ranks. Xi Jinping traveled to the United States and spent time in Iowa with an American family, learning the finer points of agriculture and tourism. After his return, he served as vice mayor of Xiamen in Fujian, where in 1987 he married folk singer Peng Liyuan, who also holds the rank of army general in the People's Liberation Army. The couple has a daughter, Xi Mingze, who studied at Harvard University under a pseudonym. [11]

In early 2012, Xi Jinping traveled to the United States to meet with President Barack Obama and members of his cabinet, and made a nostalgic trip back to Iowa. On November 15 of that year, he was elected general secretary of the Communist Party and chairman of the Central Military Commission. On March 14, 2013, he was elected president of the People's Republic of China. [11]

That's when Xi triggered his anti-corruption campaign targeting 100,000 officials, mostly his political opposition. [11]

10.2. Xi Jinping lies about South China Sea (Sept 25, 2015)

A significant meeting occurred between Xi Jinping and Barack Obama in the White House Rose Garden, on September 25, 2015. At that time, there were already signs that China was building illegal military bases in the South China Sea. In the joint press conference, Obama said:

> "I conveyed to President Xi our significant concerns over land reclamation, construction and the militarization of disputed areas, which makes it harder for countries in the region to resolve disagreements peacefully."

Xi, however, denied that militarization was taking place:

"Relevant construction activity that China is undertaking in the Nansha [Spratly] Islands does not target or impact any country and there is no intention to militarize.

Islands in the South China Sea since ancient times are Chinese territory. We have the right to uphold our own territorial sovereignty and lawful legitimate maritime rights and interests."

So Xi was able to pack several dangerous lies into two sentences:

- Xi claimed that China has no intention to militarize the Spratly Islands. As Xi already knew (and Obama already suspected), China was already rapidly militarizing the Spratly Islands. Xi was making a public, open lie to President Obama on the White House lawn. How stupid is Xi? Did he really think he would get away with that lie, and ever be believed again?
- Xi claimed that the Spratly Islands "since ancient times are Chinese territory." Once again, a complete lie, as described in earlier chapters. China shunned the South China Sea until Chiang Kai-shek became interested in 1947, and Mao simply copied him. Nine months after Xi gave this speech, the United Nations Tribunal in The Hague issued a ruling that all of China's claims and activities are illegal. China has ignored the ruling.
- Xi claimed "territorial sovereignty" which, according to the Tribunal ruling, is another lie.

I know that I keep saying this, but it's almost impossible to grasp the stupidity of these people. Chinese leaders whine because they aren't respected, but look at these ridiculous lies. How could anyone in the West have any respect at all for these pathetic leaders?

10.3. UN Tribunal declares China's South China Sea claims invalid (July 2016)

I've discussed this at length in earlier chapters: In July 2016, the Chinese Communist Party was thoroughly humiliated when all of their activities in the South China Sea were declared illegal by the United Nations Permanent Court of Arbitration in The Hague, which ruled that all of China's activities in the South China Sea are illegal and in violation of international law. [6]

It's worth mentioning here because I have the feeling that this was a major turning point, personally, for Xi Jinping.

Xi's lie was the Chinese equivalent to Adolf Hitler's 1938 promise to Britain's prime minister Neville Chamberlain for "Peace in our time."

Recall Deng Xiaoping's "24-Character Strategy" (24 Chinese characters):

"Observe calmly; secure our position; cope with affairs calmly; hide our capacities and bide our time; be good at maintaining a low profile; and never claim leadership."

Xi Jinping seems to have been following this strategy up to this point. He may even believe that he was following this strategy when he lied to President Obama on the White House lawn.

After the Tribunal ruling, however, Xi's policies became increasingly belligerent and high profile. Xi had been exposed as having made a very public lie, equivalent to Hitler's lie to Chamberlain, and so he must have decided that there was no longer any need to pretend. Militarization of the South China Sea became increasingly open and threatening.

Today, the Chinese military has turned the South China Sea into military bases, bristling with radar domes, shelters for missiles, warplane runways, and other heavy military equipment. The Chinese once claimed that the buildup was for tourists, but no tourists are welcome. China is openly preparing for war, and doesn't care who knows it.

10.4. Xi Jinping becomes 'the core of the leadership' of the CCP (October 2016)

By October 2016, Xi Jinping had purged enough of his opposition. At the end of the four-day sixth plenum of the Central Committee, the party called on all members to "closely unite around the party's Central Committee with Comrade Xi Jinping as the core." Xi's designation as "the core of the leadership" gave him substantial additional power, including final approval or veto power over CCP policies. [12]

10.5. Xi Jinping becomes dictator for life (March 20, 2018)

Analysts said that China entered a new era with the meeting of the National People's Congress (NPC) on March 20, 2018, when president Xi Jinping made himself a dictator for life, and the most powerful leader in China's history, possibly even more powerful than Mao Zedong.

The most significant visible change was that the constitutional limit to two terms as president was removed, essentially making Xi Jinping a dictator for life, like Mao. Furthermore, the constitution was changed to incorporate "Xi's thoughts," just like "Mao's Little Red Book of Quotations from Mao."

Xi had purged most of his opposition from the government. Xi was now in charge of all organs and branches of government, and could no longer be challenged. Many Chinese people were excited by this development, because they say that Xi has done so much to make China more powerful, and now can continue to do so.

However, many other people are pointing out. Absolute dictators are not infallible gods. Hitler was an absolute dictator, but the Holocaust was a disaster for Germany as well as the world. Mao Zedong was an absolute dictator, but Mao's Great Leap Forward resulted in the deaths of tens of millions of peasants from starvation and executions, which was a disaster for China. The problem is that absolute dictators are no different from you and me in the ability to make bad decisions, but when you and I make a bad decision then someone stops us, but no one stops an absolute dictator. Just as Mao could launch the disastrous Great Leap Forward without being questioned, Xi could launch a disastrous war without being questioned.

A good example of how delusional Xi is can be shown from this claim in his final speech to the NPC:

> "China is a socialist state under the people's democratic dictatorship led by the working class and based on the alliance of workers and peasants, noting that all power in the country belongs to the people."

This doesn't even make sense. China is a "dictatorship," but there is nothing "democratic" about it. All of China's elections are predetermined, and peasants and workers are permitted to vote only for the chosen candidate.

Xi talks about the "rejuvenation" of China through "Socialism with Chinese characteristics." He calls this a "New Long March," alluding the Mao Zedong's Long March that began in 1934 and marked the beginning of the extremely bloody 16-year Chinese civil war. According to Xi:

> "China has continuously striven for its dream of realizing great national rejuvenation for over 170 years.

> History has proved and will continue to prove that only socialism can save China. Only by sticking to and developing socialism with Chinese characteristics can we achieve the rejuvenation of the Chinese nation. ...

> Turning the grand blueprint for China into reality is new Long March. We need to uphold the great banner of socialism with Chinese characteristics. China's goal is to build a socialist, modern country by the middle of the 21st century."

The reference to "170 years" refers to the Opium Wars in the 1840s-50s, and it reveals the core resentment and bitterness towards the West that guide Xi's thinking. Xi and many Chinese blame China's poverty and backwardness on the Opium Wars with Britain in the 1840s, 170 years ago. According to this view, China would already be a great nation, if it hadn't been forced into submission by Britain at that time.

Once again, this is totally delusional on the part of Xi and other Chinese. Since the 1840s, China has had two extremely destructive generational crisis wars — the Taiping Rebellion and Mao's Communist Revolution — both of them civil wars, both of them enormously destructive to China, and neither of them the fault of Britain or anybody but the Chinese themselves. But the delusion of blaming everything on a war that occurred 170 years ago is extremely dangerous, because it can be used to justify such things as annexing other countries' regions in the South China Sea.

Xi added the following:

> "Since ancient times, the realization of the great rejuvenation of the Chinese nation has become the greatest dream of the Chinese nation. The Chinese people are indomitable, and will persevere. They have the courage for bloody fights against their enemies, and they are determined to restore their former glory. Today the Chinese people are more confident and more capable, and closer than ever before of realizing the great rejuvenation of the Chinese nation."

This is extremely ominous, since Xi is justifying in advance any pre-emptive military attacks that he may decide to make. And being an absolute dictator means that the decision will be entirely his.

Chapter 11. Xi Jinping adopts harsh, violent, dictatorial policies

Xi Jinping today is adopting the same dictatorial cult status that Mao Zedong had. He's declared himself "dictator for life," same as Mao, and he's even institutionalize those silly "Xi's thoughts," same as Mao. We could take Xi more seriously if he weren't afraid of Winnie the Pooh.

11.1. Sources of Xi's policies: Japan and Great Leap Forward

Xi's policies appear to be drawn from several sources:
- The brutal atrocities that the Japanese committed to the Chinese in the Sino-Japanese war
- Adolf Hitler's Lebensraum policy to annex regions belonging to other countries.
- Adolf Hitler's "Master Race" policy of racial superiority.
- Adolf Hitler's Holocaust policies of genocide and ethnic cleansing
- The violent policies of Mao Zedong during the Great Leap Forward, that resulted in the deaths of tens of millions of Chinese by torture, starvation and execution.

However, there are some major differences between China today, and China at the time of the Great Leap Forward. Recall that Mao referred to the 600 million people as "poor and blank," and "a blank sheet of paper." That was during a generational Recovery era, and Mao was saying that he could do anything he wanted to the people and they would accept it.

Today, China's 1.3 billion people are no "blank sheet of paper." I've received many messages from people describing on a personal level what the Chinese feel about their government. Here's one example from a South Korean:

> "Middle and upper class Chinese do not buy Chinese products. No way. They buy foreign products from Europe, Japan, The US, or South Korea. South Korea produces top notch appliances, televisions, clothing, cars, and even pharma, especially pharma. The Chinese know their products are all toxic and low grade. Only the poor Chinese buy Chinese.

> As for vacations, the Chinese want to vacation abroad so that they can smuggle out money, or even escape China and never look back.

China is a toxic and corrupt hell hole. The poor hate it. Pollution has already taken 7-8 years off of their lifespans, and they know it. Many Chinese men will never find a wife, and they know it. The Chinese government is controlled by two-bit gangsters, and the Chinese know it.

The moneyed Chinese just want to leave and never go back.

This statement encapsulates what we've seen in the statistics. China is an oppressive, corrupt dictatorship where a man can't even find a wife and have a family. Add to that the fact that you can be thrown in jail and tortured for growing a beard or praying in a Church, then you understand why this person says, "China is a toxic and corrupt hell hole."

11.2. Document #9 - China's belligerent rejection of Western values (2013)

As we've described in detail, Mao Zedong's Great Leap Forward in the late 1950s was a disaster for China, resulting in the deaths of tens of millions of Chinese through starvation, torture and execution. This led to decades of poverty for the Chinese people, while the people in Japan, Taiwan, and colonial Hong Kong thrived in economic miracles. This completely discredited Socialism, Marxism and Communism. After Mao's death, Deng Xiaoping was able to implement "opening and reform" of China, which was the end of Socialism, but the start of "Socialism with Chinese characteristics," which means "capitalism and dictatorship," like Hitler's National Socialism.

The 1989 pro-democracy demonstrations, followed by the Tiananmen Square massacre of thousands of young students, followed by the 1991 collapse of China's mentor, the Soviet Union, led to the paranoid Chinese Communist Party to crack down harshly on all religions and all pro-democracy opinion, and to start a vitriolic anti-Japan hate campaign.

By 2011, the CCP was getting extremely concerned by the infiltration of Western values in the Chinese media. The CCP announced that there were five things China would never do. These were: [159]

- no multi-party democracy
- no ideological pluralism
- no separation of powers or bicameral legislature
- no federalism
- no privatization [159]

There's always a feeling of delusional insanity when you read CCP announcements, as if this silly list of five rules could possibly change anyone's beliefs or attitudes.

However, the CCP doubled down on this reasoning when it became clear that there were still pro-democracy feelings among the Chinese people, and particularly were still being expressed in the Chinese media. In October 2013, a CCP article called for ideological uniformity, warned against 'anti-China forces' who are attempting to "Westernize" China with the aim of destabilizing it, and attacks those who have been proposing "neo-liberal economic and constitutional governance reforms." [159]

To combat this evil, the CCP's Central Committee under president Xi Jinping issued a notice: "Communiqué on the Current State of the Ideological Sphere." The Document Number 9 lists several particular aspects of this evil of these pro-democracy attitudes: [158]

- Promoting Western Constitutional Democracy: An attempt to undermine the current leadership and the socialism with Chinese characteristics system of governance.
- Promoting "universal values" in an attempt to weaken the theoretical foundations of the Party's leadership.
- Promoting civil society in an attempt to dismantle the ruling party's social foundation.
- Promoting Neoliberalism, attempting to change China's Basic Economic System.
- Promoting the West's idea of journalism, challenging China's principle that the media and publishing system should be subject to Party discipline.
- Promoting historical nihilism, trying to undermine the history of the CCP and of New China.
- Questioning Reform and Opening and the socialist nature of socialism with Chinese characteristics. [158]

Document number 9 directs communist party officials across the country to do the following: [158]

- Strengthen leadership in the ideological sphere.
- Guide our party member and leaders to distinguish between true and false theories.
- Unwavering adherence to the principle of the Party's control of media.
- Conscientiously strengthen management of the ideological battlefield. [158]

The doctrines described in Document Number were promulgated across China. In Hong Kong, which had the most free press in China, the CCP appointed Beijing officials to take control of all the newspapers.

Coinciding with the issue of Document Number 9, media organizations were informed that all journalists in China will be vetted and issued fresh press accreditation cards after they pass an examination to ascertain their political reliability. Directions were issued summoning hundreds of thousands of journalists to report for a 3-month training program where subjects include "theories on socialism with Chinese characteristics," and the "Marxist view on journalism." The journalists were directed to reject ideas of democracy and human rights, which are described as values propagated by the West and targeting China's Communist Party. They are taught that the United States is "trying to undermine" China. They were also told not to write articles favorable to Japan while discussing territorial and historical issues between the two countries. Similar instructions were given with regard to the Philippines and Vietnam. These strict controls were extended to Hong Kong, where Beijing appointed new mainland officials to take control of each of the media. [159]

The document lists the ways in which the West undermines China's communist government. I'm including this list because it's so laughable, as if taken from a comic book: [158]

- Some people have disseminated open letters and declarations and have organized petition-signings to vocalize requests for political reforms, improvement of human rights, release of "political prisoners," "reversing the verdict on '6/4'[the Tiananmen Massacre]," and other such political demands;

- they have made a fuss over asset disclosure by officials, fighting corruption with the Internet, media supervision of government, and other sensitive hot-button issues, all of which stoke dissatisfaction with the Party and government.

- Western embassies, consulates, media operations, and NGOs operating inside China under various covers are spreading Western ideas and values and are cultivating so-called "anti-government forces."

- Cooking up anti-government publications overseas.

- Within China's borders, some private organizations are creating reactionary underground publications, and still others are filming documentaries on sensitive subject matter, disseminating political rumors, and defaming the party and the national leadership.

- Those manipulating and hyping the Tibetan self-immolations, manufacturing the violent terrorist attacks in Xinjiang, and using the ethnic and religious issues to divide and break up [the nation].

- Accelerating infiltration of the Internet and illegal gatherings within our borders.

- "Dissidents" and people identified with "rights protection" are active.

- Some of them are working together with Western anti-China forces, echoing each other and relying on each other's support. [158]

So Xi Jinping ordered that this idiotic list of stuff be taught to people across China as dangerous threats to China's government.

I keep emphasizing how the people in Japan, Taiwan, South Korea and colonial Hong Kong were so much happier and wealthier than the people in China, and when you read this idiotic list of warnings, you have an idea why.

11.3. Sinicization of religion

When we look at how Japan, South Korea, Taiwan and Hong Kong have repeatedly been superior to China, one of the reasons has to do with religion. In previous chapters, I described how Taiwan enormously benefited from Catholic missionaries and charities after they were ejected from China by the insanity of Mao Zedong. In fact, many nations around the world have benefited from Western religious charities and missionaries, with China being the only major exception because of the stupidity of its leaders.

Document Number 9, described above, one of the items listed as undermining China's government those criticizing the violent crackdown on Tibetan Buddhists and Uighur Muslims. The CCP has the same view of Christian religions as well.

As I described in earlier chapters, Xi Jinping announced a new "Sinicization" policy in April 2018. That announcement, for example, makes it a crime for Christians to pray to Jesus. Since then, China's security thugs have gone on a rampage, destroying Catholic and Protestant Churches, destroying Buddhist statues and temples, and jailing, beating and torturing anyone who tries to practice his religion.

The CCP has identified what it calls the "five poisons" of society that must be controlled or stamped out. These are Tibetans, Uighur Muslims, democracy activists, Taiwanese, and Falun Gong practitioners. These are the guiding principles of China's self-destruction.

11.4. Comparison of Sinicization to Hitler's Kristallnacht

In my opinion, the adoption of Sinicization represents a major turn in anti-religion government violence that parallels Kristallnacht in Nazi Germany.

The Kristallnacht ("Night of Broken Glass") incident occurred on November 9-10, 1938. Nazis in Germany torched synagogues, vandalized Jewish homes, schools and businesses and killed close to 100 Jews. In the aftermath of Kristallnacht, some 30,000 Jewish men were arrested and sent to Nazi concentration camps. German Jews had been subjected to repressive policies since 1933, when Nazi Party leader Adolf Hitler (1889-1945) became chancellor of Germany. However, prior to Kristallnacht, these Nazi policies had been primarily nonviolent. After Kristallnacht, conditions for German Jews grew increasingly worse. During World War II (1939-45), Hitler and the Nazis implemented their so-called "Final Solution" to what they referred to as the "Jewish problem," and carried out the systematic murder of some 6 million European Jews in what came to be known as the Holocaust. [125]

When I describe the Sinicization law in detail in a later chapter, it will be clear that CCP policies toward Christianity, Buddhism and Islam became substantially more violent after the law was passed.

For example, China's storm troopers demolished a massive evangelical church using bulldozers and dynamite. The Jindengtai ("Golden Lampstand") mega-church, which reportedly had a congregation of 50,000 people, was demolished. Later, the Zion Protestant Church in Beijing was banned because the administration refused to install closed-circuit television cameras that the CCP could use to monitor all activity. [65] [64]

The violent behavior of the CCP toward Christians, Buddhists, Muslims, Kazakhs, Uighurs and Tibetans is similar to the violent behavior of the Nazis toward Jews and Roma. An interesting research project would be to compare the motivations. Almost all of the people being attacked and exterminated are/were presumably completely productive loyal citizens of China and Germany, respectively.

Generational Dynamics provides explanations from an analytical point of view. Many others have provided numerous pop psychology explanations, usually framed in ideological terms. But someone who provides a unified psychological explanation for the CCP and Nazi examples, along with hundreds of other examples, will do a great deal to explain how the world works.

11.5. Genocide and ethnic cleansing of Uighurs in East Turkistan (Xinjiang)

Xi Jinping has set up concentration camps ("reeducation centers") and crematoria in East Turkistan (Xinjiang province), similar to the concentration camps set up by Adolf Hitler in the Holocaust. It appears that the intent is the genocide and ethnic cleansing of all Uighurs and Kazakhs in East Turkistan.

As a related aside, after hearing "never again" my whole life, referring to the Nazi Holocaust targeting Jews, I consider it astonishing that there are now three countries in the world where there is full-scale genocide and ethnic cleansing going on, full-scale Holocausts, targeting Sunni Muslims in each case, with little international outrage even from Muslim countries. These are:

- China's genocide and ethnic cleansing of Sunni Muslim Uighurs in East Turkistan (Xinjiang province).

- Burma's (Myanmar's) genocide and ethnic cleansing of Sunni Muslim Rohingyas, led by Buddhist monk Ashin Wirathu.
- Bashar al-Assad's genocide and ethnic cleansing of Sunni Muslim Arabs in Syria.

This is a historic event that will have very serious consequences.

11.6. China's preparations for war

I've described many of China's preparations for war in earlier chapters. Let's summarize some of them here:

- China has been developing and deploying many nuclear intercontinental ballistic missile systems that have no purpose other than to attack American cities, American bases, and American aircraft carriers.
- China has transformed the South China Sea, which is an international waterway that China shunned before 1947 but now perpetrates a total hoax claiming that it's owned by China. China has illegally transformed this international waterway, through which trillions of dollars of commercial products travel every year, into an illegal Chinese military base, poised for a military attack on all its neighbors.
- China is conducting genocide and ethnic cleansing of Uighurs and Kazakhs in East Turkistan (Xinjiang province). The purpose isn't entirely obvious, but it presumably means that China wants to be able to capture assets in Central Asia, and to use the CPEC (China-Pakistan Economic Corridor) highway to Pakistan's Gwadar port on the Indian Ocean.
- China is subsidizing Huawei to install 5G networks throughout the world, using devices manufactured by Huawei, and containing "backdoors" that can be controlled by China's military. At a time of China's choosing, China will be able to entirely completely shut down the internet and local networks in any country where Huawei's devices are installed.

This tells you that China is actively preparing for war, and it tells you that America is one of the targets, but doesn't tell you when, or what the other objectives are.

11.7. Role of North Korea and 'denuclearization'

Historically, Korea has never been an ally of China. Korea has always been a vassal, in a tributary relationship with China, meaning that Korea paid China a great deal of money, usually gold and slaves, in return for guarantees of defense from outsiders (i.e., Japan). Although China does not directly govern the vassal, China expects the vassal to do as it's told.

After World War II, North Korea alone took on the role of China's vassal, and called on China to be its principal defender in the Korean war of the early 1950s.

North Korea pays tribute to China not in the form of gold and slaves, but in the form of massive amounts of coal and "workers," both of which are also used to provide financial aid to North Korea.

However, relations between China and North Korea took a hostile turn in October 2006, when North Korea began testing nuclear weapons. North Korea did not do as it was told, and China punished North Korea by agreeing to United Nations sanctions targeting North Korea. [148]

As I described in an earlier chapter, North Korea's dictator Kim Jong-il in 2008 demolished a 60-foot-tall cooling tower to prove that it was ending its nuclear development programs, and in reaction, the administration of president George Bush agreed to remove all sanctions. As soon as they were removed, North Korea immediately and openly resumed its nuclear and ballistic missile development. They had completely defrauded and humiliated the United States and the world, apparently including China.

Since then, North Korea has more aggressively tested many more nuclear weapons and long-range ballistic missiles. China has agreed to numerous additional sanctions in the UN Security Council. One might reasonably wonder: Why? No one serious believes that North Korea is going to use those nuclear missiles on China. They're almost certainly going to be used on Japan, South Korea, and the United States. So why does China object?

China's behavior in the last few years is that they are furious not because North Korea is developing nuclear weapons and ballistic missiles, but because North Korea openly tests them. Particularly shocking were ballistic missile tests that landed just short of Japan or overflew Japan's territory.

The reaction to these open tests is that the United States increases its military defenses in the region. What particularly infuriated the Chinese is that South Korea agreed to deploy the Terminal High Altitude Air Defense (THAAD), supplied by the United States military, to protect itself from North Korean missile attacks.

Chinese officials were infuriated and became almost hysterical. Why would the Chinese object to the deployment in South Korea of an anti-missile system that would protect South Korea from North Korean missiles? Chinese media provided the answer:

> "The X-band radar can snoop on Chinese and Russian territories as it can spot at least 2,000 km. Seoul claims that it will adopt the radar with a detectable range of 600-800 km, but the mode change can be made at any

time in accordance with the needs of the U.S military that will operate the THAAD battery in South Korea."

In other words, the Chinese were furious because the THAAD system includes "over the horizon" radar that would provide early warning to the American military of a missile attack from China.

Although South Korea is not officially China's vassal at the present time, China still punished South Korea for deploying the THAAD system. China banned tour groups from visiting China, removed popular South Korean TV dramas from the internet. China also forced the closure of 75 South Korean Lotte stores in China, resulting in $179 million in losses. China particularly ordered the Chinese living in China and in South Korea to boycott Lotte department stores, owned by Lotte Group, a South Korean multinational conglomerate. China decided on this punishment because it emerged that Lotte had agreed to a land swap that would allow THAAD to be deployed on a piece of land previously owned by the company. The enraged Chinese imposed harsh economic sanctions, particularly targeting Lotte Department Stores in China and South Korea with a boycott.

A correspondent living in Seoul wrote to me in April 2017 to describe the devastating impact of the actions by China:

> "China's economic boycott of Korea over THAAD has hit the country like a ton of bricks. I went to the flagship Lotte department store today, and it was practically empty. I have friends who own their own businesses, and they tell me they are facing bankruptcy because of the loss of Chinese customers. The thing is, Koreans, by and large, hate the Chinese. This embargo is only heightening the hatred. I think this embargo has finally woken people up to the fact that China is an existential threat to Korea. ...
>
> I can't believe how much the mood here has flipped. The word 'changed' would be inappropriate. Things are different now. I feel sick."

By November 2017, relations between China and South Korea had deteriorated substantially, and it was clear that the THAAD systems would not be removed. So China backed down. In a surprise announcement, China agreed to remove the harsh economic sanctions that it had imposed on South Korea. However, it imposed conditions, and suggested that the economic sanctions and boycotts would be reimposed if the conditions are not met.

So this is why China is so vehemently opposed to North Korean nuclear missile development — not because they care about the nuclear missiles themselves, but because of the reactions from America and the West. And Japan has also increased its militarization as a result.

It's hard to predict how Korea will act in the approaching war. North and South Korea will definitely be at war, and North Korea will be at war with Japan.

But whether the North Koreans targeted those nuclear missiles at South Korea, Japan or the United States is not clear.

11.8. Japan's and China's views of each other

It's a core principle of Generational Dynamics that, even in a dictatorship, major decisions are made by masses of people, by generations of people. The attitudes of politicians are irrelevant, except insofar as they represent the attitudes of the people.

So if we want to determine China's most probable behavior in the coming war, we can look at the attitudes of Chinese people toward other countries.

In 2014, Pew Research conducted a Global Attitudes Survey on "How Asians View Each Other." The report contained a great deal of data, but we're going to focus on how many people in each country have a "favorable view" other countries. [97]

The following table, which comes from the report, shows the percentage of the population in different Asian countries have favorable views of the following five countries: China, India, Pakistan, Japan, and the United States: [97]

```
How Asians Rate China, India, Pakistan, Japan and U.S.
                      Favorable views of...
Views in:      China   India   Pakistan   Japan    US.
                 %       %         %         %
Bangladesh      77      70        50        71      76
China           -       30        30         8      50
India           31      -         15        43      55
Indonesia       66      62        52        77      59
Japan            7      63        19        -       66
Malaysia        74      46        43        75      51
Pakistan        78      13        -         51      14
Philippines     38      50        33        80      92
South Korea     56      59        30        22      82
Thailand        72      45        27        81      73
Vietnam         16      67        36        77      76
US.             35      55        18        70      -
Source: Spring 2014 Global Attitudes survey [97]
```

If you look at the above table, you see that there are a wide range of numbers, but only two of the numbers are in the single digits: [97]

- In China, only 8% have a favorable view of Japan.
- In Japan, only 7% have a favorable view of China.

To put it as simply as possible: The Chinese and Japanese people hate each other.

This means that when a war occurs in the region, China and Japan will be particularly targeting each other. Other countries will choose up sides, of course, but the crucible of the war will be China versus Japan.

Equally important is the following observation: In China, 50% of the population have a favorable view of the United States. [97]

This supports that view that China does not want a war with the United States. This appears to contradict the fact, stated in the previous section, that China is developing and deploying many nuclear intercontinental ballistic missile systems that have no purpose other than to attack American cities, American bases, and American aircraft carriers.

The reason that China is deploying these missile systems is because the Chinese know that when they declare war with Japan, then the United States, in the role of Policeman of the World, will defend Japan, and declare war on China.

11.9. Other nations' view of China

The chart shown above about how Asians rate each other is interesting for another reason: It allows us to partition the Asian nations into two groups — those most likely to be allies of China in a future war, and those likely to be opposed.

Of the 12 countries shown in the table:

- Five have a favorability view of China above 50%: Bangladesh, Indonesia, Malaysia, Pakistan, and Thailand.
- Five have a favorability view of China below 50%: India, Japan, Philippines, Vietnam, United States.
- One has a favorability view of China near 50%: South Korea

Amy Chua, Yale University professor of Chinese descent who was born and raised in the Philippines, tells a story of the venomous hatred that Chinese and Philippine people have for each other. The story appears in her 2003 book, *World on Fire.*

Chua was a member of the élite Chinese descendant minority living in Manila. She lived in an enclave walled off from ordinary Filipinos, whom she never saw except as servants living in filth in the basement of her family's mansion. Chua describes the relationship between the Chinese and Philippine people living in Manila, and the contempt her family (the Chinese) had for the Philippine people:

> "My family is part of the Philippines' tiny but entrepreneurial, economically powerful Chinese minority. Just 1 percent of the

population, Chinese Filipinos control as much as 60 percent of the private economy, including the country's four major airlines and almost all of the country's banks, hotels, shopping malls, and major conglomerates. My own family in Manila runs a plastics conglomerate. ... They also have safe deposit boxes full of gold bars, each one roughly the size of a Snickers bar, but strangely heavy. I myself have such a bar: My Aunt Leona Federal Expressed it to me as a law school graduation present a few years before she died.

Since my aunt's murder, one childhood memory keeps haunting me. I was eight, staying at my family's splendid hacienda-style house in Manila. It was before dawn, still dark. Wide awake, I decided to get a drink from the kitchen. I must have gone down an extra flight of stairs, because I literally stumbled onto six male bodies.

I had found the male servants' quarters. My family's houseboys, gardeners, and chauffeurs — I sometimes imagine that Nilo Abique was among those men — were sleeping on mats on a dirt floor. The place stank of sweat and urine. I was horrified.

Later that day I mentioned the incident to my Aunt Leona, who laughed affectionately and explained that the servants — there were perhaps twenty living on the premises, all ethnic Filipinos — were fortunate to be working for our family. If not for their positions, they would be living among rats and open sewers without even a roof over their heads.

A Filipino maid then walked in; I remember that she had a bowl of food for my aunt's Pekingese. My aunt took the bowl but kept talking as if the maid were not there. The Filipinos, she continued — in Chinese, but plainly not caring whether the maid understood or not — were lazy and unintelligent and didn't really want to do much else. If they didn't like working for us, they were free to leave any time. After all, my aunt said, they were employees, not slaves.

Nearly two-thirds of roughly 80 million ethnic Filipinos in the Philippines live on less than two dollars a day. Forty percent spend their entire lives in temporary shelters. Seventy percent of all rural Filipinos own no land. Almost a third have no access to sanitation.

But that's not the worst of it. Poverty alone never is. Poverty by itself does not make people kill. To poverty must be added indignity, hopelessness, and grievance.

In the Philippines, millions of Filipinos work for Chinese; almost no Chinese work for Filipinos. The Chinese dominate industry and commerce at every level of society. Global markets intensify this dominance: When foreign investors do business in the Philippines, they deal almost exclusively with Chinese. Apart from a handful of corrupt politicians and a few aristocratic Spanish mestizo families, all of the Philippines' billionaires are of Chinese descent. By contrast, all menial jobs in the Philippines are filled by Filipinos. All peasants are Filipinos. All domestic servants and squatters are Filipinos. In Manila, thousands of ethnic Filipinos used to live on or around the Payatas garbage dump: a twelve-block-wide mountain of fermenting refuse known as the Promised Land. By scavenging through rotting food and dead animal carcasses, the squatters were able to eke out a living. In July 2000, as a result of accumulating methane gas, the garbage mountain imploded and collapsed, something over a hundred people, including many young children.

When I asked an uncle about the Payatas explosion, he responded with annoyance, "Why does everyone want to talk about that? It's the worst thing for foreign investment." I wasn't surprised. My relatives live literally walled off from the Filipino masses, in a posh, all-Chinese residential enclave, on streets named Harvard, Yale, Stanford, and Princeton. The entry points are guarded by armed, private security forces."

I wanted to quote this story at length because it's emblematic of story after story that I've read of the contempt that Han Chinese people feel for any other group in the world. In the case that Chua describes, Aunt Leona gets murdered.

Out of hatred, one of Chua's Filipino servants, Nilo Abique, murdered her aunt. Chua described what happened:

> "Each time I think of Nilo Abique — he was close to six feet and my aunt was four-feet-eleven-inches tall — I find myself welling up with a hatred and revulsion so intense it is actually consoling. But over time I have also had glimpses of how the Chinese must look to the vast majority of Filipinos, to someone like Abique: as exploiters, as foreign intruders, their wealth inexplicable, their superiority intolerable. I will never forget the entry in the police report for Abique's "motive for murder." The motive given was not robbery, despite the jewels and money the chauffer was said to have taken. Instead, for motive, there was just one word — "Revenge."

> My aunt's killing was just a pinprick in a world more violent than most of us ever imagined. In America we read about acts of mass slaughter and savagery; at first in faraway places, now coming closer and closer to home. We do not understand what connects these acts. Nor do we understand the role we have played in bringing them about."

As I said, I've heard many anecdotes about the contempt that Chinese people have for almost everyone else. I'll give one more example, because this one is well documented.

Kenya is one of the nations that have been targeted by China's Belt and Road Initiative (BRI), and which appears to be in danger of losing its Port at Mombasa because of "debt diplomacy." In an earlier chapter, I described the "secret" contract that Kenya had signed with China, after it had been leaked.

In country after country, what China does is loan billions of dollars to a country for an infrastructure project, too much for the country to repay, and apparently uses bribery and corruption to get the nations' leadership to sign the secret agreement. The agreement always specifies that loaned money will be used to pay Chinese workers and goods purchased from Chinese factories, so that the money is immediately returned to China, but the target country still has to repay it.

Kenya media described how the Chinese workers treated the Kenyan workers in developing an infrastructure project, the Standard Gauge Railway (SGR): [99]

- Chinese staff never permit a Kenyan to eat at the same table.
- Chinese never permit a Kenyan to enter a staff van if there's even one Chinese already on board.
- Chinese freely smoke and use mobile phones, acts that would get a Kenyan fired.
- Chinese staff urinate in the open.
- Chinese refuse to do any job they consider menial.
- Chinese never permit Kenyans to drive the train, even Kenyans with years of engineering training.
- Kenyans cannot perform maintenance tasks because all the signs are in Chinese.
- The Chinese contractor has also opted to keep most of their equipment programmed in Chinese, making it impossible for Kenyans to use it, despite being employed as technicians, engineers and drivers.
- Kenyans are grossly underpaid compared to similar jobs by Chinese counterparts. Chinese contractors lie about how much they pay Kenyan employees. [99]

The Han Chinese view the universe in three layers. The highest layer is the Kingdom of Heaven, China is the Middle Kingdom ("Zhongguo"), and the rest of the world, the non-Chinese, are the barbarians. This delusional view goes back two to three millennia, and is imbued in the Chinese consciousness. If you want to identify a core reason why the Chinese people are much poorer than their neighbors, and why the government has been so incompetent for millennia, then this delusional view that the rest of the world are all barbarians is the reason.

11.10. Mutual Defense Treaties of the United States

After World War II, the United States took on the role of Policeman of the World, and in doing so, signed some sort of mutual defense treaty with many countries: Japan, South Korea, Israel, Taiwan, the Philippines, the Marshall Islands, the ANZUS agreement with Australia and New Zealand, a special treaty with Iceland, and the NATO agreement with all of Europe. The purpose was to discourage attacks on any of these allies that would otherwise have the risk of spiraling into World War III.

This is kind of a historical irony. Following World War II, President Harry Truman announced the Truman Doctrine in 1947, essentially making America the "policeman of the world." Truman's justification was that it's better to have a small military action to stop an ongoing crime than to let it slide and end up having an enormous conflict like World War II. The Truman Doctrine was reaffirmed in President John Kennedy's famous "ask not" speech in 1961, and presidents since WW II have followed the Truman Doctrine.

The historical irony is that, while these mutual defense treaties prevented a lot of wars in the past, today they make a major war more likely. The reason is that if a major regional war occurs anywhere in the world, the US will not be able to remain neutral for long. When Japan invaded China in 1937, the US didn't get involved until Japan attacked Pearl Harbor in 1941. Today, when China is ready to attack Japan, China will have to launch its massive nuclear missile attack on American cities, bases and aircraft carriers at the same time, because the US has a mutual defense treaty with Japan.

11.11. China's desire for world hegemony

Many people believe that the Chinese want to take over the world — to gain "hegemonic dominance" over America and the West. I've said so myself in the past. But I no longer believe that to be true. In fact, the Chinese may even want people to believe that, as a smokescreen, just as everything else the Chinese say is a smokescreen to mislead people.

You can't look at the Chinese character in any obvious, rational manner. First of all, "hegemonic dominance" is not in the Chinese character, and not something they would even want. The Chinese can't even govern themselves, let alone govern colonies. Even Korea, which has been dominated by China for centuries, was never a colony, but only a vassal.

There is only one motive driving the Chinese that will never disappear — a vitriolic all-consuming uncontrollable hatred for the Japanese and an overwhelming and uncontrollable desire for revenge. That all-consuming hatred will not be quenched until they've gotten that revenge. Nothing else will matter, until the very last day of the war, and I suspect that the Japanese know it as well as the Chinese know it, even though they don't want to talk about it.

And Xi Jinping knows that unless he achieves that revenge, he will lose the Mandate from Heaven, and he's willing to pursue any fanatical, desperate policy to achieve it.

11.12. The outlook for war between China and Japan

I've now shown the following:

- China is rapidly preparing for full-scale war against Japan (and the US and the West).
- China is seeking revenge against Japan in particular and the West in general for "unfair treaties" and a "century of humiliation."
- China has been conducting a vitriolic hate campaign against the Japanese since the 1989 Tiananmen Square massacre.
- The Chinese and Japanese people have a vitriolic hatred for each other.
- The Chinese are highly racist people, even worse than Hitler's Nazis, considering everyone else in the world to be barbarians and racially inferior to the Chinese Master Race — yellow race, black hair, brown eyes, yellow skin.
- Xi Jinping is pursuing a fanatical cult of personality, like Mao's, by violently crushing any religious belief, including Buddhism, Christianity, and Islam, that involve praying to some other god besides Xi himself. The policies are highly racist, similar to Hitler's Master Race.

11.13. Winston Churchill vs Neville Chamberlain

Neville Chamberlain, returning from a 1938 meeting with Hitler, promising 'peace in our time,' holding up a signed agreement

One of the most reviled men of the twentieth century, besides dictators like Adolf Hitler himself, is British Prime Minister Neville Chamberlain who, in 1938, "appeased" Adolf Hitler.

When I was in school in the 1950s, and then later in college and in bitter politics of the 1970s, I heard Neville Chamberlain's name over and over. He had appeased Hitler. Hitler had fooled him. He had permitted Hitler to annex Austria in the *Anschluss*, then the Rhineland and Sudetenland. He should have listened to Winston Churchill, an MP (Member of Parliament) who kept warning his colleagues about Germany's rapid militarization. This is what we were told many times.

It's worthwhile taking a look at what happened.

Chamberlain met with Hitler in Munich. He returned to Croydon Airport on Sept. 30, 1938, waving the piece of paper with the agreement that he and Hitler had signed. (See picture.)

When he arrived at 10 Downing Street, he read the written agreement and made this statement:

> "My good friends, for the second time in our history, a British Prime Minister has returned from Germany bringing peace with honour.
>
> I believe it is peace for our time.
>
> Go home and get a nice quiet sleep."

The written agreement said the following:

> We, the German Führer and Chancellor, and the British Prime Minister, have had a further meeting today and are agreed in recognizing that the question of Anglo-German relations is of the first importance for our two countries and for Europe.
>
> We regard the agreement signed last night and the Anglo-German Naval Agreement as symbolic of the desire of our two peoples never to go to war with one another again. We are resolved that the method of consultation shall be the method adopted to deal with any other questions that may concern our two countries, and we are determined to continue our efforts to remove possible sources of difference, and thus to contribute to assure the peace of Europe."

This agreement was met with worldwide praise, because a peaceful solution had been found by means of diplomacy and negotiation. Churchill, on the other hand, was met with worldwide vitriolic scorn and hatred when he advised Chamberlain to reject the agreement.

What the world didn't know was that Hitler was actively planning for war: on the same day that Hitler met with Chamberlain, he also met with Mussolini to plan the invasion of Britain.

In retrospect, it was completely obvious that Churchill was right. Hitler was building a vast air force in violation of treaties that Germany had signed after World War I. It was completely obvious to anyone who looked, but almost all people acted like ostriches, not wanting to see the obvious, and pouring scornful abuse and hate on people like Churchill who pointed out the obvious.

Throughout my life, people my age have wondered how it was possible for Hitler to have fooled the British people for so long. Today, it's clear how it happened in 1938, because the same thing is happening today.

Hitler annexed Austria, the Rhineland and Sudetenland, in violation of and contempt for international law. Xi Jinping is annexing the South China Sea in violation of and contempt for international law.

Hitler declared Germans to be the Master Race, and began genocide against Jews. Xi Jinping has said that Han Chinese (yellow race, black hair, brown eyes, yellow skin) are a superior race, and has begun genocide against the Uighurs and Tibetans.

Hitler began a massive militarization program, including a huge air force. Xi Jinping is in a massive militarization program, including the deployment of several missile systems that have no purpose except to attack and destroy American cities, aircraft carriers and bases. Xi Jinping and the Chinese Communist Party (CCP) are doing exactly the same things that Adolf Hitler and the Nazis did before World War II.

There's another issue here. People who don't believe that China is preparing to launch a war also, as far as I can, don't believe that there will be a world war at all, as if the politicians had solved the problem of war once and for all.

There were two "world wars" in the last century, and as I wrote in the introduction, there have been massive wars on every continent for millennia. That there will be one or two massive world wars in this century is absolutely certain. This war might begin in the Mideast, Central Asia, or elsewhere, but sooner or later China will be involved, and will use the war as a basis to attack Taiwan, Japan and the United States.

The current political situation in the United States seems to be a terminal state of idiocy. There are many people on the left who claim to believe that the earth is going to end if the "climate change" problem isn't solved in 12 years. The same people who make this moronic claim would deny that there's any chance of a world war.

What we're seeing is a powerful paradigm that has been repeated throughout history. The Biblical Jeremiah predicted the destruction of Jerusalem, probably because it was a perfectly obvious as an approaching world war is today. But Jeremiah was beaten and thrown into a pit for making these predictions.

According to the Biblical book of Jeremiah, his message aroused great hostility and death threats, even from his own family. Jeremiah was beaten and put in the stocks. Later, spiteful men obtained the king's approval to arrest Jeremiah for prophesying disaster. These men then lowered Jeremiah by ropes into a cistern, and he sank into a layer of mud, where he almost starved to death before he was freed.

The mythical Cassandra is an archetype of such "prophets of doom," such as Jeremiah and Winston Churchill. When her father, King Priam of Troy, ordered that the Trojan Horse be brought within the gates of Troy, Cassandra warned that the Trojan Horse contained Greek soldiers, and that bringing it inside would be a disaster. Cassandra was considered insane and she was ignored and reviled.

Surely Cassandra's prediction must have been pretty obvious. Why would the Greeks have built a giant wooden horse in the first place? Surely it was suspicious enough to merit a complete examination and inspection before bringing inside the walls of Troy, and then the Greek soldiers would have been discovered and Troy would not have been destroyed.

After the destruction of Troy, Cassandra was blamed for the disaster, and she was beaten and raped. She became the slave and mistress of the Greek king Agamemnon. She warned Agamemnon that if they return to Greece then his wife, Clytemnestra, would kill them both. They returned to Greece, and Clytemnestra killed them both.

For obvious reasons, these stories of Jeremiah, Winston Churchill, and Cassandra are very personal to me. I've received an enormous amount of hatred, scorn and abuse for the same reasons. I have no expectations of my life except of personal disaster. I only wish my life to end peacefully, without having been beaten, tossed into a pit, assaulted or raped. People like me cannot hope for anything better.

11.14. Timing of the war between China and Japan

We've shown that the Chinese Communist Party has become highly xenophobic and nationalistic, and is preparing to launch a war on Japan and the West at a time of its choosing, when they consider it most advantageous.

So when will China launch this war? There are a number of possible scenarios:

- As I'll describe in great detail in a later chapter, World War II began in 1937 with the Marco Polo Bridge Incident. I described that at length because it was triggered when a Japanese soldier unexpected had to pee, leading to an escalating series of misunderstandings, and full scale war within two month. The level of hatred between Chinese and Japanese today is so great that any trivial incident could trigger a similar escalation. For example, there could be a confrontation around the Senkaku Islands, or a confrontation in Central Asia between Japanese assets and the Chinese. Such a trivial incident could occur tomorrow, next week, next year, or thereafter.

- From the point of view of generational theory, China is overdue for a massive civil war, and the CCP would immediately use nationalism to turn that into a war against Japan and the West. The Taiping Rebellion (1850-64) was a massive civil war that enveloped all of China, killing at least 20 million people. China's next massive civil war was Mao's Communist Revolution (1934-49), killing tens of millions more. In 2019, another 70 years will have passed since 1949, the end of the Communist Revolution, so China is due (in fact overdue) for its next massive civil war. Concerns and fears about a massive new civil war are a major factor in Chinese Communist Party paranoia today.

- Tensions between India and Pakistan in Kashmir are growing, with the same mutual hatred between Indians and Pakistanis as between Chinese and Japanese. A war between India and Pakistan could start for the same reasons as a Chinese-Japanese war, forcing everyone else to choose sides. China and Saudi Arabia would side with Pakistan, while Russia and Iran would side with India, resulting in rapid escalation.

- In fact, war in the Middle East or anywhere in the world could similarly escalate into a much larger war within a few months.
- China could simply decide that the time to strike is now (whenever "now" is).

Any of these scenarios could lead to a world war in days, weeks, months or a couple of years.

It's important to emphasize that China's policies are not rational, and verge on near total insanity. They're like children running around the streets with loaded machine guns and grenade launchers. You can be sure that no good will come of it, and in fact nothing will come of it except that many, many people will be killed.

As I quoted earlier, Friedrich Nietzsche said, "Insanity in individuals is something rare - but in groups, parties, nations and epochs, it is the rule."

We can't predict the exact timing, and we can't predict the exact scenario, but we can predict with absolute certainly that war is coming.

Part III. China's preparations for war

Chapter 12. China's war preparations through cyber war

12.1. Theft of intellectual property

During the last ten years, there have been hundreds of stories of China's illegal theft of American intellectual property. Apparently, Chinese engineers under the CCP are so incompetent, they're unable to develop technology and have to steal it. And they wonder why nobody respects China.

On December 20, 2018, the Dept. of Justice accused hackers working for China's Ministry of State Security (MSS) of a massive international hacking scheme that penetrated commercial and military systems in at least 12 countries, including Brazil, Canada, Finland, France, Germany, India, Japan, Sweden, Switzerland, the United Arab Emirates, the United Kingdom, and the United States. [161]

An indictment charged two Chinese nationals, Zhu Hua and Zhang Shilong, with conspiracy to commit computer intrusions, conspiracy to commit wire fraud, and aggravated identity theft. [161]

According to the indictment:

"Over the course of the Technology Theft Campaign, which began in or about 2006, Zhu, Zhang, and their coconspirators in the APT10 Group successfully obtained unauthorized access to the computers of more than 45 technology companies and U.S. Government agencies based in at least 12 states, including Arizona, California, Connecticut, Florida, Maryland, New York, Ohio, Pennsylvania, Texas, Utah, Virginia and Wisconsin. The APT10 Group stole hundreds of gigabytes of sensitive data and information from the victims' computer systems, including from at least the following victims: seven companies involved in aviation, space and/or satellite technology; three companies involved in communications technology; three companies involved in manufacturing advanced electronic systems and/or laboratory analytical instruments; a company involved in maritime technology; a company involved in oil and gas drilling, production, and processing; and the NASA Goddard Space Center and Jet Propulsion Laboratory. In addition to those victims who had information stolen, Zhu, Zhang, and their co-conspirators successfully obtained unauthorized access to computers belonging to more than 25 other technology-related companies involved in, among other things, industrial factory automation, radar technology, oil exploration, information technology services, pharmaceutical manufacturing, and computer processor technology, as well as the U.S. Department of Energy's Lawrence Berkeley National Laboratory.

Finally, the APT10 Group compromised more than 40 computers in order to steal sensitive data belonging to the Navy, including the names, Social Security numbers, dates of birth, salary information, personal phone numbers, and email addresses of more than 100,000 Navy personnel." [161]

The indictment focused on the theft of commercial and military technology, and how that will be used by China's state-run companies and military. These technologies will be useful to the Chinese as they build weapons systems and prepare to launch a war on the United States.

Another indictment was specifically targeted at employees of the Chinese technology firm Huawei. It showed how Huawei employees, in the US and China, stole information about Tappy, a robot that T-Mobile used to test its own smartphones. Huawei even tried to steal poor Tappy's arm: [162]

- In May 2012, Huawei asked T-Mobile to sell them Tappy technology. T-Mobile refused.
- There were Chinese Huawei employees working at T-Mobile, and Huawei asked them to illegally collect information about Tappy, including pictures and specifications.
- By January 2013, Huawei USA employees informed China that T-Mobile was getting angry about all the questions they were asking, and the photos they were taking, and they'd have to stop.
- In May 2013, Huawei China sent an engineer from the headquarters to join its USA team. This Chinese engineer gained unauthorized access to Tappy's lab, stole Tappy's arm and took it home. He took multiple photographs and measurements of the stolen arm, and sent them to China. The next day, when confronted with T-Mobile, the Chinese employee said he carried the arm by "mistake." [162]

These two indictments show that China's criminal activities are not just the acts of individual rogue employees, but are official policy of Huawei and China's government.

12.2. Huawei's hack of African Union headquarters

Starting from 2006, China's government built and financed a $200 million project to build the 20-story headquarters of the African Union in Addis Ababa, Ethiopia. It would be an enormous office complex, capable of accommodating 15,000 officials and representatives from various entities visiting the AU Commission for summits, meetings and other events each year.

In January 2012, the completed building was handed over to the African Union (AU), with this statement:

> "The international community should provide support and help to the resolution of African issues. China believes that such help should be based on respect for the will of the African people and should be constructive. It should reinforce, rather than undercut, Africa's independent efforts to solve problems. Interference in Africa's internal affairs by outside forces out of selfish motives can only complicate the efforts to resolve issues in Africa."

As with most statements from Chinese officials, this was simply a lie. China's intention was to gain control of the AU IT infrastructure and, with it, interconnected servers and networks throughout Africa, and in some cases elsewhere in the world.

Huawei installed the entire IT infrastructure, including computing, storage sharing, WiFi, networking, and unified resource allocation services through Huawei's cloud data centers. An investigation in 2017 revealed that China had installed "backdoors" in the servers and computers that they had installed, allowing the Chinese military to spy on them, to steal data, and to take control of them if desired. Furthermore, the investigation revealed that between 2012-2017, servers in Shanghai were hacking into the servers in Addis Ababa, and stealing data every single night from 12-2am. [165]

The AU was forced to put out a bid to replace all the servers and computers, and for the "supply, installation, configuration, testing and implementation of next generation firewall data center for the African Union Commission." The bidding document explained that:

> "African Union's Data Center is a very critical asset for the African Union. The data stored and systems hosted in this data center need to be protected from any form of internal or external threats and unauthorized access." [165]

12.3. China's National Intelligence Law (June 27, 2017)

Huawei is now the largest telecommunications equipment manufacturer in the world. Their products are in everything from hand-held phones to huge 5G networks, in over 170 countries, according to claims by company executives. They win contracts because they develop low-cost products with subsidies from the Chinese Communist Party (CCP).

But increasingly many countries are blocking Huawei from bidding on infrastructure projects, because it's increasingly perceived that Huawei products are part of China's military, and that the low prices are a way to "own" servers and networks around the world.

Huawei executives claim that they're being unfairly excluded from IT projects, and are demanding that the West prove that Huawei products are a security risk. As I'll describe in the next sections, Huawei could install backdoors in all its products, and they wouldn't be detectable until it's too late — until they are activated.

But in fact, China's own law require Huawei and every other Chinese company to cooperate with the military. Article 7 of China's 2017 National Intelligence Law declares: [164]

> "Article 7. All organizations and citizens shall, in accordance with the law, support, cooperate with, and collaborate in national intelligence work, and guard the secrecy of national intelligence work they are aware of. The state will protect individuals and organizations that support, cooperate with, and collaborate in national intelligence work. ...
>
> Article 14 The state intelligence work organization shall carry out intelligence work according to law, and may require relevant organs, organizations and citizens to provide necessary support, assistance and cooperation. ...
>
> Article 24 The State shall provide proper resettlement for those who contribute to the national intelligence work and need to be resettled." [160]

Combine that with the fact that Huawei was founded by Ren Zhengfei, who was previously an officer and engineer in China's People's Liberation Army (PLA), there's no question that, despite their protestations, all of Huawei's products are part of the military. It's required by law. [164]

The CCP will send a Muslim Uighur to a concentration camp for the "crime" of growing a beard, or punish a Christian for the "crime" of praying to God, so there can be little doubt that the CCP will harshly punish any individual or organization who doesn't cooperate with China's military, even when doing so is illegal.

The National Intelligence Law is a real "f--k you" to the West. It shows complete contempt for the West, because it says that China will force any citizen or any business to commit any crime in any country to bring back intelligence to the Chinese military.

12.4. China's weaponization of Huawei

I first wrote about this subject back in 2012, when the House Intelligence Committee warned against doing business with Huawei and ZTE, and were warning about a "Cyberwar Pearl Harbor attack" from China. At that time, Secretary of Defense Leon Panetta warned that chips manufactured by Huawei or ZTE could be controlled remotely by the Chinese, and develop tools that could "cause panic and destruction and even the loss of life." For example, working remotely, China could "derail passenger trains or even more dangerous, derail trains loaded with lethal chemicals."

Statements like this received plenty of ridicule, including from people who should have known better, claiming that if Huawei chips could be controlled remotely, that would be revealed in testing. That claim is completely false.

I've spent a part of my career developing chip-level operating system software for embedded systems, so I know exactly how to do what Panetta is suggesting. Furthermore, I can tell you that not only is it doable, it's not even particularly difficult for someone with the right skills.

Huawei could develop a chipset that works exactly as described in the public specifications. The chipset could be subjected to thousands of tests, and they would all work perfectly.

But what Huawei could do is install a "backdoor" into the chipset. When the chip receives, say, a certain secret 1024-bit code, then it will execute commands sent to it by China's military. Thus, the Chinese are then in control of any devices with Huawei or ZTE chips.

As I said, this is not only doable, it's easy to do. The "backdoor" could not be detected until an attack had been launched, and then it would be too late.

And since it CAN be done, I'm absolutely certain that it HAS been done. In fact, under China's National Intelligence Law, quoted above, Huawei MUST do it, since it's required by law. And Since Huawei was founded by Ren Zhengfei, an officer and engineer in China's military, there's absolutely no doubt that it was done.

What I'm saying is that every device produced by Huawei, or which contains Huawei's chips, has a "backdoor" with certainty, and that this backdoor will allow China's military to hack, spy on and control those device at a time of its choosing.

To put it another way, China is subsidizing the manufacture of Huawei routers so that they're cheaper than competing routers, so that they'll be installed on networks around the world. At a time of its choosing, China's military would be able to completely shut down the internet and all networks in many parts of the world, where the Huawei routers are installed, causing worldwide chaos.

China has been preparing for war with the U.S. in every possible way. They've built large, illegal military bases in the South China Sea, and repeatedly lied about them. They've developed numerous nuclear-tipped ballistic and hypersonic missile systems designed to successfully strike and destroy American aircraft carriers, American cities, and American bases. They've demonstrated a capability to destroy American communications and GPS satellites. They have thousands of missiles ready to launch against Taiwan and Japan, and they have large military deployments in western Tibet ready to invade India.

In February 2018, FBI directory Christopher Wray testified:

> "We're deeply concerned about the risks of allowing any company or entity that is beholden to foreign governments that don't share our values to gain positions of power inside our telecommunications networks.

> That provides the capacity to exert pressure or control over our telecommunications infrastructure. It provides the capacity to maliciously modify or steal information. And it provides the capacity to conduct undetected espionage."

A Huawei spokesman responded in a statement:

> "Huawei is aware of a range of U.S. government activities seemingly aimed at inhibiting Huawei's business in the U.S. market. Huawei is trusted by governments and customers in 170 countries worldwide and poses no greater cybersecurity risk than any ICT vendor, sharing as we do common global supply chains and production capabilities."

He didn't even deny that Huawei could maliciously modify and steal information, and conduct undetected espionage. And 170 other governments are stupid enough to allow it.

China has been preparing in every possible way for years for a successful pre-emptive military strike against the United States, and there is absolutely no doubt that they would also prepare by installing "backdoors" in all the chips and switches and other electronic devices that they sell. Leon Panetta's warning that China could launch a "Cyberwar Pearl Harbor" is quite plausible, and is probably being planned.

12.5. Installing a hardware backdoor - Technical details

In 2005, the US Dept of Defense first issued a report expressing concern that microelectronics components sourced from other countries expose the military to security risks: [167]

> "The conclusion is a call for the U.S. government in general, and the DOD and its suppliers specifically, to establish a series of activities to ensure that the United States maintains reliable access to the full spectrum of microelectronics components, from commodity and legacy, to state-of-the-art parts, and application-specific Integrated Circuits special technologies. These activities must provide assurance that each component's trustworthiness (confidentiality, integrity and availability) is consistent with that component's military application. ...

> It is clear from recent trends in the microelectronics industry that a significant migration of critical microelectronics manufacturing from the United States to other foreign countries has and will continue to occur. The rate of this technology migration is alarming because of the strategic significance this technology has on the U.S. economy and the ability of the United States to maintain a technological advantage in the Department of Defense (DoD), government, commercial and industrial sectors. Our greatest concern lies in microelectronics supplies for defense, national infrastructure and intelligence applications." [167]

There are Chinese officials on public relations tours these days claiming that Huawei devices have no backdoors, since those would have been detected by experts in other countries. But the whole point of an undetectable backdoor is that it can't be detected, so these Chinese officials are just blowing hot air.

Basically, there are two ways to install backdoors into a chip or device, hardware or software.

There's been quite a bit of research in recent years in adding "hardware Trojans" to integrated circuits: [166]

> "In recent years, hardware Trojans have drawn the attention of governments and industry as well as the scientific community. One of the main concerns is that integrated circuits, e.g., for military or critical-infrastructure applications, could be maliciously manipulated during the manufacturing process, which often takes place abroad. However, since there have been no reported hardware Trojans in practice yet, little is known about how such a Trojan would look like, and how difficult it would be in practice to implement one." [166]

Simply adding additional circuitry to a device can often be detected by means of optical techniques (e.g., a microscope). A newer, experimental method of inserting hardware Trojans is "by changing the dopant polarity of existing transistors." According to the scientists, "our family of Trojans is resistant to most detection techniques, including fine-grain optical inspection and checking against "golden chips." [166]

12.6. Installing an undetectable software backdoor - Technical details

The problem with making a hardware change to a chip to install a Trojan or backdoor is that it may be possible to detect that the chip has been physically changed. The researchers quoted above claim that the "dopant polarity" method is not detectable with current technology, but that could change at any time. From the point of view of the Chinese military, this is highly undesirable, since once a hardware Trojan is detected in one Huawei chip, Huawei will be completely discredited.

My own past experience includes five years implementing board-level software for embedded systems. So I know how easy it would be to implement an undetectable software-only backdoor.

As I said in an earlier section, the software backdoor would be activated when the Chinese military sends, say, a secret 1024-bit key. At that time, the Chinese military could shut the router down completely, or could command it to spy or work in a different way.

The most obvious, simplest implementation would be to use public/private key encryption. The public key could be embedded in the code, and even someone in possession of the source code could not derive the private key, which would be the secret key in this case. That's just one way of doing it. There are many others.

Of course, it wouldn't be embedded in the code in an obvious way. I could write C++ code that would baffle the experts. Someone might be able to reverse engineer the code, and might even be suspicious that there's a hidden algorithm in there, but it would never be more than a suspicion and they'd never be able to prove it. This means that the backdoor is undetectable, for all practical purposes.

Remember that China's National Intelligence Law forces any company to cooperate with the military in acquiring foreign intelligence. Of course, the Chinese military have studied and developed numerous hardware and software methods to insert backdoors, and we have to assume that any Huawei device installed in the last five years contains a backdoor that can be activated China's military at a time of its choosing.

China has been subsidizing Huawei products so that Huawei can underbid other companies and gain a competitive advantage, and install Huawei devices with backdoors as widely as possible. Huawei would sell thousands of routers to some country or some company, all of them with backdoors that could be activated by China's military at any time of its choosing. This would give China's military an enormous advantage in time of war.

Chapter 13. China's Social Credit Score system

13.1. Development of China's Social Credit Score system

China is selling its "Social Credit Score" system as nothing more than a variation of the American practice of credit ratings, used for people who apply for loans or credit cards. However, the American credit rating system is severely restricted to financial issues, and is highly regulated, including a legally-mandated appeal system to correct errors. [163]

In China, everything is done for military purposes, as required by law, and the military purposes are always obscured. For example, in 2015, China's president Xi Jinping said that the artificial islands in the South China Sea had no military purpose and would be used by tourists. Xi is a total liar. Today the South China Sea is bristling with Chinese military bases and weapons, and the Chinese are threatening anyone who passes through, even though the United Nations Hague Tribunal has declared that China's activities are illegal. And there are no tourists in sight.

So when China says that its "social credit score system" will be used only for benign purposes, to help the Chinese people get through the day, you can be sure that there is a military purpose, and at the very least it will be used to punish Christians, Buddhists, Muslims, or anyone who does anything that the government doesn't approve of.

According to the Chinese, the system will reward "pro-social behaviors," such as volunteer work and blood donations. The system will penalize things like violating traffic laws or charging under-the-table fees. Agencies like tourism bodies, business regulators and transit authorities are supposed to work together. These agencies will provide data on private citizens to the central system, and will then use the credit score to reward or punish citizens. In fact, the system is already partially in place, in that people with unacceptable credit scores have already been blocked from booking more than 11 million flights and 4 million high-speed train trips. According to reports, other punishments include slower internet speeds, reducing access to good schools for individuals or their children, banning people from certain jobs, preventing booking at certain hotels and losing the right to own pets. [163]

The way to understand where this is going is to look at the technology. The Chinese are creating a "big data" database containing detailed information about all aspects of the lives of everyone in China. By the time it's completed in 2020, this enormous database will have information from every private database and data stream in China, including information about train, plane or bus trips, purchases, mail deliveries, online activities, and so forth. It can even use facial recognition of CCTV cameras to track everyone simply walking down the street. In a sense, China's military will be able to determine at any time where any China citizen is at that time, and what he or she is doing. [163]

We already see China using a non-computerized version of this system in the targeting of Uighurs and Kazakhs in East Turkistan (Xinjiang province). Police and even ordinary people spy on other people, and report everything to the authorities. This is going on today. If someone shaves his beard or even just decides to stop smoking, then those actions are considered proof that he's learning to become a terrorist, and he can be arrested and forced to join the over 100 million other Uighurs and Kazakhs in concentration camps, where he will be beaten and tortured.

13.2. Huawei's 'big data' cloud database

Ever since the United States saved China from defeat in World War II, American public attitude toward China has been mostly positive. China's turn toward a harsh Communist government caused a great deal of hostility in the West, but there was broad willingness to grant concessions to China in the hope that they would open up commercially and become responsible members of the international community.

For decades, an enthusiastic Western proponent supporting China has been Hungarian-born left-wing billionaire George Soros. But in January 2019, Soros gave a speech indicating that he had made a complete reversal of opinion. My belief is that Soros' speech is extremely significant, not because one person's opinion has changed, but because Soros's reversal is emblematic of a widespread public reversal in Western sentiment towards China. [202]

The issue that triggered Soros's sudden reversal was the "Social Credit System": [202]

> "A lot of things have happened since last year and I've learned a lot about the shape that totalitarian control is going to take in China. ...

> All the rapidly expanding information available about a person is going to be consolidated in a centralized database to create a "social credit system." Based on that data, people will be evaluated by algorithms that will determine whether they pose a threat to the one-party state. People will then be treated accordingly.

> The social credit system is not yet fully operational, but it's clear where it's heading. It will subordinate the fate of the individual to the interests of the one-party state in ways unprecedented in history.

I find the social credit system frightening and abhorrent. Unfortunately, some Chinese find it rather attractive because it provides information and services that aren't currently available and can also protect law-abiding citizens against enemies of the state.

China isn't the only authoritarian regime in the world, but it's undoubtedly the wealthiest, strongest and most developed in machine learning and artificial intelligence. This makes Xi Jinping the most dangerous opponent of those who believe in the concept of open society. But Xi isn't alone. Authoritarian regimes are proliferating all over the world and if they succeed, they will become totalitarian." [202]

In his speech, Soros went on to talk about his childhood, escaping from the Nazis and implied that the Chinese are turning into Nazis. [202]

The Chinese military and Huawei are taking advantage of new "cloud" technologies where vast databases can be created using multiple servers located in dozens or hundreds of sites across the country. These databases are linked together, and provide China's military with the ability to extract any data records at any time.

As we said before, this vast cloud database will merge information from many other databases, streams, sources and feeds, and will have information about every citizen in China, including information about train, plane or bus trips, purchases, mail deliveries, online activities, and so forth. It can even use facial recognition of CCTV cameras to track everyone simply walking down the street.

13.3. China extends its 'social credit score' system to Americans and Westerners

Supposedly, Huawei's social credit score system applies only to Chinese citizens, or to anyone within China's physical boundaries. Once again, we make the point that Huawei is required by China's National Intelligence Law to use its technology for intelligence gathering for the military. They must do this, or be in violation of the law.

This is not rocket science. In fact, it's relatively easy for software engineers with the right skills to extend China's system to every person on the internet, collecting data by hacking into foreign databases, and by taking advantage of "backdoors" in Huawei equipment that is installed anywhere in the world.

And since that's relatively easy to do, and because doing it is required by Chinese law, we have to assume with 100% certainty that China is doing that.

I'd now like to return to the December 20, 2018, indictment described several pages back of hackers working for China's Ministry of State Security (MSS) to implement a massive international hacking scheme that penetrated commercial and military systems in at least 12 countries. [199]

In addition to the theft of commercial and military technology, the indictment says that a hack of navy computers stole names, Social Security numbers, dates of birth, salary information, personal phone numbers, and email addresses of more than 100,000 Navy personnel. [199]

In the Marriott hotel data breach last year, China's Ministry of State Security (MSS) stole names, addresses, telephone numbers, credit card numbers, passport numbers, birthdates, passport photos, hotel arrival and departure dates, and information on where people traveled and with whom on roughly 500 million guests. [199]

Other data breaches attributed to China's MSS include a 2017 Equifax hack that collected detailed credit information on 145 million people, a 2013 Target breach that exposed payment card and contact information for 60 million customers, and a 2015 hack of the Office of Personnel Management (OPM) that collected detailed personal information on more than 20 million government employees, family members and applicants. There were other breaches of health-care institutions, including Anthem and CareFirst, that provided health data. [199]

That's just the hacking done in the United States. China's military is stealing the same kind of data from countries around the world.

In other words, China is hacking databases around the world so that it can track any "important" individual in any country.

So, for example, if China wants to launch a war, it could start out by simultaneously assassinating leading politicians and military officers in many countries, using data from their "big data" database to locate each of them. Even if such an operation were only 50% successful, it could partially cripple the defense capabilities of many countries.

More prosaically, China's military can use the information in its cloud database to bribe or extort anyone to provide secret information that they want.

An investigation revealed that in 2018 there were 6,515 publicly disclosed data breaches, and that more than 5 billion records were exposed. Not all of these data breaches were done by China, of course, but we can be certain that China's servers and database contain detailed personal real time data on tens of millions of America, and that China's military is in control of most of their smartphones.

13.4. China's economy — Huawei the only money making private company

Many people believe that since China is a Communist dictatorship, they can't have a recession because the Chinese Communist Party (CCP) will control the economy enough to prevent it. It doesn't work that way. Like every Socialist economy, China's economy was headed for disaster until it was opened to free markets in the 1970-80s. In fact, every Socialist economy has either opened up to free markets to some extent, or ended in disaster and massive bloodshed. Today, only Venezuela and North Korea have refused to open up to free markets, and both of those are disasters, with bloodshed in the future.

China today is subject to the same market forces and the same generational forces as every other country. People fool themselves into believing that politicians can actually change things. In China, only the politics will be different, but the outcomes will be the same.

In a speech given in early December by Professor Xiang Songzuo, Deputy Director and Senior Fellow of the Center for International Monetary Research at China's Renmin University in Beijing, it was credibly claimed that China's economy is in worse shape than reported. The speech was quickly censored by the CCP. [200]

The headline statistic in Xiang's speech is his claim that China's GDP rate of growth is at most 1.67%, or may even be negative. China's official National Bureau of Statistics claims that China's rate of GDP growth is at 6.5%. This one statistic alone could explain why the CCP felt it necessary to censor Xiang's speech. [200]

Nobody is surprised that China lies about statistics. Mao Zedong lied about agricultural statistics during the Great Leap Forward in 1958-59, with the result that tens of millions of Chinese died from starvation or were executed.

The problem is that you can lie about statistics only for a while, and then reality causes a financial crisis, which is what Xiang is predicting.

Since the CCP can pump money into any business at will, it would seem that any financial crisis can be prevented. The problem is that any business that can count on being bailed out has no motivation to become efficient, and so loses money.

Xiang says that this has happened with almost all Chinese businesses: [200]

> "Look at our profit structure. To put it plainly, China's listed companies don't really make money. Then who has taken the few profits made by China's more than 3,000 listed companies? Two-thirds have been taken by the banking sector and real estate. The profits earned by 1,444 listed companies on the SME board and growth enterprise board are not even

equal to one and half times the profit of the Industrial and Commercial Bank of China. How can this kind of stock market become a bull market?

When we buy stocks, we are buying the profits of the company, not hype and rumors. I recently read a report comparing the profits of China's listed companies with those in the U.S. There are many U.S. public companies with tens of billions dollars in profits. How many Chinese tech and manufacturing companies are there that have accomplished this? There is only one, but it's not listed, and you all know which one that is. [Xiang is referring to Huawei, the Chinese tech company.] What does this tell us?" [200]

Xiang says that "Basically China's economy is all built on speculation, and everything is over leveraged," and predicts that China's stock market is facing a huge crash greater than America's 1929 crash. [200]

Chapter 14. United Front Work Department (UFWD) and Magic Weapons

14.1. China's biggest resource: billions of expendable people

I've written thousands of articles on China in the last two decades, and one thing that comes through to me is that the Chinese Communist Party (CCP) views its population quite differently than Western democracies view their populations. Whereas a Western country values each human life, China views its people as expendable cogs in a wheel.

This was really brought home to me in August 2006 when Sha Zukang, the Chinese ambassador to the U.N., was asked during a BBC interview about Taiwan declaring independence. Sha was literally screaming in his reply:

> "The moment that Taiwan declares independence, supported by whomever, China will have no choice but to [use] whatever means available to my government. Nobody should have any illusions on that.
> ...
>
> It's not a matter of how big Taiwan is, but for China, one INCH of the territory is more valuable than the LIVES of our people."

This is a message that I've seen in many different ways. With China having 1.3 billion people, the CCP considers people to be just another resource, like soybeans or coal, with no intrinsic value except to be thrown at problems.

14.2. History of China's United Front

The "United Front" concept was adopted by Russia's Lenin in the 1920s as a tool for supporting the Communist movement in China. As we'll describe later, China in the 1920s was split between the Kuomintang (KMT) Nationalist party and the Communist party. The United Front concept was promoted by the Communists to coopt the Nationalist agenda, in the hope of "converting" the Nationalists into Communists. [152]

That didn't work, of course, and there was a major split between the two in 1927, with the Nationalists defeating the Communists. However, when the Sino-Japanese war began in 1937, the Communists revived the United Front concept again, to unite all factions to fight the Japanese. [153]

The Communists internationalized the United Front concept in 1937 by extending it to Hong Kong (which was a British colony) and the Chinese diaspora around the world. Through capitalist Hong Kong, China was able to reach businesses and governments around the world, and ask for their help in obtaining arms and other support for the fight against the Japanese. Mao was able to use the "United Front" program to unite numerous factions in support of his communist party, while leaving the Nationalists to fight the Japanese. The result was that the Nationalists were weakened, and Mao won the civil war in 1949. [153]

After the war ended, the Communists founded an industrial business club, with many local businessmen involved in its functions and activities. In addition, from 1947 to 1984, the Hong Kong Branch of the official Xinhua News Agency carried out both open and underground operations in Hong Kong, in anticipation of its being under Chinese sovereignty, as happened in 1997. On the one hand, the Chinese Communists did not recognize the unequal treaties which established Hong Kong as a British colony, but on the other hand, they understood that Hong Kong was a significant source of foreign exchange and thus continued the previous policy of pragmatism toward the territory. [153]

The Communists continued to work within Hong Kong's capitalist system, as they had been doing since the war against Japan. The local Xinhua office served as a quasi-diplomatic organization for governmental communication, helping Communist cadres understand the workings of colonial rule and making known Beijing's policies to local authorities. In the 1980s, the Xinhua office gained greater significance when it focused on reaching out directly to a broader swathe of middle class Hong Kong society. It continued pursuing united work among the business, commercial, industrial and professional groups. The united front strategy continues to the present day, and was expanded to include Taiwan and Macao. [153]

Today, the UFWD is one of five departments directly under the CCP Central Committee. (The other four are the Propaganda Department, the International [Liaison] Department, the Organization Department and the Central Commission for Discipline Inspection.) The UFWD plays a low-profile but important role. [152]

In plain words, the UFWD's role is to collect information (and it necessarily would involve intelligence collecting), co-opt non-CCP élites into the political center, and control them accordingly. Generally speaking, each individual outside of the CCP with fame, wealth, or influence on public opinion can be a "target" of the UFWD. The most common way of co-opting such people is "recommending" the elites to the Chinese People's Political Consultative Conference (CPPCC), an advisory group that recommends policies to the CCP, and also broadcasts CCP policies back to the elite's constituency. Yet, it's worth noting that those who are absorbed into the UF are not regarded as loyal followers of the party either. They are just considered not to be "direct enemies." [152]

In theory, the UF will ultimately disintegrate or absorb all the party's "enemies," enhance the state's legitimacy, and keep society stable. That's why, as Xi Jinping said, "the United Front is an important magic weapon for the party's victory." [152]

The United Front Work Department (UFWD) today is a complex set of institutions and organizations that act not only as key elements of surveillance and political influence, but also as a means of consultation with and representation of those outside the Party. This system is an important reason the CCP's control is so effective and regarded as legitimate, and why the dramatic social and economic changes in China since the late-1980s have been integrated smoothly. [154]

Today the system of united front work is more expansive than ever, incorporating important new social interest groups, neutralizing potential trouble makers, soliciting advice from experts and having key representatives model their support for the CCP to others in their constituencies. As lawyers in China became more important with the rise of a new legal system, and some activists embarrassed the Party-state about human rights, they also became a special target of united front work in order to neutralize their apparent anti-state tendencies. Social media celebrities in China have also recently been made special targets of UFWD co-optation and this is one reason for their decline. Cooperation, for many, becomes more attractive than becoming targets of official lawfare or other forms of retaliation. [154]

14.3. United Front Work Department in New Zealand

The United Front Work Department (UFWD) is no longer just a China-only military organization. It has expanded far outside China, to many countries around the world.

With 1.4 billion people, perhaps China's greatest "weapon" is its massive manpower. China's president Xi Jinping has described them as "Magic Weapons," controlled by an arm of China's military called the United Front Work Department (UFWD).

Officially UFWD focuses on building support for the Communist Party in China, but it has become a coercive propaganda tool targeting Chinese globally, especially those living in Australia, New Zealand, the U.S., and Canada, but in other countries as well. The agency particularly surveils and targets Chinese students abroad and foreign universities to adopt language that favors pro-Beijing policies, such as delegitimizing Taiwan, and Western ideals and values, such as liberal democracy, Christianity, or the Falun Gong. [155]

Thanks to Chinese emigration, there are now large communities of Chinese people in Australia and New Zealand. Chinese propaganda has been so thoroughly successful that Chinese media in Australia is now almost overwhelmingly pro-Beijing, and is promoting Chinese values ("socialism with Chinese characteristics"), rather than Western values of liberal democracy and freedom. United Front Work attempts to sway elections so that pro-Beijing policies are adopted.

A report entitled "Magic Weapons: China's political influence activities under Xi Jinping," by New Zealand analyst Anne-Marie Brady, describes in detail how Chinese propaganda works in New Zealand: [155]

> "There are currently around 200,000 ethnic Chinese resident in New Zealand, out of a population of 4.5 million New Zealanders. The majority of Chinese in New Zealand live in Auckland, where they make up around 10 percent of the population. Chinese consular authorities keep a close eye on all Chinese community activities, but especially in Auckland. They have achieved this through close links with core pro-Beijing Chinese community groups, and by maintaining oversight over other Chinese community groups, ethnic Chinese political figures, and Chinese language media and schools in New Zealand. Moreover, during the Xi era, the PRC embassy has supported the setting up of new organizations that report back to united front bodies in China, and, according to two former Australian-based Chinese diplomats, by placing supporters and informers in New Zealand Chinese organizations that are more independent minded and pose a potential threat to China's interests. This is classic CCP party-building and organization work; one of the three "magic weapons" of the CCP. The current level of supervision over the ethnic Chinese community in New Zealand is a remarkable achievement. All throughout the Cold War years, with only a few exceptions, Chinese New Zealanders were neither pro-CCP nor pro-PRC, even if they were not necessarily pro-Chinese Nationalist Party or pro-ROC,76 and New Zealand's Chinese-language media, community groups, and language schools were proudly independent. ...

> The organization most closely connected with the PRC authorities in New Zealand is the Peaceful Reunification of China Association of New Zealand (PRCANZ), founded in 2000. ... The name of the organization is a reference to the "Peaceful Reunification" of mainland China and Taiwan. However, the organization also engages in a range of activities which support Chinese foreign policy goals, including block-voting and fund-raising for ethnic Chinese political candidates who agree to support their organization's agenda. When Chinese senior leaders visit New Zealand, it is united front-affiliated organizations such as PRCANZ who organize counter-protest groups to shout down pro-Falun Gong, pro-

Tibet, or any other group critical of China who come to protest when China's senior leaders visit New Zealand." [155]

Brady's report also gives a detailed account of Chinese officials in New Zealand's government.

14.4. China's infiltration of Australia

Relations between China and Australia have been increasingly tense for a number of reasons. One is that China's illegal militarization of the South China Sea is seen as a military and commercial threat to Australia.

A book titled "Silent Invasion: How China Is Turning Australia into a Puppet State," written by Clive Hamilton, a left of center professor of public ethics at Charles Stuart University. The book documents the extent to which Chinese nationals have infiltrated Australia's government, and influences its policies. Several publishers withdrew offers to publish the book because of pressure from the Chinese Communist Party.

As one Australian commentator pointed out, he could walk into any bookstore or library in Australia and find a dozen books that accused the CIA of controlling Australia's government and institutions, and no one would care. However, just one book about China's activities caused a furious, threatening response from China.

The book was supposed to be published in November 2017 by Australian publisher Allen & Unwin, which had published 8 previous books by Hamilton. However, the publisher's chief executive, Robert Gorman, cancelled plans at the last minute to publish Hamilton's book. He wrote an e-mail message to Hamilton saying:

> "We have no doubt that Silent Invasion is an extremely significant book. [But we are concerned about] potential threats to the book and the company from possible action by Beijing. ... The most serious of these threats was the very high chance of a vexatious defamation action against Allen & Unwin, and possibly against you personally as well."

The publisher told Hamilton that he would have to heavily edit the book and remove large portions of the text to get it published. According to Hamilton:

> "Last week Allen & Unwin did express some legal concerns but despite that I thought they were resolved to publish it, so it was a complete shock.
>
> The Chinese government's campaign is far more extensive than ever previously understood. If you're going to analyze how Beijing is influencing Australian society and politics you have to analyze that

activity of individuals and name names, and that's what I've done. It's a factual book with 1,100 footnotes and it has been meticulously researched, but short of redacting 100 names from the book there's always the possibility someone might launch a vexatious legal act against the publisher, in this case Allen & Unwin."

In January 2018 another publisher, Melbourne University Press, became the second leading publisher to cancel plans to publish the book. Reportedly, a university official was concerned about Beijing's ability to dissuade students from attending the university if MUP published the book.

There are very real concerns about publishing material not approved by the Chinese Communist Party. Within China itself, every publication is closely censored, and writing or even reading any unapproved publication can land a person in jail subject to severe and repeated torture.

But China's censorial reach extends past the mainland. In 2015, five Hong Kong booksellers whose shops contain books critical of Xi and the CCP were abducted and thrown into jail in Beijing. Four were eventually released – three "confessed" and have remained mute, while one spoke of his torture. The fifth is still imprisoned.

Foreign citizens are not immune. In January, Swedish citizen Gui Minhai, a Hong Kong book publisher, was arrested in China while accompanied by Swedish diplomats. Sweden's foreign minister Margot Wallstrom said the "brutal intervention" against Swedish consular support for Gui took place despite Chinese promises. But this is an ordinary example of how the Chinese cannot be trusted about anything.

Clive Hamilton's book was finally published in February 2018, thanks to pressure from alarmed members of the Australian parliament's national security committee. His research revealed evidence of CCP influence and infiltration in politics, culture, real estate, agriculture, universities, unions, and even primary schools. The book lists more than 40 former and sitting Australian politicians allegedly doing the work of China's totalitarian Government, if sometimes unwittingly.

In response, Australia is increasingly trying to restrict China's "United Front Work Department" (UFWD), which is the international Chinese coercive propaganda organization of Chinese citizens in the diaspora who are described by Chinese leaders as "Magic Weapons," as we've previously described The UFWD is in contact with over a million Chinese expats in countries around the world. It uses a variety of techniques to coerce them to influence local politicians and media to support China's policies in a variety of areas, including Taiwan policy, criminality in the South China Sea, One Belt One Road, the Dalai Lama, and so forth.

The Chinese claim that Australia's opposition to the use of its UFWD is just the latest manifestation of anti-Chinese racism.

Australia has a long history of antipathy towards Chinese in Australia since European settlement, starting with race riots amid the gold rush of the 1850s and '60s. With hundreds of Chinese prospectors injured and evicted from mining sites, the unrest prompted immigration rules that led to the infamous "White Australia" policy, which existed in various forms from 1901 until 1973.

Chinese activists have increasingly been saying that anti-Chinese racism is rising again, and that it's the cause of anxiety about Chinese influence in Australia, New Zealand, Canada, the United States, Europe, and other countries.

However, there are plenty of reasons for anxiety about China's intentions having absolutely nothing to do with racism. China is conducting well-publicized illegal activities in the South China Sea, building a massive military force with the intention of taking control of the whole region. China is also making military threats against Taiwan, India, Japan and other countries where the Chinese government wishes to confiscate a portion of the regions those countries govern.

14.5. United Front Work Department (UFWD) in Australia — mind control

There are 150,000 Chinese students in Australia, and there have been numerous incidents where Chinese students complained to school officials that lectures or course materials made them "feel uncomfortable" because they didn't "show respect" for China. They've complained about materials that describe Taiwan as a country, about a map that shows Indian territory claimed by China as Indian territory. These complaints were accompanied by demands that the materials be changed.

Now imagine any Western country trying the same thing. Imagine an agency in the Trump administration telling American students in universities overseas to complain when the university lectures and course materials contradict American policy as defined by the Trump administration. The international outrage would be enormous, and none of the American student expats would do as they had been told anyway.

By Western standards, what China is doing appears to be almost like mind control. It's amazing that an agency like the UFWD exists, and it's amazing that Chinese students around the world do as they're told — although the latter could be explained by the fact that China can threaten severe punishment for any student that disobeys orders.

America does have an agency that sends people to countries around the world — the Peace Corps. "The Peace Corps is a service opportunity for motivated changemakers to immerse themselves in a community abroad, working side by side with local leaders to tackle the most pressing challenges of our generation."

I've never heard anyone describe the Peace Corps as a "Magic Weapon" or as any kind of weapon. America has the Peace Corps, to help bring peace, and China has the "Magic Weapon Corps" to coercively spread Chinese propaganda.

So if people in Australia, Canada, the US or any other country are anxious about the Chinese, the Chinese have only themselves to blame, and it has nothing to do with racism.

China's policies could have serious consequences for Chinese expats. In World War II, the American government interred Japanese-American citizens but not German-American citizens. There are probably a lot of reasons for that, not the least of which is that there were too many German-Americans to even think about interring. But the main thing is that there was a great deal of mutual American-Japanese xenophobia prior to the war, and that turned into internment during the war. China's coercive propaganda policies applied to Chinese expats to the point of apparent mind control could, in some future circumstances, lead to the internment of Chinese expats in Australia, Canada or the United States. So the Chinese policies may be "Magic Weapons," but they could have severe consequences for the Chinese themselves.

14.6. University of North Florida closes its Confucius Institute

The University of North Florida (UNF) announced that it will cut ties with the China-funded Confucius Institute on its campus. Others of the approximately 100 colleges and universities hosting Confucius Institutes are considering doing so as well, or have already done so. [198]

Ostensibly, Confucius Institutes are apolitical partnerships between American and Chinese universities, giving American students opportunities to learn to speak Chinese or study abroad. But the Chinese themselves say that they serve as "an important part of China's overseas propaganda," and they also serve as outposts of China's intelligence and surveillance operations, as FBI Director Christopher Wray testified to the US Senate in February.

Closing UNF's Confucius Institute was a blow to the local Chinese community. Wen Raiti of the Jacksonville (Florida) Chinese Association says that the local Chinese community is a small, close-knit group that, until recently, included the institute. She says: [156]

> "This is disturbing to us who live here," says Raiti. "I participate in the political process and civil engagement. I would not want my sisters and brothers to be accused of being spies. Not everyone is part of the central

government. A lot of people are just like us, they are ordinary people. A lot of people have dissatisfaction with what [China's] government has done. I do not feel like I have to restrain myself or what I say about the Chinese government." [156]

Raiti says that she does not feel restrained about criticizing China's policies, but I doubt that this goes very far. Suppose she criticizes China's genocide of the Uighur Muslims? I suspect that she'd be in serious trouble.

Wen Raiti's husband, Jon, an American who lived in China for three years and frequently returns there on business adds: [156]

"I think it's pretty absurd to think that all [Chinese] students are spies. I think there's probably some, but not all. So you're painting the entire canvas with the same giant brush. I would suspect that it's a gross simplification." [156]

I actually feel sympathy for Chinese-Americans, since they're caught in the middle of a huge dilemma. When there's a war between China and Japan, whose side with Chinese-Americans be on, and which side will they support? China, obviously.

But when that war extends to a war between China and the United States, whose side will Chinese-Americans be on? They'll undoubtedly be split, but they will be treated with enormous suspicion by most Americans, and they may be interned as the Japanese were during World War II. It will be up to the Chinese themselves to prove that they're more American than Chinese.

So when Jon Raiti says that "it's pretty absurd to think that all [Chinese] students are spies," he's right. But he's condemned himself through his own words. When he uses the word ALL, he tacitly agrees that SOME Chinese students are spies. Closing the Confucius Institute will prevent China's UFWD to radicalize more students to be Chinese spies.

14.7. Controversy over China's Confucius Institutes

In addition to the 100-plus Confucius Institutes in the US, China runs about 500 "Confucius Classrooms" at American K-12 schools. In Australia, New Zealand, Canada, the United States and other countries, China runs 1,500 Confucius Institutes and Classrooms, with 40% of them in the US, more than any other country. [198]

The Confucian Institutes are one of the programs of Beijing's international coercive propaganda agency, the United Front Work Department (UFWD). Every aspect of the Confucian Institutes is tightly controlled by the Hanban agency, the Chinese Communist Party agency that oversees all Confucius Institutes. Teachers and teaching materials are all supplied by China. Taiwan and Tibet are portrayed as undisputed territories of China, with no alternate views permitted. The 1989 Tiananmen Square massacre, the one million Uighurs in re-education camps, and the human rights abuses in China are all forbidden subjects.

The Pentagon has been working with Confucius Institutes in some colleges, and even co-funding some programs, in order to develop Chinese-speaking students. However, the 2019 National Defense Authorization Act, signed in August, contains provisions barring any U.S. university from using Pentagon resources for any program involving Confucius Institutes. In many cases, this will force universities to choose between receiving funding the Pentagon and funding from Hanban. [198]

Steve Bannon, formerly the chief strategist and advisor to president Donald Trump, has researched the extent to which Chinese engineers are working on American weapons systems.

According to Bannon, many Chinese workers in the US start out as students in American colleges, through Confucius Institutes, controlled by the Chinese Communist Party (CCP) through Beijing's international coercive propaganda agency, the United Front Work Department (UFWD), and funded by China's military. Every aspect of the Confucian Institutes is tightly controlled by the CCP. Teachers and teaching materials are all supplied by China. Taiwan and Tibet are portrayed as undisputed territories of China, with no alternate views permitted. The 1989 Tiananmen Square massacre, the one million Uighurs in re-education camps, and the human rights abuses in China are all forbidden subjects. [197]

Bannon says that Chinese students study in colleges to get access to the latest scientific research to be passed back to the CCP. After graduation, these students become contractors to get access to the latest American weapons systems, once again for the CCP. According to Bannon, Defense Department reports on the infiltration of China into our research universities and our weapons labs shows extensive infiltration:

> "I don't think people understand these reports. These reports are essentially declassified reports that showed that the 300,000 students are here on student visas and the 10,000 contractors that we have the weapons labs — I think that up to 2/3 of them could be intelligence assets, intelligence officers or agents.
>
> This is political correctness and greed and avarice writ large. How did contractors — and let's call them out — Booz Allen and all these contractors — how do these contractors and these big government programs get so many Chinese nationals working into our weapons labs? Our weapons labs are at the cutting edge of national security. How did it happen? ...

The political correctness of it all-- the Financial Times of London leaked the other day that my colleague, Stephen Miller, who's a terrific young man, actually had the plan in place to get all 300,000 Chinese students out of the country with a way to cut the visas off right away. Not that we we're going to execute on it, but it was even in thinking.

And obviously, it got leaked. In the Times, it goes around the State Department, et cetera. Look at all the appeasers. I am so glad. I take great pride that someone like Susan Thornton now owns a farm up in Maine because she was part of this kind of irrational accommodationist, this softness in the Defense Department, in the State Department, in our intelligence services that basically went along with what China wanted to do and looked the other way."

Chapter 15. Belt and Road Initiative and Debt Trap Diplomacy

"Belt and Road Initiative" (BRI), originally called "One Belt One Road" (OBOR), and sometimes called "the New Silk Road," has a romantic appeal because it's a modern day version of the ancient "Silk Road," a collection of trade routes regularly used between 100 BC to 1400 AD by traders carrying goods back and forth between China and Europe. The name comes from the popularity of Chinese silk in the Roman Empire.

Unlike the original Silk Road, the new Silk Road is not simply an overland route. The Belt and Road Initiative project consists of two parts:

- The Economic Belt is a collection of hugely ambitious land-based infrastructure projects, including a train line stretching from eastern China to London.
- The Maritime Silk Road is a sea-based network of shipping lanes and port developments throughout the Pacific and Indian oceans to the Mediterranean Sea and Europe.

The BRI includes infrastructure projects that have already been under development since the 1990s. China says it plans to invest hundreds of billions of dollars over the next 50 years or so to complete the project.

15.1. Debt Trap Diplomacy

Whether the BRI project will ever be completed is, of course, open to doubt. There has already been one large, spectacular failure. In 2009, China invested $1.2 billion in Sri Lanka's Hambantota seaport.

Sri Lanka had expected to repay the debt through profits earned by the port, but the slowdown in trade throughout the entire region in the last few years has meant that Sri Lanka has been unable to repay the debt. In retrospect, the estimates of profits were completely unrealistic to start with, and China may have been aware of that, but may have bribed Sri Lanka officials to get the project approved anyway.

However the deal got approved, Sri Lanka was forced to give China control of the Port of Hambantota in lieu of repayment of the debt. Since almost all the labor on the port had been performed by Chinese workers, now Sri Lanka has a large seaport controlled by China, and a large Chinese enclave with hundreds of Chinese families, with no benefit to Sri Lanka or to Sri Lankans. [189]

Because BRI is so expensive, so long-term, and so unrealistic, many people are suspicious that China's motives are more complex. The Sri Lanka port project shows what can happen — China invests a lot of money in an infrastructure project in a country, and thereby gains political influence or sovereignty in the country, or even ownership of the infrastructure. Even if the BRI is never completed, a successful outcome for China would be a strong economic and military grip in dozens of countries throughout the region.

There are examples in Africa as well.

In 2007, Democratic Republic of Congo (DRC) entered into a $10 billion resource-financed infrastructure agreement with China, where copper and cobalt mining licenses would be allocated to a Chinese consortium. In exchange, the consortium would secure financing of $6.56 billion worth of infrastructure projects and invest $3 billion in mining projects. The agreement came to light only when DRC could not make the debt payments, and China's Exim bank took control of a portion of the mines. [189]

In 2010, the government of Ghana informally secured $3 billion loan from China without parliamentary scrutiny and over 15 years Ghana would supply 750 million barrels (13,000 barrels per day) for servicing the debt. When oil prices crashed, China's Exim bank demanded that the amount of oil used to service the debt would increase from 13,000 to 15,000 barrels per day, and that the agreed fixed price to be paid would be reduced from $100 to $85 per barrel According to Ghana's then Finance minister, that $15 difference would have seen Ghanaians pay $6.4 billion to repay a $3 billion loan. Ghana was forced to cancel half of the agreed $3 billion loan. [189]

15.2. The secret BRI deals and Debt Trap Diplomacy

In all three of these cases, the details of these agreements were kept secret, per China's demands, until they were revealed because debt repayments could not be met, and China then enforced repayment by seizing assets.

For months I've been describing the onerous details of such contracts, based on incomplete reports or vague statements by politicians. It's always been clear that the reason why China demanded total secrecy was because these contracts are extremely favorable to China and are used for "debt trap diplomacy," allowing China to take control of a country's infrastructure when countries are unable to make the loan payments.

After studying what happened in several countries, the outlines of the debt trap diplomacy became increasingly clear:

- China offers the country's leaders big financial incentives to accept the deal. (The technical word for this is "bribery.")
- The terms of the contract are to be kept secret.

- China loans the country tens of billions of dollars to pay for the building of infrastructure projects, such as railways, ports, highways, pipelines, mines, and so forth — projects that are designed in such a way that China will benefit, such as by being able to extract resources or to take control of a strategic seaport.
- China demands that the work be done by Chinese workers, and that parts and services be purchased from Chinese factories and businesses.
- China demands that the loaned money be used to pay Chinese workers' salaries and to purchase parts and services from Chinese factories and businesses. So instead of benefiting the local factories and workers, the money goes back to China to benefit factories and people in China.
- And yet, the country still has to repay the loan, having gotten nothing out of it. This means that the country is repaying the loan twice.
- The contract specifies that when the country is unable to make payments on the loan, China can take possession of the infrastructure projects.

As I research BRI projects in several countries, there were differences in details, but they all generally followed the above pattern which gave China control of the infrastructure project through "debt trap diplomacy."

15.3. The Belt and Road (BRI) contract in Kenya

Kenya went on a borrowing binge in the mid-2010s, having borrowed a total of $50 billion. These loans have been used to build roads, ports and railways, and were to be repaid with the revenue from this infrastructure, but as with many of these Chinese loans, hopes were dashed and promises were not kept. [189]

In 2014, China granted to Kenya a five-year grace period for in repaying the loan, until July 2019, when Kenya's loan repayments to China will triple to $900 million per year. Those who remember the financial crisis of the mid-2000s decade will recall that a major cause was the "sub-prime mortgage loan," where the homeowner would make only small payments at first, and then the payments would increase substantially after a couple of years. Those loans were called "confiscatory" and "debt traps" because it was obvious from the start that they would not be repaid. So China granted Kenya a "sub-prime loan," under the condition that loan repayments triple in July 2019. [189]

By January 2019, there were rumors spreading that Kenya was going to lose its Port of Mombasa to China. China denied that anything like that would happen, but then the "secret" BRI contract was partially leaked, and its terms were far worse than anyone had imagined. [190]

The headline revelation in the leaked contract is that all Kenya's assets, within Kenya or abroad, are now subject to Chinese seizure if Kenya can't make its debt payments. Up until now, Kenyans had worried that its Port of Mombasa, which would be extremely valuable to China for use as a military base, was in danger of seizure by China. But the leaks reveal that any Kenyan asset can be seized. [190]

The leaked document refers to the Standard Gauge Railway (SGR) project, a railway from Mombasa to Nairobi, funded by two separate $1.6 billion loans from China. The debt was to be repaid from revenue from the SGR, but that revenue has been far below the optimistic estimates made in 2014. Clause 5.5 of the "Preferential Buyer Credit Loan Agreement on the Mombasa-Nairobi SGR" says the following:

> "Neither the borrower (Kenya) nor any of its assets is entitled to any right of immunity on the grounds of sovereignty or otherwise from arbitration, suit, execution or any other legal process with respect to its obligations under this Agreement, as the case may be in any jurisdiction."

Strictly interpreted, this clause forfeits all of Kenya's rights, sovereign or otherwise, to any Kenyan asset, whether the Port of Mombasa, another asset within Kenya, or a Kenyan asset abroad. None of the news reports I've seen provides a list of foreign assets that might be vulnerable, except to suggest that all of them are. According to legal experts, in case of default, China can take over many critical resources — anything from airports and natural resources to embassies abroad.

Other clauses of the leaked contract reveal the following:

- Kenya must keep the contract secret. Clause 17.7: "The borrower (Kenya) shall keep all the terms and conditions hereunder or in connection with this agreement strictly confidential. Without the prior written consent of the lender (China), the borrower shall not disclose any information hereunder or in connection with this agreement to any third party unless required by applicable law."
- The agreement is governed by Chinese law. According to one Kenyan lawyer: "The agreement is being made in Kenya, the railway is built in Kenya and the assets they are talking about are in Kenya, so why is it being governed by the laws of China? Had there been more transparency or choices of who funds the railway then Kenya may have got a better deal."
- Any disputes can be resolved only by a Chinese agency, the China International Economic and Trade Arbitration Commission (Cietac). According to the agreement, "The arbitration award shall be final and binding on both parties. The arbitration shall take place in Beijing." In normal contracts, disputes are settled by a neutral and impartial arbitrator. For example, in 2017 Kenya signed a pipeline security

commercial contract with Israel, and disputes will be submitted to an arbitrator in London.

- Kenya pays the China Road and Bridge Corporation (CRBC) $10 million per month to run the railway. As is usual in China's BRI contracts, the Kenyans are not permitted to run their own railroad or to hire their own workers. This despite the fact that CRBC has been repeatedly accused of abusive behavior towards Kenyans, and of "neo-colonialism, racism and blatant discrimination." Kenya's Auditor-General Edward Ouko has repeatedly violated Kenya's laws by not releasing regular reports on payments to CRBC.

- Kenya is compelled to import goods, technology and services from China. This is standard practice for China's BRI deals. China loans a huge amount of money to a country like Kenya. Kenya must use the money to pay Chinese workers, and buy goods, technology and services from China. So all the money goes right back to China and benefits Chinese factories and workers, rather than Kenyan factories and workers. And yet, Kenya still has to repay the loan, which means that it's repaying the loan twice, or else have all its assets seized and confiscated by the Chinese.

- China is charging considerably more for the project than would be standard in other countries. This is a sign of corruption.

- If Kenya tries to pay off the loan with alternate funds (I assume this means a loan from another country), then China can refuse to accept that payment. [190]

The agreement contains other clauses that protect China, and almost guarantee that the loan will not be repaid, allowing China to seize Kenyan assets. [190]

According to various reports, other African countries that have fallen to China's "debt diplomacy" traps are Madagascar and Zambia.

Chapter 16. China's claims to the South China Sea

As I said in the introduction, this was to be the entire subject of this book, originally. However, it has turned out to be just a small part of what we need to know about China.

16.1. China's Nine-Dash Map

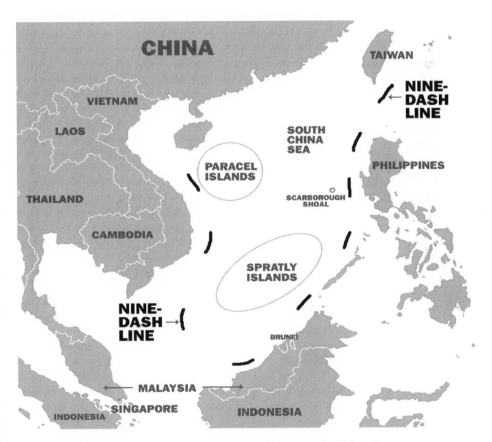

China's Nine-Dash Map of the South China Sea

China's so-called "historic claims" to the South China Sea are actually not "centuries old," but only go back to 1947, when China's Nationalist leader

Chiang Kai-shek, showing admiration for Nazi Germany's Lebensraum policy, drew an "eleven-dash line" on a map of the South China Sea, and claimed the entire region as China's sovereign territory — including areas that clearly belonged to other nations. [1]

Later, Chiang's map got simplified into a Nine-Dash Map, similar to the one shown above. [1]

Just to take one example of the arbitrariness of China's claims, let's take its claim to Indonesia's Natuna Island. In 2016, China sent its coast guard warships to ram Indonesian vessels in the Natuna Sea, and there was a naval clash between Indonesia and China in what is clearly the exclusive economic zone or EEZ of Indonesia. What's going on here is that the Natuna Sea has extremely rich fishing grounds. The Natuna Sea is clearly Indonesia's territory, since it's very far from China, but that makes no difference to China. It's amazing that here in the 21st century, China is doing exactly what the Nazis did.

16.2. China's 'ironclad proof' of South China Sea claims revealed as hoax

By early 2016, it was becoming clear to researchers (outside of China) that China had no claim whatsoever to the South China Sea, and that China hadn't even shown an interest in the South China Sea until 1947, with Chiang Kai-shek.

The Philippines had brought a case to the Tribunal of the United Nations Permanent Court of Arbitration in The Hague to adjudicate China's claims. In early 2016, it was becoming increasingly clear, that China was going to lose that case.

Chinese authorities became increasingly desperate to find any evidence — ANYTHING — that might support their claims. They came up with a fantastical story about a 600 year old handwritten book by a fisherman named Su Chengfen, who uses the book as a guide to the various routes between the islands, according to the China Daily article, which claimed that the book provided "ironclad proof" of China's claims. [4]

When those claims were published, the BBC decided to investigate, and tracked down the fisherman, to determine whether the claim was real.

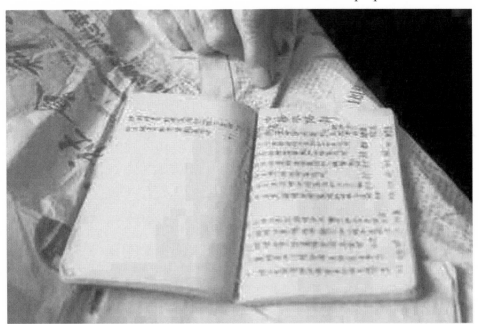

Supposedly, this is a picture of Su Chengfen's 600 year old book (China Daily)

For several weeks, China's state media repeatedly made a big deal about an "ancient book," 600 years old, that proves that Chinese fishermen were fishing in the Paracel Islands and beyond. From there, according to a leap of logic that was never clear to me, China says that this is "ironclad proof" that the Paracel Islands belong to China. So even if the book existed, it still wouldn't mean anything.

Here's the description from Chinese media: [4]

> "Su Chengfen has spent all his life fishing in the reef-filled South China Sea, guided by a handwritten book more than 600 years old that depicts routes to various remote islands from Hainan province.
>
> The former fishing vessel captain, who lives in the town of Tanmen, cherishes the book, wrapping it in layers of paper even though at 81 it is impossible for him to return to the sea.
>
> He has always known it is precious, as it contains detailed information handed down over the generations, but at first he had not realized its true significance.
>
> Specialists say the information the book contains is undeniable proof of China's sovereignty over Huangyan Island.
>
> "Unlike other versions, it depicts the exact route to Huangyan Island. It clearly proves that generations of Chinese fishermen have worked on the island," said Zhou Weimin, a retired professor at Hainan University." [4]

Another Chinese official says, "It is ironclad proof. ... We can deduce China's historic fishing and sailing rights in the South China Sea, as well as ownership."

Huangyan Island is China's name for Scarborough Shoal, a reef that is a little less than 200 kilometers from Subic Bay, well within the Philippines' exclusive economic zone or EEZ. So there's absolutely no way that that this book provides "ironclad proof" of anything. Even if the book is as described, it only proves that Chinese fishermen were fishing centuries ago in waters that clearly belong to the Philippines, just as they're doing today, illegally. It wouldn't be surprising if someone discovered that Philippines fishermen fished in Chinese waters centuries ago, but that doesn't mean that China is the Philippines' sovereign territory.

In the sixth decade BC, Julius Caesar's army conquered France, as he described in his *Gallic Wars*. But that doesn't mean that France belongs to Italy. So Su Chengfen's book, even if it existed, would have no value whatsoever.

However, the BBC sent its China correspondent, John Sudworth, to visit 81 year old Su Chengfen in the town of Tanmen on Hainan island. He wanted to speak to Su, and see this wonderful book for himself. According to Su, as told to Sudworth: [5]

> "It was passed down from generation to generation. From my grandfather's generation, to my father's generation, then to me.
>
> It mainly taught us how to go somewhere and come back, how to go to the Paracels and the Spratlys, and how to come back to Hainan Island."

OK. So Sudworth asked to see the book, but Su tells him the book doesn't exist.

> "Although the book was important, I threw it away because it was broken.
>
> It was flipped through too many times. The salty seawater on the hands had corroded it... In the end it was no longer readable so I threw it away."

According to Su, the book was thrown away in the late 1980s. [5]

So apparently the whole thing is a hoax. The picture from Chinese media, shown at the top of this article, is some other book. The layers of paper, in which the "cherished book" was wrapped, don't exist either. The "cherished book" was simply thrown out in the 1980s, according to Su.

In particular, all the information depicting the "exact route" to the Scarborough Shoal is only a 30 year old memory in the head of the 81 year old Su.

Some Chinese media reports claim that there are other books, but look again at the paragraph quoted above:

"Unlike other versions, it depicts the exact route to Huangyan Island. It clearly proves that generations of Chinese fishermen have worked on the island," said Zhou Weimin, a retired professor at Hainan University." [4] So the other books do not depict the route to Scarborough Shoal.

So China's "ironclad proof" consists of a book that doesn't exist, that may or may not have ever existed, and whose contents if it existed can only be guessed at. And even if it did exist, it only proves that Chinese fishermen were fishing in waters belonging to the Philippines, much as they're doing today, illegally.

I feel sorry for Su Chengfen. He must have been in on the hoax with the Beijing authorities from the beginning. So one day a BBC reporter shows up and asks to see the book, and he must have totally freaked out, knowing that if he said the wrong thing he would be punished severely. So he made up the story about the book being thrown out. If he'd been smart, he would have said that the book was being preserved in Beijing, but he didn't think of that.

The moronic story about Su Chengfen's mystical 600 year old book shows how totally desperate the Chinese are.

16.3. China's humiliating repudiation by UNCLOS court

In July 2016, the Chinese Communist Party was thoroughly humiliated when all of their activities in the South China Sea were declared illegal by the United Nations Permanent Court of Arbitration in The Hague, which ruled that all of China's activities in the South China Sea are illegal and in violation of international law. [6]

The following are some excerpts from the "Conclusion" section of the ruling: [6]

"D. CONCLUSION

The Tribunal considers it beyond dispute that both Parties are obliged to comply with the Convention, including its provisions regarding the resolution of disputes, and to respect the rights and freedoms of other States under the Convention. ...

[The Tribunal] DECLARES that, as between the Philippines and China, China's claims to historic rights, or other sovereign rights or jurisdiction, with respect to the maritime areas of the South China Sea encompassed by the relevant part of the 'nine-dash line' are contrary to the Convention and without lawful effect to the extent that they exceed the geographic and substantive limits of China's maritime entitlements under the Convention.

[The Tribunal] DECLARES that Scarborough Shoal, Gaven Reef (North), McKennan Reef, Johnson Reef, Cuarteron Reef, and Fiery Cross Reef, in their natural condition, are rocks that cannot sustain human habitation or economic life of their own, and accordingly that [they] generate no entitlement to an exclusive economic zone or continental shelf.

[The Tribunal] FINDS that none of the high-tide features in the Spratly Islands, in their natural condition, are capable of sustaining human habitation or economic life of their own ...; that none of the high-tide features in the Spratly Islands generate entitlements to an exclusive economic zone or continental shelf; and that therefore there is no entitlement to an exclusive economic zone or continental shelf generated by any feature claimed by China that would overlap the entitlements of the Philippines in the area of Mischief Reef and Second Thomas Shoal; and DECLARES that Mischief Reef and Second Thomas Shoal are within the exclusive economic zone and continental shelf of the Philippines.

[The Tribunal] FINDS that, in May 2013, fishermen from Chinese flagged vessels engaged in fishing within the Philippines' exclusive economic zone at Mischief Reef and Second Thomas Shoal; and that China, through the operation of its marine surveillance vessels, was aware of, tolerated, and failed to exercise due diligence to prevent such fishing by Chinese flagged vessels; and that therefore China has failed to exhibit due regard for the Philippines' sovereign rights with respect to fisheries in its exclusive economic zone; and DECLARES that China has breached its obligations under Article 58(3) of the Convention;

[The Tribunal] FINDS that Scarborough Shoal has been a traditional fishing ground for fishermen of many nationalities and DECLARES that China has, through the operation of its official vessels at Scarborough Shoal from May 2012 onwards, unlawfully prevented fishermen from the Philippines from engaging in traditional fishing at Scarborough Shoal.

[The Tribunal] FINDS, with respect to the protection and preservation of the marine environment in the South China Sea: that fishermen from Chinese flagged vessels have engaged in the harvesting of endangered species on a significant scale; that fishermen from Chinese flagged vessels have engaged in the harvesting of giant clams in a manner that is severely destructive of the coral reef ecosystem; and that China was aware of, tolerated, protected, and failed to prevent the aforementioned harmful activities.

[The Tribunal] FINDS further that China's land reclamation and construction of artificial islands, installations, and structures at Cuarteron Reef, Fiery Cross Reef, Gaven Reef (North), Johnson Reef, Hughes Reef, Subi Reef, and Mischief Reef has caused severe, irreparable harm to the coral reef ecosystem; that China has not cooperated or coordinated with the other States bordering the South China Sea concerning the protection and preservation of the marine environment concerning such activities; and that China has failed to communicate an assessment of the potential effects of such activities on the marine environment, within the meaning of Article 206 of the Convention.

[The Tribunal] DECLARES that China has breached its obligations ... with respect to China's construction of artificial islands, installations, and structures at Mischief Reef: FINDS that China has engaged in the construction of artificial islands, installations, and structures at Mischief Reef without the authorization of the Philippines; and DECLARES that China has breached Articles 60 and 80 of the Convention with respect to the Philippines' sovereign rights in its exclusive economic zone and continental shelf.

[The Tribunal] FINDS, with respect to the operation of Chinese law enforcement vessels in the vicinity of Scarborough Shoal: that China's operation of its law enforcement vessels on 28 April 2012 and 26 May 2012 created serious risk of collision and danger to Philippine ships and personnel; and DECLARES that China has breached its obligations under Article 94 of the Convention; and that, during the time in which these dispute resolution proceedings were ongoing, China: a. has built a large artificial island on Mischief Reef, a low-tide elevation located in the exclusive economic zone of the Philippines; b. has caused—through its land reclamation and construction of artificial islands, installations, and structures—severe, irreparable harm to the coral reef ecosystem ...; and has permanently destroyed—through its land reclamation and construction of artificial islands, installations, and structures—evidence of the natural condition of Mischief Reef, Cuarteron Reef, Fiery Cross Reef, Gaven Reef (North), Johnson Reef, Hughes Reef, and Subi Reef. [6]

Part of China's claim to the South China Sea was a kind of leapfrogging from island to island. China would claim one island close to the mainland, then claim another island is close to the first island, and so forth, across the South China Sea.

The Tribunal ruling was that these so-called islands are not islands. They're simply uninhabited rocks, and so they do not qualify to be claimed by anyone.

The ruling makes the following points: [6]

- The Spratly Islands are little more than rocks, uninhabited, and so do not "generate entitlements to an exclusive economic zone or continental shelf."
- China purposely and illegally permitted its own vessels to fish in the Philippines EEZ.

- China purposely and illegally prevented fishermen from the Philippines to fish around Scarborough Shoal, a traditional fishing ground for many nationalities. China put Philippines' fishermen's lives at risk.
- China has harvested endangered species "on a significant scale." China has been "severely destructive of the coral reef ecosystem."
- China's construction of artificial islands is almost totally illegal, because of environmental destruction and because they violate "Philippines' sovereign rights in its exclusive economic zone and continental shelf." [6]

China's response to the court ruling at the time was that it was "completely a political farce staged under legal pretext," and it was "plotted and manipulated by certain forces outside the region," which could mean either the Europeans or the Americans or both. The spokesman at the time continued, "Its purpose is clearly not to seek proper settlement of disputes with China, but to violate China's territorial sovereignty and maritime rights and interests and put peace and stability in the South China Sea in jeopardy."

The logic of the Chinese statement is that China's "territorial sovereignty" over the region are a given, and any challenge puts "peace and stability in the South China Sea in jeopardy."

That of course is a threat: Any challenge will be met with a military response.

16.4. China's claims in South China Sea — Nationalism, Rejuvenation, Lebensraum

The above story about Su Chengfen is so crazy and farcical that I would barely believe it happened if I hadn't verified that the claims were made on several Chinese media sites and were refuted on the BBC site, as well as on the televised BBC World News, which showed Sudworth's actual interview with Su. And yet it did happen.

I keep coming back to the sheer insanity of the Chinese Communist Party (CCP). For example, they're locking up millions of Muslim Uighurs in East Turkistan (Xinjiang province) in concentration camps. That is about the stupidest policy of any nation in the history of the world, and yet they're doing it. And how ridiculous is the CCP that they're afraid of Winnie the Pooh. Can you imagine Donald Trump or any other Western leader being afraid of Winnie the Pooh? What are we to make of the CCP government that adopts policies, one after the other, that are dangerous, insane and stupid?

For years, media and analysts in the West have been completely confused by China's claims to the South China Sea, as in "What the heck are they talking about?" The reason for so much confusion is that China never had any interest whatsoever in the South China Sea until 1947. One historian Mohan Malik analyzes it as follows: [1]

"And finally, China's so-called "historic claims" to the South China Sea are actually not "centuries old." They only go back to 1947, when Chiang Kai-shek's nationalist government drew the so-called "eleven-dash line" on Chinese maps of the South China Sea, enclosing the Spratly Islands and other chains that the ruling Kuomintang party declared were now under Chinese sovereignty. Chiang himself, saying he saw German fascism as a model for China, was fascinated by the Nazi concept of an expanded Lebensraum ("living space") for the Chinese nation. He did not have the opportunity to be expansionist himself because the Japanese put him on the defensive, but cartographers of the nationalist regime drew the U-shape of eleven dashes in an attempt to enlarge China's "living space" in the South China Sea. Following the victory of the Chinese Communist Party in the civil war in 1949, the People's Republic of China adopted this cartographic coup, revising Chiang's notion into a "nine-dash line" after erasing two dashes in the Gulf of Tonkin in 1953." [1]

However, another historian, Jacqueline Newmyer Deal, says that Chinese nationalism predates the Nazis:

"The reality is more nuanced than either the image of European-style fascism or the theory of Chinese democratization, though it is unfortunately closer to the former than the latter. Today's Chinese nationalism is a direct descendant of intellectual currents that predate the rise of Nazi Germany, but these currents were in circulation in Weimar Germany and may have helped Hitler ascend to power. This thinking is essentially illiberal and hence certainly not a sign of liberalization. Moreover, as Christopher Hughes of the London School of Economics has noted, even before Tiananmen Square [June 1989 massacre] the post-Mao CCP had begun to promulgate nationalism as a way to fill the vacuum left by the erosion of the Great Helmsman's [Mao's] cult of personality. Before succumbing to the CCP's crackdown, in fact, the student protesters of June 1989 actually tried to invoke the slogans of early twentieth-century Chinese nationalists that the party had recently trumpeted. But the forcefulness of the CCP's response made it clear that the elites had no intention of letting nationalism become a lever of popular influence. That remains the case today, as the current exponents of rejuvenation and Chinese nationalism follow in the autocratic footsteps of their late imperial Chinese forebears." [2]

She says that China's quest for the South China is wrapped up in the term "national rejuvenation." Her article, written in 2011, explains it this way: [2]

"Even in the absence of an official explanation from the CCP, it is at least possible to consider the origins and evolution of the term. Despite its currency today, national rejuvenation is not an invention of the party. Its pedigree in China actually dates back to the formative period of Chinese nationalism, from the latter stages of the nineteenth century through the early twentieth century. But it was repopularized by Premier Zhao Ziyang at the Thirteenth Party Congress under Deng Xiaoping in 1987. It then became a watchword during the tenures of Deng's two successors as CCP general secretary, Jiang Zemin and Hu Jintao. As the Harvard historian Mark Elliott has pointed out, use of the term increased dramatically, both in official party language and in the popular culture, over the last decade, starting in 2001 when Jiang declared that the party was leading the "great rejuvenation of the Chinese nation." There followed a popular CCTV television series, a three-volume book and a "song-and-dance epic" at the National Theater, all called the "Road to Rejuvenation." In March 2011, a permanent exhibit with the same name opened at the National Museum of China in Beijing. The preface to the exhibit concludes, "Today, the Chinese nation is standing firm in the east, facing a brilliant future of great rejuvenation. The long-cherished dream and aspiration of the Chinese people will surely come to reality." In the course of a single 2011 speech marking the one hundredth anniversary of the 1911 Chinese revolution, Hu mentioned rejuvenation twenty-three times. It was Chinese nationalists who took power following that revolution, and understanding their worldview turns out to be a critical requirement in order to fill out the picture of national rejuvenation." [2]

According to Deal, Sun Yat-Sen, the hero of China's 1911 Republican revolution, developed in 1905 his "Three Principles of the People" (i.e., nationalism, democracy and welfare). Sun was consciously trying to emulate Abraham Lincoln's idea of government "of the people, by the people, for the people." Despite all that, Sun added the following: [2]

"The greatest force is common blood. The Chinese belong to the yellow race because they come from the blood stock of the yellow race. The blood of ancestors is transmitted by heredity down through the race, making blood kinship a powerful force."

This concept of "yellow race" and "yellow skin" is a strong part of Chinese chauvinism, with Chinese defined as descendants of the Yellow Emperor, the heirs of a glorious civilization who will recover their preeminence. [2]

Chapter 17. America's preparation for war

Few people are even aware that the foreign policies being followed by president Donald Trump are motivated by the need for America to prepare for war with China. Whether you like Donald Trump or hate him, you should be relieved to know that he's been preparing America to defend against the inevitable attack by China.

We live in a very strange time when people in the media have absolutely no idea what's going on in the world. The media are completely baffled by Trump's policies when they talk about things like "chaos," "Trump out of control," "Trump is crazy," "the wheels are coming off," "Trump should be impeached," and so on. I have heard or read these remarks every day for almost three years.

At the same time they promote truly moronic theories, like the one currently widely held that the world will end in 12 years because of "climate change."

In the last two years, I've pointed out many times that Trump's policies make perfect sense when viewed from the point of view of Generational Dynamics. Trump himself is familiar with Generational Dynamics analyses, because he was educated about them by his former chief strategist and advisor Steve Bannon, with whom I worked off and on for several years.

Actually, this one is pretty easy. The Generational Dynamics prediction has always been that we're headed for a "Clash of Civilizations world war." The "allies" will be the United States, India, Russia and Iran, while the "axis" will be China, Pakistan, and the Sunni Muslim countries.

I've written about the reasons for this hundreds of times, and the summary behind the reasoning is as follows: China is very closely allied with Pakistan, which is very closely allied with the Sunni states. China and India are bitter enemies, as are Pakistan and India. Russia and India are very closely allied, and India is very closely allied with Iran, as Hindus have been allied with Shia Muslims going back to the Battle of Karbala in 680. Connecting the dots, the US is going to be allied with India, Russia and Iran, versus China, Pakistan, and the Sunni Muslim states. If that seems surprising, remember that Russia was our bitter enemy before WW II, was our ally during WW II, and was our bitter enemy after WW II, so you can't judge from today's political alignments how nations will act when they're facing an existential crisis in the form of a generational crisis war.

So that's the Generational Dynamics prediction, and we assume that Trump is aware of it and believes it, as he should. Now we take note of the of the following:

- ISIS is not an existential threat to America.

- Al-Qaeda is not an existential threat to America.
- Iran is not an existential threat to America.
- Russia is not an existential threat to America. (It may be an existential threat to Ukraine, but not to America.)
- The Taliban in Afghanistan is not an existential threat to America.
- There will always be disparate individuals conducting terrorist attacks, and in that sense the "war on terror" can never be won.
- China, backed by North Korea, IS an existential threat to America.

So if you're baffled by Trump's withdrawal policy, just read the above list. When you look at that list, it makes perfect sense to withdraw some resources from Syria and Afghanistan, in order to allocate them to the approaching war with China. It makes perfect sense to prepare for the coming preemptive attack by China on the United States. Keeping troops in Syria does not do that.

On the international level, the mainstream media and many politicians have been completely baffled by Trump's policies, and I've written numerous articles explaining that many of Trump's policies are for example the kind of preparations that I'm talking about now, including the following:

- Withdraw troops and resources from Syria and other regions to make them available for war with China.
- Maintain forward air bases in Afghanistan (Bagram and Kandahar International Airport)
- Maintain THAAD anti-missile defenses in South Korea
- Use negotiations with Xi Jinping and Kim Jong-un to slow preparations for war
- Use tariffs to slow China's preparations for war
- Use sanctions to slow North Korea's preparations for war

All of these things are consistent with the Generational Dynamics predictions, particularly the prediction that America is headed for a world war against China.

17.1. Will America survive world war with China?

I used to think that America might lose to China, but after years of research into China's history and policies, I no longer think so. China may be good at killing people with missiles, but they're almost totally incompetent at governing themselves.

Chinese missiles will destroy many American cities, but America itself will survive. The Imperial Japanese were much stupider than the Nazis, and the Chinese Communist Party is even stupider than the Japanese were, so the Chinese and their nuclear missiles will bring massive destruction to themselves and the entire world, but they will lose the war, and end up lying prostrate before the world.

17.2. Will America's young people refuse to fight for their country?

People sometimes say that America can't win a war because the country is so divided, just as it was in the 1960s-70s during the Vietnam war.

In fact, just the opposite is true. When the United States faces an existential threat, today's young people will rush to defend their country, and in fact will become the new "greatest generation."

From the point of view of Generational Dynamics, you can't compare today's America to the 1960s, the time of the Vietnam war. The 1960s was a generational Awakening era. The fault line was horizontal, generational and political, pitting the war survivors (older generations) versus the younger generation (Boomers).

Another example of an Awakening era war is Germany during World War I. The German people rose up against the government in 1918, and forced Germany to capitulate. Once again, that was an Awakening era war, like our Vietnam war, and it was extremely unpopular almost from the beginning. (See *Im Westen Nichts Neues*, All Quiet on the Western Front.) [205]

Today in America the major fault line is vertical, the red states versus the blue states but, still, it's purely political, not military. No red state is going to raise an army and invade a blue state, or vice versa.

America in the 1930s was just as politically divided as it is today. There was still a north-south divide left over from the Civil War. There were endless violent left-wing riots by the unions and the communists. It was the middle of the Great Depression, and people were living under bridges. And, most important, FDR was even more divisive than Trump is today. FDR actually tried a semi-coup by packing the Supreme Court, which would have given him control of two branches of government if he had succeeded.

But despite the divisiveness of FDR, the country was quickly united behind FDR, first by the attack on Pearl Harbor, and then by the Bataan Death march. In generational theory, this is the "Regeneracy," which refers to the regeneration of civic unity for the first time since the end of the previous crisis war.

So, exactly the same thing will happen today. If there's an attack on American soil, or a major military defeat overseas, then Americans will put aside their political differences and unite behind Trump (or the next president) overnight.

I used to say stuff like this during Obama's presidency, saying that the country would be instantly united behind Obama. I remember the fury I heard from the conservatives at this suggestion, with one person saying that if he were "behind Obama," then he would shoot. Nonetheless, a Regeneracy event like Pearl Harbor or the Bataan Death March would immediately unify the country behind Trump, or whoever is president.

Some people claim that today's younger generations hate America so much that they would never be willing to fight for America in a war. That may have been the case during the Vietnam war in the 1960s Awakening era, when young people's hostility was actually directed at their parents, as described by the commonly used phrase "generation gap." But today's kids, most of whom are so poorly educated that they'd have difficulty picking out China on a map, do not hate America but are simply confused.

Once again, this is no different than the way young people felt in the 1930s. But once the Regeneracy events occurred, they turned into "The Greatest Generation" and rushed out, without complaining, to fight against the Nazis and Imperial Japanese.

So those who are afraid that young people today will refuse to fight for their country should understand that, quite the opposite, today's young people will be "The New Greatest Generation."

17.3. Preparing yourself and your family for war

It's kind of a joke to say that there's no easy way for an individual person or family to prepare for a world war, but that in fact is the case.

My study of history has led me to believe that WW III will not begin with some major unexpected massive attack, like the bombing of Pearl Harbor. Instead, my expectation is that it will begin with a minor clash — possibly between China and Japan or between India and Pakistan or between Iran and Saudi Arabia — that spirals into a larger clash, and keeps getting escalated into a world war. I've previously discussed this in conjunction with the Marco Polo Bridge incident that started World War II.

The importance is that this minor event can happen at any time — next week, next month, next year, or thereafter. So if you rush to move into a bunker somewhere, you may be there for much longer than you needed to be. On the other hand, if you wait too long, then you may miss an opportunity, such as for example of all the planes leaving town are fully booked.

For most people, that means you should just live your life as usual, and just take the view that God will decide what happens to you. In any case, it would be a good idea to prepare for not having electricity for at least a month, by stocking up on food, water and medicines, enough for you and your family.

Many people may decide to move away from their current homes. There are many strategies for this. I was told by one person that he doesn't want to live through a world war, and so he's going to move near a military base or big city, a place that's likely to be hit by an early missile.

But for most people, moving away means moving away to some place safe. It's impossible to predict what places will be safe, and it depends on your skills. If you have farming skills, then a good choice might be a remote farm. If you have carpentry skills, then a good place might be a small town where homes are being built.

This is as good a time as any to mention that having a "real" skill that can be used anywhere may save your life by providing a living. If you've only lived in big cities your whole life, your best bet is probably to stay where you are, and stock up on supplies.

Working in a foreign country can raise issues, if it's a potential war zone. For example, I've had online discussions with a couple of Americans working in Seoul, the capital city of South Korea, a potential target of attack by North Korea. One of them decided to give up his job in Seoul and move back to the United States, rather than put his family at risk. The other is simply undecided what to do. If he moves back right away, then Seoul might be at peace for a year. But if he waits until the North actually attacks, then all the planes will be booked up.

If you do decide to move to another country where you believe you'll be safe, keep in mind that you'll be a stranger in a strange land. If you don't know anyone in the neighborhood, and you don't speak the language or you speak it with an accent, then you may be robbed or targeted with violence. If you have relatives or friends in some "safe" country, then that might be the best choice.

Wherever you live, if there's a breakdown in public order, then you may have to defend yourself from marauding gangs. This could happen without a war, of course. Floods, earthquakes and hurricanes can cause a breakdown in public order for a period of time.

However, some people want to be more proactive in defending themselves. Owning a gun is almost always a political issue in most jurisdictions, but even cities where carrying a gun is illegal may permit a resident to own a gun if it's kept only in the home for self-defense.

I've known several people have gone a lot farther and have become survivalists by moving to well-defended home in remote place in America's midwest.

For an even more extreme example, here's a comment that was posted as a comment on one of my articles:

> "My sister and her husband are doomsdayers. They have multiple properties in mountainous rural areas each with 2 cargo containers buried and reinforced with really cool entry and separate exit points. Bryan is an excellent electrician, has his own bulldozer and a Federal Firearms Dealer License, (seriously he has old .45 Browning Tommy Guns in mint condition, AKs etc) the containers are chock full of

generators, fuel, weapons and ammo out the gazoo. Water, food, water filters, medical supplies, venting systems — it's truly amazing. They tell me there is a whole subculture of people like this, although they are the only ones I know personally. Anyway, I know where I'm going if s h i t hits the fan."

A different commenter posted the following bit of advice to a young man wishing to move somewhere safe:

"Based on the information you provided, since you are young (presumably wouldn't have a lot of money to invest) and you think a nuclear war is probable, I would suggest you first "invest in yourself" and your survival. One idea for consideration in that regard is to set yourself up to be able to get to a safe haven outside the US. A couple countries that come to mind are Chile and Namibia. One way to do that would be to try to meet a woman in a country you determine to be a safe haven who has a reputable and well connected family. Know how you are going to get to her family's home within 24 hours and have the money set aside to do that, your bags packed and an idea of what news would make you ready to act."

So you can see that there are a lot of choices. Once you've figured out what your choices are, you have to pick one of them and decide to live with it. If you decide to do nothing, live with that. If you decide to move somewhere, live with that. Just make up your mind and do it. And I really mean it when I say that doing nothing may be the best choice, since no place is really safe from a world war, so why bother?

Part IV. Theory of War: The phases of World War III

We're now going to do two things in parallel: We're going to develop a "theory of war" according to principles from Generational Dynamics theory, and then we're going to apply that theory to make some tentative predictions about how World War III will proceed.

By jumping back and forth between these two subjects, the exposition is sometimes a little difficult to follow, so it's recommended that anyone wishing to master this material should read the following chapters twice, once to get the big picture, and once to get the details.

Chapter 18. How do world wars begin in general?

A major topic that we haven't yet touched on is when and how the next world war will start.

My study of history has led me to believe that the most likely way for the next world war to start will not be because of some massive attack, like the bombing of Pearl Harbor, but rather because of some minor confrontation that escalates. There will still be massive attacks, but they won't come until weeks or months later.

We've described that there's a historical imperative for a world war, we've described how China's thirst for revenge against Japan is the crucible for the coming world war, and now we're going to discuss when and how a world war is likely to start.

Spoiler alert: A world war might begin next week, next month, next year, or thereafter. In other words, you can try to guess, but you can never be certain until it actually occurs (and sometimes not until after it has occurred).

If you ask someone with some knowledge of history how a world war starts, he would most likely refer back to World War II, and Hitler's invasion of Poland in 1939 and then Japan's bombing of Pearl Harbor in 1941. So a world war starts with some major attack or invasion of one country on another.

But that's not true. World War II began in 1937 with a trivial incident, when a Japanese soldier unexpectedly had to pee. This led to misunderstandings, accusations, a shooting, escalations, and finally a full-scale invasion of China by Japan, quickly followed by the "Rape of Nanking," in the Sino-Japanese war (1937-45).

My study of history has led me to believe that major wars much more often begin with trivial incidents that escalate rather than with massive attacks. The start is thus spontaneous, unexpected and organic. Something happens, there is a misunderstanding, then someone attacks, someone responds with reinforcements, and the situation escalates into full-scale war.

We'll give three examples — WW I, WW II, and the 2006 Israel-Hezbollah war.

18.1. How World War I started (1914-18) - an unexpected assassination

In the early 1910s, it was plausibly believed by many that war had ended. This was "La Belle Époche" in Europe, when life was beautiful. Then, unexpectedly, a high school student decided to shoot and kill a Serbian Archduke. Within a few months, ten million guns got loaded, and World War I exploded (Jacques Brel). So, if we follow the WWI example, we can see that an assassination can trigger a world war.

World War I started in a spontaneous, unexpected and organic way when a Serb high school student, Gavrilo Princip, shot and killed Archduke Franz Ferdinand, the heir to the Austro-Hungarian empire, and his pregnant wife Sophie. Assassinations were not uncommon in the world, then or now, but to most of the world's complete astonishment, this assassination triggered World War I. [112]

Three weeks after the assassination, the Austria-Hungary's government unexpectedly issued an ultimatum to Serbia to demand that the assassin be brought to justice. Serbia refused to comply. Austria-Hungary declared war on Serbia on July 28, 1914. Russia, bound by treaty to defend Serbia, mobilized its army. Germany, allied to Austria-Hungary by treaty, viewed the Russian mobilization as an act of war against Austria-Hungary, and unexpectedly declared war on Russia on August 1. France, bound by treaty to Russia, found itself at war with Germany and Austria-Hungary. Germany declared war on France on August 3, and invaded neutral Belgium to reach Paris. [112]

Belgium appealed to Britain for help under their 75-year-old treaty. Britain was thus at war with Germany and Austria-Hungary. Britain's colonies and dominions — Australia, Canada, India, New Zealand and the Union of South Africa — offered military and financial assistance. Japan, honoring a military agreement with Britain, declared war on Germany on August 23. Two days later Austria-Hungary responded by declaring war on Japan. [112]

Italy used a treaty technicality to avoid entering the war on the side of Germany and Austria-Hungary, and ended up joining in May 1915, on the side of the Allies. The US only entered the war on April 6, 1917. [112]

This illustrates the general principle that a world war can start in a "small" way, and escalate step-by-step into something a lot larger. The war does not start with a full-scale invasion, but the full-scale invasion comes several weeks or months after the "small" event, which is then followed by other invasions.

Today, many countries have mutual defense treaties with each other.

There's a historical irony. After World War II, the United States took on the role of "Policeman of the World," and in doing so, signed mutual defense treaties with many countries: Japan, South Korea, Israel, Taiwan, the Philippines, the Marshall Islands, the ANZUS agreement with Australia and New Zealand, a special treaty with Iceland, and the NATO agreement with all of Europe. The purpose of these treaties was to discourage attacks on any of these allies that would otherwise have the risk of spiraling into World War III.

So today, since those are mutual defense treaties, all of those countries actually have an obligation to defend the US in a war with China. Even if they stay neutral, any incident could trigger a larger war. Furthermore, the extreme xenophobia in China makes it more likely that the Chinese will interpret the mutual defense treaties in a way that will cause them to attack those countries. The irony is that these mutual defense treaties were supposed to prevent World War III, but instead they make World War III more likely. In that sense, the mutual defense treaties have backfired.

18.2. How the Israel-Hezbollah war started (2006) - an unexpected abduction

In 2006, Israel had a surprise, unexpected war with the Hezbollah terror group in Lebanon. For those people who think that "this time it's different" in these modern days with e-mail, iphones and twitter, and that politicians today won't act the way they did in the past, this is a modern example that shows that nothing is different.

The war was triggered when Hezbollah unexpectedly abducted two Israeli soldiers near the Lebanon border. Israel went into a state of total panic, and launched the war in Lebanon within four hours, with no plan and no objectives. This war didn't escalate to a world war, but if it had been up to Israel it might have. The war fizzled in a few weeks because Israel's opponents were in a generational Awakening era and reacted much more rationally than Israel did. [191]

The war began after Hezbollah abducted two Israeli soldiers on the southern Lebanon border, resulting in an Israeli response, and a Hezbollah counter-response.

Israel is in a generational Crisis era, since the survivors of the 1948 war between Jews and Arabs had almost all retired or died. The Israelis panicked and fought it as an "existential" war, and with a great deal of fury and passion. At first Israel was planning to defeat Hezbollah by using air power alone. Then, when that wasn't working, they started calling up reservists, turning it into a ground war. The size of the ground war kept increasing, as Israel had to change course and bring up more reservists. After the U.N. passed a ceasefire resolution, Israel increased the ground war still further to gain as much ground as possible before the ceasefire took effect. [191]

Lebanon had fought an extremely bloody crisis civil war and war with Syria from 1976, climaxing in 1982 with a massacre, and so Lebanon was in a generational Awakening era, and so were the fighters in Hezbollah. As I described at the time, they fought the war, as "a war from the comfort of home." They sent thousands of missiles into Israel, launching from sites near their own homes. Hezbollah approached the war in a cool, methodical manner, implementing plans that had been in place for years, in contrast to Israel's "hot," panicky war style. [191]

Instead of fizzling, this might have escalated to a larger regional Mideast war with a slight change of circumstances. For example, if Hezbollah had adopted Israel's war style, then a mass of their soldiers would have crossed the border to attack and kill Israeli families in their homes. They might even have called on allies in Iran, Syria, Egypt or another Arab country to enter the war on their side, and this would have been a major escalation. But Lebanon was in a generational Awakening era, with vivid memories of the recent civil war, and so they decided that a full-scale war with Israel was futile. [191]

Lebanon's last crisis war climaxed in 1982 when Christian Arab forces, allied with Israel, massacred and butchered hundreds or perhaps thousands of Palestinian refugees in camps in Sabra and Shatila in Lebanon. That experience has overshadowed Lebanon's policies for decades, and that continues today. The Lebanese people were strongly opposed to allowing Hezbollah expand the war, and were ambivalent toward Hezbollah. One the one hand, they felt an obligation to support Hezbollah in order to maintain national unity, but on the other hand many Lebanese were appalled and infuriated at Hezbollah for launching its missile war against Israeli civilians. [192]

One of the most touching moments occurred ten days into the war, when Lebanon's president Émile Geamil Lahoud was asked in an interview why he didn't order Lebanon's army to enter the war against Israel on the side of Hezbollah. He said that doing so would split Lebanon's society, and he alluded to the civil war and the Sabra and Shatila massacre when he said that despite the destruction from Israeli warplanes, nothing was more important than Lebanon's unity: [193]

> "And really all the time, massacres are happening in Lebanon. All the infrastructure is being hit and we are paying very high price. We have women, children, all are being hit by planes. And they never stop,

people think that they will stop for a few hours. They go out to get their food or anything and suddenly they are hit again. This is a real massacre.

It is getting much worse, and day after day more targets are getting hit. As you know the airport has been hit, all bridges, big bridges, small bridges, and now the roads. Only yesterday, only 200 meters from here, at 11 at night, they hit the road. Just like this, they are creating fear and, really, it is cycling to the point of no return. That is why that as soon as possible we are asking that there be a cease-fire. ...

Believe me, what we get from our side is nothing compared to if there is an internal conflict in Lebanon. So out thanks comes when we are united, and we are really united, and the national army is doing its work according to the government, and the resistance is respected in the whole Arab world from the population point of view. And very highly respected in Lebanon as well." [193]

It's really amazing, in my opinion, that the president of Lebanon can describe the massive destruction that Israeli warplanes were causing in Lebanon, and then conclude, "what we get from our side is nothing compared to if there is an internal conflict in Lebanon." That kind of emotional state shows how much shock he felt because of the 1982 massacre. [192]

There are many similar examples in history of the sharp contrast in fighting styles between a country that is in a generational Crisis era versus a country in a generational Awakening or Unraveling era. Those interested in the subject might look at Napoleon's invasion of Russia in 1812. France was in a generational Crisis era, but Russia was in a generational Unraveling era, and Russia won the war — not by fighting Napoleon, but by evacuating Moscow and letting Napoleon's army take it without a fight, and then binge itself into self-destruction.

Leo Tolstoy's monumental work *War and Peace*, which describes Napoleon's invasion of Russia, shows the contrast between France and Russia by describing the almost uncontrolled actions of the French soldiers:

"The French soldiers went to kill and be killed at the battle of Borodino, not because of Napoleon's orders but by their own volition. The whole army - French, Italian, German, Polish, and Dutch - hungry, ragged, and weary of the campaign, felt at the sight of an army blocking their road to Moscow that the wine was drawn and must be drunk. Had Napoleon then forbidden them to fight the Russians, they would have killed him and have proceeded to fight the Russians because it was inevitable. ...

And it was not Napoleon who directed the course of the battle, for none of his orders was executed and during the battle, he did not know what was going on before him. So the way in which these people killed one another was not decided by Napoleon's will but occurred independently of him, in accord with the will of hundreds of thousands of people who took part in the common action. It only seemed to Napoleon that it all took place by his will. And so the question whether he had or had not a cold has no more historic interest than the cold of the least of the transport soldiers."

So the 2006 war between Israel and Hezbollah was triggered by a small event — the abduction of two Israeli soldiers by Hezbollah. World War II was also started by an apparent abduction of a soldier, as we'll describe below. But this shows that things like hormones, DNA and desire for revenge have not changed in the past century, and that things are the same.

18.3. How World War II started (1937-1945) - someone had to pee

World War II also began when the apparent abduction of a soldier triggered the Sino-Japanese war (1937-1945).

Most people will say that World War II began on September 1, 1939, when Hitler's Germany invaded Poland. That's when WW II in Europe started, but WW II really started in Asia. And WW II in Asia started on July 7-9, 1937. That's when a simple misunderstanding between Japanese and Chinese soldiers caused the Marco Polo Bridge Incident, triggering Japan's full-scale invasion of China. [129]

The Marco Polo Bridge is located about 15 km southwest of Beijing, and has that name because the original bridge, constructed in 1192, was visited and praised by the 13th century Italian Silk Road trader, Marco Polo.

In 1937, there were small numbers of Japanese and Chinese troops around the bridge. The Japanese troops were there to protect a Japanese diplomatic legation, and the Chinese soldiers were part of a small camp in the city of Wanping. [129]

Late one evening, on July 8, a Japanese soldier was absent from a roll call, and he could not be found. The Japanese assumed that the Chinese had abducted him, and demanded to search the city of Wanping. The Chinese refused, and there was a brief battle between the two groups of soldiers. A peace was negotiated, but both sides called in reinforcements. The situation rapidly escalated within a month, and after that, Japan and China were at full-scale war (Sino-Japanese War (1937-45)). [129]

Soon after that, the Japanese attacked the major Chinese city Nanking. The result was the "Rape of Nanking," where hundreds of thousands of innocent civilians, including women and children, were tortured, beaten, raped and slaughtered. The Japanese were already using Chinese women as "comfort women." At the same time, Japan's Unit 731 was conducting gruesome, horrific chemical and biological warfare experiments on thousands of abducted Chinese men, women and children. The Japanese were truly barbaric monsters. [128]

And what about that missing Japanese soldier? It turned out later that he had had to pee, and he went into the woods to relieve himself, and got lost. By the time he got back, the roll call was over, and the sequence of events leading to war had already been launched. [127]

So World War II was well under way when Pearl Harbor was bombed (1941) and when Poland was invaded (1939). It started in 1937 when a misunderstanding occurred because someone unexpectedly had to pee.

18.4. Do genocide and ethnic cleansing start a world war?

One would think that acts of genocide and ethnic cleansing might trigger a larger war, and even a world war, as countries identifying with the targeted ethnic group come to its defense.

But if you believe something like that, then you may also believe in the tooth fairy. The Nazi Holocaust of Jews did not trigger World War II. In fact, most of the West ignored the reports of the ongoing genocide and ethnic cleansing of the Jews.

All my life, whenever the Holocaust was mentioned, it was accompanied by the words, "Never again!" And yet, there have been many Holocausts since then — by Mao Zedong in China in the Great Leap Forward (1958-59), by Pol Pot in Cambodia (1975-79), the Rwanda genocide (1994).

Today there are actually three full-scale cases of genocide and ethnic cleansing going on, in three different countries, and they're all targeting Sunni Muslims:

- China's genocide and ethnic cleansing of Sunni Muslim Uighurs in East Turkistan (Xinjiang province).
- Burma's (Myanmar's) genocide and ethnic cleansing of Sunni Muslim Rohingyas, led by Buddhist monk Ashin Wirathu.
- Bashar al-Assad's genocide and ethnic cleansing of Sunni Muslim Arabs in Syria.

There are 50 Muslim-majority countries in the world, but nowhere are any of them expressing outrage at any of these three genocides and ethnic cleansing of their own identity groups. So it's probably safe to say that genocide and ethnic cleansing do not trigger a world war, although it's still possible for an unexpected need to pee to do so.

18.5. Neutrality

World War II began with Japan vs China in 1937. It spread to Britain vs Nazis in 1939. The United States did not enter the war until Japan bombed Pearl Harbor in 1941, four years after WW II had already begun.

As a practical matter, everyone will try to stay neutral as long as possible. Switzerland was preparing to fight the Nazis, but ended up being successful at staying neutral.

In a non-crisis era, countries can more easily be successful at staying neutral, like a disease that can't spread because everyone is vaccinated. But in a Crisis era, nationalism and xenophobia are extremely high everywhere, and the disease spreads very rapidly, because no one is vaccinated.

Chapter 19. The early and middle phases of World War III

Obviously we can't precisely predict the phases of a future World War III, but we can make pretty reasonable inferences, based on what happened in wars historically.

19.1. The early days — neutrality and the salami method

As we said, a relatively minor incident can trigger a series of events that led to world war. I've given three examples — World War I, World War II, and the 2006 Israeli-Hezbollah war — to show that major wars start with very minor events or misunderstandings, in two cases because soldiers may have been abducted. Big invasions and attacks occur later, several weeks or months after the initial incidents occur. Even WW II was started because a soldier unexpectedly had to pee.

There are a thousand trivial misunderstandings each year. What does it take for a trivial misunderstanding to lead to war?

For comparison purposes, I like to point to the 1929 stock market panic and subsequent crash. Monday, October 28, 1929, was really no different than any other date, but there was a stock market panic that day, and the Dow Jones Industrial Average fell 13.47% on that day, and another 11.73% on Tuesday.

To this day, 90 years later, experts have no idea why the stock market panic occurred on that particular day, rather than a few months earlier or later. The conditions had been there for a long time, including a growing stock market bubble, but nobody knows what trigger caused a panic to burst the bubble on that particular day.

For a "trivial event" to launch war requires a similar panic, as in the three examples that I previously gave, and there's no way to know what trivial event will trigger a panic. For example, in the 1937 Marco Polo Bridge incident, a Japanese soldier absent from roll call triggered one panic that went step-by-step from a trivial incident to full-scale Sino-Japanese war.

This is where Generational Dynamics theory enters the picture. During the 1990s, a generational Unraveling era, the world was still being managed by survivors of World War II. They would never have permitted a trivial event to lead to full scale war.

Today, as in the 1930s, the world is being managed by young people with no understanding of what full-scale war is like, and why even a trivial incident can be dangerous. Therefore, a full-scale war could start today, even though it would have been impossible in the 1990s. That's what happens in a generational Crisis era.

19.2. The euphoria phase: The declaration of war

Now let's suppose a trivial event occurs, and the situation starts to escalate. In the 1990s, the people in charge would have stopped the escalation today, but in today's generational Crisis era, the populations of most nations have become severely nationalistic and xenophobic, and more likely to cheer on an escalation than to try to stop it.

The population in the 1990s, who were still led by survivors of World War II, might have dreaded an escalation that leads to war, but in a generational Crisis era like today, the population is likely to become euphoric.

Here's how historian Wolfgang Schivelbusch describes how the euphoria at the beginning of a war is itself highly delusional in his 2001 book, *The Culture of Defeat: On National Trauma, Mourning, and Recovery*:

> "The passions excited in the national psyche by the onset of war show how deeply invested the masses now were in its potential outcome. Propaganda had reinforced their conviction that "everything was at stake," and the threat of death and defeat functioned like a tightly coiled spring, further heightening the tension. The almost festive jubilation that accompanied the declarations of war in Charleston in 1861 [American Civil War], Paris in 1870 [Franco-Prussian war], and the capitals of the major European powers in 1914 [World War I] were anticipatory celebrations of victory — since nations are as incapable of imagining their own defeat as individuals are of conceiving their own death. The new desire to humiliate the enemy, noted by Burckhardt, was merely a reaction to the unprecedented posturing in which nations now engaged when declaring war.

> The deployment of armies on the battlefield is the classic manifestation of collective self-confidence. If both sides are not convinced of their military superiority, there will be no confrontation; rather, those who lack confidence will simply flee the field. Accordingly, the battle is decided the moment the confidence of one side fails. The will to fight ("morale") evaporates, the military formation collapses, and the army seeks salvation in flight or, if it is lucky, in organized retreat. The Greek term for this point in space (on the battlefield) and time (the course of the

battle) was trope. The victors demarcated the spot with the weapons of the vanquished and later with monuments, yielding the term tropaion, from which we get our word trophy." (p. 6-7)

The euphoria goes on until something goes wrong, usually some kind of military disaster, such as the Battle of Bull Run in 1861 or the Bataan Death March in April, 1942

19.3. The public panic phase: The Regeneracy

Public euphoria goes on as long as it can − until something goes terribly wrong. A military disaster destroys the euphoria in a flash, and leads to public fury and panic. In his 1832 book, *On War*, General Carl von Clausewitz describes what happens:

> "The effect of defeat outside the army − on the people and on the government − is a sudden collapse of the wildest expectations, and total destruction of self-confidence. The destruction of these feelings creates a vacuum, and that vacuum gets filled by a fear that grows corrosively, leading to total paralysis. It's a blow to the whole nervous system of the losing side, as if caused by an electric charge. This effect may appear to a greater or lesser degree, but it's never completely missing. Then, instead of rushing to repair the misfortune with a spirit of determination, everyone fears that his efforts will be futile; or he does nothing, leaving everything to Fate."

From the point of view of Generational Dynamics, the events that cause this "sudden collapse" and "total destruction" of self-confidence are called "regeneracy events," because they regenerate civic unity for the first time since the end of the preceding crisis war, usually 60-80 years earlier.

In Generational Dynamics theory, the "Regeneracy" is a specific process that occurs near the beginning of a generational crisis war, and it's triggered by some kind of military disaster. The word "regeneracy" itself refers to the regeneration of civic unity for the first time since the end of the preceding crisis war.

At the end of a generational crisis war, the nation or society is unified behind the leadership of the government. Win or lose, the genocidal explosive climax of the war has traumatized the entire population to the point where they simply don't want to fight a war any more.

In the case of World War II, the firebombing of Dresden and the destruction of Berlin were the climax of the war in Europe, resulting in the Nazi surrender. In Asia, the nuking of Hiroshima and Nagasaki were the climax, resulting the surrender of Imperial Japan. Once those events happened, nobody wanted to fight any more.

But as the decades passed, new generations were born, and the national politics have become increasingly divisive.

For example, in America in the early 1980s, it was quite a joke that Republican President Ronald Reagan and Democratic Speaker of the House Tip O'Neill would say nasty things about each other at press conferences, but that the two Irishmen would get together in the evening, have beers and tell jokes to one another.

In fact, the Republicans and Democrats did get things done in the 1980s. The Democrats and Republicans got together and passed a tax reform law. They cooperated with each other to change the Social Security system to make it a sounder system. After that, they cooperated again to specify new rules to control the budget deficit. Even as late as 1996, Democratic President Bill Clinton cooperated with the Republican congress to eliminate the welfare entitlement.

This was all accomplished by people in the G.I. generation that fought in World War II, and by the Silent generation that grew up during World War II. These people defeated the Nazis and beat the Depression, and they set up structures like the United Nations, World Bank, and World Health Organization to manage the world. Those organizations worked as long as they were being run by the Heroes of World War II.

Today in 2019, can you imagine Nancy Pelosi getting together with Donald Trump and telling jokes to one another? Politics today have become bitterly divisive, and almost nothing can get done, with each side blaming the other.

The thing that will change this is the Regeneracy, which regenerates civic unity again. It occurs when events become so serious that the entire country becomes once again united behind the leader.

America in the 1930s was just as politically divided as it is today. There was still a north-south divide left over from the Civil War. There were endless violent left-wing riots by the unions and the communists. It was the middle of the Great Depression, and people were living under bridges. And, most important, FDR was just as divisive as Trump is today. FDR actually tried a semi-coup by packing the Supreme Court, which would have given him control of two branches of government if he had succeeded.

But despite the divisiveness of FDR, the country was quickly united behind FDR, first by the attack on Pearl Harbor, and then by the Bataan Death March. In generational theory, this is the "Regeneracy," which refers to the recreation of civic unity for the first time since the end of the previous crisis war. [184]

So, exactly the same thing will happen today. If there's an attack on American soil, or a major military defeat overseas, then Americans will put aside their political differences and unite behind Trump (or the next president) overnight.

I used to say stuff like this during Obama's presidency, saying that the country would be instantly united behind Obama. I remember the fury I heard from the conservatives at this suggestion, with one person saying that if he were "behind Obama," then he would shoot. Nonetheless, a Regeneracy event like Pearl Harbor or the Bataan Death March would immediately unify the country behind Trump.

Let's be clear: If a nuclear missile from North Korea or China lands on San Francisco, the country will be immediately united behind the president in declaring war and striking back. That means both political parties, all races, all ethnicities, all genders, all sexual orientations, citizens, legal immigrants, illegal immigrants, and so forth. That's what a "Regeneracy" means.

Those of you who are old enough to remember 9/11/2001 may recall that President Bush declared war on Afghanistan within 24 hours, with the support of both parties and pretty much all Americans. The unity continued through the Afghan war and only began fraying because of the Iraq war.

And just as the "greatest generation" rushed out, without complaining, to fight against the Nazis and Japanese, there will be a new "greatest generation" that will not hesitate to step up to fight today's enemies.

19.4. Moral degeneration during a generational crisis war

We've now described the three early phases of a world war:

- A trivial event results in a minor clash that escalates into a major clash.
- There's a declaration of war and public euphoria.
- There's a military reversal causing a public panic and regeneracy of civic unity behind the country's leaders.

Once these three steps occur, the generational crisis war is in full swing.

Moral Deterioration: During the crisis period from Regeneracy to Climax, typically 4-5 years, the population becomes increasingly desperate and impatient for a victory. If you remember 9/11, then imagine what it would be like to have a 9/11 attack every day for years (like the bombings of London in WW II). At the beginning of this period, the rules of war are observed and individual human lives are still valued. By the time the climax is reached, the only thing that matters is the survival of the country or society and its way of life. The value of an individual human life goes to zero, and any number of individuals are expendable. For all participants in the war, genocide and atrocities, particularly torture and rapes, become increasingly acceptable and excusable.

A generational crisis war is more than just a war. It's a highly emotional conflict where the passions are so high that the value of an individual human life drops to zero, particularly as the war reaches a climax, because absolutely nothing else matters besides victory. So there may or may not be a huge loss of life, depending on the circumstances, such as the surrender of one side.

Once the euphoria turns to panic, the conflict turns into an all-out generational crisis war, where the life of an individual human being will have no value at all, and the only thing that matters is survival of the nation and its way of life, no matter how many tens or hundreds of thousands of people get killed. Both sides become genocidal, and both sides end up later regretting their own actions as well as the enemy's actions.

In World War II, America sent tens of thousands of soldiers across the English Channel onto the beaches of Normandy in France, knowing that thousands of them would be immediately shot dead by the Germans. The American generals were willing to simply sacrifice the lives of thousands of American soldiers in order to get the war over with. That's what happens after several years of a generational crisis war.

One historian described Allied actions in a message to me: In World War II, the Allies, especially the normally restrained British, were attempting to kill as many German civilians as possible. This was the crux of Air Marshal Harris' bombing campaign. The firebombing of Hamburg and Dresden, let alone the carpet bombing of everything we could think of was part of this. In the Pacific Theater, we firebombed every city in Japan with a population of more than 100,000 or so. The plan for the invasion of Japan included using poison gas on the civilian population. In the case of both Germany and Japan, we were ready, willing, and ultimately capable of killing every last one of them. And if that is what is was going to take, we were going to do it.

Many people reading the last couple of paragraphs might think that the British and Americans don't act that way, but that's not true. After five years of generational crisis war, everyone acts that way — all nations, religions, races, and ethnicities. Acting that way is part of the human DNA. Nature has provided human beings with a sex drive to create more human beings, and with a desire for genocide to get rid of extra human beings. No one is excluded from this.

Once the generational crisis war ends, there is often little sense of victory, even on the winning side. They're just glad it's over. Even the victors are horrified with themselves over the atrocities they had committed to win the war, just as the people on the losing side are horrified with the atrocities they committed to prevent that victory.

Once the generational crisis war ends, then the traumatized survivors on both sides regret everything they did to allow the war to happen, and they spend the rest of their lives doing everything possible to keep anything like it from happening again. The children who grow up after the war have no personal memory of the trauma and motivations that led to the atrocities on both side. All they hear about are the atrocities. This triggers a new generational saeculum.

America has had three generational crisis wars: the Revolutionary war, the Civil war, and World War II. Other wars were non-crisis wars: Mexican-

Part IV. Theory of War: The phases of World War III

American war, Spanish-American war, World War I, Korean War, Vietnam War, Iraq war.

Chapter 20. World War III in Asia - Forecasts and predictions

We now want to go from the general and the theoretical to the specifics.

Of course it's impossible to predict the path that World War III will take. I've asked several experts to give me their views of some of the more likely scenarios.

20.1. A divided America - is civil war in America possible?

During my lifetime, I've heard repeated complaints from people who say that America is no longer willing to fight a war, usually comparing something to World War II. But that's exactly the point of a non-crisis war. World War II was a crisis war, and America was willing to send tens of thousands of soldiers onto the Normandy beaches, knowing that thousands would be mowed down immediately by German gunfire; and America was willing to firebomb Dresden and Tokyo, and nuke Hiroshima and Nagasaki, knowing that millions of civilians would be killed. But that's what happens in a crisis war — when the value of an individual human life goes to zero, and nothing is more important than winning, to preserve the nation and its way of life. Regrets come after the war ends.

Many people believe that America no longer has the will to fight a war. One person put it as follows:

> "When fighting an enemy who is willing to keep going, literally down to the last person, unless you are willing to do the same you will lose. The value that the US places on human life in a non-crisis war reduces our military's ability to fight against country's who don't place the same value on human life. We will quit fighting after a certain percentage of loss in a battle. Our enemies (especially in Asia and the middle east) will not quit until their last soldier is dead. If we are not willing to do the same thing, we will NEVER defeat an enemy in Asia or the middle east. Our human compassion will be our own undoing."

That's what happened during the Vietnam war, for example. The war was a non-crisis war for America, but a crisis war for the North Vietnamese. That's why the North Vietnamese won the war.

> "I believe that by now enough people in the US hate their own country that there are enough for an insurgency should an outside party attack.

They want to see the established systems destroyed or overturned, and would be happy to help out whoever is attacking us.

The current political divide is much worse than at any time since Vietnam, and the CCP will be happy to exploit this. The political vitriol will only escalate in the climate of a financial meltdown, as each side will blame the other for it happening. I do not believe that the "insurgents" will be anywhere near a majority, but I believe there will be enough of them to seriously impede our war-fighting ability for quite some time. I predict they will primarily target the power grid, as it is our Achilles' heel."

However, you can't compare today's America to the 1960s. The following is some technical information from Generational Dynamics theory.

The 1960s was a generational Awakening era, meaning that the country was being led by the GI Generation (also known as the "Greatest Generation"), who had fought and survived World War II. These leaders vowed to make sure nothing like that ever happened again, and they set up austere rules, procedures and institutions to guarantee that nothing like that ever happened again. They created the United Nations, World Bank, Green Revolution, World Health Organization, International Monetary Fund, and so forth.

The reason that the 1960s-70s is called a generational Awakening era is that the younger generations, growing up after the war, oppose their parents' austere rules and awaken the society with new ideas. So, in an Awakening era, the fault line is horizontal, generational and political, pitting the war survivors (older generation) versus the younger generation (Boomers).

Today in America the fault line is vertical, the red states versus the blue states but, still, it's purely political, not military. No red state is going to raise an army and invade a blue state, or vice versa.

America in the 1930s was just as politically divided as it is today. There was still a north-south divide left over from the Civil War. There were endless violent left-wing riots by the unions and the communists. It was the middle of the Great Depression, and people were living under bridges. And, most important, president Franklin D. Roosevelt was just as divisive as Trump is today. FDR actually tried a semi-coup by packing the Supreme Court, which would have given him control of two branches of government if he had succeeded, something that Trump hasn't tried (yet).

But despite the divisiveness of FDR, the country was quickly united behind FDR, first by the attack on Pearl Harbor, and then by the Bataan Death march. In generational theory, this is the "Regeneracy," which refers to the recreation of civic unity for the first time since the end of the previous crisis war.

So, exactly the same thing will happen today. If there's an attack on American soil, or a major military defeat overseas, then Americans will put aside their political differences and unite behind Trump (or the next president) overnight.

I used to say stuff like this during Obama's presidency, saying that the country would be instantly united behind Obama. I remember the fury I heard from the conservatives at this suggestion, with one person saying that if he were "behind Obama," then he would shoot. Nonetheless, a Regeneracy event like Pearl Harbor or the Bataan Death March would immediately unify the country behind Trump.

And just as the "greatest generation" rushed out, without complaining, to fight against the Nazis and Japanese, there will be a new "greatest generation" that will not hesitate to step up to fight today's enemies.

20.2. 'Mass Incidents' and civil war in China

Although a civil war in America is highly unlikely or impossible, a civil war in China is highly likely.

Map of China showing regions of White Lotus and Taiping rebellions

China's history is filled with huge, massive internal rebellions (civil wars), the most recent of which were the White Lotus Rebellion (1796-1805), the Taiping Rebellion (1850-64) and Mao's Communist Revolution (1934-49). China is overdue for a new massive civil war, and any sort of economic setback could be the trigger. That's why the Chinese Communist Party (CCP) are so paranoid about "mass incidents," which are incidents where dozens of Chinese citizens protest or get into fistfights with one another. Chinese police quell these protests quickly, often violently.

The number of mass incidents in the decades following World War II and the Communist Revolution, the generational Recovery and Awakening eras, was relatively low. However, two incidents occurred shortly after the beginning of the generational Unraveling era that made the CCP completely paranoid.

In May 1989, exactly 70 years after the May 4th movement, millions of young Chinese students crowded into Beijing to demand greater democracy and less repression. On June 4, Chinese troops and security police stormed through Tiananmen Square, firing indiscriminately into the crowds of protesters. Thousands of students were killed, and tens of thousands were arrested.

The second incident that occurred around that time was perhaps even more serious. On December 26, 1991, the Soviet Union collapsed, and all the former Soviet republics became independent self-governing nations.

Arguably, the collapse of the Soviet Union was more traumatic to the CCP than even the Tiananmen Square massacre. Suddenly, the leadership of the CCP were staring death in the face, as they considered the fact that something like the Tiananmen Square protests could force the Chinese Communist Party to collapse as well. Ever since the 1917 Bolshevik Revolution, Russian communism had always been the role model for Chinese communism. If Russian communism could collapse, then so could Chinese communism.

In the 1990s, Socialism with Chinese Characteristics began to take on a whole new and far darker and more sinister meaning. The CCP leadership became increasingly paranoid, and began seeing ghosts. Religious persecution surged. The Buddhism-based Falun Gong movement was and is particularly targeted, after millions of people became practitioners of their form of meditation. The CCP has increasingly cracked down on Christianity and even Daoism, for fear their practice could lead to overthrow of the CCP.

China used to publish the number of "mass incidents" occurring in the country. The number of "mass incidents" of unrest recorded by the Chinese government grew from 8,700 in 1993 to about 90,000-120,000 in 2010, according to several government-backed studies. The government stopped publishing the figures in 2010, but it's reasonable to believe that the number of mass incidents per year is well into the hundreds of thousands. If even just one of these mass incidents occurred in America or Europe, it would be international news, so the fact that hundreds of such mass incidents occur in China EVERY DAY indicates how socially unstable China is. [150]

Because China stopped publishing official figures, two researchers named Lu Yuyu and Li Tingyu researched computed his own figures, based on reports in Chinese media across the country. Starting around April 2012, Lu Yuyu collecting information about events around the country, and publishing them. His reports were picked up by international media. [151]

For instance, in June 2013 Lu recorded 53 mass incidents in which people fought for the protection of their rights. Among these, nearly half involved violent clashes. The majority were in response to expropriation of land and forced demolitions, as well as labor protests, with 13 and 11 incidents in each category. In June, 2017, Lu Yuyu was thrown into jail for four years by the CCP on charges of "picking quarrels and provoking trouble." [151]

20.3. Chinese Civil war and the United Front

The number of mass incidents has been growing exponentially since the beginning of the generational Unraveling era in the 1990s, and with China no longer willing to report the figures, it's reasonable to believe that the exponential growth has continued, and the number is now well into the hundreds of thousands. And with China's history full of one civil war after another, China is close to its next civil war.

China's last civil war was fought between the Nationalists in the south, led by Chiang Kai-shek, versus the Communists in the north, led by Mao Zedong. The civil war began to pick up strength in 1934 with Mao's symbolic Long March.

When the Japanese invasion began in 1937, the civil war had to be put on hold. The Communists used the "United Front" concept that it had used in the 1920s to argue that the Nationalists and Communists should fight together against the Japanese. This turned out to be a strategy by the Communists. The Nationalists were allowed to do all the fighting, which weakened them, so that the Communists won the civil war after the war with Japan ended. The population supported the Communists, because the Nationalists had been governing the country brutally, beating, torturing, raping and executing political opponents.

Today, the situation is quite the opposite. It's the CCP that has been governing the country brutally, beating, torturing, raping and executing political opponents. If the Communists try Mao's United Front strategy again, they'll be the ones weakened by fighting the Japanese, and the population will support an opposition rebellion.

Another reason is that the CCP has become increasingly paranoid and desperate about rebellions from Christians, Buddhists and Muslims. In a sense, China is already in a civil war, committing genocide and ethnic cleansing of the Muslim Uighurs in East Turkistan (Xinjiang province).

The CCP are so paranoid that they make themselves ridiculous. One is the fear of Winnie the Pooh, who looks like Xi Jinping. This is actually a real fear, because the deeply paranoid CCP leaders are actually afraid that Winnie the Pooh can be used as a symbol for an internal revolt to overthrow the CCP. Can you imagine Donald Trump or any other national leader being afraid of Winnie the Pooh or some other cartoon character? But that's the state of insanity of China's CCP government. A government is that is frightened of Winnie the Pooh is going to be ridiculed and opposed by a lot of people in a civil war.

It's also widely believed that the reason that the general public in China have not yet begun rebelling against the CCP is because most Chinese are still well fed. However, China is no more immune to an economic recession than any other country is, and any economic setback could be the trigger for a widespread rebellion, or even a new Long March.

Going beyond the civil war against its own people, the CCP would have its hands full fighting many of its neighbors, in addition to Japan. One can imagine a scenario where China launches lots of missiles, and destroys a lot of American cities and aircraft carriers, but still loses the war because they have their hands full fighting its neighbors. Vietnam won the last war against China, and they're certainly prepared to fight a new war. The Indians lost their last war against China, but they're certainly prepared to fight. Philippines, Australia, and Russia.

In Central Asia, China has made lots of enemies by exterminating the Uighurs and Kazakhs. Russia will support much of Central Asia, as it was part of the Soviet Union, and Putin still thinks they should be part of the Russian empire. Britain would be on the West's side.

Pakistan, Cambodia and Laos would be on China's side.

20.4. Civil war in China and its effect on Taiwan

Taiwan's president Tsai Ing-wen leads the governing Democratic Progressive Party (DPP), which was formed as a reaction to the 1989 Tiananmen Square Massacre in Beijing, where several thousand peacefully protesting students were brutally murdered by Chinese security forces in a huge bloodbath. The DPP have been "pro-independence" from the beginning, but in official government positions when winning elections, they've adopted the 1992 "One China Consensus" which says that China and Taiwan are one country, but which leaves the meaning of that phrase ambiguous.

However, since winning the presidential election early in 2016, Tsai Ing-wen has gone farther than previous DPP politicians by refusing to endorse the 1992 consensus, instead saying that she "respected ... the common understanding" between China and Taiwan, without saying what that means. Her refusal to endorse the 1992 consensus has triggered the usual stream of hysterical screaming threats from Chinese officials, and relations between China and Taiwan have been deteriorating steadily.

Time is not on China's side. For years, polls have shown a steady decline in the number of people who want Taiwan to be a province of China, and an increase in the number who want Taiwan to be independent. The reason for this trend is that the people who favored joining China were in the generations that fled China in 1949 through Hong Kong to Formosa, which became Taiwan. As those people have died, and new generations have replaced them, the young people are much more pro-independence than their grandparents were. This trend was greatly boosted as young college students watched in horror the 1989 Tiananmen Square massacre, and decided that they never wanted to be part of that country (China).

There's even a new pro-independence trend, with rallies organized by a new pressure group called the Formosa Alliance. The trend actually represents a split in the pro-independence movement because Tsai has been taking a relatively cautious approach to China, while the Formosa group want to take steps toward independence more quickly.

In 2005, China passed the Anti-Secession Law, which orders the army to invade Taiwan if any Taiwanese official makes any move toward independence, whether by word or by deed. Taiwanese officials have said many things since 2005 that, arguably, could trigger the anti-secession law, and Saturday's independence rally adds one more. [173]

China is committed to a military invasion of Taiwan to force it to be part of China. This invasion might occur before or during a war with Japan or America. The question that we want to address here is the interaction between a civil war in China along with a Chinese invasion of Taiwan.

When thousands of Chinese fled through Hong Kong to Formosa in 1949, they were in the Hokkein (Hakka) ethnic group. I wanted to know how the Hakka people in Taiwan would react to a Chinese invasion. A man living in Taiwan with a Hakka wife wrote the following to me:

> "My wife loves China and seems to be completely blind to their evil. She thinks if they take over, Taiwan could spend less on military and would prosper economically. I don't know anyone else in Taiwan that holds that opinion, me included.
>
> The other data point is that Tsai Ing-wen is Hakka and she is very against reunification. And she is doing something about it to include more weapons and changing military strategy to one of fortifying beach

head landing sights of which Taiwan has few and resistance by guerrilla warfare based in the mountains if the beach heads are breached. So I think that may be more indicative of the Hakka attitude.

As I'm sure you know, Taiwan as a whole does not consider itself to be a part of China anymore than Chicago is a part of China. And that attitude is getting stronger with time. They will not willing reunify.

I think if China wants Taiwan they will have to kill ever last Taiwanese to take it. And I am fairly certain Taiwan is a nuclear armed country based on facilities I have seen while working for their airforce. A war with China would not be quick and easy. It would be long and costly and frankly I don't think China currently has the ability to win."

He's not alone in believing that Taiwan would defeat China if the latter invaded. *Foreign Policy* has published a detailed analysis by which Taiwan can win a war with China. The Taiwanese, Japanese and American leaders will have 30-60 days' notice of an impending invasion, because China will have to make preparations. So the Taiwanese will be prepared with booby traps, explosives, sea mines, and the Taiwanese soldiers will be far better prepared than their Chinese counterparts. [174]

Because China's armed forces are several times bigger than Taiwan's, it's generally believed that China would easily defeat Taiwan in a war, especially if the US did not honor its commitment to mutual defense. The quick win would be achieved first by a barrage of missiles striking government and military targets, followed quickly by special forces ferried across the strait for a quick kill.

However, when China is facing war with Taiwan, Japan, Vietnam, India, and other countries, that quick win would be elusive.

20.5. America and China — Preparedness for war

Since World War II, America has been involved in numerous ground wars, in North Korea, Vietnam, Iraq and Syria. Pursuing a foreign war is a huge logistical enterprise, and America has a great deal of experience doing so.

China has never fought a foreign war, and has no experience doing so. Furthermore, China's military was completely incompetent when invaded by Japan in World War II, and had to be saved by the United States military.

For those reasons, many people believe that America would win a war with China. Of course China would launch thousands of nuclear missiles targeting American aircraft carriers, bases and cities, but in the end there would be a ground war that China would lose.

In the Generational Dynamics forum, "Burner Prime" wrote:

"Despite the loss of life and treasure, the US has been honing her fighting skills since Gulf War I. Prior to that there were a lot of shortcomings that were only uncovered by field operations and actual combat. Now our armor, weapons, tactics and electronic coordination, drone use, etc. is superior to any adversary. There are major problems with our Navy but those issues are known and being addressed."

However, "Navigator," a retired American Army Colonel 30 years experience as an Army Officer, and with and my secondary career as a military simulation creator/publisher, and blogs at http://www.comingstorms.com, posted a response:

"While our individual Soldiers are brave and competent, we will be in big trouble in a real war. We are only experienced at fighting counter insurgency, and we did a pretty bad job at that. Our Army is very over-reliant on electronics, and the Chinese will know how to exploit this. Our military is infantry deficient, and over reliant on AirForce ground support. Support the Army probably won't have, as the F35 is such a lemon, we won't have Air Superiority over the battlefield for the first time since 1942. Our force on force tactics have not changed much since WW2, and are very "broad front" centric. And the Navy is not addressing the disaster of the LCS's and over-reliance on extremely vulnerable CV battlegroups."

Burner Prime answered:

"I don't dispute anything you wrote. I have watched many hours of Afghanistan combat footage and the default is "call in air strike", where a squad of US infantry can easily get pinned down by 2-3 well-hidden shooters. I would mention that despite that, China has zero combat experience and as shown throughout history, experienced troops and commanders nearly always beat inexperienced counterparts. You should also note that every deficiency you mentioned has been exposed by actual combat operations. China likely has as many or more deficiencies that no one, not even their own leaders know about. They won't show up until tested in battle. For example maybe their SAM systems underperform against the F-35 stealthy lemon. Aside from that a world war would not be fought the way US forces have in the Gulf - as a counter insurgency. It would be all-out brutal maximized carnage without the care to protect life as there is now. Soldiers will be expected to engage much more aggressively and the extreme care to protect civilians would vanish. I think John has brought up this point many times. Battles are fought differently depending on the era.

Actually I would dispute one point: "We are only experienced at fighting counter insurgency." I don't believe this is correct. Gulf War I was no counter-insurgency. Major head-to-head tank battles took place without the benefit of air support. The US commanders, crews and equipment performed brilliantly. That is only one example. It's true Iraq had old Soviet era tanks and used outdated tactics, but they had recent experience fighting the Iranians. This did not help them. Since then our armor and equipment reliability has improved, and learned lessons applied."

Navigator replied:

"The Gulf War was completely one sided because the Iraqi forces were below incompetent. I cannot stress this too strongly. There has not been a force on force conventional conflict where both sides were competent since 1973 Yom Kippur war.

Our forces learned nothing from the Iraq war regarding conventional warfare, because it was so completely one-sided. Our tanks are from 1982, and our tactics/operational execution is a high tech version of 1944.

I believe the Chinese will have the same kind of success initially that they had when they entered the Korean War in late 1950. They will overwhelm whatever we send, though they will suffer high casualties."

The preparedness of America's military is widely debated today, particularly after the government budget sequestration in the early 2010s decade. The above exchange gives a flavor of the debate.

20.6. China's military strategy

Navigator also provided his thoughts on the details of how a war with China would proceed:

"I believe that ground wise the Chinese have 3 directions they will attempt to go initially.

1 - Cross over to Taiwan. They will need to eliminate USN ability to intervene, so they will tac nuke the USN carrier groups at sea, and possibly those at Pacific ports. However, they do not have the ability to sea lift their entire Army, so only a portion of it will go this route.

2 - Move through North Korea into South Korea, so as to threaten, if not attempt to invade Japan. Their Army would try to time things so as to be through South Korea by the time the sea lift capability used in invading Taiwan would again be available, this time for invading Japan.

3 - Through Vietnam to get towards Thailand, Malaysia, and Indonesia. The idea here would be to punish the Vietnamese, and to be able to support/elevate Chinese minorities in SE Asia.

The Chinese will not be able to contain their "offensive spirit" and, I believe, they will also engage India. This will happen both in SE Asia (Thailand/Burma) and across the Himalayas, though across the mountains is nearly impossible logistically.

In response, the American ground forces will attempt to deploy to Taiwan and South Korea. We would first send the Marines, and then the Army. 2 Divisions of Marines and maybe 4-6 Army Divisions. These forces are woefully inadequate to deal with the overwhelming masses the Chinese will employ, and they will probably suffer the same fate as "Task Force Smith" from the early days of the Korean War.

South Korea will fall. I think there is about a 70% chance that Taiwan would too. Attacking Taiwan, and dissipating their strength into SE Asia would give the US the time to mobilize somewhat and do what it could to assist Japan.

Secondary Chinese thrusts could be from Taiwan towards the Philippines, or more likely, from Malaysia into Indonesia.

The Philippines would be a good staging area for Americans looking to get into China, as would Japan.

Tactically, the war will be much more like WW1, where defensive weapons and tactics are ascendant, than WW2. Meaning that once forces become majorly engaged, tactically it becomes a stalemate for quite a while.

Invading China would eventually be attempted, probably at the northern peninsulas of either Liaoyang (think Port Arthur) or Shandong (think German Tsing-tao) and South at Hainan island followed by the peninsula just north of that island.

However, moving into the heart of China would be beyond problematic. Much better to go for a combination of starving China and creating internal divisions."

That's how the war might proceed on the ground. Here are the issues for the war on the sea and in the air:

"All wars are decided primarily on land. Even in the Pacific in WW2. The Naval War there might have been dominant, but the navies either allowed (or failed to interdict) land force projection. (Japanese in Dutch East Indies, SE Asia and Philippines; US in island hopping, New Guinea, Philippines).

That said, I am actually glad the Chinese are wasting such vast resources on building a Navy. I think the strategy is greatly misguided and does not play to their primary strengths. I think they following the path of the German Kaiser in his pre-World War One ideas of becoming a power with global force projection capability. The Imperial German fleet, while impressive, and certainly highly competent, was a waste of their military resources.

Most of the money we are now spending on our Navy (not unlike much of it spent for the Army and Air Force) is being wasted on weapon systems designed not for battlefield efficiency but for maximizing the profit of defense contractors. We need to pressure our representatives in Congress and the appointees in the Defense Department to push for truly cost effective weapons, ships and aircraft. Our Sailors, Soldiers and Airmen need effective modern weapons. The key word being 'effective.'"

At the start of US involvement in WW2, most of our aircraft were substandard (P-39, P-40), our tanks were substandard (M2, some M3's), and none of the torpedoes actually worked. We eventually developed and fielded great equipment, but it took a while. In most cases that development started because the British were pushing us for better equipment to buy from us, and we had a couple of years to start to get it through development before we were actually involved.

This time we will lose a lot of life and suffer greatly because the forces that we will have will be improperly or poorly equipped."

20.7. World War III lineup: 'The Allies' vs 'The Axis'

For almost 15 years, I've been describing the two sides in the approaching Clash of Civilizations world war, based on a Generational Dynamics analysis, to be as follows:
- "The Allies": America, the West, Japan, India, Russia, Iran
- "The Axis": China, Pakistan, Saudi Arabia, Sunni Muslim countries

Many people have questioned this lineup, especially our expected alliance with Iran and Russia.

Here's a brief summary of the Generational Dynamics analysis:
- China is very closely allied with Pakistan. Diplomats from China and Pakistan always refer to each other as "all-weather friends." One politician said that their friendship is "higher than mountains, deeper than oceans, stronger than steel, sweeter than honey, and dearer than eyesight."

- Pakistan and Saudi Arabia are long-time close allies.
- China and India are bitter enemies, as are Pakistan and India.
- Russia has historically viewed itself as a protector of India.
- India is very closely allied with Iran, as Hindus have been allied with Shia Muslims going back to the Battle of Karbala in 680.

Connecting the dots, the US is going to be allied with India, Russia and Iran, versus China, Pakistan, and the Sunni Muslim states.

If that seems surprising, remember that Russia was our bitter enemy before WW II, was our ally during WW II, and was our bitter enemy after WW II, so you can't judge from today's political alignments how nations will act when they're facing an existential crisis in the form of a generational crisis war.

Now would be a good time to briefly reprise the reasons for the prediction that Iran will be an American ally. There are two major categories of reasons.

- First, Hindus and Shia Muslims have allied against Sunni Muslims at least as far back as the seminal Battle of Karbala in 680, which was the battle that firmly created what became the Shia-Sunni split. India is also very closely allied with Russia. America will be allied with India, and so with Russia and Iran.

- Second, college students in Iran started holding pro-Western and pro-American protests in the late 1990s, at the beginning of Iran's generational Awakening era. The Iran hardliners brutally suppressed those protests, but doing so didn't change minds. Today, those students are 30-40 years old, and have risen to positions of power, ready to take over when the current hardline leadership dies off. They are generally pro-Western and pro-American, and consider Saudi Arabia to be an existential threat.

Now would also be a good time to reprise the three events of 1979 that shook the Muslim world in the Mideast and beyond, and how they affect events today:

- Prior to 1979, Iran had been an important ally of the US and UK in the Mideast. However, Iran's Great Islamic Revolution brought a radical theocratic Shia government to Iran, threatening to take over the leadership of the Islamic world from Saudi Arabia, turning the entire political infrastructure around.

- In November 1979, 500 young Salafist terrorists took over Saudi Arabia's Masjid al-Haram, or the Grand Mosque. It took two weeks for a massive Saudi army effort to retake the Mosque. By the end, the official death toll was 127 soldiers and 117 militants. Unconfirmed reports indicate that over 1,000 civilians lost their lives. The Jihadists were re-fighting a crisis war that had occurred in the 1920s between the al-Saud family and a Salafist group known as the Wahhabis. At that time, the crisis war was resolved with an agreement that the al-Saud family would rule Saudi Arabia, but would follow the strict, austere demands of the Wahhabis.

The attack on the Grand Mosque destroyed that agreement, and let the fuse for 9/11.

- The third epochal event of 1979 was the Soviet invasion of Afghanistan, which was seen by Saudi Arabia's Salafists as a Christian invasion of a Muslim country. After the violent takeover of the Grand Mosque, the al-Saud government started encouraging Salafists in Saudi Arabia to travel to Afghanistan to fight the Russians. The Russians were mainly fighting the Pashtun tribes that later formed the Sunni Muslim Taliban, and they were mainly fighting against what became the Northern Alliance of Tajiks, Hazaras and Uzbeks in northern Afghanistan, many of whom were Shias allied with Iran. At that time, the U.S. considered both Russia and Iran to be enemies, the latter because of the Iranian hostage crisis, and so the Americans supported the Pashtuns in Afghanistan (and Iraq in the Iran/Iraq war). The Afghan war led to the rise of Osama bin Laden, 9/11, and the Taliban.

Needless to say, Americans today are totally oblivious to the events described here, but these were epochal events in the history of the Arab, Persian and Muslim worlds in the Mideast and beyond, and they define what's happening in the Mideast today.

Based on analysis of previous wars, including world wars, I estimate that the war will last around five years About 3-4 billion people will die in the war, from nuclear weapons, conventional weapons, ground war, riots, disease and famine, leaving behind 4-5 billion people to hold an international peace conference and rebuild the world.

Part V. China's ancient dynasties

Chapter 21. Reference list of China's dynasties

In reading anything about China's history, whether in this book or elsewhere, it helps to keep a reference list of all China's dynasties, since they're mentioned frequently.

Xia Dynasty (unconfirmed) (ca. 2100–1600 B.C.)
Shang Dynasty (ca. 1600–ca. 1050 B.C.)
Zhou Dynasty (ca. 1050–256 B.C.)
Western Zhou (ca. 1050–771 B.C.)
Eastern Zhou (ca. 771–256 B.C.)
Spring and Autumn Period (770–ca. 475 B.C.)
Warring States Period (ca. 475–221 B.C.)
Qin Dynasty (221–206 B.C.)
Han Dynasty (206 B.C.–220 A.D.)
Six Dynasties (220–589) A.D.
- Three Kingdoms (220–265) A.D.
- Western Jin Dynasty (265–317) A.D.
- Period of Northern and Southern Dynasties 386–589 A.D.
Sui Dynasty (581–618)
Tang Dynasty (618–906)
Five Dynasties (907–960)
- Later Liang (907-923)
- Later Tang (923-936)
- Later Jin (936-947)
- Later Han (947-951)
- Later Zhou (951-960)
Liao Dynasty (907–1125)
Song Dynasty (960–1279)
- Northern Song (960–1127)
- Shenzong (1086-1127)
- Southern Song (1127–1279)
Yuan Dynasty [[Mongols]] (1279–1368)
Ming Dynasty (1368–1644)

Qing Dynasty [[Manchus]] (r. 1644–1911) [40]

Chapter 22. China's population

While European nations are at most a few hundred years old, China has been identifiable as a nation for over 2,000 years. How could such a vast, populous territory be managed and governed? What is the paste that held this nation together all this time?

The answer would have to be a relatively homogeneous population (that is, no major fault lines along religious or ethnic lines), and Confucianism, an ingenious religion, philosophy, and set of social rules. It gave each person a specific place in society, and defined specific duties and modes of conduct. For example, it defined Five Relationships of superiors over inferiors: prince over subject; father over son; husband over wife; elder brother over younger brother; and friend over friend. As long as each individual knew his place, and knew how to act, it would not be necessary for someone else to direct his activities, thus simplifying government.

As China was ruled alternately by warriors of different regions, or dynasties, all were tied together by the rules devised by Confucius in the fifth century BC. In the last thousand years, for example, China was ruled by warriors from Mongolia (1271-1368) in the north, from the south of China (1368-1644), and then from the north again by warriors from Manchuria (1644-1912).

Population of China (Millions)

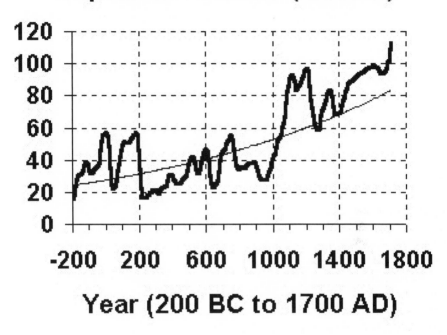

Population of China in millions of people from 200 BC to 1710 AD (Peter Turchin)

However, as this graph shows, the population of China has had wild swings throughout its history. It's hard for contemporary Americans to even imagine this, but wars, famine and disease have, at various times, killed tens of millions of Chinese people in a relatively short period of time.

The complexity of managing China's huge population is inescapable. China is geographically slightly smaller than the US, but has almost five times the population — 1.3 billion people. When you're dealing with numbers that large then, like it or not, the full force of mathematical complexity theory must be applied in order to make sense of what's going on and what happens to be done.

Even in 1800, China had about 400 million people — 300 million farmers, plus 80-100 million city folk: artisans, merchants, landlords, scholars and government officials. [34] p. 23

That's why, even as late as the year 1800, a typical Chinese village pretty much took care of itself — handling contracts, real estate transfers, boundary disputes, and organizing collective actions such as irrigation projects or business enterprises — without reference to any government officials. [34] p. 51

This explains why Communism has been such an enormous disaster for China since World War II. Communism requires a central dictatorship that controls all commercial activity, and it's easy to prove from the mathematics of complexity theory that controlling 1.3 billion people in that way is mathematically impossible.

Chapter 23. Early civilizations of the world

The modern human species, Homo Sapiens, evolved from apes over the last six million years. Humans first evolved in Africa, and much of human evolution occurred on that continent. The fossils of early humans who lived between 6 and 2 million years ago come entirely from Africa. The ability to walk on two legs evolved over 4 million years ago. Early humans first migrated out of Africa into Asia probably between 2 million and 1.8 million years ago. They entered Europe somewhat later, between 1.5 million and 1 million years. [13]

However, what we now know as modern humans evolved much later. Important human characteristics — such as a large and complex brain, the ability to make and use tools, and the capacity for language — developed more recently. Many advanced traits — including complex symbolic expression, art, and elaborate cultural diversity — emerged mainly during the past 100,000 years. [13]

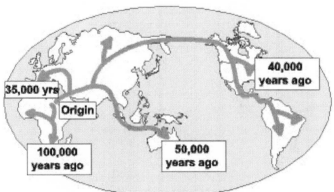

The spread of humans from north Africa around the world

Anatomically modern human beings began to appear in North Africa around 100,000 years ago. From there they spread around the world — south into Africa, into Europe 35,000 years ago, south to Australia 50,000 years ago, north to Russia, and then east across what is now the Bering Strait (there used to be a land bridge there), to populate the Americas 40,000 years ago.

Species of modern humans populated many parts of the world much later. For instance, people first came to Australia probably within the past 50-60,000 years and to the Americas within the past 30-40,000 years or so. The beginnings of agriculture and the rise of the first civilizations occurred within the past 12,000 years. [13]

Samuel Huntington, in his 1996 book *The Clash of Civilizations and the Remaking of World Order*, identified eight major civilizations in the world, with the following population in 1993:

- Sinic (Chinese): 1,340,900 million
- Islamic: 927,600 million
- Hindu (Indian): 915,800 million
- Western: 805,400 million
- Latin American: 507,500 million
- African: 392,100 million
- Orthodox: 261,300 million
- Japanese: 124,700 million

As humans migrated out of Africa, they formed civilizations. The earliest known civilizations are [14]:

- Mesopotamian civilization, 3500-550 BC
- Egyptian civilization, 3000-550 BC
- India: Indus civilization, 2500-1500 BC and Vedic age, 1500-500 BC
- Aegean civilization ca. 2000-1200 BC and Greek age, 1200 BC-0
- Ancient China, 2000 BC - 221 BC — Xia, Shang and Zhou dynasties

23.1. Peking Man (700,000 BC)

China was inhabited by pre-human Homo erectus more than 1 million years ago. In the 1920s and 1930s, Chinese scientists discovered a community of at least 40 hominids, labeled Peking Man, in a cave near Beijing (known as Peking at that time), and estimated to be about 700,000 years old. They could handle fire, engage in creative behavior, use tools, develop cultural aspects of their society including funeral rituals, and hunt large mammals. Almost all of the fossils were lost in December 1941 at the end of the four-year Sino-Japanese War. [15]

Chapter 24. Earliest dynasties

24.1. Xia dynasty (c. 2070-1600 BC)

The Xia dynasty (c. 2070-1600 BC) is often referred to as a 'legendary' dynasty because there is disagreement about its actual existence. On the one hand, there are archeological artifacts that supposedly prove its existence, but on the other hand, it can't be proven that these artifacts didn't really belong to the next dynasty, the Shang Dynast. [16]

Whether it actually existed or not, the Xia Dynasty is a powerful symbol for China's culture. According to the ancient historian Sima Qian (145-86 BC), there was once a great ruler named Huang-ti, better known as the Yellow Emperor. [16]

The Yellow Emperor emerged from the tribal system in pre-historic China to rule the region of Shandong between 2697-2597 BC. The Yellow Emperor created Chinese culture and established a form of government that would last for centuries. He is credited with inventing musical instruments, developing the production of silk, instituting law and customs, and the development of medicine and agriculture. Upon his death, he was buried in Huangling County, Shaanxi Province in the mausoleum which is today a popular tourist attraction. [16]

Huang-ti was succeeded by his grandson Zhuanxu, one of the famous Five Emperors, who founded the Xia tribe. After defeating their rivals, the Xia established the first dynasty in China under the leadership of the Emperor Yao. Yao ordered great palaces to be built and small villages of huts grew into urban centers. He is considered a great philosopher-king who ruled his people wisely and worked in their best interests following the precepts of Huang-ti. Yao is also celebrated because during his dynasty he set up a series of dykes and canals that controlled the flooding of the Yellow River. Yao's rule is considered the beginning of the Xia Dynasty and he is celebrated for his victories over the flood, and the establishment of stable government. [16]

24.2. Shang Dynasty (c.1500 - 1050 BC)

According to the story, whether legendary or not, the Shang dynasty began when a tribal chief named Tang defeated the Xia Dynasty, which was under the control of a tyrant named Jie. This victory is known as the Battle of Mingtiao, which is sometimes assigned the date 1766 BC. Jie survived the Battle of Mingtiao, but died later of illness. Tang is known for establishing a low number of drafted soldiers in the army and for beginning social programs to help the kingdom's poor. [18]

The Shang dynasty (1500 - 1050 BC) was the first historically documented dynasty. The Shang used bronze and the first examples of Chinese writing were found on turtle shells and oracle bones dating from this period. [37]

Culturally, the Shang lacked things that were to become typical of a "Chinese" civilization, in terms of family structure, and its agrarian religion. There were even words in Shang writing that disappeared later, indicating that the Shang language may have been different from the Chinese language to come. [32]

During the Shang Dynasty, there were several large settlements, including Zhengzhou and Anyang, though these are not believed to be as densely urban as Mesopotamian settlements during the same time. [18]

Anyang became the capitol around 1300 B.C. under King Pan Geng and at the time was called Yin. Zhengzhou is renowned for its walls, which ran for four miles and were 32 feet high and 65 feet thick. [18]

Anyang is believed to be the city that Shang kings ruled from for more than two centuries, with altars, temples and palaces located at the center. Surrounding the political center were artisans comprising an industrial area of stone carvers, bronze workers, potters and others, and then small housing structures and burial sites. [18]

The stability of the country during the Shang Dynasty led to numerous cultural advances such as industrialized bronze casting, the calendar, religious rituals, and writing. The first king, Tang, instantly began to work for the people of his country instead of for his own pleasure and luxury and provided a role model for his successors. These men created a stable government which would continue for 600 years but eventually, according to the records of the Chinese historians, they lost the mandate of heaven which allowed them to rule. [17]

Chapter 25. Zhou dynasty (1050 - 221 BC)

Following the Shang dynasty, it is Zhou dynasty. Zhou dynasty is usually referred as Western Zhou before 771 BC and Eastern Zhou after 771 BC. This is based on the location of the capital city. Western Zhou was a peace reign while Eastern Zhou had massive wars. Eastern Zhou can be further divided into Spring and Autumn period and Warring States period.

The Zhou dynasty began as a small realm in central Shensi (Shaanxi) province, a region of many "non-Chinese" tribes. As they grew, they moved eastward. An analysis of their tribal composition at the time of their conquest of the Shang seems to indicate that the ruling house of the Zhou was related to a Turkic group of tribes, and that the population consisted mainly of Turks and Tibetans. [32]

Finally, about 1028 B.C., the Chou ruler, named Wu Wang ("the martial king"), crossed his eastern frontier and pushed into central Honan. His army was formed by an alliance between various tribes, in the same way as happened again and again in the building up of the armies of the rulers of the steppes. Wu Wang forced a passage across the Yellow River and annihilated the Shang army. He pursued its vestiges as far as the capital, captured the last emperor of the Shang, and killed him. [32]

Thus was the Zhou dynasty founded, and with it we begin the actual history of China. The Zhou brought to the Shang culture strong elements of Turkic and also Tibetan culture, which were needed for the release of such forces as could create a new empire and maintain it through thousands of years as a cultural and, generally, also a political unit. [32]

Since the Zhou conquerers were an alien minority among the Shang, they had to march out and spread over the whole country. Moreover, the allied tribal chieftains expected to be rewarded. The territory to be governed was enormous, but the communications in northern China at that time were limited to narrow footpaths from one settlement to another. Under such conditions, the simplest way of administering the empire was to establish garrisons of the invading tribes in the various parts of the country under the command of their chieftains. [32]

25.1. Western (1070-771 BC) and Eastern (770-221 BC) Zhou dynasties

The Zhou dynasty aimed to create a single Chinese state. However, in 771 BC the Zhou lost control of western China and moved their capital to the east. As a result, the Zhou period is divided into Western Zhou (1050-771 BC) and Eastern Zhou (770-221 BC). [37]

25.2. Eastern Zhou: China's Spring and Autumn period (770-476 BC)

The Eastern Zhou period itself is divided into two parts, the Spring and Autumn period (770-476 BC), named after a work by Confucius, the Annals of Spring and Autumn, followed by the Warring States period (475-221 BC).

The Spring and Autumn period was the time of China's great philosophers - Sun Tzu, Laozi, and Confucius. These three philosophers lived toward the end of this period, but their texts and work became extremely popular during the subsequent Warring States period.

We'll come back to these three great philosophers when we describe the history of religious and cultural teachings in China.

25.3. Eastern Zhou: China's Warring States period (481/403 - 221 BC)

The last three centuries of the Zhou dynasty are known as the Warring States period.

The Warring States period describes the three centuries when various rival Chinese states battled viciously for territorial advantage and dominance. Various historians specify a starting point of somewhere between 481 BC and 403 BC. [28]

Seven major states vied for control of China: the Chu, Han, Qi, Qin, Wei, Yan, and Zhao during this period. It's generally agreed that the Warring States period ends in 221 BC when one of the states, the Qin state, defeated all the others, and established the first unified Chinese state. [28]

During the Warring States period, China enjoyed no political unity and suffered from the internecine warfare of small states, remnants of the once-great Zhou polity that collapsed after "barbarian" invasions in 771 BCE. For more than three hundred years after the alleged year of Confucius' birth, the Chinese would fight each other for mastery of the empire lost by the Zhou. In the process, life became difficult, especially for the shi ("retainer" or "knight") class, from which Confucius himself arose. [20]

As feudal lords were defeated and disenfranchised in battle and the kings of the various warring states began to rely on appointed administrators rather than vassals to govern their territories, these shi became lordless anachronisms and fell into genteel poverty and itinerancy. Their knowledge of aristocratic traditions, however, helped them remain valuable to competing kings, who wished to learn how to regain the unity imposed by the Zhou and who sought to emulate the Zhou by patterning court rituals and other institutions after those of the fallen dynasty. [20]

Chapter 26. Qin (Chin, Ch'in) Dynasty (221-206 BC)

Out of the chaos of the Zhou dynasty and the Warring States period there arose the feudal state of Qin (or Chin or Ch'in) that defeated all the other feudal states around it, and united all of China for the first time. The name "China" comes from the state of "Chin" or "Qin." [32]

In 256 B.C. the last ruler of the Zhou dynasty abdicated in favor of the feudal lord of the state of Qin. Some people place the beginning of the Qin dynasty in that year, 256 B.C.; others prefer the date 221 B.C., because it was only in that year that the remaining feudal states came to their end and Qin really ruled all China. [32]

The Qin Dynasty established the first empire in China, starting with efforts in 230 B.C. during which they engulfed six Zhou Dynasty states. The empire existed only briefly from 221 to 206 B.C., but the Qin Dynasty had a lasting cultural impact on the dynasties that followed. [29]

It was at this time that the Chinese came into close contact with Turkistan (Central Asia). The Qin state was at the center of a rich cultivable zone which was the route through which all traffic from and to Turkistan had to pass. The state of Chin had never been so closely associated with the feudal communities of the rest of China as the other feudal states. A great part of its population, including the ruling class, was not purely Chinese but contained an admixture of Turks and Tibetans. The other Chinese even called Qin a "barbarian state." But this hostile environment turned out to make Qin one of the economically strongest among the feudal states, and provided the impetus to end the feudal system and set up a bureaucratic system. [32]

The Qin did many things to unify China: [29]

- Conquered the other feudal states. [29]
- Standardized non-alphabetic written script across all of China, replacing the previous regional scripts. [29]
- Standardized weights and measures, casting bronze models for measurements and sending them to local governments, who would then impose them on merchants to simplify trade and commerce across the empire. [29]
- Created bronze coins to standardize money across the regions. [29]
- Began the Great Wall of China along the northern border. [29]
- Created the Terra Cotta Army, an army of life-size statues: 8,000 terra cotta warriors, 600 terra cotta horses, plus chariots, stables and other artifacts. [29]

The Qin Dynasty had enormous influence on the subsequent history of China, but it ended almost as quickly as it began.

The warlord Xiang Yu defeated the Qin army in battle in 206 BC. Xiang Yu gave another king, Liu Bang, the Han River Valley to rule. In 202 B.C., Xiang Yu committed suicide, and Liu Bang assumed the title of emperor of the Han Dynasty, adopting many of the Qin dynasty institutions and traditions. [29]

According to one legend, Xiang Yu captured Liu Bang's father and sent a final warning to Liu Bang, assuring that his father would be boiled alive unless Liu Bang surrendered. Liu Bang's answer suggests that he did not get along very well with his father: "Send me a cup of the soup", he replied. In the end, Liu Bang's father was not turned into soup, and Xiang Yu decided to end his own life by committing suicide in 202 BCE. Some accounts say he was defeated in battle, while others tell us he was never defeated in battle but was gradually undermined by the popular support for Liu Bang; Liu Bang was the first Chinese emperor who was originally a commoner. [31]

The Qin dynasty (221-206 BC) lasted 15 years. It was defeated by the ruler of the Han River Valley, Liu Bang, who assumed the title of emperor of the Han Dynasty. [29]

Chapter 27. Han Dynasty (206 BC - 220 AD)

The four centuries of the Han Dynasty are considered a golden age for China. Chinese calligraphy developed into an art. Confucianism was made the official state ideology. Thousands of Confucian academies were built, spreading Confucian ethics across China and most of East Asia and would dominate Chinese ethics during the centuries to come. Even today, Confucian academies are China's most effective means for spreading Chinese culture around the world. It only ended in 220 AD when the imperial order collapsed after a series of palace intrigues. [31]

27.1. The Silk Road

In 138 B.C., a man named Zhang Qian was sent on a mission by Emperor Wu to make contact with tribes to the west. Zhang was captured by a local tribe and continued west, to a region in Afghanistan called Bactria, under Greek control, having been conquered by Alexander the Great. In Bactria, Zhang Qian saw bamboo and textiles brought from China and asked how they had gotten there. He was told that the items came from a kingdom in Afghanistan called Shendu. Thirteen years after he had left, Zhang Qian made his way back to the Emperor, told him of what he had seen and mapped out a route to send an expedition back there. The map and this route was used more and more, and developed into the international trade route known as the Silk Road. [30]

27.2. Invention of paper

Paper was invented during the Han Dynasty. A screen was dipped into a vat of watery oatmeal-like pulp made of rice straw and inner tree bark. When the screen was raised, it had a layer of dripping slush on top, which was later pressed and dried. The end result was a sheet of paper. [31]

Other accomplishments of the Han Dynasty include conquest of Central Asia, northern Vietnam, Inner Mongolia, southern Manchuria, and most of Korea. [31]

27.3. Yellow Turban uprising - 184 AD

After the first century AD, there were a number of different natural calamities such as tremors, floods, and grasshopper plagues, which were seen as manifestations of the anger of heaven. This led to a big protest of thousands of members of the Confucian academy against the corruption of the government. [31]

About 170 AD, a student of Daoism, named Chang Kioh, by pretending to supernatural powers in magic, and curing diseases, gained a large number of followers, in the northeast of China, who regarded him as a God. The number of his adherents continued to increase rapidly, and in 184 AD they raised the standard of rebellion. An immense army of them wearing yellow turbans and divided under thirty-six generals, marched and acted so rapidly, that in a month they had subdued the whole north of China. These were the famous Yellow Turban Rebels who played such an important part in bringing about the downfall of the after Han dynasty. [48]

By the way, the Yellow Turban rebellion is linked to today's Triad Society. The rebels ushered in the turbulent times of the three kingdoms. And it was in the struggle against these rebels that Kwan Yii, since deified as Kwan Ti, the God of War, Liu Pei and Chang Fei, leaders in the wars of the Three Kingdoms, took the solemn oath in the peach garden, to fight and live and die together. This oath was often referred to by the Triad Society, and its members were exhorted to emulate the faithfulness to each other and loyalty to their cause, of the heroes who took it. [48]

27.4. End and legacy of the Han Dynasty

The Yellow Turban Rebellion led to a series of battles between warlords. A warlord named Dong Zhou seized control of the imperial capital, and the Han Dynasty collapsed in 220 AD. Wars between warlords and states continued and China would have to wait around 350 years to be unified again. [31]

Because the Han Dynasty was considered a glorious period in China's history, in the centuries following the end of the Han Dynasty, the phrase "Han Chinese" was used to identify a particular group of the Chinese population. However, there is no distinct Han Chinese ethnic group, as there is for example an Arab ethnic group or a Sinhalese ethnic group.

In some ways, "Han Chinese" are like "Americans," a mixture of anyone who happens to live in a particular place at a given time. However, the difference is that the geographic boundaries of "Americans" are defined by the boundaries of the United States, while the geographic boundaries of the Han

Chinese have been defined for centuries by whatever the warlord at a particular time and place want for Han Chinese to be. So at different times in Chinese history, a warlord would designate his subjects as Han Chinese, while the subjects of the opposing warlord would be "foreigners." [41]

Today, Han Chinese are any people who pledge to worship the Chinese Communist Party (CCP) and Xi Jinping. I've seen Chinese officials stumble over themselves, criticizing someone who referred to Tibetans, saying that Tibetans were Chinese but not Han Chinese. Here's another irony: The Manchus (people of Manchuria) were foreigners when they ruled China during the Qing Dynasty, but today have become Han Chinese to protect themselves.

Chapter 28. Sui Dynasty (581-618 AD) and Korea's Goguryeo Kingdom

Before we switch directions and focus on China's religious and cultural teachings, we wish to describe one more of China's many dynasties: The Sui Dynasty (581-618 AD).

The Sui Dynasty is important for two reasons — because it unified northern and southern China, and because it was decisively defeated by Korea's Goguryeo Kingdom at the Battle of Salsu River in 681.

28.1. Reunification of Northern and Southern China

Once the Han Dynasty had collapsed, there were three centuries when China was split into warring states, with the last period known as the "Period of Northern and Southern Dynasties" (386–589 AD). [81]

In 581, one commander, known then as Yang Jian (aka Yang Chien), amassed an army and seized government, unifying the North. Yang Jian's army then continued down the Yangtze river and conquered the South in 589. So China was unified for the first time in centuries. [81]

So the Sui Dynasty consisted of only two emperors: Wendi (aka Wen or Wen-ti), who reigned 581-601 AD, and his son Yangdi (aka Yang Guang or Yang-ti) who reigned from 604-618 AD. [81]

Yangdi reinforced the Great Wall of China, to protect his kingdom from Turkic invaders from the west, built the massive Grand Canal to join the Yangtze and Yellow Rivers, and conquered territory from the Annam and the Champa in southern Vietnam.

28.2. Defeat by Korea's Goguryeo Empire (37-688) and Battle of Salsu River (612 AD)

The second reason that the Sui Dynasty is important is because of an abortive invasion of Korea.

Historical records indicate that the Goguryeo (Koguryo) Kingdom was founded in northern Korea in 37 AD. The kingdom grew through conquest, and it saw its greatest period during the reign of Gwanggaeto (391-413), when it dominated northern Korea, most of Manchuria, and a portion of Inner Mongolia — including parts of northeastern China and Russia's Far East. Goguryeo was one of the three kingdoms of ancient Korea, along with Baekjae and Silla [84]

The Sui launched a series of attacks on the Goguryeo kingdom, starting in 598 and again in 611, and was pushed back both times. [84]

The war between the Sui and the Goguryeo empire climaxed in 612, when Yangdi himself led a massive army invasion of Korea. when the Koreans under general Ulchi Mundok won a great victory against the Chinese with the Battle of the Salsu River. According to legend, of the 300,000-strong Sui army, only 2,700 returned to China. Two more attacks we rebuffed in 613 and 614 CE and Goguryeo built a 480-km (300 miles) long defensive wall in 628 CE so as to deter any further Chinese ambitions. [81]

28.3. The Goguryeo Stele

The reason that Korea's Goguryeo Kingdom is relevant to today's news is that in January 2013, an ancient memorial stone or gravestone, the Goguryeo stele, was unearthed in northeast China. [83]

This reopened an explosive dispute between China and South Korea over whether the Goguryeo Kingdom was really Korean, or whether it was actually governed by China with a Korean population. In 2004, China's claims to this effect caused enormous Korean hostility to China. By 2013, the dispute had quieted down, but the discovery of the stele, and its investigation by Chinese researchers has reopened it. [83]

There is no sign that China plans to claim North Korea as part of China. Although this dispute seems purely symbolic, it has aroused strong nationalism in South Korea, and it could play a part in a possible future war involving North Korea, South Korea, and China. [82]

Part VI. Religious and cultural teachings in China

Chapter 29. China's harsh 'Sinicization' policy of religions (April 2018)

We're now going to change direction.

We want to look at China's history since the Han Dynasty, but from the point of view of Generational Dynamics, we're not looking for a simple list of warlords, emperors and battles. We're interested in the things that drive the attitudes and behaviors of the population, and in the case of China, that's almost always religion.

We'll start by looking at how the Chinese Communist Party (CCP) deals with religion today.

In June 2018, China passed a "Sinicization" law that required all religious practices to conform strictly to harsh CCP regulations, including forbidding worship of "outsiders," such as Jesus Christ.

We're going to look at different aspects of this law, but the bottom line is that, like so many things from China's government, the law is completely delusional. No serious Christian is going to worship Xi Jinping instead of Jesus Christ.

29.1. Number of religious believers in China

The law provides a summary of religious activity in China: [42]

"The major religions practiced in China are Buddhism, Taoism, Islam, Catholicism, and Protestantism; with a total of nearly 200 million believers and more than 380,000 clerical personnel. China has numerous Buddhist and Taoist believers, but it is difficult to accurately estimate their numbers as there are no set registration procedures which ordinary believers must follow as part of their religion. There are around 222,000 Buddhist clerical personnel and over 40,000 Taoist clerical personnel. The 10 minority ethnic groups, the majority of whose population believe in Islam, total more than 20 million, with about 57,000 clerical personnel. Catholicism and Protestantism have 6 million and 38 million followers in

China respectively, with 8,000 and 57,000 clerical personnel. China also has many folk beliefs which are closely linked to local cultures, traditions and customs, in which a large number of people participate. There are approximately 5,500 religious groups in China, including seven national organizations which are Buddhist Association of China, Chinese Taoist Association, China Islamic Association, Chinese Catholic Patriotic Association, Bishops' Conference of Catholic Church in China, National Committee of the Three-Self Patriotic Movement of the Protestant Churches in China, and China Christian Council.

Conditions of places of worship have been notably improved. The State requires the registration of places of worship for group religious activities in accordance with the law, so as to provide legal protection and ensure that all activities are carried out in an orderly manner. At present, there are about 144,000 places of worship registered for religious activities in China, among which are 33,500 Buddhist temples (including 28,000 Han Buddhist temples, 3,800 Tibetan Buddhist lamaseries, and 1,700 Theravada Buddhist temples), 9,000 Taoist temples, 35,000 Islamic mosques, 6,000 Catholic churches and places of assembly spread across 98 dioceses, and 60,000 Protestant churches and places of assembly. ...

[T]here are 91 religious schools in China whose establishment was approved by the State Administration of Religious Affairs (SARA), including 41 Buddhist, 10 Taoist, 10 Islamic, 9 Catholic and 21 Protestant schools. There are six national level religious colleges, namely, the Buddhist Academy of China, High-level Tibetan Buddhism College of China, Chinese Taoist College, China Islamic Institute, National Seminary of the Catholic Church in China, and Nanking Union Theological Seminary. At present, more than 10,000 students study in these religious schools whose graduates total more than 47,000." [42]

Those numbers are not large in a population of 1.4 billion people. Outsider estimates are much higher. By one estimate, China's Christian population has swelled from a few million in the early 1980s to 100 million this year – in comparison, the Communist Party has 90 million members.

We know from experience in other countries that attempts to suppress religion are never successful. Russia, for example, was an Orthodox Christian country for centuries. The Bolshevik Revolution in 1917 supposedly turned Russia into an atheist country. But anecdotal evidence shows that Christians simply held secret religious ceremonies in their homes. There's plenty of anecdotal evidence that the same thing is happening today in China, which explains the difference between the official and unofficial numbers of believers.

29.2. Equivalence of Islam, Christianity and Buddhism to CCP

Starting in 2017, the CCP became increasingly bloody and violent against the four supposedly "approved" non-indigenous religions, Islam, Buddhism, Catholicism, and Protestantism. [65]

When I've written about this subject in the past, some commenters criticized me for implying that Islam and Christianity are equivalent in some way. Actually, nothing that I wrote implies that. The point was that the Chinese Communist Party (CCP) considers Islam and Christianity to be equivalent, and the same for all of the non-indigenous religions.

In China's multi-millennial imperialistic history, China has always been at war or close to it — invading neighbors to exterminate them and take their land, or planning and preparing for such an invasion, or being invaded by a neighbor, or in the midst of a massive internal civil war. China's indigenous "religions" — Sun Tzu's Art of War, Confucianism and Daoism — are all aimed at unifying behind the government and winning wars.

Each one of the non-indigenous religions has been used at one time or another, sometimes successfully, sometimes not, as a belief system to create a populist movement to overthrow a dynasty or a government.

This became particularly frightening to the CCP on June 4, 1989, when tens of thousands of students from all over China traveled to Beijing and rallied in Tiananmen Square, causing the CCP to viciously murder thousands of students, creating a bloodbath. This show of mass protest showed the Chinese leadership how easy it would be for them to be toppled by a mass movement, and so they've been extremely vicious towards all non-indigenous religions. And then when the Soviet Communist Party collapsed in 1991, they went into full-scale panic and paranoia.

So to the CCP, Islam, Buddhism and Christianity are exactly the same as one another and all the non-indigenous religions. They're all alien religions, differing only in details. And they're all a threat to the government, since they can form the basis of a popular mass movement that overthrows the government.

Therefore, to keep them from overthrowing the government, they all must be subject to "Sinicization," which means that they must conform to Chinese government policies or face jailing or destruction. [42] [65]

29.3. CCP administrative control of religion

In March 2018, China's government issued its Sinicization decree, called by the Orwellian name "China's Policies and Practices on Protecting Freedom of Religious Belief." [42]

There are six areas of Sinicization: intensifying political identification, integrating religion into Chinese culture, establishing theological thought with Chinese characteristics, setting up a management system for the church with Chinese characteristics, exploring liturgical expression with Chinese elements, and using Chinese aesthetics in church buildings, pictures and sacred music. [42]

According to the decree: [42]

> "It also means guiding religious groups to support the leadership of the CPC and the socialist system; uphold and follow the path of socialism with Chinese characteristics; develop religions in the Chinese context; embrace core socialist values; carry forward China's fine traditions; integrate religious teachings and rules with Chinese culture; abide by state laws and regulations, and accept state administration in accordance with the law."

This paragraph gives complete administrative control of the religion to the CCP, and permits the CCP to monitor all religious activities. The crackdown has been particularly brutal this year.

In 2018, China's storm troopers demolished a massive evangelical church using bulldozers and dynamite. The Jindengtai ("Golden Lampstand") mega-church, which reportedly had a congregation of 50,000 people, was demolished. Later, the Zion Protestant Church in Beijing was banned because the administration refused to install closed-circuit television cameras that the CCP could use to monitor all activity. [65] [64]

In mid-2018, churchgoers in the Beijing district were given notice that the "great masses of believer must respect the rules and regulations and attend events in legally registered places of religious activity." This notice particularly targets the millions of Chinese people who attend "underground churches," not registered with the government. [64]

Any person who violates the government's rules can be tortured or jailed or sent to reeducation or concentration camps. The most extreme example of this so far is Xinjiang province, where a million ethnic Uighurs are being tortured, raped and beaten in concentration camps.

I was listening to a BBC report in 2018, interviewing someone who had a number of Uighur friends living in Xinjiang province. He rattled off a list of the offenses that could get you sent to a concentration camp, things like not saying "hello" to a Chinese official when you pass him in the street. He also mentioned "giving up smoking." It turns out that if you give up smoking, then it means that you're planning to become an extremist and terrorist, so you have to be sent to a concentration camp.

29.4. CCP attitude toward religion

The following sentence, near the beginning of the Sinicization law, lays out the general attitude of the CCP towards religion:

> "The state protects citizens' right to freedom of religious belief, normal religious activities and the lawful rights and interests of religious groups, bans illegal religious activities, prohibits the dissemination of extremist thought and engagement in extremist activities in the name of religion, resists the infiltration of hostile foreign forces taking advantage of religion, and fights against illegal and criminal activities under the guise of religion. Believers should abide by the Constitution, laws, rules and regulations of the country. Religious activities should be carried out within the bounds of the law. No religion should interfere in the implementation of administrative, judicial and educational functions of the state. No abolished religious and feudal privileges should be resumed. "

Under this clause, any thing said or done by a believer could be deemed "extremist" by government officials.

Furthermore, any government official can punish believers by accusing them of interfering with the "administrative, judicial and educational functions of the state."

> "The Regulations prescribe the rights and responsibilities of religious organizations, places of worship, and religious believers when establishing places for and holding religious activities, setting up and running religious institutions, applying for legal person status, publishing and distributing religious books and periodicals, receiving donations, managing religious property, conducting charity activities, and carrying out exchanges with other countries."

This makes it clear that every aspect of religion is rigorously controlled by the CCP through "Regulations."

29.5. Pope's betrayal of Chinese Catholics

In the March 2018 law, there are six areas of Sinicization: [58]
* intensifying political identification,

- integrating religion into refined, sophisticated Chinese culture,
- establishing theological thought with Chinese characteristics,
- setting up a management system for the church with Chinese characteristics,
- exploring liturgical expression with Chinese elements,
- using Chinese aesthetics in church buildings, pictures and sacred music. [58]

This mega plan covers every aspect of Catholic life, including theology, church-state relations, church administration, church education, formation of church personnel, and church arts. [58]

Chinese Catholics feel betrayed and abandoned by the Pope after he reached an agreement in 2018 to retire all Chinese Bishops appointed by the Vatican, and allow them all to be replaced by Bishops appointed by the CCP. [61]

29.6. Imperialist China view of religion

Because of China's long history as a militaristic, imperialistic society going back millennia, it's not surprising that the CCP's view of religion and cultural teachings has nothing really to do with religion, but has to do with fighting and winning wars, or with anti-government protests that could lead to internal civil war.

In the following chapters, we'll be looking mainly at the following cultural teachings and religions:

- Sun Tzu and the Art of War. China's "bible" for always being prepared for winning a war.
- Confucius and Confucianism. This is the "pro-government" cultural teaching. It tells both peasants and government leaders how to maintain a "Mandate from Heaven" for a unified society that wins wars.
- Lao Tzu and Daoism. This religion was a reaction to Confucianism, teaches peasants how to maintain harmony with nature without the harsh Confucian rules, whether you're pro-government or anti-government, and so Daoism has sometimes been the core of anti-government protests.
- Buddhism. As a religion imported from India, not indigenous in China, it has historically been the most important vehicle for anti-government protests. Major historical anti-government branches of Buddhism were the White Lotus Society, Tibetan Buddhism, and Falun Gong, all of which have been violently suppressed by the government as major threats.

- Catholicism. This has existed in China since the 600s AD. It became very popular in China, thanks to Jesuit missionaries, but the Chinese government has always considered it a major threat because it requires allegiance to an outsider — the Pope. Since 1949, the government has been harshly hostile to Catholicism, and has demanded to control all functions, including appointments of bishops and priests. So today, there are two Catholic churches in China, the Chinese Catholic Church, and the underground Catholic Church, with allegiance to the pope.
- Protestantism. The massive Taiping Rebellion (1850-64) civil war was launched by a Protestant convert who believed he was the brother of Jesus. Since 1949, China has harshly controlled Protestantism, even to the point of replacing worship of Jesus with worship of Xi Jinping.
- Islam. China's wars with the Turkic tribes in Central Asia have almost always been against Muslims. Today, the Chinese government has opened concentration camps ("reeducation camps") for millions of Muslim Uighurs in Xinjiang province, and Uighurs are regularly raped, tortured and slaughtered.

29.7. Chinese government attitude towards non-indigenous religions

In the West, we consider Buddhism, Catholicism, Protestantism and Islam to be completely different religions, sometimes at war with each other, with different beliefs, with different histories, and with different geopolitics.

For the Chinese Communist Party (CCP), those religions are all the same. They're all invaders from outside China, they all (except for Buddhism) use the same Bible, they all have been used historically to guide populist movements to overthrow Chinese governments, and they all are viewed today by the CCP as an existential threat.

So for the CCP, there's no difference between Catholicism, Protestantism, Buddhism and Islam except at the level of detail. They're all the same, and they're all threats.

29.8. Rules governing Christian Churches in China

Under Sinicization, Christianity isn't really Christianity any more, so much as a set of Confucian rules for obedience to the CCP. The following rules apply specifically to Protestant Churches (known as Three Self churches), but the rules apply generally to all Christian Churches: [63]

- The Communist Party is the head of the church in China (Three Self churches report to the Three Self Patriotic Movement, which in turn reports to the State Administration for Religious Affairs (SARA), which is controlled by the Chinese Communist Party).
- The Communist Party decides how many people can be baptized per year.
- The Communist Party has the final say on who can preach and what can be preached.
- Preaching should focus on the social rules and the social benefits of Christianity.
- Preaching about the resurrection of Jesus is forbidden.
- Preaching about the second coming of Jesus is forbidden.
- Preaching against religions that deny the deity of Jesus is forbidden.
- Preaching that atheist Communist heroes went to hell is forbidden.
- Preaching cannot deny that all good Communists go to heaven.
- Preaching against abortion is forbidden.
- Preachers can preach only at the Three Self church to which they are assigned.
- Worshipping outside Three Self churches and official "meeting points" is forbidden.
- Importing Bibles is forbidden, even if they are given away for free.
- [16]Printing Bibles is forbidden, even if they are given away for free.
- Evangelizing or giving out tracts is forbidden.
- Government officials cannot be Christian.
- Police officers cannot be Christian.
- Soldiers cannot be Christian.
- Teachers cannot be Christian.
- Children cannot become Christian.
- Teenagers cannot become Christian. [63]

As an example of how these rules are applied, Chinese police have stormed into people's homes and replaced the pictures of Jesus Christ and other religious symbols with pictures of Xi Jinping, with the implication that people should be worshipping Xi Jinping as God. [65]

Chapter 30. Sun Tzu / The Art of War (500 BC)

We've just summarized the CCP view of religion today. Now we turn to historical development of religion in China.

It says a lot about China's culture that for more than two millennia, the most important and significant work in China's history is a military treatise that lays out a series of recipes for imperial conquest.

30.1. The Art of War

The Art of War, written by Sun Tzu around 500 BC, is a military treatise written covering all aspects of warfare. It seeks to advise commanders on how to prepare, mobilize, attack, defend, and treat the vanquished. One of the most influential texts in history, it has been used by military strategists for over 2,000 years and admired by leaders from Napoleon to Mao Zedong. [19] [24]

The Art of War is divided into 13 chapters or pian which cover different aspects of warfare from planning to diplomacy. The work is not shy on the use of deception which runs through many of the suggested stratagems. Still, the book is not a glorification of warfare, and an important point, raised several times in the work, is that actual combat only results from the failure of other strategies to defeat the enemy and is always an undesirable waste of men and resources. [19]

An important concept in the Art of War is "qi" (pronounced zhih), which is the "breath" or essence of life in Chinese thought. Its relevance to warfare is that commanders must energize the qi of their own troops while at the same time drain it from the enemy. Thus, the psychology of warfare is recognized as a vital factor in the overall success of campaigns. In a later chapter, we'll discuss "qigong," a set of exercises to energize one's own qi. [19]

As much of the advice relates to deploying troops with imagination and daring based on a good prior knowledge of the terrain and enemy, withdrawals and counter-offensives, and the importance of psychology, The Art of War is often cited as the go-to source for those engaging in guerrilla warfare. For this reason, Sun Tzu's ideas have continued to be relevant to the conduct of war no matter the developments in technology or increase in the destructive power of weapons. Wherever soldiers come face to face with the enemy Sun-Tzu's ideas may be applied. [19]

30.2. Sima Qian's biography of Sun Tzu

Sima Qian (145 or 135 BC - 86 BC) was a Chinese historian who wrote a biography of Sun Tzu. The following famous excerpt from his biography, whether precisely true or not, illustrates the public perception of Sun Tzu, and explains the Chinese admiration for Sun Tzu: [24]

"Sun Tzu Wu was a native of the Ch`i State. His ART OF WAR brought him to the notice of Ho Lu, King of Wu. Ho Lu said to him: "I have carefully perused your 13 chapters. May I submit your theory of managing soldiers to a slight test?"

Sun Tzu replied: "You may."

Ho Lu asked: "May the test be applied to women?"

The answer was again in the affirmative, so arrangements were made to bring 180 ladies out of the Palace. Sun Tzu divided them into two companies, and placed one of the King's favorite concubines at the head of each. He then bade them all take spears in their hands, and addressed them thus: "I presume you know the difference between front and back, right hand and left hand?"

The girls replied: Yes.

Sun Tzu went on: "When I say "Eyes front," you must look straight ahead. When I say "Left turn," you must face towards your left hand. When I say "Right turn," you must face towards your right hand. When I say "About turn," you must face right round towards your back."

Again the girls assented. The words of command having been thus explained, he set up the halberds and battle-axes in order to begin the drill. Then, to the sound of drums, he gave the order "Right turn." But the girls only burst out laughing. Sun Tzu said: "If words of command are not clear and distinct, if orders are not thoroughly understood, then the general is to blame."

So he started drilling them again, and this time gave the order "Left turn," whereupon the girls once more burst into fits of laughter. Sun Tzu: "If words of command are not clear and distinct, if orders are not thoroughly understood, the general is to blame. But if his orders ARE clear, and the soldiers nevertheless disobey, then it is the fault of their officers."

So saying, he ordered the leaders of the two companies to be beheaded. Now the king of Wu was watching the scene from the top of a raised pavilion; and when he saw that his favorite concubines were about to be executed, he was greatly alarmed and hurriedly sent down the following message: "We are now quite satisfied as to our general's ability to handle troops. If We are bereft of these two concubines, our meat and drink will lose their savor. It is our wish that they shall not be beheaded."

Sun Tzu replied: "Having once received His Majesty's commission to be the general of his forces, there are certain commands of His Majesty which, acting in that capacity, I am unable to accept."

Accordingly, he had the two leaders beheaded, and straightway installed the pair next in order as leaders in their place. When this had been done, the drum was sounded for the drill once more; and the girls went through all the evolutions, turning to the right or to the left, marching ahead or wheeling back, kneeling or standing, with perfect accuracy and precision, not venturing to utter a sound. Then Sun Tzu sent a messenger to the King saying: "Your soldiers, Sire, are now properly drilled and disciplined, and ready for your majesty's inspection. They can be put to any use that their sovereign may desire; bid them go through fire and water, and they will not disobey."

But the King replied: "Let our general cease drilling and return to camp. As for us, We have no wish to come down and inspect the troops."

Thereupon Sun Tzu said: "The King is only fond of words, and cannot translate them into deeds."

After that, Ho Lu saw that Sun Tzu was one who knew how to handle an army, and finally appointed him general. In the west, he defeated the Ch`u State and forced his way into Ying, the capital; to the north he put fear into the States of Ch`i and Chin, and spread his fame abroad amongst the feudal princes. And Sun Tzu shared in the might of the King." [24]

This anecdote encapsulates the Chinese view of Sun Tzu and the art of war today, and is a good illustration of the imperialist culture of the Chinese people.

My purpose here is to use the Sun Tzu history as a way of understanding China's millennia-old culture of imperialism. The Art of War, combined with Sima Qian's biography of Sun Tzu, are revered by the Chinese people, apparently without reservation.

Chapter 31. Confucius (551-479 BC)

The historical Confucius, born in the small state of Lu on the Shandong peninsula in northeastern China, was a product of the "Spring and Autumn Period" (770-481 BCE). We know him mostly from texts that date to the "Warring States Period" (403-221 BCE). [20]

The Chinese consider Confucius to be the greatest philosopher in history. Today, China uses the Confucius name to spread Chinese culture around the world. China runs 1,500 Confucius Institutes and Classrooms in Australia, New Zealand, Canada, the United States, and other countries, with 40% of them in the US, more than any other country. According to the Chinese, they serve as "an important part of China's overseas propaganda." [186]

31.1. Confucius sayings and aphorisms

Before getting into deep subjects, let's introduce the subject of Confucius in a lighter way. Many people know nothing about Confucius except his sayings, whether or not he actually said them.

"Confucius say" sayings are often meant to be funny, and can often be found as sayings in fortune cookies served after meals in a Chinese restaurant. Here are some examples: "Confucius say: Man with one chopstick go hungry." or "Confucius say: Man who cut self while shaving, lose face. " or "Confucius say: Man who jump off cliff, jump to conclusion! " or "Confucius say: Man should not sleep with woman with more troubles than he have."

Those sayings are meant to be funny, but he probably never said them.

However, there is a large body of real Confucius sayings that carry a great deal of wisdom, even though they were written down 15 centuries ago. In fact, many of them have become common sayings. Here are some examples: [23]

- "Your life is what your thoughts make it."
- "What you do not want done to yourself, do not do to others." (This is an early form of the Golden Rule.)
- "The journey with a 1000 miles begins with one step."
- "Choose a job you love, and you will never have to work a day in your life."
- "Learn avidly. Question it repeatedly. Analyze it carefully. Then put what you have learned into practice intelligently."

- "If you are the smartest person in the room, then you are in the wrong room."
- "Act with kindness but do not expect gratitude."
- "I slept and dreamt life is beauty, I woke and found life is duty."
- "Respect yourself and others will respect you."
- "By nature, men are nearly alike; by practice, they get to be wide apart."
- "Only the wisest and stupidest of men never change."
- "Do not impose on others what you yourself do not desire."
- "To see the right and not to do it is cowardice."
- "When anger rises, think of the consequences."
- "If we don't know life, how can we know death?"
- "Give a bowl of rice to a man and you will feed him for a day. Teach him how to grow his own rice and you will save his life."
- "Never give a sword to a man who can't dance." [23]

31.2. Confucius Analects

Because of the importance of Confucius to Chinese history, it is ironic that so little is known about his life. What is known is the contents of the sayings and biographical fragments recorded in the texts known as the Confucius Analects. [20]

As with the person of Confucius himself, scholars disagree about the origins and character of the Analects, but it remains the traditional source for information about Confucius' life and teaching. Most scholars remain confident that it is possible to extract from the Analects several philosophical themes and views that may be safely attributed to this ancient Chinese sage. These are primarily ethical, rather than analytical-logical or metaphysical in nature, and include Confucius' claim that Tian ("Heaven") is aligned with moral order but dependent upon human agents to actualize its will; his concern for li (ritual propriety) as the instrument through which the family, the state, and the world may be aligned with Tian's moral order; and his belief in the "contagious" nature of moral force (de), by which moral rulers diffuse morality to their subjects, moral parents raise moral children, and so forth. [20]

What Confucius claimed to transmit was the Dao (Way) of the sages of Zhou antiquity; in the Analects, he is the erudite guardian of tradition who challenges his disciples to emulate the sages of the past and restore the moral integrity of the state. Although readers of the Analects often assume that Confucius' views are presented as a coherent and consistent system within the text, a careful reading reveals several different sets of philosophical concerns which do not conflict so much as they complement one another. [20]

31.3. Confucius theology: Tian and the Mandate from Heaven

Confucius and Sun Tzu were contemporaries during China's Spring and Autumn period, and it's worthwhile to look at the relationship between their works.

Sun Tzu was a brilliant war strategist and tactician. From deception to beheadings, every tactic is on the table for winning wars. Compromise or mercy are never possible. If Sun Tzu's work was the recipe for imperialist warfare, Confucius' work was the theology of imperialist warfare. Confucius lived at the time of the Zhou Dynasty, about five centuries after it had beaten the Shang Dynasty. How were the Zhou able to defeat the Shang? Much of Confucius' work is devoted to answer that question in a theological framework.

The Shang worshiped a heavenly ancestor called Shangdi ("the Lord on high"), and kings were permitted to rule under the power of this god. When the Zhou defeated the Shang, they replaced (or merged) Shang Di with their own god, Tian, a sky god, a "deity above who rules the Heavens." [20]

Under the Zhou doctrine, a king is the Son of Heaven, and is allowed to rule under a Mandate from Heaven, provided that he rules reverently and virtuously. Thus, if the Zhou defeated the Shang, then the Shang king must have lost his Mandate from Heaven. An excerpt from an ancient history classic is the Zhou explanation of what happened: [22]

> "We do not presume to know and to say that the lords of Yin (Shang) received Heaven's Mandate for so many years. ... But they did not reverently attend to their virtue and so prematurely threw away the Mandate. ... Now our king has succeeded and received the Mandate. ... Being king, his position will be that of a leader of virtue. ... The Son of Heaven could not properly fulfill his functions unless his moral nature was pure and his conduct above reproach. Heaven could not be served by a tyrant or a debauchee, the sacrifices of such a ruler would be of no avail, the divine harmony would be upset, prodigies and catastrophes would manifest the wrath of Heaven."

Confucius formalized and strengthened this doctrine of Tian and the Mandate from Heaven. He wrestled with the same "theodicy" contradiction that every religion faces: If God created everything, then God created Good and Evil, so how could God be good if God created evil? [21]

For Confucius, this contradiction and its apparent manifestation in the Zhou conquests, applies to Tian. The word "theodicy" refers to any attempt to resolve this contradiction, and Confucius develops his own theodicy. He recognizes that Tian is a superhuman power in the universe, but the power depends on human agents. There are three assumptions about Tian that are deeply rooted in the

Chinese past, and Confucius adopts these three assumptions without questioning them: [20]

- its alignment with moral goodness;
- its dependence on human agents to actualize its will;
- the variable, unpredictable nature of its associations with mortal actors.

The first assumption says that "God (Tian) is good," and appears to reject any evil in Tian. However, it's the second assumption that resolves the contradiction. If Tian is dependent on human agents to actualize its will, then Tian is not omnipotent, which means that there's a part of the universe ("evil") that God (Tian) is not responsible for. The third assumption amplifies the second by making it clear that evil is the result of "mortal actors" and their unpredictable nature.

31.4. Confucius theology: Maintaining stability and harmony

The Taiping Rebellion (1850-64) was a massive civil war that enveloped all of China, killing at least 20 million people. China's next massive civil war was Mao's Communist Revolution (1934-49), killing tens of millions more. From the point of view of generational theory, each of these was a generational crisis wars, a war so bloody and massive that the survivors vow to keep it from ever happening again — and it doesn't, until these survivors all die off, usually 58-70 years later, when a new war can begin. So the Communist Revolution began 70 years after the end of the Taiping Revolution. In 2019, another 70 years will have passed since 1949, the end of the Communist Revolution, so China is due (in fact overdue) for its next massive civil war. Concerns and fears about a massive new civil war are a major factor in Chinese Communist Party policy today.

Words like "stability" and "harmony" appear in speeches from Chinese officials and news stories about Chinese policy far more than for other countries. For example, I looked at some recent news stories about China and extracted some snippets where these words are used:

- China says it wants to achieve peace, stability, harmony and prosperity in the region.
- Unions in China, such as worker's unions, student's unions, commercial unions, usually have strong ties to the government. The official mission of most workers' unions is "promoting harmony," rather than protecting workers' rights.
- The objectives of Confucius Institutes are to strengthen educational and cultural exchange and cooperation between China and other countries,

to deepen friendly relationships with other nations, to promote the development of multi-culturalism, and to construct a harmonious world.

- China's objectives in the Arctic Council include realizing harmonious coexistence between man and nature.
- Xi Jinping says that in 15 years, China will become prosperous, strong, culturally advanced, harmonious and beautiful.

From the most ancient times in China's history, China was riven with similar massive civil wars. Finding a way to prevent the next one and to maintain harmony and stability has been a problem for every warlord, king and monarch in Chinese history, and the attempt to solve that problem was an objective of the theology of Confucius.

So Confucius' reasoning is as follows: [20]

- Tian is resolutely aligned with morality, but actualization depends on the somewhat random actions of mortal human actors.
- It thus becomes the duty of the king and other government leaders to be stringently moral and virtuous. Only a moral leader can rule at the pleasure of Tian, for which the leader receives the Mandate from Heaven.
- There is a "moral force" ("de" or "te"), a quality and virtue of the successful rule.
- Aesthetic concerns for harmony and stability unites with moral force in pursuit of social goals: a well-ordered family, a well-ordered state, and a well-ordered world.
- Such an aesthetic, moral, and social program begins at home, with the cultivation and self-cultivation of the individual. [20]

Since Tian depends on human actors to implement its will, Confucius insists on moral, political, social, and even religious activism. Only through this activism will a society maintain a harmonious order. [20]

Confucius in his Analects explains how self-cultivation applies to his own life: [20]

> "From the age of fifteen on, I have been intent upon learning; from thirty on, I have established myself; from forty on, I have not been confused; from fifty on, I have known the mandate of Heaven; from sixty on, my ear has been attuned; from seventy on, I have followed my heart's desire without transgressing what is right. (Analects 2.4)"

This illustrates the gradual and long-term scale of the process of self-cultivation. It begins during one's teenaged years, and extends well into old age; it proceeds incrementally from intention to learning , from knowing the mandate of Heaven to doing both what is desired and what is right. [20]

To achieve this, Confucius emphasizes loyalty to relationships, and "self-reflection," which is explained in his own version of the Golden Rule: "What you do not desire for yourself, do not do to others." [20]

Confucius provides a comprehensive philosophy and theology for promoting stability and harmony. It starts with the moral goodness of Tian, and depends for actualization of moral properties on a "moral force" that applies to individuals, particularly government leaders, achieved through self-actualization.

However, there is a glaring unproven assumption in this flow of logic: He assumes without proof that all these steps will lead to stability and harmony for Chinese society. This assumption is unproven at two levels.

The first assumption is that the specific self-actualization rules described by Confucius are the ones required to achieve Tian's moral goodness. There are no "Ten Commandments" as there are in the Biblical Old Testament, where God specifically provides the rules for virtue in life. Apparently, the rules specified by Confucius were derived from his own mind, his own reasoning, and that's not proof of correctness.

The second assumption is that Tian's alignment with moral goodness is even supposed to imply stability and harmony. It could imply something completely different — that moral goodness means an imperialist policy of conquering and subjugating all of China's neighbors. This has in fact been China's policy for millennia.

From the point of view of Generational Dynamics, none of this talk of moral goodness and moral force is relevant. The massive, bloody civil war in Mao's Communist Revolution occurred at that time because that was the time when all the survivors of the Taiping Rebellion had disappeared. It makes absolutely no difference whether Mao Zedong had a Mandate from Heaven or not. A massive, bloody civil war of some kind was going to occur, with 100% certainty.

Since Mao won the bloody civil war of 1934-49, we have to assume that in Confucian theology Mao was following a moral force and had a Mandate from Heaven. Whether one believes that or not, Mao has to be viewed as one of the most evil Chinese leaders in history. During Mao's sociopathic Great Leap Forward (1958-59), 500 million peasants were taken out of their homes and put into communes, with children, wives and husbands all living separately, with the purpose of creating a great Communist machine, but instead resulted in tens of millions of death, including massive starvation and millions of executions.

After the disastrous failure of the Great Leap Forward, Mao launched the Red Guards, mostly students, who fought pitched battles, carried out summary executions, drove thousands to suicide, and forced tens of thousands into labor camps, usually far from home.

There's a particular irony to the case of Mao Zedong. During the 1960s, Confucianism fell into disfavor, and leftist students in America, Europe and around the world were carrying around Mao's Little Red Book of Quotations in their back pockets, ready to be pulled out and used to lecture someone at any time. Today, Xi Jinping and the Chinese Communist Party consider Mao to be a threat, since Mao's revolutionary policies would mean the end of the CCP. Instead, Confucius is being rehabilitated, and Xi Jinping has the Mandate from Heaven.

31.5. Relevance of Confucius and Sun Tzu to today's world

China has adopted a racist view of the world very similar to Adolf Hitler's Master Race concept of the Aryan people being superior to all other races. However, when comparing China's Master Race view to Hitler's, there's one remarkable difference: Hitler's Master Race views were known and adopted by the German people for only a few years, and were discarded after World War II, while China's Master Race views go back millennia, and are still deeply imbued in Chinese society today. These racist views and policies have been disastrous for China.

An anecdote from 1793 illustrates the problem. King George sent British diplomat George Macartney to Beijing in 1793, to present to the emperor, court and people an "extensive selection" of manufactured goods. The intention was that the Chinese would identify the products they liked and wanted, and then Britain would begin manufacturing, and selling them in the huge Chinese market. The emperor accepted all the goods as tributes from the vassal King George, but flatly refused to open China's ports to trade. The emperor is quoted as saying, "We have never valued ingenious articles, nor do we have the slightest need of your country's manufactures...Curios and the boasted ingenuity of their devices I prize not." [157]

China thus missed a great opportunity for economic growth. But more important, this insular and racist view has persisted for millennia. One can argue that China has every right to keep to itself, and has kept the Chinese people poor, while other nations, including Taiwan, South Korea and Japan, have surged ahead.

When you look at the work of Sun Tzu and Confucius, and use their work to analyze modern events, you see that both philosophers lack any idea of a "peace conference" or a "United Nations." Since the Chinese king was the Son of Heaven, the Ruler of All Under Heaven, and received its Mandate from Heaven to rule, it would not make sense to sue for peace with anyone else, because no one else had the Mandate from Heaven.

But if there's no peace, it's still possible to take advantage of a "peace process." Sun Tzu said that "All warfare is based on deception," and he advocated the use of deception first, and actual war as a last resort.

So for China today, the United Nations is not a tool to bring about peace, but a tool to be used with deception to win the war. For example, China treats international law with contempt, saying that its own law supersedes international law as in the South China Sea, where China is criminally violating international law, but still references international law when it favors China. This is a perfect example of deception and manipulation. China is contemptuous of international law, but still uses it as a tool of deception. Sun Tzu would be proud.

31.6. North Korea denuclearization - deception and manipulation

North Korea has followed the same policy of deception and manipulation for decades over the issue of denuclearization.

The current dictator, Kim Jong-un, appears to be replaying the same fraudulent script that his father Kim Jong-il followed in 2008. At that time, the North demolished a 60-foot-tall cooling tower to prove that it was ending its nuclear development programs. In reaction, the administration of president George Bush agreed to remove all sanctions. As soon as they were removed, North Korea immediately and openly resumed its nuclear and ballistic missile development. They had completely defrauded and humiliated the United States and the world.

Chapter 32. Laozi (Lao Tzu) (-533 BC) and Daoism

Laozi or Lao Tzu is the author or editor of the Daodejing (Dao de jing, Classic of the Way and its Power). It's not known with certainty whether Laozi actually existed, or whether the Daodejing was written by a collection of people. Either way, the Daodejing over time evolved into Daoism, a countervailing philosophy and religion to Confucianism.

Since the earliest times, the word "Dao" ("tao") mean a way or a path, the core value that underlies the entire universe. Much of Chinese philosophy deals with the question of understanding Dao, and living in conformity with Dao.

32.1. Confucians vs Daoists

Confucians gave an "activist" meaning to Dao, speaking of how people should behave in an ethical and moral way in society, and how these same values should be imposed on government leaders, who were expected to govern in an ethical or moral manner. [43]

Daoism was a strong reaction to the activism of Confucianism. In Daoism, the Confucian concept of Dao was too limited. Daoists preferred to understand the Dao as the Way of Nature as a whole. They believed that Confucians, by insisting on a purely human Dao, exaggerated the importance of man and failed to pay attention to the lessons which Nature has to offer about time and change, gain and loss, the useful and the useless. [26]

32.2. Description of the Dao de jing

The Dao de jing is often a vague and inconsistent book and it is sometimes tempting to wonder whether its authors really had any special insight to offer, or whether they just wanted to sound impressive. But the book does in fact articulate ideas of great originality and interest, ideas that have had enormous influence on Asian culture. [25]

Here are some of the major points of the Dao de jing:

- The nature of the Dao. There exists in some sense an overarching order to the cosmos, beyond the power of words to describe.
- To understand the nature of human ignorance, it is necessary to undergo a fundamental change in our perspective. To do this, we need to

disentangle ourselves from beliefs we live by that have been established through words and experience life directly.

- If we were able to escape the beliefs we live by and see human life from the perspective of the Dao, we would understand that we normally view the world through a lens of value judgments — we see things as good or bad, desirable or detestable. The cosmos itself possesses none of these characteristics of value. All values are only human conventions that we project onto the world. Good and bad are non-natural distinctions that we need to discard if we are to see the world as it really is.

- The selfishness of our ordinary lives makes us devote all our energies to a chase for possessions and pleasures, which leaves us no space for the detached tranquility needed to join the harmonious rhythm of Nature and the Dao.

- As the Daoist sage comes effortlessly to subdue the world, he will necessarily be treated as its king. The rule of such a king will be to discard all human institutions and social patterns that are the product of human intellectual effort and value judgments. The people will be returned to a simple and primitive state close to animal society, and this social environment will itself nurture in the population a stance of wuwei. Ultimately, the world will return to the bliss of ignorance and fulfillment in a stable life of food gathering, food consumption, and procreation, all governed by the seasonal rhythms of Nature and the Dao.

32.3. Excerpts from the Dao de jing

The following are some selected verses from the Dao de jing: [27]

The Dao that can be spoken is not the eternal Dao.
The name that can be named is not the eternal name.
The nameless is the origin of heaven and earth
While naming is the origin of the myriad things.

Heaven and Earth are not humane,
And regard the people as straw dogs.
The sage is not humane,
And regards all things as straw dogs.
The space between Heaven and Earth is just like a bellows:
Empty it, it is not exhausted.

Squeeze it and more comes out.
Investigating it with a lot of talk
Is not like holding to the center.

Get rid of learning and there will be no anxiety.
How much difference is there between yes and no?
How far removed from each other are good and evil?

Human beings follow the Earth.
Earth follows Heaven
Heaven follows the Dao
The Dao follows the way things are.

Accomplish but don't boast
Accomplish without show
Accomplish without arrogance
Accomplish without grabbing
Accomplish without forcing.
When things flourish they decline

Victory is never sweet.
Those for whom victory is sweet
Are those who enjoy killing.

The softest thing in the world
Will overcome the hardest.
Non-being can enter where there is no space.
Therefore I know the benefit of actionless action.
The wordless teaching and actionless action
Are rarely seen.

Do without doing.
Get involved without manipulating.
Taste without tasting.
Make the great small,
The many, few.
Respond to anger with virtue.
Deal with difficulties while they are still easy.
Handle the great while it is still small.

When people are born they are gentle and soft.

At death they are hard and stiff.
When plants are alive they are soft and delicate.
When they die, they wither and dry up.
Therefore the hard and stiff are followers of death.
The gentle and soft are the followers of life.
Thus, if you are aggressive and stiff, you won't win.
When a tree is hard enough, it is cut. Therefore
The hard and big are lesser,
The gentle and soft are greater.

True words are not fancy.
Fancy words are not true.
The good do not debate.
Debaters are not good.
The one who really knows is not broadly learned,
The extensively learned do not really know.

The five colors blind men's eyes,
The five tones deafen men's ears,
The five flavors numb men's mouths,
Racing at a gallop in pursuit of the hunt maddens men's minds.
Rare objects obstruct men's conduct.

Confucianism stresses patriarchy, family relationships and hierarchical structures, Daoism stresses that individual happiness, not laws and regulations, is the basis of a good society. For many Chinese, Daoism was the "anti-Confucius" religion, which meant that it could be the "anti-government" religion.

As we described in an earlier chapter, the Yellow Turban uprising in 184 AD against the Han Dynasty was launched by a student of Daoism. For that reason, the CCP is as suspicious of Daoism, which is an indigenous religion, as it is of the non-indigenous religions.

Chapter 33. Buddhism

33.1. Justification for Buddhism in China

Buddhism has always been a major problem for the governments of imperial China simply because it was not an indigenous Chinese religion like Confucianism or Daoism. A group forcibly conquered and subjugated by the imperial Chinese are not going to be tempted by China's indigenous religions. Buddhism, which originated in India, is the perfect choice for a subjugated people, in part because it promises an afterlife that's better than the current life.

When a major new religion arises and becomes popular, it's often a reaction to the existing state religion. In Europe, for example, the Protestant religions arose in reaction to the Catholic religion. Protestants maintained many of the beliefs and rituals of the Catholics, from Sunday worship to the divinity of Jesus Christ, but rejected the one they find most politically objectionable, in this case the supremacy of the Pope.

From the point of view of generational theory, religion provides a way of creating identity groups, and providing a justification for war. A leader who wants his people to conquer, subjugate, torture, rape and exterminate another group of people has to give a reason. The Muslims say that their enemies are "infidels," and so must be killed. The Chinese say that their enemies have lost (or never had) the "Mandate from Heaven" to govern, and so must be killed.

Confucianism arose in the 2nd century BC, providing harsh rules for both individuals and leaders to maintain the Mandate from Heaven, and thus avoid social unrest. Daoism arose at about the same time, as a reaction to Confucianism's harshness, but providing a path for people and leaders to maintain harmony with nature, and thus avoid social unrest. Over time, Confucianism and Daoism have mostly merged, but in a political context, Confucianism is pro-government and Daoism is (usually peacefully) anti-government.

But both of them were still entirely Chinese. Buddhism was not, and provided a political pathway for peasants who wanted to oppose Chinese rule entirely. [32]

Buddhism began to enter China in the 300s AD, mostly in the region of northwestern China occupied by the Xiongnu tribes and the Tibetan tribes. [32]

The Xiongnu were a nomadic tribe from Central Asia that settled in today's Mongolia and repeatedly challenged the Han Chinese in northern China, at times victorious, for centuries beginning around 300 BC, until the Han completely vanquished them in 329 AD. From that point on, they were dominated by the Chinese. Historians have long suggested that the Xiongnu were the same tribe as the Huns that swept across Central Asia and attacked the Roman Empire, led by Attila the Hun. In the last quarter century, that view has become largely discredited. Older histories of China still refer to this northern tribes as "the Huns." [44]

The Tibetans were also a Central Asian ethnic group of tribes living since around 2000 BC on the high Tibetan plateau, occupying much of what is today western China. China claims that they've been part of China since the Han dynasty, although there was no identifiable Tibetan empire until the 600s. [45]

Both the Tibetans and the Xiongnu were subjugated by the Chinese, but they were "aliens," not Chinese. In the fourth century, when Confucianism and Daoism were flourishing in southern China, there was little interest in those two philosophies among the Xiongnu and Tibetans.

Buddhism had its own history, or course. Buddhism itself was a reaction to the harsh caste system of Hindu India, so Buddhism emphasized that all people are equal, and that those who are evil in this life will be punished in the next life. As Buddhism spread from India, it became the equalizer between the peasants and the kings.

Buddhism came to China overland and by sea during the Han dynasty. The missionary Buddhist monks who came from abroad with the foreign merchants found little approval among the Chinese gentry. They were regarded as second-rate persons belonging, according to Chinese notions, to an inferior social class. Thus the monks had to turn to the middle and lower classes in China. Among these they found widespread acceptance, not of their profound philosophic ideas, but of their doctrine of the after life. This doctrine was in a certain sense revolutionary: it declared that all the high officials and superiors who treated the people so unjustly and who so exploited them, would in their next reincarnation be born in poor circumstances or into inferior rank and would have to suffer punishment for all their ill deeds. The poor who had to suffer undeserved evils would be born in their next life into high rank and would have a good time. This doctrine brought a ray of light, a promise, to the country people who had suffered so much since the later Han period of the second century A.D. Their situation remained unaltered down to the fourth century; and under their alien rulers the Chinese country population became Buddhist. [32]

33.2. Secret Societies

Every government in every country has some popular opposition, and most of the time opposition can be expressed openly. But in China, opposition views of any kind have almost always been suppressed, often violently, with the violent suppression being justified, ironically, as being necessary to maintain an open, harmonious society. Thus, in China historically, underground anti-government protests have been forced to go underground, where they are referred to as "secret societies." [49]

Throughout China's history, two of the longest-lasting and most important of these were the White Lotus Society and the Triad Society. But there were also many short-lived secret societies.

At the beginning of the first century AD, Chih Met or Carnatian Eyebrow Rebels attempted to overthrow the government. Before going into battle, their members painted their eyebrows with vermilion, in order to make themselves more terrible in appearance. They were defeated by a ruse: They were drawn into an ambush of soldiers dressed and painted with the same painted eyebrows. By this stratagem the real Chih Meis were unable to distinguish friend from foe and in the confusion which ensued they were completely routed. [49]

The Yellow Turban rebellion, which played an important part in 184 AD in bringing down the Han Dynasty, as we've previously described, was a Daoism-based secret society.

Secret Societies were often splinter groups from established religions, usually Buddhism, but also Daoism and Protestantism. The splinter sects often had a messianic quality, with a zealous leader or at least a set of spiritual and supernatural beliefs that could be used to claim the much-desired Mandate from Heaven.

A good example occurred in 1102-1110, when a secret society was formed by a band of rebels, of whom Sung Chiang and Ln Chiin-i were the chiefs. According to the legends surrounding this secret society, 108 leaders took the following oath: [49]

> "We are one hundred and eight persons assembled in this hall who regard the Stars as our brothers, and Heaven and Earth as our father and mother, and though unlike in features we are alike in stateliness. We possess one hundred and eight hearts, and every heart is spotless. We bind ourselves to share each other's happiness and bear each other's sorrow. We arrange our names before Heaven and must not become a laughing-stock for men. The information of one day being found reliable must be acted upon with life-long courage. Should any of us harbor unkindness in our hearts and sever ourselves from our great cause, or say one thing at home and another abroad : or begin without continuing to the end, may Heaven above look down on us and devils by our sides watch us : may knives and swords cut our bodies and thunder-bolts blot out every trace of us; may we everlastingly sink in hell and not be reborn as human beings for a myriad ages. May such be the retribution of those of us who break our oath. Let Heaven and all the gods look down on us while we swear."

The oath being delivered they swore to it, and said they would meet in every life, and never, in any age, separate. They then drank each other's blood in wine. [49]

This is a good example of the supernatural nature of many Chinese secret societies.

33.3. White Lotus Society and Red Turban Rebellion (1351-68)

Early traces of the White Lotus Society can be found as early as the fourth century, with the rise of the Mahayana branch of Buddhism. It was, however, only during the middle of the 12th century that a Buddhist monk by the name of Cizhao founded the White Lotus Society. Some of this new movement's practices include the veneration of the Amitabha Buddha, the observance of the five Buddhist rules of discipline, and the illustration of Buddhist teachings via drawings and pictures. The teachings of this school were simple and easy to understand, and the use of images and drawings made the teachings of the Buddha accessible to all. As a result, many people became adherents of the White Lotus Society. [47]

The Chinese government did not officially recognize this new religious movement, but after the conquest of China by the Mongols, and the establishment of the Yuan Dynasty by Kublai Khan, the Mongol rulers acknowledged and even sponsored the White Lotus Society. [47]

In time, corruption grew in the Yuan government, and so the teachings of the White Lotus Society became more anti-government, with the notion that the Buddha would descend from Heaven to bring salvation to mankind. As the number of anti-government uprisings by its followers increased, the Yuan Dynasty outlawed the society early in the 1300s. [47]

The Yuan Dynasty was overthrown by the Red Turban Rebellion (1351-68), which used White Lotus Society teachings as its religious basis. White Lotus followers defeated the Mongols and established the Ming Dynasty. [47]

The Ming Dynasty became bureaucratic and corrupt by the beginning of the 1600s, and in the 1620s, small uprisings and rebellions occurred frequently. One rebel tried to employ the White Lotus Society to overthrow the dynasty, but he was slain in battle, and so the Society was inactive, as the Manchus invaded and conquered China in 1644. [49]

33.4. White Lotus Rebellion (1796-1804)

After that, the White Lotus Society was no longer as prominent, although it continued to exist and served as the religious underpinning of numerous small uprisings for centuries.

The Manchus (people from Manchuria) had invaded and conquered China in 1644 and formed the Qing Dynasty, but by the late 1700s had become increasingly bureaucratic and corrupt. The Manchus had suppressed the White Lotus Society, and the Manchu army had become quite skilled at suppressing small uprisings. However, a major White Lotus rebellion began in 1796, and spread too rapidly for the Manchus to put it down quickly. They were able to crush it finally by 1804, but ironically only by calling on Chinese militia to help. They crushed the uprising, but the White Lotus Rebellion had exposed the weakness of the Qing government, weakened the power of the dynasty, and diminished its wealth. [47]

33.5. Tibetan Buddhism

Tibetan Buddhism is a form of Mahayana Buddhism that developed in Tibet and spread to neighboring countries of the Himalayas. Tibetan Buddhism is known for its rich mythology and iconography and for the practice of identifying the reincarnations of deceased spiritual masters. [51]

Tibetan Buddhism is a form of Mahayana Buddhism combined with an indigenous religion called Bon. Because Tibet is a relatively isolated region in the Himalayas, Tibetan Buddhism has its own unique characteristics. Just as China was alternatively conquered by the Mongols and Manchus, Tibet was alternately an independent nation, or under the control of the Chinese, Mongols or Manchus. It was during the periods of Mongol governance that Tibetan Buddhism developed the theology of the Dalai Lama. [46]

A "lama" is a Buddhist teacher, a source of wisdom, and "dalai" is a Mongol word meaning "ocean." It is commonly believed that the Mongol leader Altan Khan originated the title Dalai Lama, meaning "Ocean of Wisdom," in 1578. The title was given to Sonam Gyatso (1543-1588), the third head lama of the Gelug school. Since Sonam Gyatso was the third head of the school, he became the third Dalai Lama. The first two Dalai Lamas received the title posthumously. The Dalai Lama leads the Tibetan Buddhists through his lifetime, and on his death is reincarnated in a new Dalai Lama. [50]

For over three centuries since then, a succession of spiritual and political leaders, each known as the Dalai Lama reincarnated from the previous Dalai Lama, has led the Tibetans from the capital city Lhasa. In the early 1900s, Tibet was an independent nation, but it was invaded and subjugated by Imperial China in 1950. [50]

In 1950, Tibetan Buddhists were led by the fourteenth Dalai Lama, who was born in Amdo, Tibet in 1935, and is still alive today (2018) at age 83.

Although Imperial China uses harsh, violent methods to control any non-indigenous religions, it has a particular problem with Tibetan Buddhism that is similar to the problem that it has with Catholicism. Since 1949, China has harshly suppressed any Catholic churches that pledge allegiance to the Pope in the Vatican, China is also terrified by the Dalai Lama because they fear he could lead an anti-government separatist rebellion.

The Dalai Lama is particularly sensitive to China's leadership, because the Dalai Lama has historically had a close relationship with the Mongols, and the Mongols conquered and subjugated the Chinese for several centuries. In November 2016, the Dalai Lama visited Mongolia's capital city Ulaanbaatar for a six-day visit. China's reaction was furious, imposing harsh economic sanctions on Mongolia by closing part of the border, leaving hundreds of trucks carrying copper and coal backed up on the highway in sub-zero temperatures. Mongolia's government was forced to apologize quickly for allowing the Dalai Lama to visit. [188]

After Imperial China's army invaded and subjugated Tibet in 1950, there were frequent clashes between China's army and Tibetans. These clashes culminated in Tibet's extremely bloody generational crisis war, the 1959 uprising in Lhasa, Tibet's capital city. [187]

In March 1959, China's army invited the Dalai Lama to visit army headquarters for a theatrical performance and tea. Many Tibetans believed that the army planned to kidnap the Dalai Lama and possibly kill him. On March 10, 300,000 Tibetans confronted China's forces, which some reports number up to a million. The Dalai Lama escaped to India, and in the war that followed, tens of thousands of Tibetan men, women and children were slaughtered by China's army. China also destroyed Lhasa's major monasteries along with thousands of their inhabitants. [187]

Allowing the Dalai Lama to escape has been a continuing humiliation to China. China keeps hoping he'll drop dead, but at age 83, he has refused to do so, so far. [187]

However, the successor to the Dalai Lama has become a major issue. The current Dalai Lama is the 14th. Each Dalai Lama is believed to be a reincarnation of the previous one. Each Dalai Lama can choose the person who will select the next Dalai Lama after he dies. The current Dalai Lama did select a six-year-old boy in the 1995 for this role, but the boy and his family were immediately kidnapped and killed by the Chinese government. [187]

China now wants to take control of the succession process, and essentially to select the next Dalai Lama when the current one dies. However, it's not likely that the Tibetan people will accept the choice of the Chinese government.

33.6. Qigong and Falun Gong

Xi Jinping and the CCP feel a special terror of the Falun Gong spiritual movement. This is an offshoot of Buddhism that began in 1992 in reaction to the government's bloody crackdown in Tiananmen Square. In 1999, when there were tens of millions of practitioners, China began to arrest, torture, rape and kill practitioners. Human rights advocates claim that hundreds of thousands of practitioners have been killed for the purpose of organ harvesting — to provide fresh organs to be transplanted into other people.

Qigong (pronounced ZHEE gong) is a general term referring to different sets of regulated, controlled breathing exercises. The major premise of Qigong is that all forms of life are animated by an essentially like-force called qi. Qi also means "breath" and "air", similar to the Hindu concept of prana. Invisible, tasteless and odorless, qi nonetheless permeates the entire cosmos. In general, Qigong is a set of gymnastics to promote health and cure diseases by combining physical exercises with self-massaging and regulated, controlled breathing. [54]

Qigong was originally named "Dao Yin," and these movements are known to have been part of the Chinese culture and Chinese medicine for several millennia. They were modified and adapted by several religions, including Daoism, and several branches of Buddhism. Qigong was often an identifiable element in anti-government uprisings. [55]

For that reason, the atheist Chinese Communist Party (CCP) outlawed Qigong when it came to power in 1949. Anyone practicing Qigong could be thrown in jail and tortured. [55]

However, a change occurred in the 1980s, when the CCP discovered a "scientific" explanation for the benefits of Qigong, and after numerous scientific studies were conducted by the China Qigong Science Association, Qigong became extremely popular and was taught openly. [55]

The Falun Gong anti-government movement began in 1992. It was founded by Li Hongzhi as a new combination of Buddhist teachings combined with qigong. Like other anti-government movements throughout China's history, Falun Gong has a spiritual and supernatural core that can be used to claim the much-desired Mandate from Heaven.

The word "Fa" is the Chinese translation of the Sanskrit word "dharma," meaning "Buddhist teachings." The word "Lun" translates the Sanskrit word "chakra," meaning "wheel." Therefore Falun is the dharma chakra, the wheel of

Buddhist teachings. In order to practice and propagate Buddhist teachings, one much turn the Falun, the wheel of the Buddhist teachings. [53]

Previously, in the chapter on Sun Tzu's "The Art of War," we described "qi," the "breath" or essence of life in Chinese thought. The word "gong" means skill, so "qigong" is "the skill of controlling qi." Putting these words together, "Falun Gong" means "a qigong method that spreads Buddhist wisdom." [53]

Falun Gong practitioners go farther than that. The falun is also a spiritual energy center in the lower abdomen. The gymnastic and regulated, controlled breathing exercises form an "energy ball" that massages the internal organs, relaxes the diaphragm (causing a deepening and slowing down of the breath), and awakens an awareness of the body's untapped potentials. [53]

By the year 1999, Falun Gong had attracted more than 70 million practitioners, and groups of practitioners were openly performing these breathing exercises in public gatherings. Between 1992 and 1999, he has established 39 general teaching centers with more than 1,900 instruction stations and more than 28,000 exercise spots in different provinces, autonomous regions, and municipalities. Thus, a complete and systematic organization was formed. [52]

At this point, the Chinese Communist Party (CCP) panicked and decided that Falun Gong was a major threat to them. In a way, this isn't surprising, given the CCP mentality. As we've described before, they were already in a state of high anxiety because of the collapse of the Soviet Union, and of course they were well aware that many dynasties had fallen from just the kind of mass movement that the Falun Gong represented. In a democracy like America, leaders don't like it when they lose elections to a populist movement, but they don't react by jailing, raping and torturing ordinary people in the populist movement. But the leaders of the CCP think that they're so special that no one can replace them, and anyone who tries deserves to be thrown into a pit and be hanged by his thumbs.

On July 22, 1999, the CCP banned Falun Gong and branded it an "evil cult" and "a threat to social stability," and any party member who believes in Falun Gong will "fall captive to idealistic heresies and finally lose credit as a communist." The CCP issued prohibitions against: [53]

- hanging or posting Falun Gong pictures, insignias, signs, or advertisements
- distribution of books, magazines, audio and video products, or Falun Gong promotional materials
- assemblies of people for the purpose of promoting Falun Gong
- activities such as parades, demonstrations, or petitions that protect or advertise Falun Gong
- any activities that incite the public to disturb social order through fabricating or distorting facts" or spreading rumors

- organizing, linking up, or directing activities that contest relevant government decisions. [53]

The Chinese embassy web site still describes Li Hongzhi, the founder of Falun Gong, as an evil figure who, by deceiving, has been seriously disrupting social order and sabotaging the hard-earned social stability of China. [52]

Li Hongzhi fled to America a couple of years before the sect was banned, and remains active. In a speech in June 2018 to thousands of followers at a stadium in Washington, he praised practitioners in China for keeping their faith despite repression by the "evil" party. [56]

Chapter 34. Christianity — Catholicism and Protestantism

By one estimate, China's Christian population has swelled from a few million in the early 1980s to 100 million this year – in comparison, the Communist Party has 90 million members. [60]

34.1. Catholicism

Catholicism has existed in China since the 600s AD. It was introduced first with Persian Nestorian monks in the seventh century, followed by Catholic Franciscans in the 12th century, and Jesuits in the 16th century. But the Chinese government has always considered it a major threat because it requires allegiance to an outsider — the Pope. [66]

Catholic scholars consider the first evangelization in China to be when an Assyrian monk, Alopen, brought Christianity across the Silk Road to what is now Xi'an, China, in the seventh century. The period was commemorated with the erection of the Nestorian Stone, a 10-foot-high tablet that describes Christian doctrine and ceremonies, the development of Christianity in China and the support Christianity was given by some emperors of the Tang Dynasty. The stone contains doctrinal, historical and eulogistic contents that most scholars say could be accepted by all Christians today. The stone is preserved in the Provincial Museum of Shaanxi, in Xi'an. [57]

A significant Christian presence occurred in the 13th century, when Mongols conquered China and founded the Yuan Dynasty. The Mongol court was open to Christian missionaries and even turned over the administration of parts of northern China to Christian tribesmen from Central Asia. From Rome, the pope also sent Franciscan missionaries in an effort to establish ties with Eastern Christians and to form an alliance with the Mongol empire. Italian merchants also founded some Catholic communities in major trading centers; among them were two brothers from Venice, Niccolo and Maffeo Polo, who brought along Niccolo's son, Marco. China's second period of Christian growth came to an end when its protectors, the Mongols, were expelled by the armies of the Ming Dynasty. [59]

Toward the end of the Ming dynasty, a new wave of Jesuit missionaries came to China. They established schools and hospitals, and more or less openly proselytized. The most prominent among these new missionaries was the Italian

Jesuit Matteo Ricci, who learned to speak and write Chinese and managed to become the first Westerner invited into the Forbidden City. [59]

By 1635, other religious orders began arriving in China, and soon the country was divided into territories for the religious orders. By 1700 the Catholic Church had about 200,000 Chinese members, but the so-called Chinese Rites Controversy stunted development of the church. Franciscans, Dominicans, Augustinians and members of the Paris Foreign Mission Society objected to Jesuit acceptance of Chinese rituals used to honor ancestors as well as to Chinese names for God. Papal decrees in 1715 and 1742 banned the Chinese Rites, and the emperor reacted by prohibiting the preaching of Christianity and by ordering the deportation of missionaries who did not use them. [57]

Once Mao Zedong came to power in 1949, the Chinese Communist Party (CCP) began cracking down violently on Catholics in China. The CCP insisted that anyone who wanted to remain Catholic had to split from Rome and the papacy. The Chinese state only recognizes the Patriotic Catholic Association, which was established by the Communist authorities in 1957. Meanwhile, the underground church which remained loyal to the Vatican was forced to hold mass in private. It functions in a legal gray zone, being more or less tolerated by the state depending on the political situation. [62]

34.2. Catholicism and Taiwan

The Sinicization document issued in April 2018 says the following: [42]

> "Religious groups and religious affairs are not subject to control by foreign countries.... This principle is a historic choice made by Chinese religious believers in the Chinese people's struggle for national independence and social progress, as Catholicism and Protestantism, which were known as foreign religions in China, had long been controlled and utilized by colonialists and imperialists." [42]

This rule has been particularly applied to Catholics, since Catholics have allegiance to the Pope in the Vatican, and the Pope is presumably either a colonialist or imperialist, as far as the CCP is concerned.

There are about twelve million Catholics in China. Seven million of them belong to the Chinese Catholic Patriotic Association, which is actually a CCP political organization, and is "Catholic" in name only. The other five million belong to "underground" Catholic churches, which are barely tolerated by the government, but which retain allegiance to the Pope.

In the last few decades, many Catholic priests in China have gone to jail for years and been tortured for their refusal to reject their vows and the guidance of the Pope.

So many of these people feel betrayed by the Pope, because the Vatican last year agreed to a "compromise" where the Vatican recognized seven bishops who were ordained by the CCP without the approval of the Vatican. There was another part to the deal, where China promised to accept some bishops in the "underground" church who had been ordained by the Vatican, but China has so far not fulfilled that promise.

It appears that the Vatican has completely given in to China in order to gain approval from China.

This has raised concerns in Taiwan that the Vatican will go further in giving in to China by cutting ties with Taiwan.

Taiwan has about 300,000 Catholics, and Taiwan, unlike China, has complete freedom of religion. The Taiwanese government apparently does not fear that the Catholics will form a secret society whose purpose is to overthrow the government, which is what has happened many times in China. If, as many fear, the Vatican withdraws its recognition from Taiwan, then the Pope will lose all credibility with the Catholics in Taiwan, and will be held in contempt by millions of people in "underground" Catholic churches in China.

34.3. Protestantism - Taiping Rebellion (1850-64)

Catholicism has been present in China since the 600s, and it's always been a big problem to China's government because of one major thing — the Pope. Chinese government officials cannot tolerate even the thought of Chinese people having allegiance to or being influenced by someone so distant and alien as the Pope in the Vatican in Europe. [66]

Protestantism arrived in China with missionary Robert Morrison (1782-1834), who arrived in China in 1807. At first, Protestantism must have seemed ideal to the Chinese rulers: If the people want Christianity, then let them be Protestants, and we won't have to deal with the Pope. But whatever love they felt for Protestantism, it must surely have disappeared after the Opium Wars and the Taiping Rebellion.

Hong Xiuquan was born in 1814. As a youth, he studied Confucianism assiduously, but he was unable to pass the civil service exams. In 1836, at age 22, Hong was exposed to Christianity through Edwin Stevens, a missionary. He was given a number of religious pamphlets, but according to reports he kept them but didn't read them. [67]

The next year, in 1837, he became extremely ill, and went to bed suffering from hallucinations. In his dreams, he went to heaven and learned from his father that demons were destroying humankind, and he led the fight that killed the demons. When he awoke after several days and told his dreams, he was thought to be insane. [67]

The First Opium War (1839-42) was an invasion by Britain to force China to open up to international trade. It had the side effect of allowing an influx of Christian missionaries from the West to enter the country and begin proselytizing. The war ended with the Treaty of Nanking, which was a major humiliation to the imperial government, damaging its prestige. [67]

This humiliation affected Hong, and in 1843 he returned to the Christian pamphlets he had received several years earlier. This changed his view of Chinese society and Confucian values, and convinced him that the father in his hallucinatory dreams of years before was the God of Christianity, and that he (Hong) was the son of God, and was the younger brother of Jesus. Hong Xiuquan became the very charismatic leader of the God Worshipping Society, in a domain of southern China called Taiping Tianguo (Heavenly Kingdom of Eternal Peace). He gained thousands of followers as his word spread, leading to the massive Taiping Rebellion. [67]

As in the case of many rebellions, the Taiping Rebellion was not a religious conflict. It was an ethnic conflict between the ethnic Hakka people, who were a marginalized subset of the Han Chinese with their own dialect, living in far southern China in Guangdong and neighboring provinces. In any rebellion, if the leader wants to motivate his followers to torture and kill the opposition then he needs to give them a reason, and often it's a religious reason, calling the opposition "nonbelievers" or "infidels." So Hong described Confucianism, Buddhism and Daoism as superstitions that blinded men to the true God. [68]

Hong was a member of the ethnic Hakka people, who had fled the Mongols in the 13th century and the Chinese at other times, and became an enclave treated as separate from regular Chinese society. They were primarily destitute laborers who sought protection from oppression. [67]

The Hakka's original place of residence was the Central Plains in the Huang (Yellow) River Basin. There were five mass migrations of Hakkas, the first starting as early as 200 BC in the Qin dynasty. The fourth Hakka migration took place at the beginning of Qing dynasty, as the Manchurian armies were sweeping southward. The fifth mass migration occurred as a result of the Taiping Rebellion. Since the 1700s, the Hakka have been migrating to Taiwan. [70]

Hong Xiuquan was able to mobilize the Hakka through the God-Worshippers. Hong did not begin with a desire to overthrow the Qing government. After realizing the connection between his dream and the Christian tracts, Hong was able to persuade people of his spiritual powers charismatically and through a strong religious conviction. He began to preach his message to the public and formed the Society of God Worshippers in an isolated area of eastern Guangxi province with one of his first converts in 1847. Hong's movement then spread and drew converts from the Hakkas in the province. By 1849, he had attracted around 10,000 followers. [68]

This mobilization of the Hakkas by the God Worshipping Society was the immediate precondition to the uprising and the founding of the Taiping Heavenly Kingdom. The imprisonment of six God Worshippers became the trigger that turned this religious movement into a rebellion, and led to the formation of the Taiping Army. [68]

As the Taiping Army and the Qing forces clashed, Hong proclaimed 1851 as the first year of the "Taiping Heavenly Kingdom." Hong's forces grew to 60,000, and he became more dictatorial. Hong declared that his followers should not "commit adultery or be licentious" and should reject "the cast of amorous glances, the harboring of lustful thoughts about others, the smoking of opium and the singing of libidinous songs" or be punished with beheadings. He decreed the separation of men and women, with beatings for anyone who defied him. [67]

In 1852, Hong conducted a series of bloody battles, giving him control of a large region. With two million followers, he conquered Nanking, and established an administration there. The Taiping army held Nanking for 11 years, until Hong was found dead in 1864. Nanking was put under siege and fell several months later, with the Taiping occupiers massacred. The Chinese imperial army eventually put down the rebellion with the aid of Western military advisers. Estimates vary, but the Taiping Rebellion is believed to have claimed between 20 million and 70 million lives, due to warfare and starvation, making it one of the deadliest conflicts in human history. [67] [59]

Part VII. China's 'Century of Humiliation'

Chapter 35. China today: Xi Jinping's view of the Century of Humiliation

35.1. Xi Jinping's speech to National Peoples' Congress (March 2018)

In March 2018, China's president Xi Jinping addressed a meeting of the National People's Congress (NPC), and announced that he was making himself an absolute dictator by modifying the constitution to allow him to be president without limitation.

The speech he gave was not a declaration of war on the West, but it was a lengthy justification for a future war with the West, at a time of China's choosing. Since then, Xi has ordered his army to prepare for war in the South China Sea.

Absolute dictators are not infallible gods. Hitler was an absolute dictator, but the Holocaust was a disaster for Germany as well as the world. Mao Zedong was an absolute dictator, but Mao's Great Leap Forward resulted in the deaths of tens of millions of peasants from starvation and executions, which was a disaster for China. The problem is that absolute dictators are no different than you and me in the ability to make bad decisions, but when you and I make a bad decision then someone stops us, but no one stops an absolute dictator. Just as Mao could launch the disastrous Great Leap Forward without being questioned, Xi could launch a disastrous war without being questioned. And Xi's speech indicates that's where he's headed.

A good example of how delusional Xi Jinping is can be shown from this claim in his final speech to the NPC:

> "China is a socialist state under the people's democratic dictatorship led by the working class and based on the alliance of workers and peasants, noting that all power in the country belongs to the people."

This doesn't even make sense. China is a "dictatorship," but there is nothing "democratic" about it. All of China's elections are predetermined, and peasants and workers are permitted to vote only for the chosen candidate.

Xi talks about the "rejuvenation" of China through "Socialism with Chinese characteristics." He calls this a "New Long March," alluding the Mao Zedong's

Long March that began in 1934 and marked the beginning of the extremely bloody 16-year Chinese civil war. According to Xi:

> "China has continuously striven for its dream of realizing great national rejuvenation for over 170 years.
>
> History has proved and will continue to prove that only socialism can save China. Only by sticking to and developing socialism with Chinese characteristics can we achieve the rejuvenation of the Chinese nation. ...
>
> Turning the grand blueprint for China into reality is new Long March. We need to uphold the great banner of socialism with Chinese characteristics. China's goal is to build a socialist, modern country by the middle of the 21st century." [7]

Once again, this has all the characteristics of a hysterical rant. China has repeatedly been destroyed by wars for millennia, and now China is trying socialism. That doesn't prove that Socialism can save China. To the contrary, Socialism has been a disaster for every country that's tried it, and the same is true for China.

A core part of Xi's delusion is the reference to 170 years, an allusion to the Opium War of the 1840s. The Chinese delusion is that the Opium War launched the "Century of Humiliation" that is causing all of China's problems today.

It would be more accurate to talk about "Many centuries of humiliation." China is a very weak, divided country that has often been overrun by foreigners from Asia. The Mongols ruled China from 1271-1368, and the Manchus ruled China from 1644-1911.

These invasions are by foreigners who bloodied and subjugated China for centuries, but Xi doesn't blame them. He blames the Opium Wars, whose purpose was to open China to foreign markets, not to subjugate China. You can blame the West for many things, including exploiting China commercially, but the humiliation imposed by the Mongols and Manchus was many times worse.

The Chinese also blame the West for the Taiping Rebellion. Why? Because it was led by Hong Xiuquan, a Chinese nutcase who believed he was the son of God and the younger brother of Jesus. Are the Chinese really dumb enough to believe that this was a Western invasion of some kind?

Finally, it's arguable that the West saved China from the Manchus. The Opium wars opened up China to foreign concessions, and educated the Chinese elite in European schools. If it were not for Western intervention, China might still be ruled by the Manchus today. (However, China might be better off, since the Manchus knew how to govern, but the Chinese obviously do not.)

I've gone into these details to show how Xi's speech to the NPC doesn't even make sense, and appears to be completely delusional. At the end of the speech, he added the following:

"Since ancient times, the realization of the great rejuvenation of the Chinese nation has become the greatest dream of the Chinese nation. The Chinese people are indomitable, and will persevere. They have the courage for bloody fights against their enemies, and they are determined to restore their former glory. Today the Chinese people are more confident and more capable, and closer than ever before of realizing the great rejuvenation of the Chinese nation." [8]

Besides being delusional, this is extremely ominous, since Xi is justifying in advance any pre-emptive military attacks that he may decide to make at a time of his choosing. And being an absolute dictator means that the decision will be entirely his, no matter how delusional.

Since he made that speech in March 2018, it's been increasingly apparent that the NPL speech was a major pivot point in Xi Jinping's foreign policy, in that he's increasingly impatient and wants to prepare for war. In fact, he said exactly that in a speech seven months later in October 2018. The speech was addressed to the army's Southern Theatre Command, which is the branch of the army that would be conducting war against Taiwan and in the South China Sea. Xi told them:

"It's necessary to strengthen the mission ... and concentrate preparations for fighting a war. We need to take all complex situations into consideration and make emergency plans accordingly.

We have to step up combat readiness exercises, joint exercises and confrontational exercises to enhance servicemen's capabilities and preparation for war." [9]

China's activities in annexing the South China Sea and building large, powerful military bases there are criminal activities, as ruled by the United Nations Tribunal in 2016. The United States, Australia, Japan and the UK have been sailing "freedom of navigation" ships through the South China Sea to publicly challenge China's illegal claims. China has reacted with furious temper tantrums to these freedom of navigation trips, as if Xi Jinping were an immature teenager. What his speeches increasingly indicate is that, immature teenager or not, Xi is moving from furious temper tantrums to full-scale war.

35.2. Do the Chinese have only themselves to blame?

The Chinese refer to the century beginning with the 1840 Opium War until the 1945 end of World War II as its "Century of Humiliation," by the Japanese and by Western powers. There are plenty of reasons for the Chinese to say this, and we'll discuss them here.

But there's an old saying: "Fool me once, shame on you. Fool me twice, shame on me." The meaning of that saying is that if you're humiliated, then you should learn a lesson and take steps to make sure it doesn't happen again, because it's your own fault if you're fooled a second time by the same person.

And this is the problem. The Chinese never seem to learn. They alternate between admiring the West and hating the West. Their foreign policy is a combination of admiration, imitation, deception and fraud, all at the same time. They never seem to figure out how to become, if not a "Western nation," then at least a nation that operates successfully within the global infrastructure that has evolved in the West. They're either being attacked by an outside nation or, as they are today, preparing to attack outside nations, which will cause a world war that will be a catastrophe for China and the entire world.

Chapter 36. China and Japan prior to 1840

36.1. The 'Middle Kingdom' and China's tributary system

Is there such a thing as a "national DNA"? We believe that Germany and Japan have changed their national behaviors and attitudes since the 1930s and World War II, but we also know that much of their behavior today is the direct result of centuries or even millennia of history. In fact, any generational crisis war is so devastating and so traumatizing that populations do undergo deep behavioral and attitudinal changes as a result. But there are always core attitudes that remain constant, and some of the behavioral changes that occurred as a result of the war sometimes come back decades later when the survivors of the war retire and die. In other words, a nation or society seems to have a core that does guides all behaviors back to a certain norm, just as the Law of Mean Reversion drives long-term financial values back to their historical trend lines.

Since at least the time of Confucius, and probably centuries earlier, China viewed the universe in three layers. The highest layer is the Kingdom of Heaven, China is the Middle Kingdom ("Zhongguo"), and the rest of the world, the non-Chinese, are the barbarians. The ancient Chinese were unaware of the growing civilizations in Europe and elsewhere — the Babylonians, the Greeks, the Romans, the Persians — and believed that China occupied the middle of the earth, surrounded by barbarians. [33]

As we've previously described, the Zhou dynasty developed the view that an Emperor of China could govern the Chinese only as long as he had a "Mandate from Heaven," and a poor leader would lose that Mandate, and could no longer govern. Later, Confucianism held that the social and political order, on the one hand, and the natural order on the other hand, were integrally connected, and that the primary function of the Emperor was to uphold this overall cosmological order. Therefore, the Emperor was held responsible not only for any major disturbances in the social and political life of his empire, but also for natural disturbances and calamities such as floods, droughts, earthquakes, etc. [33]

The exact boundaries of the Middle Kingdom were never precisely defined, as they could vary, depending on invasions and wars. Also, the definition of "barbarians" had some flexibility. As happened with the Mongol conquest in the 13th century and the Manchu conquest in the 17th century, the conquerors basically assumed the exalted location of the Emperors of China themselves. As long as the rulers governed according to Confucian principles, life accepted on as usual. [33]

Ancient China was not aware of the civilizations in Europe, but it was aware of its barbarian neighbors. Chinese textbooks say that the Middle Kingdom was the oldest and most advanced civilization in the universe, that it was at the very center of the universe, surrounded by lesser, partially Sinicized states in East and Southeast Asia, whose leaders must pay tribute to the Emperor of China. Having such a delusional view of the entire rest of the world has led frequently to belligerent and imperialistic policies, often based on a revisionist interpretation of history, in its diplomatic efforts to achieve foreign policy objectives, especially to extract territorial and diplomatic concessions from other countries. Almost every contiguous state has, at one time or another, felt the force of Chinese arms — Mongolia, Tibet, Burma, Korea, Russia, India, Vietnam, the Philippines, and Taiwan — and been a subject of China's revisionist history. [1]

36.2. European trade with China 1557-1838

Portuguese explorer Ferdinand Magellan arrived in the Philippines and claimed it for Spain in 1521, after which Magellan went on to Indonesia and other conquests. Direct maritime trade between Europe and China began with Portugal, starting roughly when the Portuguese leased an outpost in Macau in 1557. Other European nations soon followed, competing with Arab and Japanese traders. After Spain's conquest of Manila in 1565, trade between China and western Europe accelerated dramatically. [33]

Both the Ming and Qing dynasties were suspicious of maritime trade. Qing attitudes were also further aggravated through traditional Confucian disdain (even hostility) towards merchants and traders. Qing officials claimed that trade incited unrest and disorder, promoted piracy, and threatened to compromise information on China's defenses. In the late 1600s, Qing instituted a set of rigid and partial regulations concerning trade at Chinese ports, setting up four maritime customs offices and a sweeping 20 percent tariff on all foreign goods. These policies only succeeded in establishing a system of kickbacks and purchased monopolies that enriched the Chinese officials who administered coastal areas. [33]

Although foreign merchants and traders dealt with low stage Qing bureaucrats and mediators at specified ports and entry points, China's relations with foreign governments were organized through the tributary system. The tributary system affirmed the Emperor as the son of Heaven with a mandate to rule on Earth; as such, foreign rulers were required to present tribute and acknowledge the superiority of the imperial court. In return, the Emperor bestowed gifts and titles upon foreign emissaries and allowed them to trade for short periods of time throughout their stay within China. [33]

Foreign rulers agreed to these conditions because trade with China organized in this way was very lucrative and exempt from customs duties. But as time passed, Qing authorities became increasingly arbitrary in granting trade privileges, and assigned to European embassies a "tributary" status that became increasingly unacceptable to European nations, particularly Britain. [33]

From 1700–1842, Guangzhou, a port city near Hong Kong also known as Canton, came to control maritime trade with China, and this era became recognized as the "Canton System". The British empire conducted trade with China through its East India Company. [33]

Opium has been recognized in China since the 7th century and for centuries it was used for medicinal purposes. In the 17th century, the practice began (by copying the Europeans) of mixing opium with tobacco, resulting in increased use of opium. Although China began prohibiting opium in the 1700s, the usage kept growing.

In 1810, the Qing government issued the following decree: [33]

> "Opium has a harm. Opium is a poison, undermining our good customs and morality. Its use is prohibited through law. Now the commoner, Yang, dares to bring it into the Forbidden Municipality. Indeed, he flouts the law! Though, recently the purchasers, eaters, and consumers of opium have become numerous. Deceitful merchants buy and sell it to gain profit. The customs home at the Ch'ung-wen Gate was originally set up to supervise the collection of imports (it had no responsibility with regard to opium smuggling). If we confine our search for opium to the seaports, we fear the search will not be sufficiently thorough. We should also order the common commandant of the police and police- censors at the five gates to prohibit opium and to search for it at all gates. If they capture any violators, they should immediately punish them and should destroy the opium at once. As to Kwangtung and Fukien, the provinces from which opium comes, we order their viceroys, governors, and superintendents of the maritime customs to conduct a thorough search for opium, and cut off its supply. They should in no methods consider this order a dead letter and allow opium to be smuggled out!" [33]

The decree had little effect. The Qing government, seated in Beijing in the north of China, was unable to halt opium smuggling in the southern provinces. A porous Chinese border and rampant local demand only encouraged the all-too eager East India Company, which had its monopoly on opium trade recognized through the British government. There was a rapid rise in the 1830s, and in 1838 the Emperor ordered the arrest of opium dealers in Guangzhou, and all opium stocks destroyed. [33]

Public opinion in Britain, influenced by missionaries in China, was largely against the trade practices. The British government did nothing to stop the trafficking, since it was highly taxed, accounting for one-third of national revenue in the 1830s. [39]

When the British refused to end the trade, the Chinese government blockaded the British traders in their factories and cut off supplies of food. As well as seizing supplies in the factories, Chinese troops boarded British ships in international waters outside Chinese jurisdiction, where their cargo was still legal, and destroyed the opium aboard. In 1839, the government published an open letter to Queen Victoria questioning the moral reasoning of the British government: "Your Majesty has not before been therefore officially notified, and you may plead ignorance of the severity of our laws, but I now provide my assurance that we mean to cut this harmful drug forever." [33]

This situation is remarkable for its similarity to the situation in the United States today. The use of drugs is becoming an important issue today, especially opioids manufactured in China. Just as China couldn't close its border to opium Britain, the US is finding itself unable to close its southern border to drugs. I would imagine that many officials in China are taking a great deal of pleasure in seeing America today struggle with opioids from China, despite giving lip service to the opposite.

36.3. Japan's Tokugawa era or Edo era (1603-1868)

Japan was not involved in China's opium war, but the Japanese public was well aware of the war, and sympathetic to the Chinese side. Japan at that time was nearing the end of the Tokugawa era or Edo era (1603-1868), named after the Tokugawa clan that ruled for that period.

During the Tokugawa era, Japan was ruled as a collection of fiefdoms under the Tokugawa shogunate, a military dictatorship that was based in Edo (present day Tokyo). Society was highly stratified, with the feudal warlords, or daimyo, at the top, and the samurai warrior class just below them. Merchants, artisans, and farmers were at the bottom. The emperor, residing in Kyoto, in practice had very little political power. [74]

Japan was militarily weak, technologically backward, and almost entirely closed off from the outside world in a policy known as sakoku, or "locked-up country." Driven in part by a fear of the spread of Christianity after Europeans first landed in the 16th century, any contact with foreign countries was almost entirely limited to a port in Nagasaki. [74]

For two and a half centuries Japan under the Tokugawas thrived and urbanized with little foreign interaction. The Western powers were excluded with only the Dutch allowed limited access. Diplomatic dealings were maintained with Korea and China and a limited trade sustained with these countries as well. Internally, Japan was divided into 244 autonomous han, or estates of daimyo (landowners), sometimes called fiefdoms. There were a bewildering number of currencies and even the dialects spoken differed greatly. The social classes were fixed and free movement restricted. It was in many ways a world within walls. These restrictions were in part responsible for the extraordinary extensive duration of Tokugawa rule. [33]

However, it would be wrong to ignore the signs of change and development. Peace allowed trade and commerce to flourish within Japan, creating a national market with linkages among the han. In practice movement between han appears to have been frequent and both thoughts and people crossed han boundaries. These very changes in society and the inability of the political structure to creatively respond to the new situations generated thoughts and philosophies which laid the foundation for undermining the hegemony of the Tokugawa rulers. [33]

It is hard to have an overall assessment of the era. Though, we necessarily consider the question that whether the system lasted because of secure supervision and heavy repression or because of the lack of government interference. For instance, seclusion worked not because the world was also indifferent towards Japan. Likewise the towns and villages regulated themselves without much interference from the Bakufu.

Yet, the era laid the foundation for the development of modern Japan in that the skills and institutions urbanized the skill of the people to accept new thoughts and grasp the opportunities presented to them. [33]

The Tokugawa period contains a bit of a puzzle, as historians typically refer to it as two and one-half centuries of total peace. From the point of view of Generational Dynamics, that's impossible. The population always grows faster than the food supply, there is increased competition for food, water and other resources, and larger populations build houses on farmland, additionally reducing food production. So over time, wars and especially crisis wars are necessary to decide who will get the resources.

In fact, while Japan had no country-wide wars during this period, there were many regional uprisings. There were one or two regional rebellions or wars per year in the 1600s. The number kept increasing, and by 1790, there were more than six of these regional wars per year. [33]

The period 1477-1600 is known as the "Warring States" or "Sengoku" era of Japan, characterized by political anarchy and battles between warlords consolidating their holdings. The Warring States Era ended with a crisis war climaxing with the Battle of Sekigahara (October 20, 1600). [33]

The Battle of Sekigahara was won by the warlord Tokugawa Ieyasa, and the victory initiated the Tokugawa era, uniting Japan, and ending the Warring States era. In order to maintain peace and prevent a return to warring states, in 1615 Tokugawa Ieyasa instituted a system of political management known as the "baku-han" system. The "baku" part refers to the Bakufu, which is the central

Tokugawa government. The "han" refers to the 244 autonomous han, or estates of daimyo (landowners), sometimes called feudal fiefdoms. So the baku-han system described a federal relationship between the central government in Edo (Tokyo) and individual han fiefdoms across the country. It was a complete system that ensured that no rival power could threaten the supremacy of the central Tokugawa government, and contributed to its amazing longevity. [33]

In brief, the baku-han system was as follows:

- The emperor of Japan, living in Kyoto, was totally devoid of power. The emperor and his court should confine themselves to academic and cultural affairs
- The han would be permitted no contact with foreigners.
- There was restricted social mobility and frozen social dealings in the well-recognized shi-no-ko-sho system (samurai, farmers, artisans, and merchants).
- The feudal lords (daimyo) in the hans could not build or repair fortifications or contract marriages without the Tokugawa approval. They were forbidden to harbor fugitives from other fiefdoms. [33]

A crucial component of the baku-han system was the family "hostage" requirement.

At the core of Tokugawa strength was the armed might of some 60,000 armed vassals. The daimyo who were considered loyal to the Tokugawa were given strategically significant lands, while those daimyo who had been defeated in war had their fiefdoms confiscated or forced to change provinces. Throughout the 1600s, more than 200 daimyo lost a part of all of their territory for offences. [33]

The central Tokugawa government maintained social control by means of a family hostage system. It required the daimyo (warlords) to reside in the capital city Edo (present day Tokyo) for defined periods. When a daimyo was absent from the capital, he had to leave his family as hostage to ensure his loyalty to the Shogun. This family hostage system seems to have been successful in protecting the Tokugawa central government. [33]

The baku-han system was backed by a complex administrative structure that gave the Tokugawa control of crucial regions of foreign dealings, coastal defense, and key urban centers as well as the sources of gold and silver. There were still "uprisings" and rebellions in regions across the country, and some of these must have been generational crisis wars in those regions, but at least for the central government, this system brought two and a half centuries of peace and stability. [33]

The visit by American Commodore Matthew Perry in 1853 forced Japan to open its ports to the west. It particularly resulted in the end of the restriction against contact with foreigners, and brought down the baku-han system, leading to the Meiji Restoration — the return to government by the emperor.

Chapter 37. Clash of civilizations: China vs Japan after the Opium Wars (1840-70)

What China calls "the century of humiliation" begins with the first Opium War in 1839.

37.1. The 'bad marriage' of China and Japan

Prior to 1840, China and Japan were always acutely aware of each other, but kept themselves distant from one another, except to interact with one another, and Russia, in respective invasions of Korea. In addition, nations in the West were already economic, political and trading powerhouses, having gone through the Industrial Revolution (1760-1840). But China and Japan were almost completely oblivious to what was going on outside of their own countries.

As we described earlier, the Chinese won a major naval victory over Japan that must have been well remembered by both the Chinese and the Japanese. In the 1500s, Korea was a tributary state to China, meaning that Korea paid gold and slaves to China in return for guarantees of defense from outsiders (i.e., Japan). Japan attacked Korea in 1592 and 1597 with the intention of using it as a stepping stone to the conquest of China. In 1597, the Koreans, supported by the Chinese, won a brilliant naval victory against the Japanese, using technologically advanced "turtle ships," believed to be the world's first ironclad warship. [85]

This was a major humiliation for Japan, and after 1870 must have been a major motivation to become technologically more advanced than China, and to get revenge against China. On the other side, it was a glorious, incredible victory for the Chinese, and must have been a major reason for overconfidence, obviating the need for further technological development.

In fact, the 1597 war must have been so climactic for Asia that it may well be the most important battle in Asia for the entire millennium (prior to WW II), just as the 1453 Ottoman conquest of Constantinople was possibly the most important battle in Europe. After the 1597 war, both China and Japan went into a kind of "hibernation," with the Manchus taking charge in China, and the Tokugawa clan taking charge in Japan.

What happened to China and Japan after 1840 is almost comparable to a bad marriage where a couple get married despite the fact that they hate each other, and then get a divorce and fight to the death over custody of the kids.

During the years 1850-70, both China and Japan suffered extremely bloody generational crisis wars. In both cases, the core reasons were the same: China and Japan were forced to deal with the West, which meant that centuries of out-of-date policies and decaying bureaucracies in the Qing and Tokugawa governments, respectively, had to collapse. So it may be said that the Opium Wars and the Commodore Perry visits "triggered" these generational crisis wars, but these wars had to happen one way or another.

During this period, both China and Japan were forced to open up to the West. This was a "clash of civilizations" with the west for both countries, but it was also a clash of the Chinese and Japanese civilizations with each other. Opening up to the west was highly significant for both countries individually, but it was also highly significant for them jointly: Their destinies became thoroughly entangled, bringing them to their next generational crisis wars — World War II in Asia.

An outline of the steps is as follows:

- Britain demanded that China open up to trade. China refused, and Britain forced China to open up with the First Opium War (1839-42).
- The Japanese public followed the Opium War, and pictured it as the barbaric British using superior military strength to defeat brave, heroic Chinese soldiers led by the corrupt and inept Qing government.
- American Commodore Matthew Perry demanded that Japan open up to trade. The Japanese, having watched what happened in China, agreed without any war (1853-54).
- From 1870-1945, China and Japan were in acrimonious competition with each other. Continuing with the bad marriage analogy, Japan was the battering husband who was part of the evil patriarchy (the West), controlling the money by being economically developed, and controlling the children (Korea, Taiwan, Shandong, Manchuria) by being militarily superior. China was typical victim feminist, becoming weaker and more victimized by constantly turning against the evil patriarchy (the West) that she despised.
- Continuing with the analogy, after the World War II the two sides were completely divorced, and are once again living apart with as little interaction as possible. Japan accepted the restraining order, which prevents militarization except for self-defense. China has remained a victim feminist, still despising the evil patriarchy (the West), and has remained backward economically, blaming the West for its troubles.
- In 1978, China finally "opened up," a century after Japan opened up. Unfortunately, we now understand that this opening up was based on dishonest trade policies and stealing intellectual property.
- Japan has become a responsible member of the international community. China is repeating the disastrous mistakes that Japan made prior to the

war — looking for revenge against China, militarizing, and turning into barbaric monsters. China will bring an even worse disaster to itself and the world than Japan did in World War II.

History doesn't repeat itself, but it rhymes.

37.2. First Opium War (1839-42)

China's history is filled with wars — rebellions, invasions, and being invaded. But the Anglo-Chinese wars, or Opium Wars, were different. They were an enormous culture shock because they were against a nation that refused to pay tribute, and which they were unable to defeat.

The Opium Wars of 1840-42 are portrayed as a shameful incident in British history, and indeed, they were shameful because of the trade in opium. But as usual, the situation is far more complex, and much of its outcome would have had to occur anyway, even if opium hadn't been involved.

From Britain's point of view, the issue was open and free trade. The Industrial Revolution had made England had become the world's greatest industrial power. Ever since Adam Smith had published *Wealth of Nations* in 1776, many policy makers believed that free trade was best for everyone, and adopted what might be called "the imperialism of free trade." And so forcing free trade on a backward China was a natural extension of the expansionist policies of the day. [34]

It should first be pointed out that China was not entirely isolated from international commerce in the early 1800s. It's just that all commerce was controlled as tightly as possible by the national and regional governing entities, especially by the imposition of stiff import tariffs. On the export side, tea, silk and porcelain was getting very popular in Europe, and all this resulted in a fairly substantial balance of trade deficit, which favored China's rulers. With the Industrial Revolution proceeding in England, Europe and America, it was only a matter of time before someone found some product or products that would be irresistible to the Chinese, and would reverse the balance of trade deficits. [34] 97-99

Unfortunately, that product turned out to be the addictive drug opium, which not only became very popular, but also was not subject to import tariffs, since it entered the country via pirates in violation of Chinese laws. Opium was already illegal in England, so it's hard for the English to claim innocence in selling opium to the Chinese. But complicating the issue were the attitude of the Chinese rulers, who treated outsiders as inferiors, and who did not always live up to the terms of previous treaties.

The war was triggered in 1840 when the government confiscated tons of opium and blockaded the ports, not just to opium but also to all outside trade.

That was too much for the English, who declared war. The First Opium War lasted until 1842, when Beijing was forced to capitulate and sign a treaty. The treaty forced all ports open to foreign trade and gave Hong Kong to the British. (It was not returned until 1997.)

Britain was offended anyway by the tributary system, and in response to the destruction of opium stocks and actions taken against traders, the British government sent expeditionary forces from India, with a large portion of British force consisting of Indian 'sepoys' (soldiers) in the British Indian Army. The British press made almost no mention of this, but Japanese reports on the war color-coded the British forces as "White and black men" or "black and white barbarians." Contemporary English writings about the first Opium War did not ignore plunder and pillage by the British side; and, indeed, collections in British museums today contain some of the better samples of this loot. The word loot itself comes from the Hindu "lut," and entered popular usage as an English word at this time. [76]

The British forces ravaged the Chinese coast and dictated the conditions of resolution. The Treaty of Nanking in 1842 not only provided the means for further opium trade, but ceded territory including Hong Kong, unilaterally fixed Chinese tariffs at a low rate, granted extraterritorial rights to foreigners in China, and granted diplomatic representation. [33]

The British victory in the Opium war was politically divisive in both the UK and US, because it appeared to have as its purpose to force an opium addiction on the Chinese people. In Britain's House of Commons, a young MP William Ewart Gladstone wondered if there had ever been "a war more unjust in its origin, a war more calculated to cover this country [Britain] with permanent disgrace, I do not know, and I have not read of." The Foreign Secretary, Lord Palmerston, replied through saying that nobody could "say that he honestly whispered the motive of the Chinese Government to have been the promotion of moral habits" and that the war was being fought to stem China's balance of payments deficit. In other words, the motive was not to make the Chinese people addicted, it was to make money, with addiction being a side effect. [33]

In America, John Quincy Adams commented that opium was "a mere incident to the dispute... the cause of the war is the kowtow — the arrogant and insupportable pretensions of China that she will hold commercial intercourse with the rest of mankind not upon conditions of equal reciprocity, but upon the insulting and degrading shapes of the dealings flanked by lord and vassal." [33]

Not surprisingly, the Treaty of Nanking in 1842 is considered by China to be the first of the "unequal treaties," and the beginning of the "century of humiliation." [39]

37.3. Taiping Rebellion (1852-64) and the rise of Marxism

We've previously discussed the Taiping Rebellion and its connection to a Protestant missionary movement. Karl Marx was aware of the Taiping Rebellion, and in 1853 he wrote an article, published in the New York Daily Tribune, describing the rebellion in progress and blaming it on the Opium War, and its effect on the "barbarous and hermetic" Chinese people:

> "Whatever be the social causes, and whatever religious, dynastic, or national shape they may assume, that have brought about the chronic rebellions subsisting in China for about ten years past, and now gathered together in one formidable revolution the occasion of this outbreak has unquestionably been afforded by the English cannon forcing upon China that soporific drug called opium. Before the British arms the authority of the Manchu dynasty fell to pieces; the superstitious faith in the eternity of the Celestial Empire broke down; the barbarous and hermetic isolation from the civilized world was infringed; and an opening was made for that intercourse which has since proceeded so rapidly under the golden attractions of California and Australia. At the same time the silver coin of the Empire, its lifeblood, began to be drained away to the British East Indies.

> Up to 1830, the balance of trade being continually in favour of the Chinese, there existed an uninterrupted importation of silver from India, Britain and the United States into China. Since 1833, and especially since 1840, the export of silver from China to India has become almost exhausting for the Celestial Empire. Hence the strong decrees of the Emperor against the opium trade, responded to by still stronger resistance to his measures. Besides this immediate economical consequence, the bribery connected with opium smuggling has entirely demoralized the Chinese State officers in the Southern provinces. Just as the Emperor was wont to be considered the father of all China, so his officers were looked upon as sustaining the paternal relation to their respective districts. But this patriarchal authority, the only moral link embracing the vast machinery of the State, has gradually been corroded by the corruption of those officers, who have made great gains by conniving at opium smuggling. This has occurred principally in the same Southern provinces where the rebellion commenced. It is almost needless to observe that, in the same measure in which opium has obtained the sovereignty over the Chinese, the Emperor and his staff of pedantic mandarins have become dispossessed of their own sovereignty. It would seem as though history had first to make this whole people drunk before it could rouse them out of their hereditary stupidity." [69]

This was published five years after Marx's book Communist Manifesto was published, and one can see from Marx's rant on the rebellion that he was trying to sell his politics and trying to sell books. Despite Marx's contemptuous view of the Chinese and "their hereditary stupidity," the Chinese have largely adopted Marx's view, because it fits their own political view that everything that happened in China for the entire century was the fault of the West. [68]

However, the Taiping rebellion was no more caused by a Protestant missionary than was the White Lotus rebellion sixty years earlier, or the Communist Revolution seventy years later. These are generational crisis wars that occur regularly, in one form or another, as populations grow and compete with each other for food, water, land and other resources.

Marx lived in Europe and America, far from China, and knew little about what actually was happening. In particular, he did not know about the Hakka ethnic group, which led the Taiping Rebellion against the mainstream Han Chinese, as we described in an earlier chapter. [68]

So the Taiping Rebellion, or something like it, would have occurred with or without the Opium wars. But since one occurred shortly after the other, that's enough for a Chinese mind in a state of paranoia to conclude causality and, in particular, to blame the West for the Taiping Rebellion, as part of its Century of Humiliation.

The Taiping Rebellion did not mean the end of Manchu rule or the Qing dynasty. The bureaucracy of the Manchu government prevented any real modernization to occur, with the result that China was many decades behind Japan, leading to repeated humiliation, and eventually to World War II.

37.4. Japanese view of China's Opium War

Japan was not involved in China's opium war, but the Japanese public was well aware of the war, and sympathetic to the Chinese side. Popular Japanese media at the time described the virtuous and valorous Chinese soldiers in heroic terms, describing victories against the British that never actually occurred. China's humiliating defeat at the hands of the British was blamed on China's corrupt and inept Qing government. [76]

Even worse, the Japanese media accounts suggested that the Tokugawa government in Edo was equally corrupt and inept, and incapable of countering a similar threat. Furthermore, the suggestion was that Japan would receive a visit similar to the one that Britain made to China. One Japanese writer wrote, "I have read Western books, and I know that their rapacious greed is not satiated.... I am afraid that their violent blaze has not burnt out." [76]

The distorted Japanese view of the war is not surprising because reports of the war sent back to the Qing government described major defeats as great, heroic victories. According to historian Julia Lovell, "The reality was that the further away you were from Beijing the freer the rein you had. It was really quite flabbergasting how fast and loose some of the emperor's servants played with the truth." [79]

37.5. American Commodore Matthew Perry comes to Japan

As we've explained, China's Taiping Rebellion may have been triggered by the Opium Wars, but would have occurred in one way or another even if the Opium Wars hadn't occurred. The same is true of Japan's Meiji Restoration, which would have occurred even if Commodore Matthew Perry had not visited Japan in 1853. So even though Perry's visit set off in Japan a period of acrimonious debate and political uprisings that lasted until the Meiji Restoration in 1868 (and sometimes afterwards), the Tokugawa government and in fact the entire baku-han system was badly out of date and due to collapse anyway.

The mid-1800s was a time when America, Europe and the West took increased interest in opening up markets in East Asia, so it's not surprising that there was a similar event to the Opium Wars occurring in Japan.

In July 1853, Perry visited China, and then Okinawa, and then entered Edo Bay with his squadron of two frigates and two sloops. He presented a letter from the US president demanding, somewhat imperiously, that Japanese ports be opened to foreign trade. [33]

As we've described the Japanese media reports of China's Opium War made it clear that the Chinese soldiers may be brave and heroic, but they could not stand up to the military firepower of British gunboat diplomacy. The widespread belief was that Japanese soldiers could not stand up to Commodore's fleet. In addition, it was believed that Japan's Tokugawa was just as corrupt and inept as China's Qing government. The Japanese gave in so quickly to Perry's ultimatums to open the country, reflecting their acute grasp of their military vulnerability. [76]

In 1854 Perry returned with greater force and after negotiations the Treaty of Kanagawa was signed on March 31, 1854. The treaty opened the ports of Shimoda and Hakodate where U.S. ships could refuel and provision their ships. The United States was also allowed to post a counselor agent at Shimoda. In October, Japan concluded a similar treaty with Britain, then with Russia, and with Holland in 1855. The US envoy Townsend Harris came to reside in Shimoda in 1856, and concluded the Harris Treaty on July 29, 1858, which opened the ports of Kanagawa and Nagasaki, and other ports. [33]

To understand the acrimony of the political debate at the time, think of the acrimony in the political debates in the US and Europe today. It had been a core rule of the baku-han structure that no foreign interaction was permitted, except through the central government. The Tokugawa government wanted to reject the treaties, even though it might risk war, because accepting them could result in social disorder. The treaties were signed, and social disorder did occur. The port openings undermined not only the foreign interaction rule, but the entire baku-han structure. [33]

The arrival of Americans was a culture shock to Japan. Since Japan had been "locked up" and Christianity forbidden for centuries, the introduction of this American culture must have been both extremely exciting and extremely terrifying. Americans demanded to trade. They showed off new customs (including the scandalous tendency of women to accompany men to public events). They practiced the previously forbidden Christian religion. And they even took sides in Japan's political disputes, which must have been baffling to the Japanese. [75]

Perry's visit disrupted the political centers and caused conflicts that at first were political and later were actual clashes. These clashes culminated in the Boshin War ("Year of the Dragon War", January 27, 1868 - April 11, 1869), a civil war where the rebel samurai army, led by Saigo Takamori, forced the surrender of Tokugawa Yoshinobu, the fifteenth and last Tokugawa shogun. This was the Meiji Restoration, as power passed from the Tokugawa leaders to the Meiji Emperor, a teenager at the time. [75]

As an aside, the samurai army leader Saigo Takamori later regretted his role and turned against the emperor. He died in 1877, as portrayed in the 2003 movie "The Last Samurai" (even though there were many other samurai still alive at the time).

37.6. Second Opium War (1856-60)

The Treaty of Nanking in 1842 was violated on both sides, especially through smuggling of opium and other goods illegally, to avoid paying customs duties. Furthermore, the Chinese still refused to accept foreign ambassadors and obstructed the trade clauses of the treaties resulting in disputes over the treatment of British merchants in Chinese ports and on the seas led to the Second Opium War and the Treaty of Tianjin. [33]

By 1856, the British were becoming impatient, and wanted to open additional Chinese ports for trade. The British wanted to renegotiate the Nanking Treaty to (among other things) open all of China to their merchants and legalize the opium trade. [39]

The context in 1856 is that the Crimean War had just ended. It had yielded no victor and had been a disaster for all participants, including Britain and France. However, the British were still in another war, and were engaged in heavy fighting against the Moguls in India, so only a small British force was involved in the war with China. China, on the other side, was completely distracted by the ongoing Taiping rebellion. [32]

In October 1856, a Chinese-owned Hong Kong-registered vessel was seized by Chinese authorities in Guangzhou and the crew were imprisoned on allegations of piracy. Rumors spread at the time that the British flag had been pulled down during the incident, an act that was regarded as an insult to the British Crown. (It was later revealed that the registration of the vessel had expired at the time of the incident.) Using this as an excuse, the British attacked Guangzhou and waged war on China. Meanwhile, a French Mission Entrangere priest was executed in Guangxi, and this incident prompted the French to join the military campaign. The first phase of the war concluded with the Treaty of Tianjin in June 1858. [77]

However, hostilities were renewed in 1860. The British and French were reinforced and launched an attack on the capital. They occupied Beijing and looted and burnt down Yuan Ming Yuan (the Old Summer Palace). The war ended with the signing of the Convention of Beijing ceding Kowloon Peninsula to Britain. Clauses also included the legalization of the opium trade, the opening of Tianjin as a treaty port, and permission for British ships to carry indentured labor to the Americas. [77]

Similar arrangements with France and America soon followed, These later became recognized as the Unequal Treaties, and the Opium Wars represented the start of China's "Century of humiliation". [33]

In Britain, the looting of Yuan Ming Yuan (the Old Summer Palace) was considered a heroic act by the British soldiers, as it was thought to prove their superiority over the Chinese. The soldiers tore into the multiple rooms, grabbing and smashing the delicate porcelain and jade works of art, ripping down the elaborate textiles, looking for gold and silver and anything else they could get their hands on. Soldiers burned the libraries and rare books, then all of the palaces: the temples, halls, pavilions, the Jade Fountain Park, and the grand Main Audience Hall with its marble floor. Much of the loot is still on view today in British museums. [78]

37.7. The 1860 Treaty of Tianjin (Tientsin) and international law

The Second Opium War was settled in 1860 with the Treaty of Tianjin, which was a bitter lesson in international law which the Chinese remember to this day. Because the terms of the 1860 had enormous effects on China's history, and still influence China's attitudes and behaviors today, it's worthwhile to list the terms of the agreement and some of their consequences.

There were many clauses humiliating to the Chinese, but possibly the most significant was the "Most Favored Nation" clause. This provided that if China granted any privilege or concession to any other nation, then that privilege or concession would automatically be granted to Britain as well. This proved to be enormously dangerous to international relations, because it made it impossible for China to conduct normal foreign relations where policy might favor one nation over another. Other clauses included: [32]

- Opium trade would be legal again.
- Numerous additional ports would have to be opened to European traders.
- Kowloon Peninsula, the strip of land on mainland China that was opposite Hong Kong, was ceded to Britain. Hong Kong itself had already been ceded to Britain in 1842.
- A British diplomatic legation would be established in Beijing. Previously, China had forbidden any embassies or diplomatic missions.
- British ships would have freedom of navigation along the Yangtze River.
- British subjects would be permitted to purchase land in China.
- British subjects who committed crimes would be subject to British courts, not Chinese courts.
- Christian missionaries would be permitted throughout the country. [32]

An immediate result of this treaty, especially because of the Most Favored Nations clause, was that China's balance of trade became increasingly adverse, since China could neither stop the importation of European goods nor set a duty on them, and on the other hand China could not compel foreigners to buy Chinese goods. This meant that China had to repay the loans by giving economic privileges, but then, under the Most Favored Nation clause, had to grant the same privileges to other states that had made no loans to China. This created a vicious spiral, which in the end could only bring disaster. [32]

37.8. Consequences today of the 1860 Treaty of Tianjin (Tientsin)

In 1860, China was still embroiled in the Taiping Rebellion, which was far more traumatizing to the public than the Treaty of Tianjin, whose terms were written in the language of international law that the Chinese were unfamiliar with and didn't really understand anyway. So it's not surprising that the decade of 1860-70 was actually a period of goodwill and cooperation between China and the Western powers. [33]

But as the decade progressed, the Chinese began to understand the language of international law, and the consequences of the treaty that they had signed under duress. The Treaty had contained a provision for the revision of the Treaty after ten years. The Chinese worked with a sympathetic American representative in Beijing, Anson Burlingame, to undertake a mission to convince the western countries to renegotiate the treaty. However, in 1870, the British government rejected any revision of the treaties. This rejection, more than the treaty itself, marked the beginning of an era of friction and disagreement, and was a major turning point in relations between China and the West, with significance to this day. [33]

China today is openly contemptuous of international law. They laughably point to international law when it can be invoked against a Western nation to serve their purpose, but when international law is invoked to point to any of China's many domestic and international crimes, they simply ignore it.

China's leaders today in the Chinese Communist Party (CCP) have adopted a collection of barbaric policies that can almost always be traced back to the 1860 Treaty at Tianjin and the 1870 refusal by Britain's government to renegotiate.

- An obvious example is that the opioid crisis in the United States is being driven by opioid manufacturing and export from China, according to US officials. Chinese officials deny this, but I would be very surprised if Chinese officials aren't enjoying this situation and doing everything they can to encourage it. [149]

- When China joined the World Trade Organization (WTO) in 2001, the hope was that China would stop cheating at trade. Instead, not only has China continued to cheat, but has purposed taken advantage of WTO rules to cheat even more aggressively. This is revenge for the trade rules imposed on China in 1860.

- China's claims to the South China Sea are a hoax and have been eviscerated by the United Nations Permanent Court of Arbitration in The Hague in a ruling that thoroughly humiliated the Chinese Communist Party. But the ruling has only emboldened the CCP to use military force by building numerous military bases. This is revenge directly for the Opium Wars and for using gunboat diplomacy to force China to sign unfair agreements.

- The CPP isn't only getting revenge on Western nations. In using "debt trap diplomacy" in its contracts with dozens of countries to build infrastructure for the Belt and Road Initiative (BRI), China uses bribes and corruption to impose contractual debts that can't be repaid. In the case of Kenya, China's contracts stipulates that in case of default, China can take possession of any of Kenya's assets, within the country or abroad. This is revenge for the unfavorable economic terms that the 1860 contract imposed on China. [190]

- Also, the same BRI contracts impose the restriction that all disputes will be settled by courts in China. This is revenge for contract terms that require certain legal actions to be resolved by British courts. [190]
- China is arresting, beating, torturing, raping and executing millions of Muslim Uighurs in Xinjiang province, with the apparent intention of committing genocide and ethnic cleansing. China also arrests, beats, tortures, rapes and executes many Catholics, Protestants and Buddhists for their religious beliefs. This behavior is revenge for a treaty term permitting Christian missionaries to proselytize throughout the country. This barbaric Chinese behavior began in 1870 with the Tianjin massacre of the Catholic Orphanage, described below.

37.9. Tianjin Massacre of Catholic orphanage (1870)

One of the major irritants for China in this era was, ironically enough, not the overtly military or economic behaviors of the Western powers, but the behaviors of several individual missionaries and missionary organizations. [33]

The treaties signed after the First Opium War permitted France to have missionaries in China, while the Treaty of Tianjin of 1860 permitted the missionaries to reside and carry out their behaviors anywhere in China. Unlike the Western diplomats and the Western merchants who congregated in selected enclaves in the ports or in Beijing, the missionaries spread out everywhere. [33]

This was especially true of the Catholic missionaries. They existed for the main part in small towns and villages, where they intervened actively in the local social and political life. They freely acquired property, and were permitted to re-inhabit lands confiscated from the Jesuit missionaries in the 18th century. They converted local residents to their faith, and then proceeded to attempt and extend their own legal immunity in criminal cases to these converts. They also set up schools and orphanages which were viewed with deep suspicion through the local population, who often whispered that the missionaries were kidnapping their children. Particularly obnoxious to the local people and the local authorities was the tendency of the missionaries to appeal to their own countries for protection and support on every issue. It became increasingly general for the gunboats of the foreign powers to sail threateningly up the rivers in an illustration of force, whenever there was a conflict between the missionaries and the local people in some part of China. [33]

Until 1860, popular hostility to the foreigners was mainly confined to the Canton region in the era between the two Opium Wars. After the 1860 Treaty of Tianjin, the hostility began to spread rapidly throughout the interior of China. The 1860s saw innumerable clashes that resulted in physical violence and killings. [33]

This culminated in the Tianjin Massacre of 1870, a day of rage where rumors of kidnapping of Chinese children led local residents to an attack on a French Catholic orphanage. In the rampage, 21 foreigners and 30 Chinese Christians were killed. Both the orphanage and a nearby cathedral were burned down. The nuns in the orphanage were dragged from their hiding places, stripped naked, repeatedly stabbed, and set on fire. [80]

The incident caused worldwide shock. It might have led to a declaration of war on China by France. In the end, China avoided war only because the French were too busy that year losing the Franco-Prussian War to muster the forces necessary to chastise Tianjin. [80]

The 1870 Tianjin Massacre was by no means the last such disagreement over missionaries. There were frequently such riots and clashes, some especially serious, like the riots in Sichuan province in Western China in 1886 and those beside the Yangtze River valley in 1891. The latter almost led to a combined Western military invasion of China, which was prevented mainly through the complete capitulation by the Qing government. This capitulation was widely resented by the Chinese, reinforcing anti-Qing sentiments, as well as the feeling that the Qing rulers were "traitors" who were in league with the foreigners. Anti-foreign currents therefore became intertwined with movements for the overthrow of the dynasty. It was precisely such a fusion of currents that led to the explosive Boxer Rebellion of 1898-1900 in North China. [33]

Chapter 38. China and Japan prior to World War I (1870-1912)

38.1. European scramble for East Asia (Late 1800s)

I'm using the phrase "Scramble for East Asia" to mimic the phrase "Scramble for Africa," which is commonly used by historians to describe the frenetic competition among European nations to colonize Africa during the late 1800s.

In the 1850s it was discovered that malaria could be controlled with quinine, and by the 1870s the floodgates opened. The "Scramble for Africa" pitted England, Belgium, France, Portugal, Italy, Spain and Germany against each other to snap up as much of the continent as possible. By the mid 1890s the Scramble had just carved up just about all of Africa, and in 1914, all of black Africa except Ethiopia and Liberia were European colonies.

So I've decided to use the phrase "Scramble for East Asia" to describe similar frenetic activity by Japan, Russia, Europe and the United States to gain influence in east Asia, especially in China, Korea, Taiwan, and various islands.

38.2. The Joseon Dynasty in Korea (1392-1910)

Korea physically separates two powerhouses, Japan and China, and Korea has always been something of a ping-pong ball between them.

Korea was unified under the Joseon Dynasty starting in 1392, and almost immediately became a tributary state of China under the Ming Dynasty. The phrase "tributary state" doesn't really apply to today's world, but prior to the 1800s it referred to a relationship between a weak nation (tributary state) and a powerful state (hegemon state). The tributary is not a colony of the hegemon, since it is not governed or controlled by the hegemon. But the weaker nation would pay a substantial tribute to the stronger nation, often consisting of gold or slaves. In return, the stronger nation would guarantee not to invade the weaker nation, and might even promise to defend the weaker nation from a foreign enemy. Despite invasions by the Japanese, Korea remained a tributary state until Japan finally succeeded in colonizing Korea in 1912. [85]

The first two major Japanese invasions occurred in 1592 and 1597, when Japan's samurai army general Toyotomi Hideyoshi. He had succeeded in unifying Japan in 1591, and wanted to go beyond that victory to the conquest of China, and to do so by going through Korea. [86]

Backed up by hundreds of thousands of troops, Hideyoshi began his first invasion of Korea in 1591. The Koreans were caught by surprise, and their swords were no match for the Japanese muskets. There emerged Korean Admiral Yi Sun-sin, who directed the building of a fleet of modern warships, led by an innovative warship called "kobuk-son" — the "turtle ship," so named because of its shape and because it is believed to be the world's first ironclad warship. [86]

In 1592, Yi's navy was able repeatedly to defeat Japan's navy on the sea. On land, guerrilla forces sprang up all across Korea to fight the Japanese, and in February 1593, a Ming Chinese army of 50,000 soldiers entered the war against Japan. This led to negotiations that froze the war in place (something that today would be called an "armistice"). [86]

38.3. Imjin Wars and Battle of Myongnyang (Myeongnyang), October 26, 1597

Arguably the most important European battle in the last millennium was the fall of Constantinople and the defeat of the Christian Byzantine Empire by the Muslim Ottomans in 1453.

In my opinion, the most important battle in Asia in the last millennium (prior to WW II) was the Battle of Myongnyang (Myeongnyang), October 26, 1597, because it was so crushing and so climactic that it must have been well remembered for centuries — with glee by the Koreans and Chinese, and with humiliation by the Japanese — and would have had a strong visceral influence on the events following the Taiping Rebellion and the Meiji Restoration.

Japan's samurai army general Toyotomi Hideyoshi launched his second invasion of Korea on August 27, 1597, with a force of 100,000 soldiers in 1000 ships to reinforce the 50,000 troops left behind in Korea after the first invasion. The climax was the Battle of Myongnyang on October 26. Admiral Yi's small contingent of twelve ships destroyed 133 Japanese vessels without any Korean losses. Admiral Yi achieved this victory after luring the Japanese fleet into a narrow channel and using the swift currents to his advantage. This victory prevented the Japanese navy from entering the Yellow Sea and re-supplying its army trying to advance towards Seoul. [86]

Even today, the battle is described in almost mythic terms, as an almost miraculous victory by Korean Admiral Yi Sun-sin, who used a tactical innovation called a "crane wing formation": [87]

"Crane Wing formation (Kor. Hagik-jin): One of Admiral Yi's famed naval formations. A Turtle-ship sails at the head of a detachment of board-roofed ships, which spread out in a curved line resembling a crane's wing when they come close to the enemy, thus surrounding him before attacking. The renowned Japanese history journal, History Studies (May 2002) revealed that Admiral Togo's 'T' formation, used in the Battle of Tsushima, was based on this formation by Admiral Yi." [87]

Joseon Korea became increasingly isolationist after defeating Japan, and was defeated in 1637 by an invading army by the Manchus in China who were forming the Qing dynasty, forcing Josean Korean to submit once more to a tributary relationship with the Manchus in China. This relationship continued until the Sino-Japanese war of 1894-95. [85]

After the climax of the war, both China and Japan went into a kind of "hibernation," with the Manchus taking charge in China, and the Tokugawa clan taking charge in Japan, and Korea in a tributary relationship with China. This stayed the same for over three centuries, until Britain initiated the Opium Wars with China, and American Commodore Matthew Perry visited Japan in 1853, forcing it to open its ports to the west.

38.4. Japan's revolutionary social, political and economic changes

After the Meiji Restoration of 1868, the Meiji period did not end until the death of the emperor in 1912. During the Meiji period, Japan experienced significant social, political and economic change — including the abolition of the feudal system and the adoption of a cabinet system of government. In addition, the new regime opened the country once again to Western trade and influence. [71]

The Meiji period was revolutionary for Japan. Far from expelling the barbarians (i.e., the West), the new leaders embraced everything foreign. The "Charter Oath" of April 1868 that formally ended feudal rule decreed that "knowledge shall be sought throughout the world". Some 50 officials set off on a tour of America and Europe to learn about administration, trade, industry and military affairs. On their return, and with foreign help, they threw their country into a race to catch up with the West, building railways and roads, pursuing land reform that redistributed the old feudal estates, establishing a Western-based system of education, and building a modern army. In 1889 the Meiji constitution, modeled along Prussian lines, enshrined both representative government and reverence for the emperor. Together, these were potent steps. Japan humiliated China in the Sino-Japanese war (1894-95), and then humiliated Russia in the Russo-Japanese war (1904-5). It was these two war victories, in particular, that cemented Western respect for Japan, and why Japan today is considered to be a "Western" country, even though it's in East Asia. [73]

These radical changes occurred in Japan after the Meiji Restoration, but no such radical changes occurred in China after the Taiping Rebellion. Whereas the young Meiji emperor encouraged changes, the old Chinese Manchu leaders resisted it. The result was that, in the last half of the 19th century, there was rapid modernization and westernization in Japan, while China remained a feudal culture with little modernization.

During this same period, Japan began its military buildup, and became increasingly imperialistic, leading to World War II. Much of Japan's military buildup victimized China, playing a major part in China's "Century of Humiliation."

A final point is that many historians look at this issue in reverse. I've been asking why China couldn't keep up with Japan in the late 1800s, but many historians point out that it was Japan that was unique, not China. At that time, only America, the European states and Japan were developed nations. The Meiji Restoration was the starting point for Japan's success. From Japan's perspective, Japan was able to adapt to the times and emerge as a modern nation during the mid-nineteenth century, while other Asian nations, including China, were not able to replicate the feat. [72]

So here's a philosophical question: Which of the two followed a better strategy? Was it the Japanese, who modernized quickly and turned into a military imperialist power which, allied with Nazi Germany, brought about global catastrophe in World War II? Or was it the Chinese, who remained feudal much longer, did not westernize, and remained a victim of the Japanese, leading to global catastrophe in World War II?

38.5. Japan's relations with Korea, China, Russia, Britain and France

Korea had been the staging ground for earlier invasions by both China and Japan against one another — for example, Kublai Khan's invasions of Japan in 1274 and 1281 or Toyotomi Hideyoshi's attempts to invade Ming China via Korea in 1592 and 1597. [88]

China's hegemony over Joseon Korea continued from 1392 into the 1870s. In 1876, Japan, China and Korea signed the Treaty of Kanghwa, giving Japan and China equal access to Korea, but in practice, Korea was still principally dependent on China. [33]

In the 1870s, two political factions developed within Korea itself, one which was conservative, anti-foreign and supported China, while the other was progressive, pro-foreign and pro-Japanese. An anti-Japan riot in 1882 served as an excuse for Japanese troops to enter Korea. With both Chinese and Japanese forces in Korea, a worsening situation was possible. In 1884, the pro-Japanese forces attempted a coup d'état, where many of the King's ministers were killed. War was prevented when an agreement, the Li-Ito Tianjin Agreement, was signed in March 1885, calling on both China and Japan to withdraw their troops. [33]

Russia was also interested in Korea (as it is today), and offered to train Korean soldiers in return for use of a Korean port, but was stopped through protests by both China and Japan. A crisis was averted until 1893. [33]

Numerous foreign powers, including Britain, France, Germany, Russia and the United States, were also watching the situation carefully. Japan had signed treaties with Britain and France that they considered unequal, and wanted to revise them as early as 1873. Britain set, as a condition, that Japan adopt Western legal codes, including the penal code, the code of criminal procedure, a civil code, and the commercial code. The main concern was that Westerners accused of personal or property crimes in Japan would be tried according to Western legal codes. [33]

Finally, Foreign Minister Aoki Shuzo went to London and signed a treaty on July 16 1894, to take effect in 1899. Similar treaties with other powers also followed. This procedure helped Japan move one step forward towards her goal of achieving an equality with the Western powers. [33]

So as Japan and China competed for influence and trade in Korea, the competition did not take place in isolation. There were many other countries in the Scramble for East Asia, including Russia, Britain, France, Germany, Russia and the United States.

38.6. First Sino-Japanese war - 1894-95

War between China and Japan over Korea had been prevented in 1885 by the Li-Ito Tianjin Agreement, which had even brought about the withdrawal of Chinese and Japanese troops. However, it was only a temporary truce.

A competition in trade became increasingly important. Textiles imported by Korea from China were mainly Western manufactured goods imported into China and re-exported to Korea. These goods rose from 19% of total Korean imports in 1885, when the Li-Ito agreement was signed, to 45% in 1892. In the meantime, Japan was developing a contemporary textile industry, and was exporting these domestic goods to Korea in competition with the Western goods re-exported from China. [33]

A crisis occurred in 1894, when a Korean terror group called the Tonghaks, who were in the anti-foreigner, pro-Chinese political faction, launched the Tonghak Insurrection, and asked for military assistance from China. Japan invoked the 1885 Li-Ito agreement and sent its own troops to Korea. Hostilities began on July 28, 1894, with the Battle of Asan. [88] [33]

Much of the First Sino-Japanese War was fought at sea, where the Japanese navy had an advantage over its antiquated Chinese counterpart, mostly due to the Manchu Empress Dowager Cixi reportedly siphoned off some of the funds meant to update the Chinese navy in order to rebuild her Summer Palace in Beijing. [88]

After numerous humiliating defeats, Qing China was forced to sue for peace. On April 17, 1895, Qing China and Meiji Japan signed the Treaty of Shimonoseki, which ended the First Sino-Japanese War. China relinquished all claims to influence over Korea, which became a Japanese protectorate until it was annexed outright in 1910. Japan also took control of Taiwan, the Penghu Islands, and the Liaodong Peninsula. [88]

In addition to the territorial gains, Japan received war reparations of 200 million taels of silver [10 million kilograms of silver] from China. The Qing government also had to grant Japan trade favors, including permission for Japanese ships to sail up the Yangtze River, manufacturing grants for Japanese companies to operate in Chinese treaty ports, and the opening of four additional treaty ports to Japanese trading vessels. [88]

However, this did not come without loss. Approximately 35,000 Chinese soldiers were killed or wounded in the battle while Japan only lost 5,000 of its fighters and service people. All of this was a huge humiliation to China, and is remembered today as part of the "century of humiliation." [88]

Alarmed by the quick rise of Meiji Japan, three of the European powers intervened after the Treaty of Shimonoseki was signed, after the Sino-Japanese war, April 17 1895. Russia, Germany, and France particularly objected to Japan's seizure of the Liaodong Peninsula, which Russia also coveted. The three powers pressured Japan into relinquishing the peninsula to Russia, in exchange for an addition 30 million taels of silver. Japan's victorious military leaders saw this European intervention as a humiliating slight, which helped spark the Russo-Japanese War of 1904 to 1905. (A tael is a weight used in East Asia, fixed in China at 50 grams or 3/4 oz) [88]

38.7. Significance of the First Sino-Japanese war (1894-95)

Although the First Sino-Japanese war is almost completely forgotten today in the West, the war was enormously significant to the countries involved, and that significance continues to influence policies today in China, Japan and Korea.

This was the first overseas battle fought by a Japanese army for 300 years (since the Battle of Myongnyang, October 26, 1597). This was also the beginnings of Japanese imperialism that led decades later to World War II in the Pacific.

That history undoubtedly weighed heavily on the minds of the Japanese after they surrendered in 1945, and agreed to a new constitution that permitted use of an army only for defensive purposes. It also explains why there is such resistance in Japan today to use the army overseas even for "collective self-defense," which permits the use of the army overseas in defense of an ally (the United States). Japan declared war on China on August 1, 1894. [90]

The Sino-Japanese war (1894-95) was the first big test for China and Japan in the late 1800s, following both their civil wars that climaxed in the 1860s. In fact, this war was a dramatic illustration of the enormous power of Japan's modernization under the young Meiji emperor, contrasted with China's refusal to modernize under the bureaucratic Manchus.

The most significant difference was that China's supposedly powerful navy turned out to be outdated when facing the smaller, faster Japanese ships. [89]

The technological gap was the deciding factor in the battle in the waters of Dadonggou. The Chinese ships were bulky and slow. It took 15 minutes for the Zhenyuan's 12-inch cannon to fire once, while the smaller cannons used by the Japanese could fire five times a minute. [89]

Much of the First Sino-Japanese War was fought at sea, where the Japanese navy had an advantage over its antiquated Chinese counterpart. Japan cut the Chinese supply lines for its garrison at Asan by a naval blockade, then Japanese and Korean land troops overran the 3,500-strong Chinese force on July 28, killing 500 of them and capturing the rest — the two sides officially declared war on August 1, 1894. [88]

According to Chen Yue, president of the Chinese Naval Historical Institute, for thousands of years China viewed its 11,180-mile coastline as a "natural Great Wall." According to Chen, "Before Great Britain, no nation had invaded China via the sea, so, as a result, the army held most of the resources and senior posts because inland threats were far more common." [89]

38.8. Treaty of Shimonoseki on April 17, 1895

After six months of war, Japan was in full possession of all of Korea and the rich Liaotung peninsula in Manchuria. China was forced to sign the Treaty of Shimonoseki on April 17, 1895, on terms greatly favorable to Japan, giving Japan hegemony and dominance over Korea and the Liaotung peninsula, control of Taiwan, and commercial access to Chinese ports and municipalities. [33]

Japan's occupation of Taiwan continued until 1945. With regard to the Liaotung peninsula, France, Germany and Russia were opposed to giving Japan control, as doing so was considered a threat to peace. The European powers forced Japan to give the Liaotung peninsula back to China in return for a monetary indemnity, but Japan's government experienced a backlash in the form of criticism and virulent nationalism which supported an aggressive foreign policy. [33]

Japan's humiliation turned into fury and open animosity when China then granted a 25 year lease of the Liaotung peninsula to Russia, for use as a warm water port (Port Arthur), as well as rights to build a railway linking it to Vladivostok. Germany and France also granted rights to France and Germany. [33]

38.9. Open-Door Policy (1899-1900)

By the end of the 1800s, China's government under the Manchus was in chaos. Different nations especially European nations, were negotiating with different warlords for trading privileges, with no recognition of China as a sovereign nation. [100]

This was the time of the "Scramble for Africa," where European colonial powers had carved up Africa into individual colonies, each governed by a European nation. In the 1890s, there was a danger that the European nations would try to carve China up into pieces in the same way.

The United States was not actively involved in this jockeying for power in China until it came into possession of the Philippines after the Spanish-American war (1898). The US took a greater interest in China after that, and wanted both to protect its own interests and to prevent China from being carved up by the European powers. [100]

President William McKinley and Secretary of State John Hay endorsed an "Open-Door Policy." Under this policy, there would be a free, open market and equal trading opportunity for merchants of all nationalities operating in China. For the United States, which held relatively little political clout and no territory in China, the principle of non-discrimination in commercial activity was particularly important. Hay called for each of the powers active in China to do away with economic advantages for their own citizens within their spheres of influence, and also suggested that the Chinese tariffs apply universally and be collected by the Chinese themselves. Although the other powers may not have agreed fully with these ideas, none openly opposed them. [101]

Although the Open Door policy was challenged by the Boxer Rebellion, it remained official U.S. policy towards the Far East in the first half of the 20th century. [101]

38.10. Boxer Rebellion (1900)

In the late 1800s, it must have occurred to many Chinese, especially the ruling Manchus in the Qing Dynasty, just how dangerous religions can be to them. The Qings had come close to being overthrown by two religion-based rebellions — the White Lotus Rebellion (1796-1804), based in the Buddhist White Lotus Society, and the Taiping Rebellion (1852-64), based in the Protestant God-Worshippers Society.

For the ethnic Chinese, these observations went farther, blaming all foreign influences. The influx of Protestant missionaries had led to the Protestant God-Worshippers Society, which led to the horrific Taiping Rebellion. The Opium Wars had opened up China to trade with the West, which led to intense international trade competition, and growing influence from the West. All of these foreign influences had weakened China, and permitted the Japanese victory in the Sino-Japanese war, another major humiliation. In contrast to Japan, which embraced the West, China shunned the West and retained its feudal ways. [39]

From the point of view of generational theory, a society follows certain prescribed patterns in the decades following a bloody, brutal generational crisis war like the Taiping revolution. What always happens first is that when the war ends, the survivors do everything possible to make sure that nothing like it happens again. This often means making undesirable compromises or imposing stifling rules on society.

After 20 years pass, a new generation has grown up with no personal memory of the war, and their voices are heard through objecting to the compromises and rules that their parents had set up to prevent a new war. This results in what is popularly called a "generation gap" or a "generational split." In generational theory it's called a "generational awakening," because the first generation growing up after a generational crisis war begins to make itself heard.

In America in the 1960s, these demonstrations became antiwar protests, anti-discrimination protests, pro-environment protests, and sexual freedom protests that were characterized by events where boys burned their draft cards while girls burned their bras.

In China, the survivors of the bloody Taiping Rebellion must have decided that the best way to proceed was to open their markets completely to foreigners, granting concessions as needed, and trusting the foreigners to keep their promises to help China become an important nation in the world, and in time to become a world leader in international commerce.

The generation gap occurred in the attitudes towards these foreigners. In China's Awakening era, young people began protesting the presence of these foreigners, whom they blamed for their troubles. In the late 1890s, a Chinese secret group with the evocative name "the Society of Righteous and Harmonious

Fists" had begun carrying out regular attacks on foreigners and Chinese Christians. This group performed calisthenics rituals and martial arts that that they claimed would give them the ability to withstand bullets and other forms of attack. Westerners referred to these rituals as shadow boxing, leading to them being given the nickname "Boxers." [102]

Although the Boxers came from various parts of society, many were peasants, particularly from Shandong province, which had been struck by natural disasters such as famine and flooding. In the 1890s, China had given territorial and commercial concessions in this area to several European nations, and the Boxers blamed their poor standard of living on foreigners who were colonizing their country. [102]

The Boxer Rebellion began in 1900, when the Boxer movement spread to the Beijing area, where the Boxers killed Chinese Christians and Christian missionaries and destroyed churches and railroad stations and other property. On June 20, 1900, the Boxers began a siege of Beijing's foreign legation district (where the official quarters of foreign diplomats were located.) The following day, Qing Empress Dowager Tzu'u Hzi (or Cixi, 1835-1908) declared a war on all foreign nations with diplomatic ties in China. [102]

Incited by the Boxers, on June 21, 1900, the Empress Dowager of the Qing declared war on the world. She besieged the Beijing legations of England, France, Germany, Austria, Italy, Russia, Japan, and the United States. These eight nations responded with an expeditionary force of 20,000 men who freed the legations, sacked Beijing, and occupied its palaces. The Celestial Court submitted to the onerous terms of the conquest, including an indemnity four times the Qing revenue, to be paid through 1940. The Boxer Rebellion was popularized in the U.S. by the movie *55 Days At Peking* with Charlton Heston and Ava Gardner, which showed China brought to its knees in humiliation by a small foreign force. [39]

Once again, a contrast with Japan was in order. By 1900, Japan was fully engaged with Western commercial interests, while China was effectively declaring war on them. Like the Sino-Japanese war, this was an illustration of the superiority of the rapid modernization and westernization in Japan, compared to China's continuing feudal culture with little modernization.

38.11. Anglo-Japanese Alliance (1902, 1905, 1911)

There were three separate treaties in the Anglo-Japanese Alliance, signed respectively on 30-January-1902, 12-August-1905, and 13-July-1911. Each treaty replaced the previous one, and the last one was formally replaced on 17-August-1923. [104]

It is one of the conclusions of this book that after 1870, the Japanese continually and repeatedly bested the Chinese in all ways — militarily, diplomatically, economically, and in governance. The Anglo-Japanese Alliance brought Japan as an important nation in the international community, and firmly established Japan's diplomatic superiority to China, which continually remained hostile to the Western world.

That Japan became militarily superior to China was already clear by 1890. Japan had already defeated China in the First Sino-Japanese war (1894-95), making several territorial gains, and receiving numerous commercial concessions as well as war reparations of 200 million taels (10 million kg) of silver. [88]

After the war, Japan continued its military buildup. By 1900, using the money from the reparations, China purchased a first-class foreign-built fleet of six battleships. The last of these, the British-built Mikasa, was perhaps the most powerful vessel afloat in its class. [105]

Diplomatically, China declared war on the world in 1900 through the Boxer Rebellion, blaming their poor economic situation on Christianity and other foreign influences.

But Japan went in the opposite direction signing, in January 1902, a treaty with Britain called the Anglo-Japanese Alliance. The Japanese public were unrestrainedly overjoyed by this treaty, because it proved that Japan had emerged from its feudalism to become a major international member, worthy of an alliance with a European power. They saw it an offensive-defensive alliance (koshu domei) in the same mold as the Franco-Russian alliance and the triple alliance of Germany, Austria and Italy, except that its bounds were unlimited. [105]

You can argue about the motivations of Britain and Japan in making this alliance — Japan wanted agreement with its commercial concessions in Korea and China, while Britain wanted to use the alliance as a lever to prevent Japanese militarism and expansionism. And you can argue about the motivations of China in declaring war on the world in the Boxer Rebellion. But whatever the motivations, this moment confirms a major contention of this book, that Japan consistently and repeatedly defeated China in international diplomacy.

38.12. Russo-Japanese War (1905)

The Russo-Japanese War held great international significance, as it was the first all-out war of the modern era in which a non-European power, Japan, defeated one of Europe's great powers, Russia. As a result, the Russian Empire and Tsar Nicholas II lost considerable prestige, along with two of their three naval fleets. Popular outrage in Russia at the outcome helped lead to the Russian Revolution of 1905, a wave of unrest that lasted more than two years but did not manage to topple the tsar's government - until the Bolshevik Revolution 12 years later. [91]

For the Japanese Empire, of course, victory in the Russo-Japanese War cemented its place as an up-and-coming great power, particularly since it came on the heels of Japan's victory in the First Sino-Japanese War of 1894-95. Nonetheless, public opinion in Japan was none too favorable. The Treaty of Portsmouth did not grant Japan either the territory or the monetary reparations that the Japanese people expected after their significant investment of energy and blood in the war. [91]

Just as important is the contrast between Japan and China, since the "invasion" by the West. Since the Meiji Restoration, Japan embraced the West and even became part of the West, to the point where it could win two major wars. China, by contrast, had the Boxer Rebellion that rejected the West, and instead paints itself as a victim of the "Century of Humiliation."

38.13. Japan's annexation of Korea (1905, 1910)

The Japanese finally got revenge for being forced by the Western powers to give up the Liaotung peninsula (Manchuria) to Russia after the Sino-Japanese war and the Treaty of Shimonoseki in 1895.

US president Theodore Roosevelt presided over the Peace Conference at Portsmouth in the USA, which began on August 10, 1905. President Roosevelt had warned France and Germany that if any moves were made against Japan, he would support Japan. The terms of the Treaty of Portsmouth were: [33]

- Recognition of Korean independence and Japan's paramount political, economic and military interests.
- Transfer to Japan of Russia's rights and bases in Liaotung and of the South Manchurian Railway.
- Withdrawal of all foreign troops from Manchuria except Japanese railway guards. Cession of south Sakhalin and special fishing rights in adjacent waters to Japan.
- Non-interference through Russia and Japan in events which China might take for commercial and industrial development of Manchuria. [33]

After the Treaty of Portsmouth, Korea appealed to the US to avoid giving control of Korea to Japan, but to no avail. In November 1905, the US closed the American Legation in Seoul and declared Korea a Japanese protectorate. The Korean King appealed to The Hague in 1907 and the New York Tribune commented that Japan's right to act as it did in Korea was "at least as good as that of Russia, France, England or any other Power to deal as they have with subject nations," referring to the numerous colonies of those nations. [33]

Japan appointed a distinguished statesman, 65 year old former prime minister Ito Hirobumi, to be Resident-General of Korea. Ito had hoped to avoid annexation and carry out the Korean government reforms with the co-operation of the Korean Court and Korean Executives. In particular, he hoped to force on Korea the same reforms that had led Japan toward modernization. However, his paternalistic attitude towards Korea, and his contempt for Koreans as well as their traditions and culture thwarted his attempts, and made him a hated figure. A conscious policy of obstructionism was followed. When Ito resigned his office in June 1909, he realized that his policies had failed. [33]

In October 1909, Ito was in Harbin China, and was assassinated by a Korean. Ito's death served as an adequate pretext to annex Korea. On August 22, 1910, Japan and the Korean King signed the Treaty of Annexation. Like Taiwan, Korea also became a colony and Japanese iron rule in Korea suppressing all demands for independence earned for her the everlasting hatred of Koreans. They remained colonies until 1945. [33]

Japan, however, was not successful an annexing Manchuria along with Korea. The USA had years earlier adopted the Open Door Policy, meant to keep trade with Asian countries open to all. Britain and the USA had financed Japan in the Russo-Japan war with the understanding that the Open Door policy would be honored, and they now believed that Japan wanted to use its military to close Manchuria off from foreign trade. In 1909 this infuriated segments of the Japanese government, which were split into two factions, for and against cooperating with Britain and the USA. The factions against cooperation won out, and despite objections from Britain and the USA. At the same time, during this period, Russia also developed economic interests in Manchuria. Once the Chinese Revolution of 1911 occurred, and there was no longer any stable government in China, Japan and Russia attained virtual control of Manchuria, closing the door to the West. [33]

38.14. Sun Yat-Sen and the Republican Revolution (1911)

An awakening era climax is often called a "Velvet Coup" or "Velvet Revolution" of "bloodless coup" because a historic change of government occurs with no bloodshed. A recent example was the peaceful 1989 uprising that ousted the Communist regime in the former Czechoslovakia. In America, the 1974 ousting of president Richard Nixon was a climax that firmly established the political victory of the younger post-war generations over the survivors of World War II.

It's also possible for the Awakening climax to go in the opposite direction. A massive peaceful student uprising in 1989 in China's Tiananmen Square was crushed by a huge massacre of thousands of student protesters, resulting in a bloodbath, establishing the victory of the Chinese Communist Party over the younger generations.

So the Boxer Rebellion was supposed to get rid of the foreigners, but instead ended in one more major humiliation of the Chinese by foreigners. Throughout the 1900s decades, the European states, Russia, America, and Japan regarded China as a field for their own plans, and in their calculations paid scarcely any attention to the Chinese government. Foreign capital was penetrating everywhere in the form of loans for railway and other enterprises. If it had not been for the mutual rivalries of the powers, China would long ago have been annexed by one of them. [32]

By 1910, a new revolutionary movement began in the south, directed against all foreigners — and this time that included the ruling Manchus in the north. The Manchu government had been so weakened, and there was no real opposition to the revolutionaries. [32]

In February, 1912, Dr. Sun Yat-sen, the hero of the revolution, took 15,000 troops and visited the tomb of the founder of the Ming dynasty (A. D. 1368-1644) situated outside the city of Nanking, the temporary capital of China. Surrounded by military and naval officers, "at high noon [he] stood reverently before the ancient altar at the tomb, while the master of ceremonies announced to the spirits of the departed monarch that China had been recovered by the Chinese people, that the power and prestige of the Manchus had been annihilated, and that a free republic had been established." [118]

China's gentry backed the revolutions, so on February 12th, 1912, the Manchu government renounced the throne of China and declared the Republic to be the constitutional form of state. That was the end of the Qing Dynasty, which had ruled since 1644. And it was the end of a 2000 year Imperial form of government. [32]

There's an interesting contrast between the Mongols, who ruled China during the Ming Dynasty (1368-1644), and the Manchus, who ruled China during the Qing Dynasty (1644-1911). The Mongols have survived as an ethnic community, and today there is still a country known as Mongolia, whose population is mostly descendants of the same Mongol tribes that ruled China. But the Manchu community did not survive, especially after Japan's invasion of Manchuria in the 1930s. The Manchu language is now dead, their lands settled by Han Chinese. The Manchu culture that expanded China's borders and established its longest individual reigns was extinguished. [39]

The Chinese empire had been conquered by about 120,000 Manchus, a force so small that Chinese are still embarrassed. Manchus viewed the Han Chinese whom they had subjugated as inferior, which the Han deeply resented. Initially, the Manchus were not allowed to mix with the Han, and intermarriage was forbidden. After the Republican Revolution in 1912, the Manchus were still blamed for society's problems. To survive, individual Manchus passed themselves off as Han if they could. Today, there are about 3 million Manchus. [Other sources say 10 million.] They can be found throughout China, but live mostly in Beijing, in the northeastern provinces of Liaoning, Jilin, Heilongjiang and Hebei, and in Inner Mongolia. [103]

In the 18th century, China's Manchu rulers lifted the ban on intermarriage, allowing Manchus and Han Chinese to get married and start families. At the same time, Manchu officials were told they had to start studying Mandarin, so the Manchu language has been fading for a long time. Today, no one in China speaks Manchu as a first language, and fewer than a hundred people can read classical Manchu fluently. But there are troves of untranslated materials written in the Manchu language, full of information about family histories, government policies, and traditional medicine during the Qing dynasty. [116]

Chapter 39. China and Japan during World War I (1910-1919)

39.1. China versus Japan at beginning of 1910s decade

The Meiji Restoration of the late 19th century had propelled Japan into the modern world. The Japanese had tapped into Western knowledge to develop an industrialized economy. Japan's military, once a barefoot army of samurai, was now a well trained Westernized armed force, equipped with modern weapons. Its government was dominated by militarists and expansionists who hoped to make Japan an Asian imperial power. [130]

Japan had used the time since the Meiji Restoration (1868) to strengthen itself economically and militarily and, most important, had changed its culture to become a part of the global governance and commerce architecture. In other words, Japan made itself a part of "the West."

China, by contrast, had done little to improve itself since the Taiping Rebellion ended (1864). Not only did it do nothing to strengthen itself economically or militarily, it actually "declared war" on the rest of the world in the Boxer Rebellion, and so it isolated itself from the West.

So it's not surprising that, in 1912, Japan was considerably stronger than China, and considered better prepared to deal with the world as World War I approached. But China's situation was infinitely worse than even that.

For three centuries, the Manchus had ruled China's empire, and the Chinese people acceded to this rule like sheep. Then, in 1912, the Manchus disappeared from power, leaving the Chinese in charge, and the Chinese had absolutely no clue how to change from sheep to rulers.

39.2. Sun Yat-Sen versus Yuan Shikai

Dr. Sun Yat-Sen (1866-1925) is remembered to this day as the hero of the 1911 revolution, as leader of the Revolutionary Alliance. He is considered to be the founding father of modern China, and also the founder of the Kuomintang (KMT) nationalist party, which has become the leading political party in Taiwan after Mao Zedong won China's civil war in 1949. [113]

Another hero at the time was Yuan Shikai (1859-1916), who had served as an army general under the Qing dynasty. When the revolution broke out in

October 1911, and regional elites throughout China rose up against the imperial dynasty, Qing rulers called Yuan back to the capital again. As prime minister and head of the Qing army, Yuan had commanded his forces into the rebel-controlled city of Wuhan by December 1911, forcing the leaders of the revolution to negotiate. [106]

Sun Yat-sen had been in the United States raising money for the Revolutionary Alliance when the revolution broke out. Yuan Shikai made a deal with the revolutionaries, and on January 1, 1912, Dr. Sun Yat-sen was inaugurated as the first president of the Republic of China, just as it had been widely expected due to his leading position in the fight against the Qing government. [106]

This ended more than 2,000 years of imperial rule in China. According to the agreement, Sun Yat-sen resigned on February 12, and Yuan Shikai became provisional president. [113]

What happens in country after country after a civil war is that whoever becomes leader after the civil war refuses to give up power, often resorting to mass slaughter, rape, torture, mass jailings, mutilations and so forth to stay in power. In today's world (2019), leaders in this category with varying levels of violence are Bashar al-Assad in Syria, Hun Sen in Cambodia, Paul Biya in Cameroon, Pierre Nkurunziza in Burundi, Paul Kagame in Rwanda, Yoweri Museveni in Uganda, Robert Mugabe in Zimbabwe, and Joseph Kabila in DRC.

Yuan Shikai was supposed to be a provisional president, staying in office long enough to write a constitution and conduct a new election. The opposition party was Sun Yat-sen's nationalist party, and Yuan was ruthless in crippling it. No constitution emerged, and Yuan Shikai is suspected of having orchestrated the assassination of the leader of the KMT in the provisional assembly. After Yuan Shikai had coerced the assembly into electing him as president (for a 5-year term) in late 1913, he expelled all nationalist delegates from further participation in it. Sun Yat-Sen was exiled to Japan. [113]

Yuan Shikai seems to have been something of a nutcase. In late 1915, in the midst of World War I, he even tried to establish a new imperial dynasty and a new empire with himself as the Great Emperor of China, complete with ceremonial robes he had made for himself. This strained the support of even his loyal followers beyond the breaking point and he had to flee from the capital a short time afterwards. In early June 1916, Yuan Shikai died from kidney failure. [113]

Yuan's death was the end of China's first attempt, following the 1911 revolution, to unify the country under a central government. Following Yuan's death, there was a 12-year period known as the warlord era, during which local generals in China's provinces continually challenged the weak central authority of the Republic of China. There was no effective central government in China between the years 1916 and 1926/1927. [106]

39.3. European and Asian alliances prior to World War I

By 1914, when the Great War (World War I) began, Europe was already a tangle of alliances. At that time, the three nations of the Triple Alliance - Germany, Austria-Hungary, and Italy - stood against the three nations of the Triple Entente - France, Russia, and Great Britain.

The Entente alliance began in 1894 with an alliance between Russia and France over concerns of Germany's military power. In the late 1890s, it became clear that Germany intended to construct a navy to match the Britain's Royal Navy, and so Britain joined what became the Triple Entente. During the war, this phrase fell into disuse as other nations joined, including Japan.

The Triple Alliance of the Central Powers grew out of the wars of German Unification in the 1860s-70s. It began with German's alliance with the Austro-Hungarian empire, and was later joined by Italy. During the war, the Central Powers alliance was joined by Bulgaria and Turkey.

Once the war began, the two sides of the war were usually described as "the Allies" versus "the Central Powers." The United States was not part of "the Allies," and did not join the war until 1917, though of course fought on the side of the Allies when it did. On April 6, president Woodrow Wilson issued a proclamation of a state of war with German, in order to make the world "safe for democracy." [107]

39.4. China and Japan in World War I

World War I broke out in Europe in 1914, during the presidency of Yuan Shikai. As we said previously, the Chinese had no idea how to govern a nation or an empire once the Manchus were gone, and in particular Yuan Shikai was a disaster as a leader.

As of the beginning of World War I in 1914, Japan had already annexed Korea, and Japan shared hegemony with Russia in Manchuria.

Many of the islands in the Pacific and Indian oceans were up for grabs by European powers, including Spain and Germany. After Spain was defeated in the Spanish-American war in 1898, Spain ceded its Pacific islands to Germany. Thus, by the beginning of World War I, Germany was in possession of several islands as colonies or at least under German protection — Micronesia, Marshall Islands, Caroline Islands, Palau Islands, Mariana Islands. Many of these islands were ceded to Japan by the 1920 Versailles Treaty after Germany was defeated in World War I. [111]

At the beginning of World War I, Japan took advantage of this situation by offering to extend the 1902 Anglo-Japanese agreement by allying with Britain and the Entente powers against Germany. This provided Japan's military an opportunity to enormously expand its sphere of influence. The Imperial Japanese Navy played a significant role in securing the sea lanes in the South Pacific and Indian Oceans against the German navy. Japan captured Germany's Micronesian territories north of the equator, and ruled the islands until 1921. During the war, the British Admiralty request naval assistance from Japan several times, and Japan provided this assistance as far way as South Africa and the Mediterranean Sea. [33]

39.5. Twenty-One Demands - May 9, 1915 - China's National Humiliation Day

To this day, the Chinese remember May 9, 1915, with bitterness and anger.

At the beginning of World War I, China's government was in a state of chaos. With the Manchus out of power, there was no government infrastructure, and president Yuan Shikai was inexperienced and naïve. Indeed, Yuan saw himself not as the democratically elected president of a republic, but rather as an all-powerful monarch serving as king to an empire. For example, in anticipation of becoming Emperor, Yuan ordered the Imperial kilns to manufacture 40,000 porcelain pieces for his palace. [33]

Japan, on the other hand, had used the 50 years since the Meiji Restoration to grow into a major international economic and military power, on par with some of the European powers. But Japan's successes in wars with China and Russia had also given Japan a feeling of imperialistic superiority that continued to grow until World War II.

The West had supported Japan in its wars and imperialism prior to World War I, but at the same time had set boundaries and red lines that Japan was not permitted to cross. Once the world war began, and the West was completely distracted, Japan was able to take advantage of the inexperience and naïveté of China's government to expand its influence. [114]

On January 18, 1915, Japan had presented to Chinese President Yuan Shikai (Yuan Shih-Kai) a list of "Twenty-One Demands" that China would have to concede. Among the demands was Japanese control of Shandong province, southern Manchuria, and eastern Inner Mongolia. Fearing a Japanese invasion of China, Yuan adopted a policy of appeasement and accepted the ultimatum on May 9, and signed the treaty on May 25. [114]

In the aftermath, May 9, 1915, became known as China's National Humiliation Day. The Twenty-One Demands nurtured a considerable amount of public ill-will towards Japan, and the upsurge in nationalism is still deeply felt today in China's handling of Sino-Japanese relations. [114]

Chapter 40. The aftermath of World War I

40.1. New Culture Movement (1915-1920)

The 1910s decade was the heart of China's generational Unraveling era, following the Taiping Rebellion that climaxed in 1864.

When a country goes through a horrific and violence civil war like the Taiping Rebellion, there is a standard generational template that the country follows. First, there's an 18-year Recovery era, when the traumatized survivors of the war work to reconstruct society and impose rules to guarantee that nothing so horrific will happen again. Next, there's a 20-year Awakening era, as the next generation of young people come of age and make their voice heard, usually in opposition to their parents' policies, resulting in a "generation gap." As the older generation of war survivors dies off, the generational differences are resolved during a 20-year Unraveling era, when the rules imposed during the Recovery era unravel.

The first major outcome of China's generational Unraveling era was the shedding of the Manchu government, and return to Chinese rule. But young people were demanding more than that. After the collapse of the old imperial order, many Chinese not only rejected the old political institutions, ideology and culture, but many traditional forms of behavior and further aspects of traditional Chinese culture as well. Nearly everything that was old was suddenly seen as problematic, holding China back from the necessary modernization and reform efforts. [113]

One of the pillars of old Chinese culture had been the use of a classical literary form of the Chinese language among the educated elite circles of society. This sophisticated form of Chinese was preserved in the around 2.000-year-old writings of Confucius, Mencius and other sages. Over the preceding centuries, the traditional attachment to this old form of Chinese among elite circles of society had led to an increasing alienation from the common speech of the ordinary Chinese people. [113]

This classical Chinese language was rejected by the younger generations, in favor of a colloquial language. Not only the use of classical Chinese, but also the values and ideas of Confucianism came to be seen as an obstacle on the path to China's modernization. The Confucian emphasis of hierarchical relationships (between ruler and subject, husband and wife etc.) began to be seen as oppressive and the - according to Confucius - reciprocal nature of these relationships (i.e. if the ruler wasn't a just ruler, he didn't have to be obeyed any longer) had been mostly forgotten. Confucianism came to be seen as a facilitating ideology in the oppression of certain groups within society (i.e. women, peasants, workers etc.), whereas it raised the societal value of other more privileged groups (like men, the educated elite etc.). [113]

40.2. The Versailles Betrayal (1919)

China's government had decided that participating in the war on the side of America and the Allies would entitle China to share in the rewards and perhaps to regain the right to manage her own destiny. At the very least there was hope that lost powers and autonomy would be recovered and perhaps that the Japanese "21 demands" could be reversed. China sent a vast labor force of 100,000 laborers to the European front to help the Allies. [33]

It actually turned out that America and the Allies — Russia, France, Britain — were all betraying China. The Allies wanted to encourage China to participate in the war, but Japan objected, based on the fear that the Allies would protect China from Japan if China helped the Allies in the war. [117]

On February 16, 1917, Britain and Japan concluded the following agreement: [117]

> "His Britannic Majesty's Government accedes with pleasure to the request of the Japanese Government, for an assurance that they will support Japan's claims in regard to the disposal of Germany's rights in Shandong and possessions in the islands north of the equator on the occasion of the Peace Conference; it being understood that the Japanese Government will, in the eventual peace settlement, treat in the same spirit Great Britain's claims to the German islands south of the equator." [117]

On March 2, France's ambassador wrote to Japan: "The Government of the French Republic is disposed to give the Japanese Government its accord in regulating at the time of the Peace Negotiations questions vital to Japan concerning Shandong and the German islands on the Pacific north of the equator." [117]

On March 5, the Russian ambassador confirmed this agreement. After these agreements, Japan saw no further objection to China's participation in the war. America was in "more or less honest ignorance" of these arrangements, and used the hope of recovering Shandong as the chief inducement to China. [117]

Hopes were raised high in China with circulation of US president Woodrow Wilson's pronouncements on questions of national self-determination and recovery of territorial rights. Wilson's rhetoric emphasizing national self-determination as one of the guiding principles of the post-war settlements, enthused Chinese youth with a new sense of idealism. They were sure that the Versailles Peace Conference would recognize China's rights in Shandong and cancel out the Japanese "Twenty-one demands." [33]

So it was a tremendous shock to the Chinese government and people that China was betrayed by the West at the Versailles Peace Conference. It turned out that there had been a secret agreement, signed by Britain, France, Italy, Japan, and China's Tuan Chi Jui government (the government that took over when Yuan Shikai resigned and died) that gave Japan major concessions in Shandong, upholding and sustaining Japan's imperialistic interests. One Chinese student was quoted as saying bitterly: [33]

> "We have been told that in the dispensation which is to be made after the war, nations like China would have an opportunity to develop their culture, industry, their civilization unhampered. We have been told that secret covenants and forced agreements would not be recognized. We looked for the dawn of this new era but no such sun rose for China. Even the cradle of the nation (Shandong, homeland of the Chinese philosopher, Confucius) was stolen." [33]

During the peace negotiations in Paris, England and France supported Japan's demands for Shandong by virtue of their secret agreements. America's president Woodrow Wilson, who had previously used the return of Shandong as an inducement, sacrificed everything to his League of Nations, which the Japanese would not have joined unless they had been allowed to keep Shandong. As we'll see, however, after the May Fourth Movement Shandong was returned to China. [117]

When combined with the New Culture Movement, this formerly secret agreement caused a huge outburst of patriotic and national outrage to what was seen as a betrayal of China.

40.3. The May Fourth Movement (1919)

With the death of Yuan Shikai in 1916, China's central government almost completely lost control. The period 1916-1928 is called the "Warlord Era," because the country was governed regionally by warlords. During this period, the central government had 24 cabinets, 5 parliaments, and 4 constitutions. [33]

With the country in chaos, and increasingly under the influence of foreign powers, there was an explosion of new ideas among students. Nothing was off the table — Liberalism, Socialism, Anarchism, Utopianism, Science, Democracy. If it was new, modern, scientific, and, preferably, foreign then it was an idea worth sharing. [115]

The era culminated in demonstrations in Beijing and other cities around the country on May 4, 1919. Students took to the streets to protest China's treatment at the Paris Peace Conferences that year and deals which had handed German concessions in Shandong over to Japan. 3,000 students from over 13 universities and schools marched to Tiananmen Square and through the streets of the capital. The movement spread to other cities and led to a general strike which lasted over a month. Authorities arrested many of the student leaders and several students were beaten and injured in scuffles with police. [115]

The demonstrating and rioting students became known as "Young China," and they became an effective anti-government political force. The Government in Beijing in 1919-20 was in the hands of the pro-Japanese An Fu party, but they were forcibly ejected, in the summer of 1920, largely owing to the influence of the Young China agitation on the soldiers stationed in Peking, causing them to hide out in the residence of the Japanese legation. [117]

Things did not go well for president Wilson, as the US Senate overwhelmingly rejected the Treaty of Versailles, on the grounds that the US should not get entangled in European politics. This "isolationist" stance continued, as the United States also did not join the League of Nations, which Wilson had conceived and pursued with zeal. [108]

Thus, neither China nor America signed the Treaty of Versailles, and so Wilson no longer felt bound to support the Allies' secret agreements that gave Shandong to Japan. As soon as the Washington Naval Conference was announced, Japan began feverishly negotiating with China, with a view to settling the Shandong question bilaterally. [117]

40.4. The Washington Naval Arms Limitation Conference (1921-22)

It was widely believed that an arms race had contributed to the outbreak of World War I, and so a way should be found to prevent a new or continuing arms race, especially in expensive naval ships such as battleships and aircraft carriers. Despite its lack of participation in the League of Nations, the United States was at the forefront of extensive efforts at disarmament during the 1920s and 1930s especially to restrict the growth of naval tonnage, considered to be a key measure of military strength. [109]

In the wake of World War I, leaders in the international community also sought to prevent the possibility of another war. Rising Japanese militarism and an international arms race heightened these concerns and policymakers worked to reduce the threat. [109]

In 1921 President Harding was elected on a platform which contained a popular naval disarmament plank. Isolationists of the day believed that prohibiting preparedness would promote peace. Republican Senator Hiram Johnson of California, "War may be banished from the earth more nearly by disarmament than by any other agency or in any other manner." Just before the Washington Conference convened on Armistice Day, 1921, several thousand women marched down Pennsylvania Avenue in Washington, DC, carrying banners denouncing war. "Scrap the battleship," their placards read, "and the Pacific problems will settle themselves." For many Americans, the Washington Arms Limitation Conference was supposed to be a substitute for the League, for alliances, and for armaments. [109]

There were many technical treaties concluded at the conference, but for our purposes we focus on the Shangtung (Shandong) Treaty. This treaty took Shandong province from Japan and returned it to China. The intention was to reassure China that its territory would not be further compromised by Japanese expansion. [109]

As a footnote to all this, in 1929 the US led the world in signing the Kellogg-Briand Pact, which outlawed war and made war illegal. Frank Kellogg earned the Nobel Peace Prize in 1929 for his work on the Peace Pact. [110]

Feel free to supply your own jokes.

Part VIII. China turns to Communism

Chapter 41. China's alignment with Soviet Russia against the West

41.1. Historic relationship between Russia and China

The Russians have hated the Chinese ever since the Mongols defeated the Chinese in 1206, and then went on to attack and conquer almost all the Russian principalities, and made them bitter vassals of the Mongol Empire, in a relationship called the "Mongol Yoke." This hated period, two centuries long, has defined the relationship between the Russian and Chinese people forever. There is no possibility that China and Russia will remain "strategic partners" for long.

In fact, Soviet Russia and China almost went to full-scale war as recently as the 1960s. As this shows, any relationship between China and Russia can never be more than a marriage of convenience.

Still, in 1920, China and Russia had several very striking similarities:

- Each has very large land masses with diverse populations.
- Each had just ended centuries of dynastic rule, under the Manchu Qing dynasty, and under the Tsars, respectively.
- Each considered itself victimized by the West, China by the Opium Wars and Russia by Napoleon's invasion.
- Each was governed by a group of young "revolutionaries" who in fact had no clue how to govern an empire.

So one might say that, despite centuries of mutual hatred, the stars were aligned in 1920 for China and Russia to reject the West and succumb to the siren song of Marxism.

Today, the major international outlaw nations are China, Russia and North Korea, and they are impoverished and consider themselves the ultimate victims of the world. By contrast, the outlaws of World War II, including Japan and Germany, seem to have repented for their crimes, and are both economic powerhouse democracies.

41.2. Aftermath of the May 4th Movement

While much of the world was occupied by the Great War in the 1910s, it provided something of an opportunity for young people in China. Since young Chinese were not involved in actually fighting the war, they were free to go to Europe, Russia, North America or Japan for either work or education.

We've already described, in the context of the "New Culture Movement," how young people were rejecting old cultural ideas including the classical Chinese language and Confucianism. For many, the answers at first lay in Western ideas of individualism, but even those were rejected by many who blamed the West for the Versailles betrayal. Rejecting these ideas created a cultural vacuum which was filled by new ideas brought in from foreign lands.

Karl Marx's Communist Manifesto had been published just 70 years earlier, in 1848, and the Bolshevik Revolution started in Russia on November 7, 1917. The ideas of anarchism and communism found fertile ground among the young people who were returning from foreign lands, where these ideas were considered quite chic and fashionable. Furthermore, popular Western thinkers like John Dewey, George Bernard Shaw and Bertrand Russell travelled through China on speaking tours in the late 1910's and early 1920's, further popularizing these left-wing views. After 1920, Marxist study groups began sprang up in large cities, supported by Russian agents and international communist organizations, resulting in the creation of the Chinese Communist Party (CCP). [113]

41.3. China's disillusionment with 'imperialism' and the West

At the beginning of the 1900s, the concept of regaining sovereign rights became central to the thinking of China's population. From the Chinese point of view, since the Opium Wars, China had been subjected to foreign attacks, each of which ended with an unequal treaty. China had to pay indemnities to the victorious powers and grant privileges, rights and even territorial concessions. The Sino-Japanese war of 1894-95 exposed China's complete weakness, and it appeared that she could not refuse anything to anybody. [33]

Then in 1900, the Boxer Rebellion was China's attempt to take back control and eject Beijing legations of eight nations — England, France, Germany, Austria, Italy, Russia, Japan, and the United States — and these nations responded with an expeditionary force of 20,000 men who freed the legations, sacked Beijing, and occupied its palaces. Despite China's physical incapability to prevent encroachments, there was a distant greater determination at this time to strengthen the country and reclaim all that had been lost. The sixty years of indignity had to be countered. [33]

Thus, China did the following: [33]

- Reasserted claim to Tibet to contain the British
- Increased emigration to Manchuria to block Japan's expansion
- Asserted sovereignty in Mongolia to block Russia. This was done through encouraging the flow of Chinese into Mongolia, and sending out Chinese garrison troops. [33]

However, the Versailles betrayal was the event that convinced China to fight Western "imperialism."

41.4. Details of the Versailles betrayal and return of Shandong

Since the Versailles treaty that came out of World War I was one of the most important events of the 20th century, leading to militarism in both Germany and Japan, it's worth making note of the details, perhaps to learn some lessons to be used in a future "peace conference."

After the war, China's first and foremost expectation was to recover all rights and privileges formerly granted under the "unequal treaties" which the Chinese believed had been forced on them by European powers. One of those treaties, signed in 1898, had given Germany a 99-year lease to control China's Shandong peninsula, including the rights to build railways, open factories and mines. When Germany lost the war, the Chinese public quite reasonably assumed that full control of Shandong would revert to China. [33]

Anyone who has ever signed a contract only to discover later that the fine print obligates them in ways they never intended might understand what happened next. In 1915, Japan had forced upon China the "Twenty-One Demands" agreement, along with associated agreements. So at the peace conference following the war, the question of the disposition of Shandong province came up, and Japan was able to produce these signed agreements. One of these was a secret agreement signed by the Beijing government that confirmed the Chinese acceptance of Japanese proposals for the financing, construction, and joint operations of two new railways in the province of Shandong. [33]

In addition, Japan was able to produce agreements that we've previously described that China signed with Britain, France, Italy that gave Japan major concessions in Shandong, upholding and sustaining Japan's imperialistic interests. During the world war Japan had given loans to the various governments and rebels, and in this way had secured one privilege after another, including these agreements. [32]

At the Versailles peace conference, China demanded the abrogation of the Twenty-One Demands and related agreements, because they had been forced on China. China also demanded the following: [33]

- Renunciation of spheres of power or interest,
- Withdrawal of foreign troops and police,
- Withdrawal of foreign post offices and telegraphic agencies,
- Abolition of extra territorial jurisdiction,
- Relinquishment of leased territories,
- Restoration to China of foreign concessions and settlements, and
- Restoration to China of tariff autonomy. [33]

In other words, China was demanding from the international community a dilution, if not a complete annulment, of the unequal treaties. These requests were rejected by the peace conference as being outside its conditions of reference. [33]

Ever since the 1915 Twenty-One Demands agreement became public, Japan was hated throughout China. At the end of the first world war Japan had a hold over China amounting almost to military control of the country. China did not sign the Treaty of Versailles, because she considered that she had been duped by Japan, since Japan had driven the Germans out of China but had not returned the liberated territory to the Chinese. In 1921 peace was concluded with Germany, and the German privileges being abolished. The same applied to Austria. [32]

During the peace conference, the United States had sided with China on the abrogation of the Twenty-One Demands agreement and the return of Shandong to China, out of fear of a militarized Japan. China refused to sign the Versailles treaty, and so did the United States — though in that case because the US Senate opposed American "entanglements" in Europe. [108]

41.5. Bolshevik government renounces privileges and interests in China

The Versailles Peace Conference (Paris Peace Conference) had begun on January 18, 1919. In March 1919, while negotiations were still ongoing, Soviet Russia renounced Russian rights and privileges to all the capitulations that had been awarded to countries from China. This was the first step in the gradual rescinding of the Capitulations; the last of them went only in 1943, as a consequence of the difficult situation of the Europeans and Americans in the Pacific produced by World War II. [32]

As we've described, Shandong province was finally taken from Japan and returned to China at the Washington Naval Arms Limitation Conference (1921-

22), in order to reassure China that its territory would not be further compromised by Japanese expansion. [109]

But diplomatically, it was the Russian renunciation in March 1919 that proved the most consequential. It created a very favorable attitude among the Chinese people towards the new Soviet State. In the beginning several Chinese intellectuals were not interested in Bolshevik theory. But then their attitudes changed, as they saw communism as a weapon — a weapon to combat militarism and imperialism. [33]

Chapter 42. Nationalists vs Communists - Chiang Kai-shek vs Mao Zedong — 1920-1949

42.1. Warlord era (1916-1927)

After the overthrow of the Manchu Qing dynasty, Yuan Shikai had attempted to unify China under a central government. When he was ousted in 1916, and then died, China's central government lost control of the country, and China entered a new "Warlord Era" — that is, the country was split into regions, with each region ruled by a warlord. [33]

The last 20 years of Qing rule had produced a steady decline towards decentralization and provincialism. After the Qing were ousted, there were two competing governments. In the north, Yuan Shikai led the Beiyang Army to power, creating a national army and a national presidency, though his attempts at unifying the country fell to his attempts to restore a monarch with himself as emperor. In the south, nationalists led by Sun Yat-sen formed a weak provisional government with some legitimacy but no means of enforcing it. [119]

When Yuan Shikai died in June 1916 it created a national power vacuum that was quickly filled by the warlords. Now leaderless, the national army itself broke apart, its regiments or divisions falling under the control of powerful provincial leaders, who claimed them as private armies. Warlords formed regional armies through conscription, coercion, or enticement (bribery). Many of these armies were simply roving bands of bandits, though others were led by progressive warlords who tried to improve people's lives, without resorting to exploitation, corruption and banditry. The warlord period was one of political division, instability, corruption and self-interest, economic stagnation and social repression. [119]

By 1925 the number of unemployed in China was estimated at more than 168 million, more than half of them peasants and farm laborers. The northern government barely existed, while Sun Yat-sen's Kuomintang (KMT) nationalist government was gaining strength in their stronghold in the southern province of Guangdong. [119]

42.2. The rise of communism

In the beginning, the May 4th Movement had Western ideological traits, but was not communistic. It was widely believed that communism had no real prospects for China, as a dictatorship of the proletariat seemed to be relevant only in a highly industrialized society and not in an agrarian one. However, attitudes changed for several reasons. First, there were the good feelings that resulted from Russia's March 1919 renunciation of all capitulations. Second, the Bolshevik Revolution in Russia was obviously a success. And third, the theoretical writings of Lenin showed the left-wing intellectuals how communism could be applied to China. [32]

For example, After 1920, Sun Yat-sen, too, became interested in the developments in Soviet Russia. However, he never actually became a communist. He believed that the soil belonged to the tiller of the soil, and this is completely forbidden by communism, which demands the abolition of individual land-holdings. Communist control of the land in China was later put into full effect by Mao Zedong with the Great Leap Forward in the late 1950s, which resulted in the deaths of tens of millions of Chinese through starvation and executions. [32]

The Third Communist International (The Comintern) was formed by Russia in March 1919 in order to control all communist parties around the world, and did so until Stalin dissolved in May 1943, and transferred its activities to other organizations. [120]

The Chinese Communist Party (CCP) was formed in 1921, and became a member of the Moscow Comintern. In the early 1920s, Sun Yat-sen's nationalists and the CCP worked closely together, along with the Moscow Comintern, from their stronghold in the southern province of Guangdong, where were preparing to move against the warlords and reunite China by force. This relationship between Sun Yat-sen's nationalists and the CCP was an alliance of convenience, tolerated by both sides until it was violently ended by the fall of Shanghai in 1927. [119]

42.3. The 1927 Nanking Incident (3/24/1927) and Battle of Shanghai

Sun Yat-sen died in 1925, and Chiang Kai-shek (who married Sun Yat-sen's wife's sister) became the *de facto* leader of the Kuomintang (KMT) nationalist government in the south, which had been organized by the Russians, and was still allied with the CCP. The nationalist and communist armies, advised by the Russians, moved north.

In 1926, after having sufficiently consolidated his power base within the nationalist party and army, Chiang Kai-shek launched an effort to reunify China, that came to be known as the Northern Expedition or the Chinese Nationalist Revolution. With most of China in the hands of warlords, the nationalists only controlled their base area around Canton in Guangdong province in the south of China at that time. From there, the nationalist army under Chiang Kai-shek's leadership followed almost the same route as the Taiping Movement during the previous century, up through Hunan province in central China to the Yangtze River Valley before turning eastwards to Nanking. [113]

By early 1927, Nationalist armies of the Kuomintang controlled half of China and were nearing the strategic cities of Shanghai and Nanking in the lower Yangtze valley. The capture of Nanking took place on Thursday, March 24, 1927, amidst anti-foreign looting, pillaging, and murder, killing six foreigners and wounding several others. Victims of the violence included nationals of Great Britain, the United States, France, Japan, and Italy. [122]

The Northern Expedition consisted of both Nationalist and Communist "revolutionary" forces, and all were fanatically xenophobic — anti-Japanese and anti-Western. As the revolutionary forces approached Nanking, British citizens — business and missionary personnel — were ordered to leave the city, while American citizens were advised to leave. Most people fled for the International Settlement at Shanghai. And all foreign homes in Nanking were extensively looted. [121]

The attack on Nanking by southern forces was a complete mêlée. Soldiers looted foreigners' homes and businesses at will. Chinese people were not targeted at all and, in fact, went about their daily activities unconcerned. [122]

One British gunboat, the HMS Emerald, and two American gunboats, the USS Noa and USS W. B. Preston, were called into action. The British consulate kept in touch with the gunboats through by radio and by semaphore messages communicated by signalmen. The gunboats launched hundreds of explosive shells at designated targets within a seventy minute period. [122]

At this point, the Sixth Nationalist Army commander, General Cheng Chien, arrived to express regrets, desiring to prevent further bombardment. The American and British demands were that they required the protection and evacuation of foreigners, the protection of foreign property, and the appearance of the Fourth Division commander to make arrangements for these demands. If the Chinese failed to comply with these demands, the naval captains threatened further military action. [122]

The evacuations took place on the following day, leaving behind six dead in Nanking. The property loss from burning and looting was substantial. No accurate estimate is possible, but the size of the loss might be indicated by the cost to the International Export Company which lost more than AC120,000 in commercial goods to looters. [122]

42.4. Aftermath of the Nanking incident (1927) — assigning blame

Historians who discuss Chiang Kai-shek's subsequent capture of Shanghai often omit discussion of the Nanking incident, or consider it a minor incident, lasting a few hours, or little significance. From the point of view of Generational Dynamics, the highly "organic" nature of mêlée actually makes it at least of equal significance. That is, the looting was completely disorganized, driven by xenophobic attitudes of the soldiers, and not directed by commanders of any of the groups involved. This spontaneous, extremely violent riot had enormous impact on both the Chinese and the foreign powers in the international community.

That international passions were stirred was clear from the headline in the New York Times on March 25, 1927, the day after the Nanking Incident: [121]

"Americans and British Killed in Attacks at Nanking; Warships Then Shell City and Rescue Some Foreigners; Allied Commanders Serve Ultimatum; All China Aflame"

Even though the riots were "organic," it was necessary to assign blame to the appropriate politicians.

The attacks by their "friends," the southern Nationalist army, had been almost completely unexpected by the foreigners. After it was over, the foreigners who had been targeted by the looters and rioters were acutely aware of the costs at Nanking in lives and property. They were certain that the "friends" who had perpetrated the attacks were Nationalists. In short, they knew what had happened at Nanking, and who had attacked them, but they did not know who ordered the attack, nor did they understand clearly the purpose of the violence. Why then, had the foreign community, been attacked? [122]

The Kuomintang-Communist alliance, formed in 1923, was always an alliance of convenience, and was opposed by factions in each camp. The Nationalists and the Comintern's Communists were both opposed to the northern government, but beyond that each looked for ways to take advantage of the other. There was also a split in Moscow between Stalin, who wanted the Chinese communists to work with Kuomintang, and Trotsky, who didn't. The bloody power struggle between Stalin and Trotsky forced Stalin to support cooperation, and so there was cooperation. [122]

Chiang Kai-shek at first blamed the northern army, and then blamed the communists. When it became clear that it was his Nationalist army that had done the looting, he developed a narrative. Chiang Kai-shek accepted full responsibility for the event. He promised to investigate the incident and punish any Nationalist soldiers involved, and unofficially he said that the communists had incited the riots. In his memoirs Chiang Kai-shek recalls that the riot at

Nanking was a "Communist engineered incident," designed to "provoke a direct clash between the foreign powers and our Revolutionary Army." [122]

This was the end of the Kuomintang-Communist alliance. Chiang Kai-shek captured Shanghai without a struggle, and then had a choice to make. On the one hand, he could take the path favored by the Communists and expropriate the money and land of the Shanghai capitalists, industrialists, landowners and financiers. [32]

One factor influencing Chiang was that he was married to Sun Yat-sen's wife's sister, and through that marriage he had become allied with one of Shanghai's greatest banking families. Chiang allied with the Shanghai financiers, and capital of the Shanghai financiers, and soon foreign capital as well, was placed at his disposal, so that he was able to pay his troops and finance his administration. At the same time the Russian advisers were dismissed or executed. [32]

The Communists formed a rival government in Hankow, while Chiang Kai-shek made Nanking the seat of his government (April 1927). In that year Chiang not only concluded peace with the financiers and industrialists, but also a sort of "armistice" with the landowning gentry. "Land reform" still stood on the party program, but nothing was done, and in this way the confidence and co-operation of large sections of the gentry was secured. The choice of Nanking as the new capital pleased both the industrialists and the agrarians: the great bulk of China's young industries lay in the Yangtze region, and that region was still the principal one for agricultural produce; the landowners of the region were also in a better position with the great market of the capital in their neighborhood. [32]

The "Great Powers" might have reacted harshly to the Nanking Incident, as they had to the Boxer Rebellion. Five days later, on March 29, the foreign ministers of five Powers — the United States, Great Britain, France, Japan and Italy — met in Nanking to create a joint list of demands: [122]

- Punishment of the commanders of the troops and other implicated persons responsible for the "murders, personal injuries, indignities, and material damage" done at Nanking,
- A written apology by the Commander-in-Chief of the Nationalist Army, and
- Complete reparation for material damages and personal injuries. [122]

The foreign ministers expected united and immediate response from their governments, but this was not forthcoming. There were months of disagreement, with many in Britain favoring military reprisal, and many in America favoring conciliation. [122]

During the remainder of 1927 and into 1928, Chiang was able out-maneuver the Communists and unify the country, with the exception of Manchuria, which was dominated by Japan. The Nationalist government in Nanking gained the confidence of the western powers, and did make some reparations. It was recognized as the official government of China, and was able get rid of the "unfair treaties" that had been signed in the past. In particular, the collection of duties on imports and exports was brought under the control of the Chinese government, instead of foreign control. This gave Nanking the freedom to collect tariffs, making it financially more independent of the provinces. It succeeded in building up a small but modern army, loyal to the government and superior to the still existing provincial armies. This army gained its military experience in skirmishes with the Communists and the remaining generals. [32]

In June, 1928, Chiang's Nationalist troops entered Beijing and drove out the last of the warlords, and so united China under a single Kuomintang government. The Nanking incident was a seminal event that changed China and also changed the international view of China. It shocked the international community into understanding the full significance of Chiang Kai-shek's victory over the Communists and the northern generals, and his achievement in unifying China. Finally, as long as Chiang was dictator over all of China, there was a single government that other governments could negotiate with. [122]

42.5. Japan invades Manchuria — the Mukden incident (1931)

On September 17, 1931, an explosion occurred near the train tracks of a Japanese owned railway in the city of Mukden in Manchuria. The Japanese blamed the explosion on Chinese Nationalists, although most historians believe that it was staged by Japanese soldiers. Even many Japanese historians today accept the latter view. [124]

Either way, Japan used the "Mukden Incident" as a pretext for the invasion of Manchuria. The Chinese Nationalist government in Nanking had only a loose association with Manchuria, and so the Nationalists were helpless to stop the Japanese invasion. Thus Manchuria was lost almost without a blow. [32]

42.6. The rise of Japan's militarism

From the point of view of Generational Dynamics, the invasion of Manchuria occurred at a significant time for Japan, because it was 63 years after the climax of the previous generational crisis war (the Meiji Restoration in 1868), which means that Japan was in the beginning years of a generational Crisis era.

Today, in 2019, many nations of the world are deep into a generational Crisis era. As I've been writing for years about country after country, many countries of the world are becoming increasingly nationalistic and xenophobic, as the survivors of World War II have almost completely disappeared. This is true today in North America, Europe and Asia. And this is not an abstract concept. It has real consequences in that the survivors of World War II were willing to compromise, but the generations growing up after World War II are not. So most countries have become more willing to escalate small crises into larger ones, and less willing to accept compromises to prevent war. An actual war is an unavoidable consequence.

Japan had considered invading Manchuria in the 1920s, but had decided against it because of, among other things, fear of Western military intervention to oppose Japan, and fear of war. So in 1931, Japan was becoming increasingly nationalistic and xenophobic, and was less concerned about Western opinion or of war. Thus, 1931 was the time of Japan's invasion of Manchuria and increasing militarism in the following years, leading to the bombing of Pearl Harbor on December 8, 1941.

At this point, it's well to mention the issue of American hostility and xenophobia towards Japan. In 1913, California had passed a law restricting land ownership to Japanese awaiting citizenship, intending to prevent the Japanese, as Gov. Hiram Johnson put it, "from driving the root of their civilization into California soil." The perceived threat to the people of Japan was real. The United States had been its main hope, its Asian neighbors with few exceptions tied to one or another of the colonial powers. [123]

The British philosopher Bertrand Russell, wrote the following in an article in 1922:

"The Japanese are firmly persuaded that they have no friends, and that the Americana are their implacable foes. One gathers that the Government regards war with America as unavoidable in the long run. The argument would be that the economic imperialism of the United States will not tolerate the industrial development of a formidable rival in the Pacific, and that sooner or later the Japanese will be presented with the alternative of dying by starvation or on the battlefield. Then Bushido will come into play, and will lead to choice of the battlefield in preference to starvation. Admiral Sato (the Japanese Bernhardi, as he is called) maintains that absence of Bushido [Bushido is the code of honor and morals developed by the Japanese samurai] in the Americans will lead to their defeat, and that their money-grubbing souls will be incapable of enduring the hardships and privations of a long war. This, of course, is romantic nonsense. Bushido is no use in modern war, and the Americans are quite as courageous and obstinate as the Japanese. A war might last ten years, but it would certainly end in the defeat of Japan."

(Compare this to some of the things that Chinese nationalists say today.)

So mutual xenophobia between Japanese and Americans was not a new thing, and entering a generational Crisis era for both nations only escalated it. However, these feelings were exacerbated by another global event the stock market crash of 1929 and the beginning of the Great Depression. Within a year, the economies of most countries of the world were suffering from the Great Depression.

Then there was the Smoot-Hawley Tariff Act. The US Congress passed this most xenophobic of laws in June 1930, supposedly to protect American jobs as the Depression worsened, although it's still debated today whether the law made the Depression better or worse. The effects were enormous. The bill erected large trade barriers for numerous products and virtually shut down product exports from other countries to the United States. Countries like Germany and Japan were going through the same financial crisis America was going through, and they were furious that America as a market was closed to them. The Smoot-Hawley act could arguably be called the first hostile act of World War II.

Japan was the hardest hit. The Great Depression was hurting Japan just as much as it was hurting America but, in addition, Japan's exports of its biggest cash crop, silk, to America were almost completely cut off by the Smoot-Hawley Act. The Japanese price of silk fell to a 34 year low. So this was a time when Japan, an island nation, was surrounded by hostile neighbors, was blocked from investments in its nearest Western neighbor, the United States, was suffering like everyone else from the Great Depression, and was apparently singled out by the US tariff policy for even special suffering. [123]

Despite Western opposition to Japan's invasion of Manchuria, Japan was correct that there was little taste in the West to intervene militarily on behalf of China in Manchuria. China protested to the League of Nations against its loss of Manchuria. The League sent a commission (the Lytton Commission), which condemned Japan's action, but nothing further happened, and China indignantly broke away from its association with the Western powers (1932-1933). In view of the tense European situation (the beginning of the Hitler era in Germany, and the Italian plans of expansion), the Western powers did not want to fight Japan on China's behalf and without that nothing more could be done. They pursued, indeed, a policy of playing off Japan against China, in order to keep those two powers occupied with each other, and so to divert Japan from Indo-China and the Pacific. [32]

All these examples illustrate the same thing: That nationalism and xenophobia were increasing on all sides in the years leading to World War II.

The final *coup de grâce* occurred on August 1, 1941, the US established an embargo on oil and gasoline exports to Japan. Three months later, Japan attacked Pearl Harbor.

42.7. The Soviet Communist Republic of China

After the Nanking Incident and the Nationalist capture of Shanghai in 1927, the former alliance of convenience between the Communists and Chiang Kai-shek's Nationalists was at an end. Under the direction and control of the Moscow Comintern, the Communists formed a Soviet Republic of China, based in Jiangxi province in the southeast. [126]

Between 1930 and 1934, the Nationalists under Chiang Kai-shek (1887-1975) launched a series of five encirclement campaigns against the Chinese Soviet Republic. Under the leadership of Mao, the Communists employed guerrilla tactics to successfully resist the first four campaigns, but in the fifth, Chiang raised a huge force and built fortifications around the Communist positions. Mao was removed as chairman, and the new Communist leadership employed more conventional warfare tactics, and its Red army was decimated. [126]

42.8. Mao Zedong's Long March (1934-35)

Mao Zedong's Long March is a story that has achieved a mythic quality, almost like the ancient Greek tale of Odysseus, with Mao himself exhibiting almost heroic qualities of bravery.

There's no doubt that it was a remarkable achievement. It began on October 16, 1934, when Mao led his Communist army of more than 85,000 troops and thousands of accompanying personnel to break through the Nationalist encirclement at its weak point. Once the Nationalists realized that the Communists had slipped past them, numerous battles ensued. [126]

After enduring starvation, aerial bombardment and almost daily skirmishes with Nationalist forces, Mao linked up with other Red army troops in Shaanxi on October 20, 1935, ending the Long March. By some estimates, 8,000 or fewer marchers completed the journey, which covered more than 4,000 miles and crossed 24 rivers and 18 mountain ranges. The Long March proved to be a powerful symbol of heroism, resulting in thousands of young Chinese traveled to Shaanxi to enlist in Mao's Red army. [126]

Chapter 43. Sino-Japanese War (1937-45) - World War II in Asia

Westerners think of World War II as having started in September 1939, with the Nazi invasion of Poland. But the early conflicts of World War II were well under way before Hitler invaded anyone. Japan invaded Manchuria in 1931, and Italy invaded Ethiopia in 1935. World War II in Asia clearly began with the Sino-Japanese War (1937-45).

43.1. Japan's conquest of Manchuria (1931)

Japan's invasion of Manchuria in northeast China in the early 1930s and the war that followed capped off decades of antagonism between the two nations. The political and economic development of Japan stood in stark contrast to that of China. The Meiji Restoration of 1868 had propelled Japan into the modern world. The Japanese had tapped into Western knowledge to develop an industrialized economy. Japan's military, once a barefoot army of samurai, were now a well trained Westernized armed force, equipped with modern weapons. Its government was dominated by militarists and expansionists who hoped to make Japan an Asian imperial power. [130]

We've previously described the Mukden incident (1931), which was almost certainly staged by the Japanese themselves. The incident in Mukden, Manchuria in September 1931 provided the Japanese with the pretext for a full military invasion of Manchuria. Once established there, the Japanese set up the puppet state of Manchukuo and installed the last Qing emperor, Puyi, as its ineffectual head of state. In May 1933 the Nationalist president Chiang Kai-shek, who was more concerned with fighting the Chinese communists than Japanese imperialists, signed the Tanggu Truce, effectively recognizing the legitimacy of the Manchukuo puppet state. [130]

International criticism of Japan for invading Manchurian incident led to Japan withdrawing from the League of Nations. After conquering Manchuria in 1931, Japan used an immense system of smuggling, currency manipulation and propaganda to establish the puppet state. Chiang Kai-shek took no action. [32]

43.2. Unit 731 - chemical and biological warfare (1936-45)

In 1936, Japan set up a horrific chemical and biological warfare in Harbin, Manchuria. Unit 731 conducted experiments on some 3,000 human beings, mostly abducted Chinese, used as guinea pigs. It was headed by a sociopathic scientist named Shiro Ishii, who had gone around the world, visiting clinics and laboratories in almost thirty countries, and developed techniques for the most gruesome chemical and biological atrocities. [131]

Ishii's experiments, tested on thousands of people, included using blood-sucking fleas to spread bubonic plague, vivisection of live prisoners, without anesthesia, amputating limbs of live prisoners to study blood loss, injecting horse's urine into prisoners' kidneys, and lethal doses of x-ray radiation. At one point, the mice kept in the laboratory were then released, which could have cost the lives of 30,000 people, since the mice were infected with the bubonic plague, and they spread the disease. [132]

The Japanese kept Unit 731 as a closely guarded secret for 40 years, until its existence was acknowledged in 1984. [131]

There are unconfirmed reports today that China is performing the same kinds of experiments as Unit 731 on practitioners of the Buddhism-based Falun Gong religion and on the Muslim Uighurs in Xinjiang province.

43.3. Marco Polo Bridge Incident (July 7-9, 1937) and Sino-Japanese War

Most people say that World War II began in 1939 when Nazi Germany invaded Poland. Well, that's when World War II in Europe began, but World War II in Asia began in 1937 with the Marco Polo Bridge incident.

The Marco Polo Bridge Incident is highly relevant to today's world, because it shows how a trivial misunderstanding could start World War III today, tomorrow, next week, or next year.

In 1937, both China and Japan were deep into generational Crisis eras, their previous crisis wars having climaxed 73 and 69 years earlier, respectively. This isn't an abstract concept. What it means is that the traumatized people who had survived the horrors of the previous crisis war were all gone. They had spent their entire lives trying to make sure that nothing so horrible ever happens again, but now they were gone, and there was nobody left who felt the same way.

Many of the details of the Marco Polo Bridge incident are trivial, but these trivial details started World War II in Asia, so they're worth reviewing because of lessons that apply to today's world.

There actually is a Marco Polo Bridge. It's located about 15 km southwest of Beijing, and it has that name because the original bridge, constructed in 1192, was praised by the 13th century Italian Silk Road trader, Marco Polo.

Both Japan and China had small numbers of troops at opposite ends of the bridge. Japan's troops were there to provide protection for a Japanese diplomatic legation. The Chinese had a small military camp there. [127]

Late on July 7, 1937, the Japanese performed a roll call of their troops, and one soldier, Private Shimura Kikujiro, was missing. According to documents released by the Japanese in 2013, Kikujiro had snuck off into the woods during the training exercise for an unauthorized bathroom break, but got lost trying to find his way back. By the time he did get back, the roll call had been performed. [127]

The Japanese assumed the worst: That Kikujiro had been abducted by the Chinese from a small military camp in the town of Wanping, at the end of the Marco Polo Bridge. The Japanese requested permission from the local Chinese to enter Wanping and search for Kikujiro. The Chinese refused. [127]

It's worth noting in passing that abductions are a big part of the news today. The Chinese particularly perform abductions not only of their own people in China from Hong Kong to Xinjiang, but also of people from other countries. Abducted people in China have no rights, and are simply "disappeared" for long periods of times, during which time they're jailed without legal representation or outside contact, and often beaten, raped and tortured. Just as the assumed abduction of Kikujiro in a generational Crisis era led to World War II in Asia, an assumed or actual abduction today can lead to war.

The Japanese entered the city of Wanping on July 8, and of course Kikujiro was not found, since he'd already reported back to his base. Low-level shooting occurred on both the Chinese and Japanese side, but both sides called for reinforcements. One hundred Chinese defenders fought to hold the bridge; only four of them survived. The Japanese overran the bridge, but Chinese reinforcements retook it the following morning, July 9. [129]

In Beijing, the two sides negotiated a settlement of the incident. That would have been the end of it any time except in a generational Crisis era. The Japanese Cabinet held a press conference to announce the settlement, in which it also announced the mobilization of three new army divisions, and harshly warned the Chinese government in Nanking not to interfere with the local solution to the Marco Polo Bridge Incident. This incendiary cabinet statement caused Chiang Kai-shek's government to react by sending four divisions of additional Chinese troops to the area. [129]

Soon, both sides were violating the truce agreement. The Japanese shelled Wanping on July 20, and by the end of July the Imperial Army had surrounded Tianjin and Beijing. Even though neither side likely had planned to go into an all-out war, tensions were incredibly high. When a Japanese naval officer was assassinated in Shanghai on August 9, 1937, the Second Sino-Japanese War broke out in earnest. It would transition in to the Second World War, ending only with Japan's surrender on September 2, 1945. [129]

A lot of people believe that World War III, if it begins, will begin in an "organized" way, similar to how WW II in Europe began: Hitler invades Sudetenland in order to "protect Germans," then promises Britain "Peace in our time." Britain warns Hitler not to invade Poland, Hitler invades Poland, Britain declares war. Very organized. And Winston Churchill foresaw it years earlier.

But World War I began in a "disorganized" way. Austrian Archduke Franz Ferdinand was assassinated by a Serb high school student, triggering a war that nobody saw coming.

And now we see that even World War II — in Asia — began in a "disorganized" way, from a random event that was triggered because a Japanese soldier needed to pee. In "normal" times, the crisis would have ended quickly. But in a generational Crisis era, small conflicts trigger larger ones in a series of tit-for-tat escalations known in generational theory as "regeneracy events," referring to the regeneracy of civic unity for the first time since the climax of the preceding crisis war.

Thus, a small event triggered tit-for-tat escalations that started a major World War in Asia, a war that soon spread to Europe.

Today, some small event in the Mideast, in Kashmir, in the South China Sea or in the East China Sea, that would normally amount to nothing could, today, trigger a tit-for-tat series of escalations leading to a new world war. That's what happens in a generational Crisis era, just as happened with the Marco Polo Bridge Incident on July 7-9, 1937.

43.4. Aftermath of the Marco Polo Bridge incident

China had already suffered a humiliating defeat to Japan in the First Sino-Japanese war (1894-95).

The Second Sino-Japanese War (1937-45) had a significant impact on the course of the Chinese Revolution. Known in China as the "War of Chinese People's Resistance Against Japanese Aggression," it was a catastrophic conflict for the Chinese people, causing up to 20 million casualties. [130]

Full-scale war between China and Japan began in July 1937, following the Marco Polo Bridge incident. When the Japanese launched an invasion in late July, the Nationalists and CCP were seven months into a shaky alliance, dubbed the Second United Front. The Nationalist armies attempted to resist the invasion but were quickly overcome by the technological supremacy and preparedness of the Japanese. China's underdeveloped industries were incapable of supplying munitions or engineering quickly or in sufficient quantities. Unlike the Japanese, the Chinese military had no tanks and only a few aircraft. The first phase of the war was a blitzkrieg of Japanese victories as their forces moved swiftly along China's east coast. Almost a half million Japanese troops moved against Shanghai, Nanking and other locations in mainland China, while Japanese military planes bombarded regions where their foot soldiers could not penetrate. In late 1937 the Nationalist government was forced to retreat from its capital, Nanking, to Chongqing in western China. [130]

43.5. Battle of Nanking / Rape of Nanking (December 13, 1937)

Once the Sino-Japanese crisis war began, it very quickly became savage.

China's Nationalist government lost Shanghai to the Japanese in November 1937, and Chiang Kai-Shek realized that his capital city, Nanking, would be next. He decided to withdraw his forces from Nanking, leaving behind an untrained force of 100,000 poorly-armed fighters. On December 10, the Japanese attacked. Hundreds of thousands of Chinese civilians were summarily beaten, tortured, raped, and slaughtered, even after surrendering. Some were blown up with mines, mowed down with machine guns, or sprayed with gasoline and set on fire. F. Tillman Durdin, a reporter for the New York Times who witnessed the massacre, reported: "In taking over Nanking the Japanese indulged in slaughters, looting and rapine exceeding in barbarity any atrocities committed up to that time in the course of the Sino-Japanese hostilities... Helpless Chinese troops, disarmed for the most part and ready to surrender, were systematically rounded up and executed... Civilians of both sexes and all ages were also shot by the Japanese." Bodies piled up in streets and alleyways, too many for any accurate count. [128]

While Chiang Kai-shek had some early assistance from Soviet Russian leader Joseph Stalin, the Nationalists had little support from foreign powers. In June 1938 Jiang ordered the dykes of the Yellow River dam to be blown, a desperate attempt to slow the advance of the Japanese invasion. While this ploy worked, it also caused a devastating flood that killed between 500,000 to one million Chinese civilians, rendered up to ten million homeless and ruined millions of acres of important farmland. The resulting food shortages, famine and human suffering only contributed to rising peasant hatred of Chiang Kai-shek and the Nationalist regime. Other problems confronting Chiang and the Kuomintang government were widespread corruption, rising inflation and high desertion rates caused by poor treatment of Nationalist soldiers, most of whom were unwilling conscripts. [130]

As the war began, American soldiers experienced the same fanatical viciousness of the Japanese. On April 9, 1942, just four months after the Pearl

Harbor attack, the US was forced to surrender Bataan Peninsula on the main Philippine island of Luzon to the Japanese. Some 70,000-80,000 Filipino and American troops were tortured and beaten by the Japanese on what became known as the Bataan Death March. The Japanese were also responsible for massacres of civilians, and the use of chemical and biological weapons. [184]

The Japanese also used suicide attacks. There were human wave attacks (called "banzai attacks" by the West), and similar suicide attacks with squadrons of "kamikaze pilots," who crashed their planes into American ships.

These atrocities, along with the Nanking massacre, and the Japanese army's use of Korean and Chinese women as "comfort women" during World War II, is still a major political issue today. Japanese troops did not leave China until they were defeated by the Americans at the end of World War II.

43.6. Regeneracy and the United Front

In generational theory, the term "regeneracy events" refers to events that regenerate civic unity since the end of the last generational crisis war. That is, within a nation or ethnic community, there may be sharp political differences that grow worse every day. This is certainly the case today (early 2019) in the United States, the UK and Europe.

However, when a nation or ethnic group faces an existential crisis at the beginning of a generational crisis war, then the groups put aside their political differences, and unite to fight the common enemy, for the preservation of the nation and its way of life.

In the United States, the entire population put aside their political differences and united behind President Franklin Roosevelt after the attack on Pearl Harbor and the Bataan Death March. In the American Civil War, the population in the North united behind President Lincoln after the bloody Battle of Bull Run.

China formalized this concept of unity with the "United Front" (UF). The idea of the UF originated from Leninism. Leninism held that people were divided by class and the communist was the representative of the proletarians; the communist's goal was to overthrow the capitalism oppressing the proletarians and achieve socialism and finally communism. However, to achieve this final goal, the communist could use some temporary expedients, such as allying with more minor enemies against the major target. From this came the idea of the United Front. [152]

In 1924, the new Chinese Communist Part allied with the Kuomintang (KMT), hoping to convert the Nationalist KMT to Communism. That failed, but when Mao Zedong took over the CCP, he extended the United Front concept to be a recruiting tool. United Front would be a coordinated effort, using tools from propaganda and "fake news" to coercion and violence to bring business leaders, industrialists, bankers, teachers, community leaders, farmers, workers and any group to support the aims of the CCP. In today's world in 2019, the most obvious international example is China's use of propaganda and "fake news," coercion and violence to force businesses and groups around the would accept China's position on Taiwan.

When China's war with Japan began in 1937, there was a regeneracy (regeneration of civic unity) as there is any society or nation at the beginning of a generational crisis war that puts the country and its way of life at existential risk. For China, this concept was taken over by the CCP under Mao Zedong using the United Front. The United Front would no longer just mean various social groups within China supporting or joining the CCP. It would also mean something much more important: That the CCP and KMT would stop fighting each other for a while, and join forces to fight the Japanese.

43.7. The United Front and Hong Kong

The CCP under Mao Zedong also significantly internationalized the United Front to include Chinese people and Chinese sympathizers overseas. Hong Kong played a crucial and unique role.

Recall that Hong Kong had been a British colony since the Opium wars in the 1840-50s meaning that, unlike China, Hong Kong was governed by a democracy with a capitalist economy. The result was that even in 1937 Hong Kong was already a thriving business, financial, and industrial center. Even at that time, China used Hong Kong in the same way that it does today — China maintains its own backward economy with incompetent government, but exploits Hong Kong as a portal to the rest of the world, and as its main source of foreign currency. [153]

The CCP's United Front effort made creating and developing alliances with Hong Kong's "big capitalists" the top priority. These efforts differed sharply from Communist ideological and other political campaigns on the mainland, and comprised a secretive part of the party's history. These "big capitalists" were business, industrial, and community leaders who had already been members of the National People's Congress (of China) and the Chinese People's Political Consultative Conference. [153]

At first, the party's fundamental goal was to use Hong Kong's special links to overseas Chinese communities to secure materials and mobilize resources for the anti-Japanese war effort. These valuable connections made Hong Kong special to the Communists and an important part of what they hoped would be a broader united front, outside the mainland's borders, in the struggle against the Japanese invaders. As one part of this effort, they established an Office of the Eighth Route Army in Hong Kong, which was the chief united front organization under the versatile leader Liao Chengzhi who, among other things, was responsible for arms purchases. In addition, Madame Sun Yat-sen (Soong Ching Ling) and many leftist scholars, writers and journalists arrived in Hong Kong from the late 1930s to 1941. They contributed significantly to the anti-Japanese resistance in the British colony and, before the Japanese occupation in 1941, Liao Chengzhi and the Communists maintained good working relations with many Hong Kong businessmen. [153]

43.8. American support for China before Pearl Harbor (1937-41)

America's long-standing friendship with China, combined with concern about Japan's militarism and invasions of Manchuria and northern China, caused America to side with China in the Sino-Japan war. However, America also had a policy of non-interference, and had no vital interests in China, and so had little desire to go to war with Japan — or with Germany in Europe, for that matter. [92]

America did not even enter the Sino-Japan war when Japan's warplanes bombed and sank the USS Panay on the Yangtze River on December 12, 1937, as it was evacuating Americans from Nanking during the Battle of Nanking (which became known as Japan's "Rape of Nanking"). This is notable because it was the first Japanese attack on an American naval vessel, and it was four years prior to the attack on Pearl Harbor. [94]

Three men on the USS Panay were killed, and 27 injured. The Japanese claimed that the attack was a mistake, but few people believe that. A newsreel of the Japanese warplanes sinking the ship "went viral" in America and shocked the public, especially because America was neutral in the war. Rather than risk America entering the war on the side of China, the Japanese apologized and paid compensation. [94]

The Japanese massacre of Nanking and the sinking of the USS Panay were shocks to the American public, but not shocking enough to change American opinion against being drawn into the war, especially after the apology. [94]

When war broke out in Europe in September 1939, President Franklin D. Roosevelt declared that while the United States would remain neutral in law, he could "not ask that every American remain neutral in thought as well." Because the American public was strongly against entering the war, Roosevelt began supplying weapons to Britain in exchange for leases on territory, and later on deferred payment terms known as "The Lend-Lease program," which would not require payment until after the war. [93]

Over the course of the war, the United States contracted Lend-Lease agreements with more than 30 countries, dispensing some $50 billion in assistance. Although British Prime Minister Winston Churchill later referred to the initiative as "the most unsordid act" one nation had ever done for another, Roosevelt's primary motivation was not altruism or disinterested generosity. [93]

The Lend-Lease program didn't originally apply to China, but in 1940-41, Roosevelt formalized U.S. aid to China. The U.S. extended credits to the Chinese Government for the purchase of war supplies, as it slowly began to tighten restrictions on Japan. [92]

The United States had been the main supplier of the oil, steel, iron, and other commodities needed by the Japanese military in China. But in January, 1940, Japan abrogated the existing treaty of commerce with the United States. This abrogation gave Roosevelt the ability to cut off or restrict the flow of military supplies into Japan. After January 1940, the United States combined a strategy of increasing aid to China through larger credits and the Lend-Lease program with a gradual move towards an embargo on the trade of all militarily useful items with Japan. [92]

In 1940, Japan announced the intention to drive the Western imperialist nations from Asia. On September 27, 1940, Japan signed the Tripartite Pact with Germany and Italy, making China an ally of the West. Then in mid-1941, Japan signed a Neutrality Pact with the Soviet Union, freeing Japan's military to move into Southeast Asia. A third agreement with Vichy France enabled Japanese forces to move into French Indochina and begin their Southern Advance. [92]

Although negotiations restarted after the United States increasingly enforced an embargo against Japan, they made little headway. Diplomats in Washington came close to agreements on a couple of occasions, but pro-Chinese sentiments in the United States made it difficult to reach any resolution that would not involve a Japanese withdrawal from China, and such a condition was unacceptable to Japan's military leaders. Faced with serious shortages as a result of the embargo, unable to retreat, and convinced that the U.S. officials opposed further negotiations, Japan's leaders came to the conclusion that they had to act swiftly. For their part, U.S. leaders had not given up on a negotiated settlement, and also doubted that Japan had the military strength to attack the U.S. territory. Therefore they were stunned when the unthinkable happened and Japanese planes bombed the U.S. fleet at Pearl Harbor on December 7, 1941. The following day, the United States declared war on Japan, and it soon entered into a military alliance with China. When Germany stood by its ally and declared war on the United States, the Roosevelt Administration faced war in both Europe and Asia. [92]

Part IX. Appendix: China's neighbors on the South China Sea

Chapter 44. History of Vietnam

Because of its prominent geographical position commanding the entire South China Sea, the history of Vietnam is crucial to evaluating the history of the South China Sea. As we'll see, Vietnam played an important part in the sailing and trading throughout the Champa Sea, which was what Asians called the South China Sea two millennia ago. While China was inward-directed, focusing on its internal wars and conquering neighboring lands in what is now Tibet, East Turkistan (Xinjiang) and Mongolia, the early occupants of Vietnam were outward-directed, sailing and trading through the region.

44.1. The earliest settlers — the Sa Huynh

Linguists have identified a family of languages, the Austronesian languages, that are spread throughout the islands of the Pacific Ocean. This is distinct family of languages, different from the Indo-European languages, spoken in countries stretching from India through Iran into and across Europe, and the Sino-Tibetan languages, spoken in China, Burma and Tibet.

The Austronesian family includes hundreds of languages, including languages spoken in Malaysia, Philippines, Australia, Indonesia, Taiwan and Madagascar. By comparing different languages, and determining similarities and differences among languages in the same family, it's possible to get a picture of how ancient populations spread.

The earliest settlers in Vietnam were the Sa Huynh, a people and culture that flourished between roughly 1000 BC and 500 AD, identified as speaking a Malayo-Polynesian language. They're believed to have arrived in Vietnam from what is today's island of Borneo. Archeological evidence has uncovered a Southeast Asian trading system that dates to at least 1000 BC. Because of the prominent geographical position of Vietnam, the Sa Huynh would have played a major role. [180] [181]

44.2. The Cham people and the Champa Kingdom

Malayo-Polynesian-speaking ancestors of the Cham are thought to have arrived in Vietnam by sea from Borneo. Most scholars believe the Cham are descendants of the [5]Sa Huynh, who occupied the same area from roughly 1000 B.C. to the second century A.D., when the Cham culture began flowering. [180]

For centuries the South China Sea was known by navigators throughout Asia as the Champa Sea, named for a great empire that controlled all of central Vietnam, from the northern border of today's Quang Binh Province to roughly the southern border of Binh Thuan Province. [180]

At the peak of the Champa empire, from around the 6th to the 15th centuries, its various kingdoms, presided over by regional royal families, also included sizable portions of eastern Cambodia and Laos. [180]

44.3. North Vietnam versus South Vietnam (Champa Kingdom)

North Vietnam (Vietnamese Kingdom) was originally populated by ethnic Chinese, while South Vietnam (Champa Kingdom) was populated by Polynesian settlers from Indonesia and Malaysia. These ethnic differences resulted in one crisis war after another over the centuries.

The major one occurred in 1471, when the (North) Vietnamese invaded Champa (in the South), captured its capital of Vijaya and massacred thousands of its people, effectively ending the existence of Champa kingdom. Tens of thousands of Cham were slaughtered in the invasion, taken into slavery and the capital was razed to the ground and burned in a genocide. The Cham population was permanently reduced to a low level of a few tens of thousands of people. Vietnamese colonists then moved south and settled in Champa by the thousands and now Vietnamese are in the tens of millions in former Champa while the Cham are only around 200,000 in Vietnam today. [180]

44.4. Unity and disunion in Vietnam

After the North Vietnamese conquered the Champa Kingdom in South Vietnam, the North and South Vietnamese people were enemies for centuries, and probably continue to be so to this day.

The next crisis war, in 1545, partitioned Vietnam into North and South again, and also drove out the Chinese Army from the north.

The country remained partitioned until the Tay-Son rebellion, 1771-1790, the most celebrated military event in Vietnamese history. In its explosive climax in 1789, the Vietnamese troops repelled a much larger Chinese army in a brilliant battle that united the country for the first time since 1545.

The generational awakening era that followed the Tay-Son rebellion changed the country enormously. The 1800s were the high point of literary culture in Vietnamese history, and, thanks to the French, Christianity bloomed, with hundreds of thousands of Catholic conversions from Confucianism and Buddhism. However, as the generational Unraveling era arrived (1850s-70s), Ember Tu-Duc relentlessly suppressed Christianity, sanctioning thousands of executions.

44.5. French conquest of Indochina (1865-85)

That lasted until the next crisis war, the French conquest of Indochina in 1865-1885. Under the French, the Catholic Church flourished, opening missions, schools and hospitals all over the country.

As usual, there were student riots in the generational Awakening era that followed, as there are in every generational Awakening era, and this time the riots and demonstrations were targeting the French colonists.

In 1904, the Duy Tan Hoi revolutionary (anti-colonial) society was formed, leading to a student uprising in Hanoi in 1908. This led to the rise of Ho Chi Minh. In 1920, Ho had been in France, where he took part in the founding of the French Communist Party. In 1925, he formed the Revolutionary Youth League. During WW II, Ho formed the Viet Minh political / relief organization, for people starving to death thanks to confiscation of goods by the occupying Japanese.

After WW II, Ho Chi Minh led the effort to drive the French colonialists from Vietnam, and succeeded with human wave assaults against a large French encampment at Dien Bien Phu in 1954.

With the French gone, Vietnam was once again partitioned into North and South. Ho controlled the North, with support from the Soviet Union and China, and over half a million Catholics migrated from the North to the South. America feared that South Vietnam would also fall under Communist control.

44.6. America's Vietnam war

When you look at the long history of Vietnam from the point of view of Generational Dynamics, it's easy to see how the 1960s-70s war had to do with events that were launched centuries ago.

This was the time when America had fought two world wars, and was desperately fearful of a third one on the horizon, this time with the Communists. It was considered essential to stop Communism before it could become too threatening, and so America endeavored to stop Communism from spreading from North to South Vietnam. America began providing advisors in the 1950s, growing to full-scale armed intervention in the 1960s. The North-South crisis civil war finally ended in 1974, with Hanoi's victory, followed by Hanoi's reign of terror.

In view of centuries of history, it's very hard to see any justification for the Vietnam war. The fear that the spread of Communism would have the same result as the rise of Hitler's Nazism was very real, and it was also strongly believed that World War II could have been avoided completely if Hitler had been killed or the Nazis had been stopped in 1935.

From the point of view of Generational Dynamics, all of those assumptions were completely wrong. World War II would have occurred with or without Hitler and the Nazis, and the Vietnam war was just a repeat of the North vs South civil wars that have been going on for centuries.

Today, North and South Vietnam are united, for the time being.

44.7. China's Vietnam war

China had previously given Hanoi steadfast support against U.S. forces in the Vietnam War. But their comradeship swiftly began to deteriorate in the mid-1970s, especially when Vietnam joined the Soviet-dominated Council for Mutual Economic Cooperation (Comecon) and signed the Treaty of Friendship and Cooperation with the Soviet Union (USSR) – then China's greatest rival – in 1978. China called the treaty a military alliance and branded Vietnam the "Cuba of the East," pursuing hegemonistic "imperial dreams" in Southeast Asia. [179]

On August 25, 1978, Chinese troops crossed the border to Vietnam to assault officers, women, and local people. Le Dinh Chinh, a local policeman, fought back with his bare hands and was stabbed to death by a group of Chinese. Chinh is thus known as the first Vietnamese soldier who fell in Vietnam's fight against the Chinese invasion. This incident sent an ominous signal of a looming armed conflict between the two brothers. After a few months of serious and careful preparation for a military ground campaign against Vietnam, in the pre-dawn hours of February 17, 1979, Chinese spearheads, supported by 400 tanks and 1,500 artillery pieces, concurrently attacked in the direction of Vietnam's border provincial capitals, when residents living there were still sleeping. [179]

On February 17, 1979, hundreds of thousands of Chinese troops crossed Vietnam's northern border to invade the country, waging a bloody strike along the 600-kilometer border that the two nations share. [179]

Owning to its large population and the huge disparity in economic and military capacity vis-à-vis Vietnam, the China's People's Liberation Army (PLA) relied on "human waves" of ragtag soldiers, a tactic used nearly three decades before during the Korean War, and a "scorched-earth" policy to conquer Vietnam. These tactics enabled Chinese soldiers to completely destroy everything in their paths, overrun population centers, and occupy strategically important mountainous areas and high spots along the boundary. These areas then became sites of low-profile yet deadly conflicts, which took place throughout the following decade. The war ended on March 16, 1979. [179]

The 1979 war and armed clashes that flared over border disputes in the subsequent years resulted in a heavy toll in terms of both casualties and economic losses for both sides. Though neither side publicized its casualties and the exact figures remain unclear, Western estimates run as high as 28,000 Chinese dead and 43,000 wounded, while the number of Vietnamese dead were estimated at under 10,000. [179]

Almost 40 years later, there has been not any official commemoration of the war in Vietnam. Yet since the escalation of tensions with China in the South China Sea in recent years, the Sino-Vietnamese war has begun receiving renewed media attention. Vietnamese people have begun using social media to vocally commemorate martyrs and civilians who died in the war, followed by debates criticizing the government for remaining silent and neglecting the war in high school history textbooks. [179]

Chapter 45. History of Philippines

45.1. China's history with the Philippines

What is possibly most remarkable about the history of the Philippines is that China doesn't appear in it, until the decades after World War II.

According to Chen Yue, president of the Society of Chinese Navy History in Beijing,, for thousands of years China viewed its 11,180-mile coastline as a "natural Great Wall." He said, "Before Great Britain, no nation had invaded China via the sea, so, as a result, the army held most of the resources and senior posts because inland threats were far more common." [89]

45.2. Ancient history of the Philippines

Theories vary about the origins of the original inhabitants of the Philippine islands, and how they arrived in successive waves of migration from Southeast Asia and evolved. [182]

In the beginning of the 3rd century, the inhabitants of Luzon island were in contact and trading with East Asian seafarers and merchants including the Chinese. In the 1400's the Japanese also established a trading post in Northern Luzon. [183]

In 1380, Muslim Arabs arrived at the Sulu Archipelago and established settlements which became mini-states ruled by a Datu (a term that designates indigenous royalty). They introduced Islam in the southern parts of the archipelago including some parts of Luzon and were under the control of the Muslim sultans of Borneo. They had a significant influence over the region for a couple of hundred years. The Malay Muslims remained dominant in these parts until the 16th century. [183]

45.3. Philippines Spanish colonial period (1521-1898)

Beginning in 1492, Spain was the first European nation to sail westward across the Atlantic Ocean, explore, and colonize the Amerindian nations of the Western Hemisphere. At its greatest extent, the empire that resulted from this exploration extended from Virginia on the eastern coast of the United States south to Tierra del Fuego at the tip of South America excluding Brazil and westward to California and Alaska. [185]

Portuguese explorer Ferdinand Magellan, serving the Spanish crown, arrived in the Philippines in 1521, and claimed it for Spain. Spain continued to send expeditions for financial gain, and in 1565, Spain's King Philip II, after whom the Philippines was named, took control of the Island. The legacy of Spain's control was the conversion of the people to Catholicism and the creation of the privileged landed class. [183]

By 1825 much of the Spanish Empire had fallen into other hands and in that year, Spain acknowledged the independence of its possessions in the present-day United States (then under Mexican control) and south to the tip of South America. The only remnants that remained in the Spanish empire in the Western Hemisphere were Cuba and Puerto Rico and across the Pacific in Philippines Islands, and the Carolina, Marshall, and Mariana Islands (including Guam) in Micronesia. [185]

The Spanish-American war of 1898 was originally fought over Cuba. The US had been interested in Cuba for decades, and by 1898 tensions between America and Spain were high. On February 15, 1898, an explosion caused the USS Maine to sink in Havana harbor. A US Naval Court of Inquiry found that a mine had blown up the Maine. On April 21 President McKinley ordered a blockade of Cuba, and four days later declared war with Spain. The Spanish-American war began on April 25, 1898.

Representatives of Spain and the United States signed a peace treaty in Paris on December 10, 1898, which established the independence of Cuba, ceded Puerto Rico and Guam to the United States, and allowed the victorious power to purchase the Philippines Islands from Spain for $20 million. The war had cost the United States $250 million and 3,000 lives, of whom 90% had perished from infectious diseases. [185]

45.4. Philippines under American control (1898-1946) and Japanese occupation (1941-45)

On June 12, 1898, Filipinos declared independence. This declaration was opposed by the U.S. who had plans of taking over the colony. And this led to a guerrilla war against the Americans that continued until 1901, when the US took control of the Philippines as a colony. The U.S. passed the Jones Law in 1916 establishing an elected Filipino legislature with a House of representatives & Senate. In 1934, the Tydings-McDuffie Act was passed by the U.S. Congress, established the Commonwealth of the Philippines and promised Philippine independence by 1946. [183]

On December 8, 1941, the Japanese invaded the Philippines hours after bombing Pearl Harbor in Hawaii. In March 1942, the Philippine government went into exile in Washington D.C. and American and Filipino forces surrendered on May 6, 1942. Soon a guerrilla war against the Japanese was fought by the Philippine & American Armies. In October 1944, Gen. Douglas MacArthur with Philippine President Sergio Osmeña returned and liberated the Philippines from the Japanese. [183]

In accordance with the Tydings-McDuffie Act of 1934, The Philippines was given independence on July 4, 1946 and the Republic of the Philippines was born. [183]

45.5. Modern generational history of the Philippines republic

The Communist Party of the Philippines (CPP-NPA) was formed in 1968, at the height of the generational Awakening era and of anti-government student protests in many countries, including the United States, France, Germany, and others. A pro-Maoist activist named José María Canlás Sison began the movement with the goal of removing from power the dictator Ferdinand Marcos, and of removing the influence of "American imperialism" and "Japanese imperialism" from the country. Japan and the Philippines had been enemies in World War II.

Violence and repression by Marcos' thugs aided the growth of the CPP-NPA, reaching about 10,000 members at its peak, and was supported by weapons, money and training from China's government. However, in 1976 the Philippines and China governments normalized relations, aided by the memory that they had both been invaded and occupied by the Japanese. The result for the CPP-NPA was that the Chinese cut off relations with them.

The Awakening era climax for the Philippines occurred after the 1986 elections, in which the presidency was won by the Corazon Aquino, widow of a popular oppositional senator who had been assassinated by Marcos' thugs. Marcos himself was forced to flee the country, and lived in exile in Hawaii until his death in 1989.

The defeat of Marcos, who had been dictator for 21 years, was considered by many to be a victory of the CPP-NPA. After that victory, the CPP-NPA began to lose its purpose, and turned against itself, with thousands of its members being killed by other members.

Today, it's estimated that there are still about 4,000 members of the CPP-NPA. Although the organization doesn't have anything like the power it had during the reign of Marcos, it can still pull off terrorist attacks to remind everyone that it's still around.

Sison, the founder of the group, still directs it at age 77, but has lived in exile in the Netherlands for many years.

Chapter 46. Brief generational history of Cambodia

Cambodian culture dates back to at least 5000 BC. During the period 500 BC to 500 AD, the Khmer people in Cambodia were strongly influenced by Indian culture, via India traders, bureaucrats and priests. When Khmer became a written language in about 300 AD, Indian characters were adapted for its alphabet. Cambodia adopted some Indian gods, but not the caste system of Hinduism. In the 1200s, there was a mass conversion of Cambodians to Theravada Buddhism, a religion that was also adopted by the neighboring Thais. There were several centuries of wars between the Khmer and the Thais, until the French arrived in the 1860s.

Cambodia became a French protectorate in 1863. Cambodia gained independence from France in 1953, and supported the North Vietnamese against the South Vietnamese and the Americans in America's Vietnam war. It's easy to underestimate the horror of what happened next, since in the vitriolic political atmosphere following the Vietnam war, leftists like Jane Fonda vocally denied it was even going on, saying "I will never criticize a Communist government."

And yet, the Buddhist society of the China-backed Khmer Rouge in Cambodia in 1975-79, led by Pol Pot, perpetrated one of the three or four top mass genocides of the 20th century, comparable to the huge genocides of Adolf Hitler, Josef Stalin, and Mao Zedong.

The Buddhist Cambodian "Killing Fields" genocide, 1975-79, killed something like 1.7 to well over 2 million people, out of a population of 8 million. So around 20% of Cambodia's population were killed, making it possibly the worst genocide, on a percentage basis, of the 20th century. By contrast, the Nazi Holocaust killed around 5 million, which was less than 3% of Germany's population. Pol Pot was trying to imitate Mao Zedong's Great Leap Forward in China, which was a genocide that killed tens of millions of people out of some two billion. Mao Zedong and Pol Pot may be comparable in their genocides. In all cases, these millions of people were the subject of almost unimaginable atrocities, including torture and rape.

By January 1979, the Khmer Rouge had so destroyed Cambodia that the country was too weak to fight off an invasion by Vietnamese forces. At the time, many Cambodians welcomed the Vietnamese invasion, because it freed them from the Khmer Rouge. The war between the Vietnamese and Cambodians was extremely bloody, until the Vietnamese finally withdrew in 1989.

In 1991, prime minister Hun Sen signed a peace agreement called the Paris Peace Accords, a document that guaranteed democracy and human rights in Cambodia. However, like other leaders we've described following an ethnic or tribal civil war, Hun Sen has become increasingly authoritative and dictatorial, using as an excuse that unlimited violence is justified to avoid returning to the violence of the civil war.

In October 2016, as Hun Sen was brutally cracking down in preparation for these new elections, he said the following in a speech:

> "Don't imagine you can hold a meeting like the Paris Peace conference again because the Paris Peace [Accords] agreement is like a ghost."

He told people to stop "dreaming" and harking back to the ideals of the agreement, because the Khmer Rouge were gone now, and so the agreement was useless "unless the Khmer Rouge returns."

Hun Sen is following the same generational pattern that I've described in numerous leaders from other countries, such as Bashar al-Assad in Syria, Paul Biya in Cameroon, Pierre Nkurunziza in Burundi, Paul Kagame in Rwanda, the military junta in Thailand, Yoweri Museveni in Uganda, Robert Mugabe in Zimbabwe, Salva Kiir in South Sudan, Joseph Kabila in DRC, as well as Hun Sen in Cambodia.

Chapter 47. Brief generational history of Thailand

Part of Thailand's history was made famous by Anna Leonowens, who came from London to Siam (as it was known then) to be the governess and teacher of the many children of King Mongkut (Rama IV) in the 1860s. In 1895, she wrote memoirs that were turned into a film, "Anna and the King of Siam" in 1946, and into the 1952 Rodgers and Hammerstein Broadway musical, "The King and I."

The play depicts a troubled king trying to lead a small country surrounded by large enemies, and willing to use invasion, torture and other atrocities.

King Rama had fought a generational crisis war in the early 1830s when he had invaded Laos and Cambodia, but ended up losing to a Vietnamese army.

Siam's next generational crisis war occurred in what is now southern Thailand. For centuries, Siam's kings had felt that the Muslims in southern Siam were a major threat to the security of the country, mainly because resistance and rebellion against Thai government rule were so strong among the Muslim population, and in fact the southern Muslims had revolted during the 1830s crisis war.

By the late 1800s this threat had been felt to be critical, and in 1902 King Rama V invaded and annexed the Malay kingdom of Patani, consisting of the four provinces of Satun, Yala, Pattani and Narathiwat. (Note: The kingdom is spelled "Patani," while the province is spelled "Pattani.") In 1909, an Anglo-Siamese Agreement established the present border between Thailand and Malaysia.

During the next few decades, Siam (which became Thailand in 1939) was faced with the problem of trying to assimilate the southern Muslim population into what is essentially a Buddhist country. During the generational Awakening era that followed, the military coup of 1932 overthrew the absolute monarchy in Siam and replaced it with constitutional monarchy. This was a representative form of government that promised a high degree of political participation of the Malay-Muslims in the South. However, as World War II (an Awakening era war for Thailand) approached, the country became more Thai-nationalistic, and the country adopted a policy of forced assimilation towards the Muslims, which had little success, as resistance and rebellion have continued since then.

The 1930s also saw a large influx of migrants from China, coming to the country to work. Over the decades, they were able to displace the indigenous people in positions of power in government, and in control of businesses. This formed an ethnic fault line between the indigenous Thai-Thai majority and the elite Thai-Chinese minority.

The next generational crisis war was the Cambodian "killing fields" war, 1975-79, in which Pol Pot's communist Khmer Rouge government, backed by China, killed 1.7-3 million people in a massive genocide. The Cambodian war spilled over into Thailand in the form of a communist rebellion that had begun in the 1960s. King Bhumibol (Rama IX) became an essential figure in the fight against the communists, although his role became more controversial in the savage anti-leftist coup of 1976, in which dozens of students were brutally killed by the security forces and royal-backed militias, and thousands forced to flee to seek sanctuary with the Communist Party.

The Cambodian "killing fields" civil war took place on Thailand's doorstep, though not on Thai soil. Still, it caused a split along the Thai-Thai versus Thai-Chinese fault line that continues to the present time. Today, Thailand is in a new generational Awakening/Unraveling era, and we're seeing a repeat of what happened in the 1930s.

During the generational Awakening era of the 1930s, the military coup of 1932 overthrew the absolute monarchy in Siam and replaced it with constitutional monarchy that gave some power to the southern Muslims, only to have it taken away a few years later.

During the current era, the 1997 constitution guaranteed free elections for everyone, including the indigenous Thai-Thai, and now that's being taken away by a military junta. History doesn't repeat itself, but it rhymes.

Chapter 48. Brief generational history of Myanmar (Burma)

The following is a brief Generational Dynamics history of Burma (Myanmar):

Crisis war: 1727-1752: Various rebellions against the Toungoo throne at Ava. The crisis war climax occurred when the Ava throne fell in 1752, after a siege by a combined army of different ethnic groups, ending the Toungoo dynasty.

Crisis war: First Burmese War, 1824-26. British victory. Britain annexes the southern portion of Burma, which becomes part of British India.

Awakening Era war: Second Burmese War, 1852-53. Britain annexed additional territory.

Crisis war: Third Burmese War + civil war, 1886-1891. The war with Britain itself ended with a quick Burmese surrender to Britain, but violent civil war among various ethnic groups continued until 1891.

Awakening: 1920 - A generational split between old and young (presumably between generational "Artists" and "Prophets") members of the Young Men's Buddhist Association. Younger members rename the organization the General Council of Burmese Associations, dedicated to anti-colonialism.

Unraveling war: World War II, 1940-45. Occupation by Japan.

1948: Independence, formation of the Union of Burma.

Note: Aung San, commander of the Burma Independence Army, is considered to be the founding father of Burma. He was assassinated six months before final independence.

Crisis war: 1948-1958: Civil war among ethnic groups, with intervention by Chinese. Climax in 1958 when the army took over power, and turned power over to a civilian government.

The army overthrew the civilian government in 1962, and has remained in power since then.

Awakening Era climax: On 8/8/88, hundreds of thousands of students in the "88 generation," joined by monks and civilians, marched against the military government. Soldiers opened fire on demonstrators with machine guns, resulting in thousands of casualties.

Note: Aung San Suu Kyi, daughter of Aung San, participated in the 1988 demonstrations, calling for democratic government. In 1989, she was placed under house arrest without charge or trial. In 1991, she won the Nobel Peace prize.

2008: On the 20th anniversary of 1988 massacre, there are massive new demonstrations in Burma, led by monks and nuns, but now joined by many ordinary citizens. The tension in Rangoon is great, and the military government is evidently trying to decide whether to let things be, hoping the demonstrations will fizzle, or repeat the violent reprisals of 1988. Since this is an unraveling era, it would seem that the demonstrations will indeed fizzle, unless the army overreacts.

2010: The army released Aung San Suu Kyi from house arrest.

2016: Aung San Suu Kyi's political party, the National League for Democracy (NLD), overwhelmingly won the national elections, making her the *de facto* leader of the country, though still effectively controlled by the army.

On August 25, 2017, Burmese army military announced the beginning of "clearance operations," which was full-scale genocide and ethnic cleansing. Burma's Buddhist army conducted a scorched earth attack on Rohingya Muslims, burning down thousands of homes and buildings, and hundreds of entire villages. The army committed massacres, torture, rapes and other atrocities that have displaced hundreds of thousands of people, with hundreds of thousands fleeing for their lives, crossing the border into Bangladesh.

Burma's government, led by the ethnic cleanser-in-chief and Nobel Peace Prize winner Aung San Suu Kyi, denied that any ethnic cleansing was taking place, and made the laughable claim that Rohingyas were burning down their own villages and killing each other.

Myanmar's genocide and ethnic cleansing program has driven over 700,000 Rohingyas out of the country, mostly into filthy refugee camps in Bangladesh, destabilizing the entire region. Aung San Suu Kyi and other Myanmar officials pretend that the problem has never even existed, despite massive evidence in the form of BBC and Reuters reporting, and interviews with thousands of refugees that fled the torture, rape and violence by the Burmese army in Myanmar.

If we compare the Buddhist genocide of Muslim Rohingya to the Buddhist Cambodian Killing Fields genocide, it may well be that the Buddhists in Burma may be borrowing some techniques from their Buddhist cousins in the 1970s Khmer rouge. This would be a historic example of one group of genocidal Buddhists learning genocide from another group of genocidal Buddhists. This comparison became even more dramatic when Burma's government announced that the government will take over the land that contained the villages that Burma's army burned down, making the ethnic cleansing permanent.

This is speculation, but there may be an even more memorable connection. The Cambodian Killing Fields genocide was based on Mao Zedong's Great Leap Forward genocide, and if the Burma genocide was based on the Cambodian Killing Fields genocide, then we have remarkable sequence of genocidal events, from the Great Leap Forward to the Killing Fields to the Rohingyas.

It's also astonishing to me that no one seems to care that there are three events of genocide and ethnic cleansing in three countries today, all targeting Sunni Muslims — in China targeting the Uighurs, in Myanmar targeting the

Rohingyas, and in Syria targeting Sunni Arabs. After hearing people talk about the Holocaust my whole life, saying "Never again," it's almost beyond belief that there are three Holocausts going on today, and nobody cares, even other Muslims.

Part X. The End

Chapter 49. About Generational Theory

49.1. Intuitive description of generational theory

The easiest way to understand generational theory is to think about American mothers in the 1950s. These mothers are almost universally stereotyped as repressed and controlled, and forced to stay at home, in the kitchen, barefoot and pregnant. This is the stereotype, but absolutely none of it is true.

A 1950s mother would have grown up during the Great Depression, surrounded by homelessness, starvation and bankruptcy. If she herself hadn't been forced to live under a bridge and depend on soup kitchens for food, then she undoubtedly had many friends who had been forced to do so.

Then, as the Great Depression ended, she saw her brothers, father and uncles tortured and maimed on the Bataan Death March, and then shot down like fish in a barrel on the beaches of Normandy. Out of patriotism, she had been forced to take "Rosie the Riveter" type jobs that she hated.

So when the 1950s arrived, a home with a white picket fence where a mother could stay at home with the kids and be safe and dry and warm and reliably supported by a working husband was a gift from heaven. This was a gift that mothers of the 1950s wanted to give to their daughters. They had suffered through starvation, homelessness and slaughter, and they had won, and they wanted to give their daughters the gift of the fruits of that victory.

Unfortunately, their daughters didn't want those gifts. Their scorn and contempt for those gifts gave rise to the women's lib and feminist movements of the 60s and beyond, holding their own mothers and their mothers' values in contempt.

Generational theory is based on the very obvious fact that children rebel against their parents, and so each generation differs significantly from the previous one. These generational changes turn out to be quite predictable, and generational theory captures those predictable changes.

In the last century, the foundational work on generational theory was done by several researchers, including Anthony Wallace, William McLoughlin, Neil Howe and William Strauss. Their research examined generational changes in England and the United States, based on intuitive conclusions drawn from reading historical diaries. Much of that work was brilliant, but there were errors and misjudgments from its lack of rigor and provability, and may critics said that it was no better than astrology.

In the 21st century, John J. Xenakis has led the development of generational theory on the web site GenerationalDynamics.com. There are thousands of generational analyses and forecasts for hundreds of countries, including Iran, Turkey, China, Pakistan, Sri Lanka, Uganda, and other countries all over the world. These analyses and forecast have proven to be extremely accurate, proving the validity of Generational Dynamics and generational theory. This body of work continues every day, providing a country by country picture of where the world is and where it's going.

This book on China provides an in-depth Generational Dynamics analysis of the history of China and its relations with its neighbors, just as his previous book provided an in-depth Generational Dynamics analysis to the entire span of Persian history, from the early Persian empires to the present time. These books also serve as additional validation of generational theory by providing a generational analysis of the entire history of other nations provided the United States and other Western nations. Books providing similar "World View" analyses of other topics and countries will follow.

49.2. Use of GenerationalDynamics.com web site

The foundational work on generational theory developed in the last century was intuitive, but because of a lack of rigor and provability contained a number of errors. Generational Theory as I've been developing it for over 15 years has had the objective of providing theoretical rigor to generational theory.

The GenerationalDynamics.com web site has been a crucial part of the theoretical development, by providing a provability platform. By 2003, I had developed the "Principle of Localization," which said that, rather than every country in the world being on the same generational timeline, every nation or society has its own generational timeline. That solved the world war problems, and many other problems. With that addition, generational theory finally made sense and seemed plausible.

That's when I set up the Generational Dynamics web site, and started writing articles that analyzed current events according to generational theory. In my own mind, the purpose was clear: If I could not use generational theory to analyze and predict current events, then I would have to assume that the entire theory was based on cherry-picking events in Anglo-American history, and was therefore worthless as astrology as a theory.

So on 5/1/2003 I posted my article on "Mideast Roadmap - Will it bring peace?" and interpreted Bush's mideast roadmap to peace through generational theory, concluding that the plan would fail. I remember thinking that this might be a completely wrong. Six months later, the Israelis and Palestinians might have shaken hands on a deal that would create two-states side-by-side blah blah blah. I predicted that it couldn't happen, and if it had happened, then I would have probably have completely dropped my interest in generational theory forever, and gone on to lead a much more normal and probably happier life.

I'll mention one place where the theory had to be changed to reflect reality. I originally said that a major war in Syria was impossible in an Awakening era, but then when the 2011 war in Syria turned out to be a major war I ended up developing an entire theory of Awakening era wars that applied to dozens of nations. So my mistake really turned out to be a huge benefit in the end.

Events actually proceeded as predicted, and so I continued development of Generational Dynamics and generational theory. Today there are almost 6,000 articles on the GenerationalDynamics.com web site, and all of them have turned out to be right or are trending right. None has been proven wrong. These analyses and forecasts have proven to be extremely accurate, proving the validity of Generational Dynamics and generational theory.

49.3. Theoretical core for Generational Dynamics

Theoretically, Generational Dynamics is non-ideological. It uses System Dynamics applied to populations. System Dynamics was developed by Jay Forrester at MIT in the 1960s. It's usually applied to analyze physical things, like the flow of water through a pipe. Applying it to population flows is a major development and advance for both generational theory and System Dynamics itself.

Another discipline used by Generational Dynamics is Chaos Theory. Whereas System Dynamics tells you how to predict and forecast things, Chaos Theory tells you what things you can and can't predict. For example, Chaos Theory tells you that you can't predict the results of elections. But when Chaos Theory concepts like fractals and cyclic attractors are applied to the generational flow analyzed by System Dynamics, then you can identify long-term trends that can be predicted, such as the ebb and flow of nationalism and xenophobia.

Another discipline used by Generational Dynamics is a special form of historical analysis. A generational analysis looks for special kinds of historical events that cause major changes in attitudes of entire populations. The most obvious are the events involved in the "Regeneracy," which is a generational theory term referring to the regeneracy of civic unity for the first time since the end of the preceding crisis war.

For example, at the end of the 1930s, America was just as politically divided under President Franklin Roosevelt as it is today under President Trump. But the bombing of Pearl Harbor and the Bataan Death March were "Regeneracy events" that caused the whole country to put political differences aside, and unite behind the president, thus "regenerating civic unity" instantly. Exactly the same thing will happen today. If there's an attack on American soil, or a major military defeat overseas, then Americans will put aside their political differences and unite behind Trump (or the next president) overnight.

Here's another example, from this book.

The first time that I read about the Battle of Myongnyang (or Myeongnyang, October 26, 1597), I was stunned. From the point of view of Generational Dynamics, this was clearly a battle of epochal importance. A small group of about 13 Korean ships lured a Japanese invading navy of hundreds of ships into a trap and destroyed them all. Such a devastating and humiliating battle would have affected Japanese policy for centuries, and certainly was a major factor in Japan's rapid militarization after the Meiji Restoration. I have called the Battle of Myongnyang the most important battle in East Asia for the entire millennium, prior to World War II, and I believe that it is.

But the Battle of Myeongnyang is barely mentioned in any of the historical documents that I looked at. To most historians, this is just another of a million battles that occurred in the millennium, but from the point of view of Generational Dynamics, it's hugely important.

Other disciplines that are used in Generational Dynamics analyses are sociology, population dynamics, economics, macroeconomics, mathematical logic (for using abstract models to apply results to the real world), technological forecasting, sociological analysis, and even the theory of evolution. What each of these disciplines does is help determine which events affect the attitudes of the entire population or entire generations. Once the important events have been selected, they can be fed back into the System Dynamics analysis to determine their effects in the future.

Chapter 50. Leon Festinger and Cognitive Dissonance

In the preceding chapter, we listed the disciplines — System Dynamics, Chaos Theory, historical analysis — that go into Generational Dynamics analysis. The purpose of this chapter is to suggest that with additional research, the study of "cognitive dissonance" can be added to that list of disciplines, and become a valuable component of a Generational Dynamics analysis.

Let's take an example from this book to show how it might be applied. We've shown the following in this book:

- Since historical times, the Chinese people have considered themselves to be superior to other ethnic groups, whom they consider to be barbarians. This concept has been imbued in the Chinese culture for three millennia.
- For almost a century, the Chinese have been completely committed to Marxism, Communism and Socialism, believing them superior to capitalism or Western economic systems.
- China's government has been deeply committed to these beliefs, and have taken major steps on those beliefs. Of particular note is the Great Leap Forward.

These deeply held and deeply committed beliefs have been completely destroyed by events. The barbarian Japanese repeatedly defeated the Chinese, diplomatically, militarily and economically, and the Great Leap Forward proved that the Chinese are wrong about Communism, Socialism and Marxism.

So this situation is the setup for the application of the study of Cognitive Dissonance: What does a person (or a country) do when deeply held and committed beliefs are disproved by reality?

There is a psychological explanation for how people can go from the first of these to the second. It's call "cognitive dissonance," and it refers to how a person reacts when deeply held beliefs are proven wrong by reality. Instead of accepting the reality, many people react by doubling down and trying to prove the deeply held but false belief by any means possible.

The 1956 book *When Prophecy Fails* by Leon Festinger can be purchased from online booksellers, or is available from https://archive.org/details/pdfy-eDNpDzTy_dR1b0iB as a free PDF. I read this book decades ago, and it made an enormous impression on me. I strongly urge everyone to read it.

First I'll describe the book's methodology and conclusions, and then I'll explain how it applies to China today.

Festinger was interested in religious cults that predict the end of the world on an explicit date, commit themselves fully to it by giving up their families and belongings, and then have to face the world again when the world doesn't end.

This is called "cognitive dissonance," when deeply held beliefs are contradicted by incontrovertible facts.

Festinger found that people in such a situation do not simply give up their beliefs because their beliefs were proved wrong. Instead, they double down on the beliefs, and look for any way to justify them. In the case of end world predictions, the easiest way is to believe that God provided the world with a reprieve provided that the chosen people begin to proselytize the new belief system. From this brief description, you can get an idea of how this applies to China, and how they might pursue war.

Festinger was aware of a religious sect that was predicting the end of the world on a specific date. Two members of Festinger's team infiltrated the religious sect. The predictions were based on messages from extraterrestrials known as the "Guardians" that one cult member, Mrs. Marian Keech, started receiving. The members of the sect would be rescued by flying saucers and then, four days later, there would be a huge flood drowning everyone left behind. The members of the sect were highly committed to this belief: Many had given up their families and all worldly belongings to join the other sect members in a vigil in a member's home, waiting for the end.

The first disconfirmation came when the flying saucers didn't show up at the predicted time. There were four wrenching days of waiting, as the saucers failed to come at each newly predicted hour, as specified by Mrs. Keech as she continued to receive "messages." The final and biggest disconfirmation came after the four days were up, and the world did not end.

Although the group were a private sect, what they were doing had become known, and they received ridicule through the newspapers, and they received visits by people who believed them and people who ridiculed them. During the four-day wait, a couple of people, the people who had joined most recently, left the group, but everyone else stayed. Here's what happened:

> Chaotic though they may seem, the days immediately preceding December 21 [the day that the floods were supposed to appear] were at least loosely organized around a dominant theme — cataclysm and salvation. By dawn on the 21st, however, this semblance of organization had vanished as the members of the group sought frantically to convince the world of their beliefs. In succeeding days, they also made a series of desperate attempts to erase their rankling dissonance by making prediction after prediction in the hope that one would come true, and they conducted a vain search for guidance from the Guardians."

Another change of behavior was equally familiar in today's politically divided world: Led by Mrs. Keech, the cult members began actively proselytizing. They had previously kept information about the cataclysm secret, "in order to prevent panic." But now they sought out even the most skeptical nonbelievers, in order to convert them. For example, one sarcastic commentator whom Mrs. Keech had repeatedly refused to speak with suddenly was welcomed with open arms. In fact, Mrs. Keech couldn't stop talking, as he recorded the interview, and she answered all his questions in detail.

Another reporter who hosted a program on women's issues asked her to comment, and she spoke at length on what's wrong with education, and how the messages from the Guardians explained how to straighten it out.

Hordes of reporters and visitors came to the house, resulting in an "amiable, manic uproar."

> One further trend was noticeable on December 21. As the day wore on, Mrs. Keech began to make more and more of the importance of some recent news items. The morning newspapers contained an article about an earthquake in Nevada that had occurred about five days earlier, pointing out that if the quake had happened in a populated area, the destruction would have been enormous. Mrs. Keech showed the story excitedly to the members of the group, emphasizing the fact that, indeed, cataclysms *were* happening.... Here, she declared, was evidence for the validity of the prediction. This theme ... grew in importance in response to further disaster news."

The next day, the group put out a press release saying that the Guardians had postponed the cataclysm, "Due to the confusion which has arisen from the prophecy we have decided to unite forces to complete the prophecy." In other words, they were proselytizing in a press release.

Festinger found that when deeply held beliefs are contradicted by incontrovertible facts, the result is not to abandon the beliefs, but to double down on them, with any possible explanation, even bizarre fantastical explanations. This is the result of cognitive dissonance.

Festinger's book lists five conditions that lead to this "cognitive dissonance" response to disconfirmation:

> "1. A belief must be held with deep conviction and it must have some relevance to action, that is, to what the believer does or how he behaves.
>
> 2. The person holding the belief must have committed himself to it; that is, for the sake of his belief, he must have taken some important action that is difficult to undo. In general, the more important such actions are, and the more difficult they are to undo, the greater is the individual's commitment to the belief.
>
> 3. The belief must be sufficiently specific and sufficiently concerned with the real world so that events may unequivocally refute the belief.

4. Such undeniable disconfirmatory evidence must occur and must be recognized by the individual holding the belief. ...

5. The individual believer must have social support. It is unlikely that one isolated believer could withstand the kind of dis-confirming evidence we have specified. If, however, the believer is a member of a group of convinced persons who can support one another, we would expect the belief to be maintained and the believers to attempt to proselyte or to persuade nonmembers that the belief is correct."

These are Festinger's five conditions for the disconfirmation of a belief in the end of the world by a religious cult.

Festinger's findings apply only in the specific situation he tested — a small group expecting the end of the world — but it's easy to see how his findings can be extended to larger groups or to entire nations, and how additional research could show that it applies to China's doubling down and preparing to launch a world war.

I've quoted the following several times, and I do so again: Friedrich Nietzsche said, "Insanity in individuals is something rare - but in groups, parties, nations and epochs, it is the rule."

Extreme cognitive dissonance is indeed a form of insanity.

Chapter 51. About John J. Xenakis

John J. Xenakis has a varied career. He started out studying mathematics at Massachusetts Institute of Technology, and completed all course and exam requirements for a PhD except the thesis. He spent most of his career as Computer Scientist and Senior Software Engineer, and also wrote thousands of articles as Technology Editor and Analyst for several business and technical publications.

After the attack on New York's World Trade Center on September 11, 2001, Mr. Xenakis became interested in work that had been done earlier on generational theory, and how it seemed to predict that something like the 9/11 attack would occur. He realized generational theory would be useless if it only applied to American and English generations. If generational theory could not be used to analyze and predict current events in all countries at all times, then we would have to assume that the entire theory was based on cherry-picking events in Anglo-American history, and was therefore worthless as a theory, no better than astrology.

He pulled together a number of disciplines — technological forecasting, system dynamics, chaos theory, historical analysis and computational complexity theory — and combined them with generational theory to produce a complete, sophisticated theory called Generational Dynamics, and used the web site GenerationalDynamics.com as a development platform. He's written thousands of analyses and forecasts showing that generational theory is a valid analysis tool for all countries at all times in history.

Mr. Xenakis admits that even he is astonished by how successful Generational Dynamics has been in analyzing and forecasting future events in one country after another. He says, "If you had asked me thirty years ago whether it was even possible to do what I'm doing today, I would have said that it's mathematically impossible." However, in brief, it was the application of Chaos Theory to generational theory that provided the breakthrough, since Chaos Theory tells you exactly what can and cannot be predicted.

The first major test occurred on May 1, 2003, when Xenakis posted an article "Mideast Roadmap - Will it bring peace?" President George Bush had just published his "Mideast Roadmap to Peace" providing specific proposals for a Palestinian state by 2005 side by side with Israel. Xenakis did a detailed generational analysis and showed that the plan would not succeed because Arabs and Jews would be refighting the 1948 war that their great-grandparents' generation had fought, following the United Nations partitioning of Palestine and the creation of the state of Israel.

Xenakis says, "When I posted that analysis, I remember thinking that it might be a completely wrong, that generational theory might be completely wrong. Six months later, the Israelis and Palestinians might have shaken hands on a deal that would create two-states side-by-side, and so forth. My prediction was that it couldn't happen, so if it had happened, then I would have probably have completely dropped my interest in generational theory forever, and gone on to lead a much more normal and probably happier life."

Now, fifteen years and thousands of "World View" analyses and forecasts on hundreds of countries later, this success has been repeated over and over, proving the validity of Generational Dynamics. These analyses can be found on the web site GenerationalDynamics.com

Chapter 52. Acknowledgments

I would like to thank Cynthia Xenakis for proofreading the draft and making valuable suggestions.

I would like to thank Professor Linnea McCord for proofreading the draft and making valuable suggestions. She is author of the book *The Wisdom of Ants: Restore the Secret Power of Trust That Made America Great Before It's Too Late*

https://www.amazon.com/Wisdom-Ants-Restore-Secret-America-ebook/dp/B01GW6JGVE

I would like to thank David Schroeder, a retired American Army Colonel with 30 years experience as an Army Officer, for his numerous contributions in the Generational Dynamics forum (http://gdxforum.com/forum) on probable likely Chinese military strategies. Schroeder has a secondary career as a military simulation creator/publisher, and blogs at the http://www.comingstorms.com web site.

Numerous other people — Chinese, Vietnamese, Japanese, Taiwanese, Korean, Indian, and others — contributed thoughtful comments in the Generational Dynamics forum (http://gdxforum.com/forum). These comments made their way into the text by influencing much of the narrative. I would like to thank all of these people for their valuable contributions.

Part XI. Footnotes / References

[FOOTNOTES]

[1] WorldAffairsJournal(6/2013): Lebensraum / Historical Fiction: China's South China Sea Claims http://www.worldaffairsjournal.org/article/historical-fiction-china%E2%80%99s-south-china-sea-claims

[2] NationalInterest(1/2/2013): Lebensraum / Sun Yat-sen / Chiang Kai-shek / Rejuvenation / China's Nationalist Heritage https://nationalinterest.org/article/chinas-nationalist-heritage-7885

[3] ChineseToLearn: Lyrics: Descendants of the Dragon / Heirs of the Dragon http://www.chinesetolearn.com/%E9%BE%8D%E7%9A%84%E5%82%B3%E4%BA%BA-heirs-dragon-song-pinyin-english-translation-dragon-symbolic-chinese-chinese/

[4] ChinaDaily(5/24/2016): Su Chengfen / Ancient book 'provides ironclad proof of Chinese ownership' http://www.chinadaily.com.cn/china/2016-05/24/content_25433846.htm

[5] BBC(6/19/2016): South China Sea: Does a book prove China's claim? http://www.bbc.com/news/world-asia-36562116

[6] UNCLOS(7/12/2016): Permanent Court of Arbitration ruling on Philippines case vs China https://pca-cpa.org/en/news/pca-press-release-the-south-china-sea-arbitration-the-republic-of-the-philippines-v-the-peoples-republic-of-china/

[7] ChinaDaily(3/20/2018): NPC / Highlights of President Xi's keynote speech http://www.chinadaily.com.cn/a/201803/20/WS5ab073aba3106e7dcc142b7b.html

[8] BBCWorldService(3/20/2018): Transcription: Xi Jinping's 'great rejuvenation' https://www.bbc.co.uk/worldserviceradio

[9] SCMP(10/26/2018): Prepare for war', Xi Jinping tells military region that monitors South China Sea, Taiwan https://www.scmp.com/news/china/military/article/2170452/prepare-war-xi-jinping-tells-military-region-monitors-south

[10] Hoover.org(10/9/2018): Uighur extermination / China's Final Solution In Xinjiang https://www.hoover.org/research/chinas-final-solution-xinjiang

[11] Biography.com: Xi Jinping Biography President (non-U.S.) (1953–) https://www.biography.com/people/xi-jinping-031016

[12] SCMP(10/27/2016): Chinese Communist Party expands Xi Jinping's political power, anointing him 'core' leader http://www.scmp.com/news/china/policies-politics/article/2040675/chinese-communist-party-expands-xi-jinpings-political?utm_content=buffer1cf0e&utm_medium=social&utm_source=twitter.com&utm_campaign=buffer

[13] Smithsonian: Introduction to Human Evolution http://humanorigins.si.edu/education/introduction-human-evolution

[14] EssentialHumanities: World History Timeline http://www.essential-humanities.net/history-overview/world-history-timeline/

[15] SCMP(12/14/2003): The significance of Peking Man https://www.scmp.com/article/438138/significance-peking-man

[16] Ancient.eu(1/10/2016): The Xia Dynasty (c. 2070-1600 BCE) https://www.ancient.eu/Xia_Dynasty/

[17] Ancient.eu(1/28/2016): Shang Dynasty (c.1600-1046 BCE) https://www.ancient.eu/Shang_Dynasty/

[18] History.com(8/21/2018): Shang Dynasty https://www.history.com/topics/ancient-china/shang-dynasty

[19] Ancient.eu(7/18/2017): Sun Tzu / The Art of War (500 BC)
https://www.ancient.eu/The_Art_of_War/

[20] UnivTenn/EncyclopediaPhilosophy: Confucius / Jeff Richey (551 – 479 B.C.E.)
https://www.iep.utm.edu/confuciu/

[21] NewAdvent: Theodicy http://www.newadvent.org/cathen/14569a.htm

[22] NewWorldEncyclopedia: Shang / Zhou / Confucius / Tian
http://www.newworldencyclopedia.org/entry/Tian

[23] Famous Confucius sayings http://www.quoteambition.com/famous-confucius-quotes/

[24] Gutenberg: Art of War, Sun Tzu, 500 BC http://www.gutenberg.org/etext/132

[25] Indiana-edu(2010): Laozi - Dao de jing and Commentary
http://www.indiana.edu/~p374/Daodejing.pdf

[26] Columbia-edu(2009): Introduction to Daoism [1][IMAGE]
http://afe.easia.columbia.edu/special/china_1000bce_daoism.htm

[27] Praxeology.net: Dao de jing / Selections from Lao-tzu (Laozi): Tao Te Ching (Daode-jing)
http://praxeology.net/laotzu.htm

[28] Ancient-eu/MarkCartwright(7/12/2017): China / Warring States Period (481/403 - 221 BC)
https://www.ancient.eu/Warring_States_Period/

[29] History.com(8/21/2018): China / Qin Dynasty (221-206 BC)
https://www.history.com/topics/ancient-china/qin-dynasty

[30] History.com(8/21/2018): Han Dynasty [206 BC - 220 AD]
https://www.history.com/topics/ancient-china/han-dynasty

[31] Ancient.eu/CristianViolatti(5/27/2013): China / Han Dynasty (206 BCE-220 CE)
https://www.ancient.eu/Han_Dynasty/

[32] Archive-org(Book,1971?): A History of China by Wolfram Eberhard
https://archive.org/details/ost-history-a_history_of_china

[33] EiilmUniversity-in: Eiilm University - History Of China And Japan 1840-1949
http://www.eiilmuniversity.co.in/downloads/History_china_and_Japan_1840_1949.pdf

[34] JohnKingFairbank(1996): John King Fairbank, The Great Chinese Revolution 1800-1985, Harper
& Row, 1986 https://www.amazon.com/Great-Chinese-Revolution-1800-1985/dp/006039076X

[35] Barrons(1980): Jean Reeder Smith and Lacey Baldwin Smith, Essentials of World History,
Barron's Education Series Inc., 1980 http://Not-available-online

[36] PeterNStearns(2001): Peter N. Stearns (Editor), The Encyclopedia of World History, 6th edition,
Houghton Mifflin Co., 2001 https://www.amazon.com/Encyclopedia-World-History-
Medieval-Chronologically/dp/0227679687

[37] BritishMuseum: History of China
https://www.britishmuseum.org/pdf/History%20of%20China.pdf

[38] PennState: Brief History of China https://www.engr.psu.edu/xinli/ENGR197/history.pdf

[39] HarvardExtension(2016): History of China https://www.edx.org/course/china-part-1-political-
intellectual-harvardx-sw12-1-0

[40] MetMuseumOfArt: List of dynasties / List of Rulers of China
https://www.metmuseum.org/toah/hd/chem/hd_chem.htm

[41] Quora(12/7/2018): Why are the Chinese people called Han Chinese? Why not Ming Chinese or
Song Chinese? https://www.quora.com/Why-are-the-Chinese-people-called-Han-Chinese-
Why-not-Ming-Chinese-or-Song-Chinese

[42] SCIO-cn(4/2018): Full text: China's Policies and Practices on Protecting Freedom of Religious
Belief http://www.scio.gov.cn/zfbps/32832/Document/1626734/1626734.htm

[43] Hoocher: Confucianism And Taoism
https://www.hoocher.com/Religion/confucianismandtaoism.htm

[44] NewWorldEncyclopedia(2013): Xiongnu
http://www.newworldencyclopedia.org/entry/Xiongnu#Juqu_.26_Northern_Liang_.28401-
460.29

[45] FactsAndDetails(2015): Early Tibetan History
http://factsanddetails.com/china/cat6/sub32/item229.html

[46] LocalHistories: A Brief History Of Tibet http://www.localhistories.org/tibet.html

[47] Ancient-Origins(6/4/2017): The White Lotus Society and the Demise of Mongol Rule in China
https://www.ancient-origins.net/history-important-events/white-lotus-society-and-demise-mongol-rule-china-008182

[48] GlobalSecurity: China / Secret Societies
https://www.globalsecurity.org/military/world/china/history-secret-societies.htm

[49] WilliamStanton-TriadSociety(Book, 1900): White Lotus Society / The Triad society; or, Heaven and earth association by Stanton, William
https://archive.org/details/triadsocietyorh01stangoog

[50] BBC(1/14/2004): Tibetan Buddhism
http://www.bbc.co.uk/religion/religions/buddhism/subdivisions/tibetan_1.shtml

[51] ThoughtCo(7/29/2017): An Introduction to Tibetan Buddhism
https://www.thoughtco.com/tibetan-buddhism-introduction-450178

[52] ChinaEmbassy(1999): Falun Gong / True Face of Li Hongzhi http://www.china-embassy.org/eng/zt/ppflg/t36564.htm

[53] QiJournal(Summer 2000): Is Qigong Political? A New Look at Falun Gong https://www.qi-journal.com/Qigong.asp?Name=Is%20Qigong%20Political?%20A%20New%20Look%20at%20F alun%20Gong&-token.D=Article

[54] Facts-cn(11/13/2007): What are the main differences between Qigong and Falun Gong?
http://www.facts.org.cn/QandA/200711/t69242.htm

[55] LeeHolden(5/2/2011): History of Qigong
http://www.leeholden.com/announcements/history-of-qigong

[56] Economist(8/30/2018): Li Hongzhi / The party's scourge - Falun Gong still worries China, despite efforts to crush the sect https://www.economist.com/china/2018/08/30/falun-gong-still-worries-china-despite-efforts-to-crush-the-sect

[57] CatholicReview(1/19/2012): Brief history of the Catholic Church in China
https://www.archbalt.org/brief-history-of-the-catholic-church-in-china/

[58] La-croix/UCANews(7/20/2018): Sinicization / How can Catholics rewrite China's bloody history? https://international.la-croix.com/news/how-can-catholics-rewrite-china-s-bloody-history/8100

[59] PBS(~2010): A Brief History of Christianity in China
http://www.pbs.org/frontlineworld/stories/china_705/history/china.html

[60] SCMP(10/2/2018): With a historic pact, the Vatican continues its battle with Beijing for Chinese hearts and minds https://www.scmp.com/comment/insight-opinion/united-states/article/2166602/historic-pact-vatican-continues-its-battle

[61] SCMP(3/30/2018): Betrayed and abandoned: why China's underground Catholics feel like Jesus on Good Friday https://www.scmp.com/news/china/policies-politics/article/2139524/chinas-underground-catholics-torn-between-hope-and

[62] DW(2/16/2018): China / Catholic / Sieren's China: Vatican makes peace with Beijing
https://www.dw.com/en/sierens-china-vatican-makes-peace-with-beijing/a-42620807

[63] BillionBibles: China - Protestant Churches - Three Self Church - Three Self Patriotic Movement
http://www.billionbibles.com/china/three-self-church.html

[64] Reuters(9/10/2018): Closed-circuit tv cameras / China outlaws large underground Protestant church in Beijing https://www.reuters.com/article/us-china-religion/china-outlaws-large-underground-protestant-church-in-beijing-idUSKCN1LQ07W

[65] DW(1/19/2018): Demolishing churches / In Xi we trust - Is China cracking down on Christianity? https://www.dw.com/en/in-xi-we-trust-is-china-cracking-down-on-christianity/a-42224752

[66] ChinaCenter(1/29/2016): China / Protestant Christianity in the People's Republic https://www.chinacenter.net/2016/china_currents/15-1/protestant-christianity-in-the-peoples-republic/

[67] History.com: Hong Xiuquan / Taiping Rebellion https://www.history.com/topics/china/taiping-rebellion

[68] JaniceYLeung(4/2013): Hakka / Xiunquan / A Critique of Marx's View of the Taiping Rebellion and Its Origins https://www.armstrong.edu/history-journal/history-journal-a-critique-of-marxs-view-of-the-taiping-rebellion-and-its-o

[69] NYDailyTribune(6/14/1853): Karl Marx: Revolution in China and In Europe https://www.marxists.org/archive/marx/works/1853/china/index.htm

[70] OverseasChineseAffairsCommittee-tw: The Hakka People http://edu.ocac.gov.tw/lang/hakka/english/a/a.htm

[71] History.com(8/21/2018): Japan / Tokugawa Period and Meiji Restoration https://www.history.com/topics/japan/meiji-restoration

[72] Diplomat(8/21/2018): Japan and the 150th Anniversary of the Meiji Restoration https://thediplomat.com/2018/04/japan-and-the-150th-anniversary-of-the-meiji-restoration/

[73] Economist(2/5/2018): After 150 years, why does the Meiji restoration matter? https://www.economist.com/the-economist-explains/2018/02/05/after-150-years-why-does-the-meiji-restoration-matter

[74] Quartz(10/22/2018): Meiji / The complicated legacy of modern Japan as it celebrates its 150th birthday https://qz.com/1423834/modern-japan-is-turning-150-heres-what-you-need-to-know/

[75] ThoughtCo(8/2/2018): Japan / What Was the Meiji Restoration? https://www.thoughtco.com/what-was-the-meiji-restoration-195562

[76] MIT(2010): The Opium War in Japanese Eyes, John Dower https://visualizingcultures.mit.edu/opium_wars_japan/index.html

[77] HongKongMarineDept: The Second Opium War and the annexation of Kowloon Peninsula https://www.mardep.gov.hk/theme/port_hk/en/p1ch3_1.html

[78] OxfordToday(3/7/2016): Yuan Ming Yuan / Old Summer Palace / The loot from China's old Summer Palace in Beijing that still rankles http://www.oxfordtoday.ox.ac.uk/opinion/loot-chinas-old-summer-palace-beijing-still-rankles

[79] PeopleDaily(3/1/2012): Lessons of the Opium War http://en.people.cn/90782/7744620.html

[80] WorldOfChinese(6/19/2016): Specter of the Tianjin Massacre [Catholic Orphanage, 1870] https://www.theworldofchinese.com/2016/06/specter-of-the-tianjin-massacre/

[81] Ancient-eu(9/22/2017): Korea / China 581-618 / Sui Dynasty https://www.ancient.eu/Sui_Dynasty/

[82] Atlantic(4/15/2013): Goguryeo empire (37BC-668AD) / How an Ancient Kingdom Explains Today's China-Korea Relations https://www.theatlantic.com/china/archive/2013/04/how-an-ancient-kingdom-explains-todays-china-korea-relations/274986/

[83] Hani-kr(1/26/2013): Goguryeo stele / China conducting closed research into ancient Korean dynasty http://english.hani.co.kr/arti/english_edition/e_international/571401.html

[84] Ancient-eu(9/29/2016): Goguryeo empire (37BC-668AD) / Korea / Goguryeo https://www.ancient.eu/Goguryeo/

[85] ThoughtCo(6/14/2017): The Joseon Dynasty in Korea [1392-1910] https://www.thoughtco.com/the-joseon-dynasty-in-korea-195719

[86] Hawaii.edu(1997): Shawn Ford / The Failure of the 16th Century Japanese Invasions of Korea http://www2.hawaii.edu/~sford/research/turtle/index.html

[87] KoreanHero(2012): The Major Naval Battle of Admiral Yi Sun-sin - Battle of Myongnyang [Western date: October 26, 1597] https://web.archive.org/web/20110928230153/http://www.koreanhero.net/en/TheMajorNavalBattles.htm

[88] ThoughtCo(7/16/2017): The First Sino-Japanese War - China's Qing Dynasty Surrenders Korea to Meiji Japan https://www.thoughtco.com/first-sino-japanese-war-1894-95-195784

[89] Telegraph(2/21/2017): Sino-Japan war 1894-95 / The war that changed Asia https://www.telegraph.co.uk/news/world/china-watch/culture/first-sino-japanese-war/

[90] HistoryOfWar(10/31/2013): First Sino-Japanese War (1894-1895) http://www.historyofwar.org/articles/wars_first_sino_japanese.html

[91] ThoughtCo(3/23/2018): Facts on the Russo-Japanese War https://www.thoughtco.com/facts-on-the-russo-japanese-war-195812

[92] State.gov: Japan, China, the United States and the Road to Pearl Harbor, 1937-41 https://2001-2009.state.gov/r/pa/ho/time/wwii/88734.htm

[93] State.gov: Lend-Lease and Military Aid to the Allies in the Early Years of World War II https://2001-2009.state.gov/r/pa/ho/time/wwii/81508.htm

[94] NPR(12/13/2007): USS Panay / Dec 12 1937 / A Japanese Attack Before Pearl Harbor https://www.npr.org/templates/story/story.php?storyId=17110447

[95] Exordio-ph(10/1/1944): Comfort women / Japanese Prisoner of War Interrogation Report No. 49. http://www.exordio.com/1939-1945/codex/Documentos/report-49-USA-orig.html

[96] JapanForward(2/23/2017): Comfort women / Japan / The Hate Farm: China Is Planting a Bitter Harvest https://japan-forward.com/the-hate-farm-china-is-planting-a-bitter-harvest/

[97] PewGlobal(7/14/2014): Chapter 4: How Asians View Each Other https://www.pewglobal.org/2014/07/14/chapter-4-how-asians-view-each-other/

[98] JournalOfCurrentChineseAffairs(1/2017): Anti-Japanese Sentiment among Chinese University Students: The Influence of Contemporary Nationalist Propaganda https://journals.sub.uni-hamburg.de/giga/jcca/article/download/1045/1052

[99] StandardMedia-ke(7/8/2018): Kenya / Revealed: SGR workers treated badly by Chinese masters https://www.standardmedia.co.ke/business/article/2001287179/revealed-sgr-workers-treated-badly-by-chinese-masters

[100] U-S-History: The Open Door Policy: Doing Business in China (1899–1900) https://www.u-s-history.com/pages/h908.html

[101] State.gov: Secretary of State John Hay and the Open Door in China, 1899–1900 https://history.state.gov/milestones/1899-1913/hay-and-china

[102] History.com: Boxer Rebellion https://www.history.com/topics/china/boxer-rebellion

[103] SACU/ChinaNow(1990): Manchus / Qing Dynasty / Barbarian Emperors http://www.sacu.org/manchu.html

[104] FirstWorldWar(8/22/2009): Primary Documents - Anglo-Japanese Alliance, 30 January 1902, 1905 https://www.firstworldwar.com/source/anglojapanesealliance1902.htm

[105] LSE(4/2002): Anglo-Japanese Alliance http://eprints.lse.ac.uk/6884/1/Anglo-Japanese_Alliance.pdf

[106] History.com(2/22/2016): Who Was Yuan Shikai? [[1859-1916]] https://www.history.com/news/who-was-yuan-shikai

[107] State.gov: Issues Relevant to U.S. Foreign Diplomacy: Unification of German States [1870] https://history.state.gov/countries/issues/german-unification

[108] State.gov: The League of Nations, 1920 https://history.state.gov/milestones/1914-1920/league

[109] GlobalSecurity-org: China / Japan / Shandong / 1921-1922 Washington Naval Conference https://www.globalsecurity.org/military/world/naval-arms-control-1921.htm

[110] State.gov: The Kellogg-Briand Pact, 1928 https://history.state.gov/milestones/1921-1936/kellogg

[111] GlobalSecurity-org: German Micronesia https://www.globalsecurity.org/military/world/oceania/fsm-history-2.htm

[112] FirstWorldWar(8/22/2009): Causes of WWI - Triple Entente - Triple Alliance https://www.firstworldwar.com/atoz/alliances.htm

[113] ChineseHistoryDigest: Republic of China (1912-1949)
http://www.chinesehistorydigest.com/republicofchina.html

[114] Diplomat(1/24/2015): Jan 18 1915 / China, Japan, and the 21 Demands
https://thediplomat.com/2015/01/china-japan-and-the-21-demands/

[115] RadiiChina(5/4/2018): May 4th Movement / Karl Marx, Cai Yuanpei, and the Legacies of May
Fourth https://radiichina.com/karl-marx-cai-yuanpei-and-the-legacies-of-may-fourth/

[116] PRI(12/3/2013): The Manchus ruled China into the 20th century, but their language is nearly
extinct PRI's The World https://www.pri.org/stories/2013-12-03/manchus-ruled-china-20th-
century-their-language-almost-extinct

[117] BertrandRussell(1922): The Problem of China By Bertrand Russell
http://www.freeclassicebooks.com/Bertrand%20Russell/The%20Problem%20of%20China.pdf

[118] ChinaAwakened(1922): Book: China Awakened: Min-ch ien Tuk Zung Tyau
https://ia600203.us.archive.org/15/items/chinaawakened00tyauuoft/chinaawakened00tyauuo
ft.pdf

[119] AlphaHistory: The Warlord Era [1916-1927]
https://alphahistory.com/chineserevolution/warlord-era/

[120] Historia.ro: March 1919, the Third Communist International / The Comintern: how Moscow
controlled communist parties around the world
https://www.historia.ro/sectiune/general/articol/the-comintern-how-moscow-controlled-
communist-parties-around-the-world

[121] WaPost(3/20/1977): Recalling the Rape of Nanking [[3/24/1927]]
https://www.washingtonpost.com/archive/lifestyle/1977/03/20/recalling-the-rape-of-
nanking/faaa8ad0-dfc7-4533-8979-0be46c19f090/

[122] ShareOk(7/1968): Carl Dorris / Nationalists And The Nanking Incident, 1927: Sources And
Impact On United States China Policy
https://shareok.org/bitstream/handle/11244/26148/Thesis-1968-
D716n.pdf?sequence=1&isAllowed=y

[123] Wnd.com(5/16/2001): Jude Wanniski to Junichiro Koizumi / Remember Pearl Harbor?
https://www.wnd.com/2001/05/9263/

[124] JapanTimes(9/17/2016): Memories of 1931 Mukden Incident remain divisive
https://www.japantimes.co.jp/opinion/2016/09/17/commentary/memories-1931-mukden-
incident-remain-divisive/#.XDYSB2l7lhE

[125] History.com(12/6/2018): Nov 9-10 1938 / Kristallnacht
https://www.history.com/topics/holocaust/kristallnacht

[126] History.com(8/21/2018): China / Mao Zedong / Long March
https://www.history.com/topics/china/long-march

[127] ChinaStudyAbroad: The Marco Polo Bridge Incident of 1937
http://www.chinastudyabroad.org/indepthchina/1040-the-marco-polo-bridge-incident-of-1937

[128] ThoughtCo(3/6/2017): The Nanking Massacre, 1937 https://www.thoughtco.com/the-
nanking-massacre-1937-195803

[129] ThoughtCo(3/8/2017): The Marco Polo Bridge Incident [[July 7-9, 1937]]
https://www.thoughtco.com/the-marco-polo-bridge-incident-195800

[130] AlphaHistory: The Second Sino-Japanese War [[1937-45]]
https://alphahistory.com/chineserevolution/sino-japanese-war/

[131] Unit731-org: UNIT 731 – Japan's Biological Warfare Project[1] https://unit731.org/

[132] MtHolyoke: Unit 731: One of the Most Terrifying Secrets of the 20th Century
https://www.mtholyoke.edu/~kann20c/classweb/dw2/page1.html

[133] State.gov: Occupation and Reconstruction of Japan, 1945–52
https://history.state.gov/milestones/1945-1952/japan-reconstruction

[134] Nippon.com(2/9/2015): Japan's Seven Postwar Decades - Lessons from the Japanese Miracle:
Building the Foundations for a New Growth Paradigm https://www.nippon.com/en/in-

depth/a04003/lessons-from-the-japanese-miracle-building-the-foundations-for-a-new-growth-paradigm.html

[135] StLouisFed(3/20/2018): How Did South Korea's Economy Develop So Quickly? https://www.stlouisfed.org/on-the-economy/2018/march/how-south-korea-economy-develop-quickly

[136] MontrealEconomicInstitute(11/2013): Hong Kong: The Ongoing Economic Miracle http://www.iedm.org/files/note1113_en.pdf

[137] Marxists.org: Mao Zedong's Little Red Book https://www.marxists.org/reference/archive/mao/works/download/red-book.pdf

[138] History.com(8/21/2018): China 1966-75 / Cultural Revolution https://www.history.com/topics/china/cultural-revolution

[139] BeijingReview(5/26/2009): The Third Plenary Session of the 11th Central Committee of the Communist Party of China - 12/18-22/1978 http://www.bjreview.com/nation/txt/2009-05/26/content_197538.htm

[140] ThoughtCo(4/14/2018): What Was the Gang of Four in China? https://www.thoughtco.com/the-gang-of-four-195613

[141] RevolutionarySocialism(4/9/2016): Tiananmen Square / Remembering the riots of spring 1976 in China – "1976 was a pivotal year for China" https://www.rs21.org.uk/2016/04/09/remembering-the-riots-of-spring-1976-in-china/

[142] MarquetteUniv: The Tiananmen Incident of 1976 https://academic.mu.edu/meissnerd/tiananmen-76.htm

[143] ThoughtCo(3/17/2017): China / 3/17/2017 / Tangshan: The Deadliest Earthquake https://www.thoughtco.com/tangshan-the-deadliest-earthquake-1779769

[144] RFI(6/3/2019): China / Thirty years on from Tiananmen: unpublished pictures of the student movement http://en.rfi.fr/asia-pacific/20190530-china-thirty-years-tiananmen-square-unpublished-photos-student-movement

[145] Brookings(3/30/2016): The end of China's one-child policy https://www.brookings.edu/articles/the-end-of-chinas-one-child-policy/

[146] EastAsiaForum(4/19/2017): China's two-child policy one year on http://www.eastasiaforum.org/2017/04/19/chinas-two-child-policy-one-year-on/

[147] History.com(2/9/2018): Why Korea was split at the 38th parallel after World War II. https://www.history.com/news/north-south-korea-divided-reasons-facts

[148] CouncilForeignAffairs(3/13/2019): The China–North Korea Relationship https://www.cfr.org/backgrounder/china-north-korea-relationship

[149] BBC(9/24/2018): Opioids / Fentanyl crisis: Is China a major source of illegal drugs? https://www.bbc.com/news/world-45564744

[150] ChinaChange(7/6/2016): What Do Lu Yuyu's Statistics of Protest Tell Us About the Chinese Society Today? https://chinachange.org/2016/07/06/the-man-who-keeps-tally-of-protests-in-china/

[151] HongKongFP(9/28/2017): Chinese Court upholds 4-year jail term for press freedom prize winner Lu Yuyu https://www.hongkongfp.com/2017/09/28/chinese-court-upholds-4-year-jail-term-press-freedom-prize-winner-lu-yuyu/

[152] Diplomat(10/24/2017): UFWD / Magic weapon / The 19th Party Congress: A Rare Glimpse of the United Front Work Department https://thediplomat.com/2017/10/the-19th-party-congress-a-rare-glimpse-of-the-united-front-work-department/

[153] CarnegieEndowment(7/2011): The Long History Of United Front Activity In Hong Kong By Cindy Yik-Yi Chu July 2011 http://carnegieendowment.org/hkjournal/PDF/2011_fall/5.pdf

[154] LowyInstitute(11/6/2017): The long reach of China's United Front Work [Department - UFWD] https://www.lowyinstitute.org/the-interpreter/long-reach-Chinas-united-front-work

[155] WilsonCenter/Anne-MarieBrady(9/18/2017): Magic Weapons: China's political influence activities under Xi Jinping https://www.wilsoncenter.org/article/magic-weapons-chinas-political-influence-activities-under-xi-jinping

[156] FolioWeekly(9/27/2018): Univ North Florida / Examining UNF's decision to close the Confucius Institute http://folioweekly.com/stories/the-case-against-confucius,20593

[157] Economist(2018?): Analysis of China's inability to govern / What China wants https://www.economist.com/news/essays/21609649-china-becomes-again-worlds-largest-economy-it-wants-respect-it-enjoyed-centuries-past-it-does-not

[158] ChinaFile(11/8/2013): Hardline ideological policy / Document 9: A ChinaFile Translation http://www.chinafile.com/document-9-chinafile-translation

[159] IPCS-in(11/14/2013): China: Document No. 9 and the New Propaganda Regime http://www.ipcs.org/focusthemsel.php?articleNo=4175

[160] NPC-cn(6/27/2017)/Trans: China / National Intelligence Law of the People's Republic http://www.npc.gov.cn/npc/xinwen/2017-06/27/content_2024529.htm

[161] DOJ(12/20/2018): Two Chinese Hackers Associated With the Ministry of State Security Charged https://www.justice.gov/opa/pr/two-chinese-hackers-associated-ministry-state-security-charged-global-computer-intrusion

[162] TeleAnalysis(1/31/2019): How Huawei Stole T-Mobile Robot Technology : A Detailed Account https://www.teleanalysis.com/analysis/how-huawei-stole-t-mobile-robot-technology-29881

[163] Wired(1/21/2019): The complicated truth about China's social credit system https://www.wired.co.uk/article/china-social-credit-system-explained

[164] ASPI(6/15/2018): Australia / Huawei highlights China's expansion dilemma: espionage or profit? https://www.aspistrategist.org.au/huawei-highlights-chinas-expansion-dilemma-espionage-or-profit/

[165] ASPI(7/13/2018): The African Union headquarters hack and Australia's 5G network https://www.aspistrategist.org.au/the-african-union-headquarters-hack-and-australias-5g-network/

[166] RuhrUniversitatBochum-de(2015): Stealthy Dopant-Level Hardware Trojans: ExtendedVersion https://www.emsec.ruhr-uni-bochum.de/media/crypto/veroeffentlichungen/2015/03/19/beckerStealthyExtended.pdf

[167] DoD(2/2005): Defense Science Board. Report of the Defense Science Board Task Force on High Performance Microchip Supply. US DoD, February 2005. https://www.acq.osd.mil/DSB/reports/2000s/ADA435563.pdf

[168] WorldBank: WorldBankDoingBusinessReport-DB2019-190317.pdf http://www.worldbank.org/content/dam/doingBusiness/media/Annual-Reports/English/DB2019-report_web-version.pdf

[169] WorldBank: World Bank 2018 Doing Business Report http://www.doingbusiness.org/content/dam/doingBusiness/media/Annual-Reports/English/DB2018-Full-Report.pdf

[170] WorldData(2010): IQ by Country https://www.worlddata.info/iq-by-country.php

[171] FraserInstitute(12/10/2018): By country / The Human Freedom Index 2018 https://www.fraserinstitute.org/studies/human-freedom-index-2018

[172] TransparencyInternational(1/20/2019): Corruption Perceptions Index - 2018 https://www.transparency.org/news/pressrelease/corruption_perceptions_index_2018

[173] China-Embassy.org(3/15/2005): China / Taiwan / Anti-Secession Law (Full text)(03/15/05) http://www.china-embassy.org/eng/zt/999999999/t187406.htm

[174] ForeignPolicy(9/25/2018): Taiwan Can Win a War With China https://foreignpolicy.com/2018/09/25/taiwan-can-win-a-war-with-china/

[175] TaiwanToday(6/1/2011): Inside the Taiwan Miracle https://taiwantoday.tw/news.php?unit=8,8,29,32,32,45&post=13965

[176] CommonwealthMag(5/29/2015): Obituary Y.C. Lo / TSMC / A Catalyst of Taiwan's Electronics Industry https://english.cw.com.tw/article/article.action?id=234

[177] WorldAtlas(5/18/2018): What Was The Taiwan Miracle? https://www.worldatlas.com/articles/what-was-the-taiwan-miracle.html

[178] Cuny(2013): Murray Rubinstein / Chapter 2 The Evolution of Taiwan's Economic Miracle 1945-2000: https://aacs.ccny.cuny.edu/2013conference/Papers/Rubenstein%20Murray_2.pdf

[179] Diplomat(2/23/2017): The Bitter Legacy of the 1979 China-Vietnam War https://thediplomat.com/2017/02/the-bitter-legacy-of-the-1979-china-vietnam-war/

[180] NationalGeographic(6/18/2014): The Cham: Descendants of Ancient Rulers of South China Sea Watch Maritime Dispute From Sidelines https://news.nationalgeographic.com/news/2014/06/140616-south-china-sea-vietnam-china-cambodia-champa/

[181] FactsAndDetails(2008): Champa And The Chams http://factsanddetails.com/asian/cat62/sub406/entry-2815.html

[182] Philippine-history.org: The First "Filipinos" http://www.philippine-history.org/early-filipinos.htm

[183] Philippine-history.org: Synopsis Of Philippine History http://www.philippine-history.org/

[184] Inquirer-ph(4/8/2019): Philippines / April 1942 / Bataan death march / Cold-blooded murder in Bataan https://opinion.inquirer.net/120634/cold-blooded-murder-in-bataan

[185] LibraryOfCongress-gov: The World of 1898: The Spanish-American War https://www.loc.gov/rr/hispanic/1898/intro.html

[186] GenerationalDynamics: 30-Sep-18 World View — University of N. Florida and Pentagon cut ties with China's Confucius Institutes http://www.generationaldynamics.com/pg/xct.gd.e180930.htm#e180930

[187] GenerationalDynamics: 3-Apr-17 World View — Dalai Lama to visit region of northeast India claimed by China http://www.generationaldynamics.com/pg/xct.gd.e170403.htm#e170403

[188] GenerationalDynamics: 29-Dec-16 World View — China punishes Mongolia for Dalai Lama visit during financial crisis http://www.generationaldynamics.com/pg/xct.gd.e161229.htm#e161229

[189] GenerationalDynamics: 3-Jan-19 World View — China may seize Kenya's Mombasa Port as debt repayments triple http://www.generationaldynamics.com/pg/xct.gd.e190103.htm#e190103

[190] GenerationalDynamics: 15-Jan-19: Kenya's leaked BRI contract reveals shocking China debt trap details http://www.generationaldynamics.com/pg/xct.gd.e190115.htm#e190115

[191] GenerationalDynamics: 23-Dec-2016: How Israel panicked in pursuing the summer 2006 Lebanon war with Hezbollah http://www.generationaldynamics.com/pg/xct.gd.e061223.htm#e061223

[192] GenerationalDynamics: 24-Jul-2006: Israel/Lebanon 2006 war with Hezbollah forces Muslims to choose http://www.generationaldynamics.com/pg/ww2010.i.060724hizbollah.htm

[193] CNN(7/21/2006): Lebanon president: We will fight invaders http://www.cnn.com/2006/WORLD/meast/07/21/cnna.lahoud/index.html?section=cnn_latest

[194] GenerationalDynamics: 13-Jul-2016: Philippines humiliates China in harsh Hague Tribunal ruling over South China Sea http://www.generationaldynamics.com/pg/xct.gd.e160713.htm#e160713

[195] GenerationalDynamics: 17-Jun-2015: China tests hypersonic missile designed to defeat American missile defenses http://www.generationaldynamics.com/pg/xct.gd.e150617.htm#e150617

[196] GenerationalDynamics: 1-Apr-2016: China close to deploying very long range DF-41 missile http://www.generationaldynamics.com/pg/xct.gd.e160401.htm#e160401

[197] GenerationalDynamics: 29-Jun-2018: Australia passes foreign influence laws, targeting China http://www.generationaldynamics.com/pg/xct.gd.e180629.htm#e180629

[198] GenerationalDynamics: 30-Sep-2018: University of N. Florida and Pentagon cut ties with China's Confucius Institutes http://www.generationaldynamics.com/pg/xct.gd.e180930.htm#e180930

[199] GenerationalDynamics: 21-Dec-2018: China hackers collect data on hundreds of millions of Americans and Westerners http://www.generationaldynamics.com/pg/xct.gd.e181221.htm#e181221

[200] GenerationalDynamics: 12-Jan-2019: China's economy destabilizes as Huawei introduces cheap smartphone http://www.generationaldynamics.com/pg/xct.gd.e190112.htm#e190112

[201] GenerationalDynamics: 15-Jan-2019: Kenya's leaked BRI contract reveals shocking China debt trap details http://www.generationaldynamics.com/pg/xct.gd.e190115.htm#e190115

[202] GenerationalDynamics: 27-Jan-2019: George Soros speech at Davos marks significant global shift against China http://www.generationaldynamics.com/pg/xct.gd.e190127.htm#e190127

[203] GenerationalDynamics: 25-Jul-2018: Defector in Kazakhstan reveals explosive information about China's 'reeducation centers' http://www.generationaldynamics.com/pg/xct.gd.e180725.htm#e180725

[204] GenerationalDynamics: 16-Nov-2018: Fifteen countries challenge China's human rights in Xinjiang province http://www.generationaldynamics.com/pg/xct.gd.e181116.htm#e181116

[205] GenerationalDynamics: 2-Jul-2006: Politicians commemorate Battle of the Somme, July 1, 1916 http://www.generationaldynamics.com/pg/xct.gd.e060702.htm#e060702

[/FOOTNOTES]

[Updated: Thursday, June 06, 2019, 15:16:11 190606 I1evJ ET, 120570 words]

Made in the USA
Columbia, SC
02 November 2019

82586056R00198